D0844669

Cincinnati: The Queen City

Bicentennial Edition

Published by
The Cincinnati Historical Society
Eden Park, Cincinnati, Ohio 45202
1988

Cover design: Tyler Davidson Fountain sketch by Ferdinand von Miller. Tyler Davidson Fountain Collection. Gift of William S. Rowe.

Frontispiece, Paul Briol. *The Fountain at Night* (c. 1935). Photograph. Paul Briol Collection.

Cincinnati looking west, Mt. Adams in the foreground. Martin Rogers, *An October Morning* from *National Geographic Magazine* (1977). Photograph. Gift of National Geographic Magazine.

Cincinnati: The Queen City

Bicentennial Edition

Preface

This bicentennial edition of *Cincinnati: The Queen City*, which is the third volume in the Bicentennial Reprint Series, includes not only the text and illustrations which proved so popular in its first and second printings but also contains a section which chronicles Cincinnati's bicentennial year from the beginning "Countdown" through the "Tall Stacks" celebration. An essay by Joseph S. Stern, Jr., Chairman of the Greater Cincinnati Bicentennial Commission, accompanied by a full color, photographic portfolio, recounts the celebration's planning, the events and the permanent legacies of the Commission from its establishment in 1982.

The celebration of Cincinnati's founding two centuries ago presented an opportunity for its citizens to recall the past as well as to look with optimism to the future. In that spirit the Commission of the Greater Cincinnati Bicentennial endorsed reprinting works of lasting interest in the history of the Cincinnati area. Volumes one and two in the Bicentennial Reprint Series are: *The WPA Guide to Cincinnati* and *The Tyler Davidson Fountain.*

While the Commission has endorsed the series, the actual selection, editing and producing of the reprints is a joint venture of The Cincinnati Historical Society and the Department of History and Center for Neighborhood and Community Studies at the University of Cincinnati.

The major portion of the proceeds realized from the sale of the reprints will fund an endowment to assist in the publication of books on the history of the Cincinnati region.

ISBN 0-911497-11-0

The Bicentennial Edition of

Cincinnati: The Queen City

is dedicated to

JOHN DIEHL

in grateful recognition of his distinguished service to

The Cincinnati Historical Society

Elected Trustee 1962

President 1974-1988

William Louis Sonntag (attr.), *View of the Ohio River at Maysville, Kentucky* (c. 1850). Oil on canvas. Gift from the estate of Helen S. Knight.

Chapter 1

Taming the Ohio Wilderness

1788-1830

Daniel Boone pointing to the rich and fertile Kentucky wilderness in 1769. James Pierce Barton, *Kentucky Landscape* (c. 1832). Oil on canvas. Gift of Mrs. W. R. Thrall.

In the 1780s southwest Ohio lay at the edge of the Northwest Territory, America's newest frontier. The frontier has always excited the American imagination. Dreams about limitless riches and fears of terrifying dangers were always just beyond the next mountain range. On the frontier, the democratic, self-reliant American identity was supposedly forged.

In most popular accounts of the American frontier, the dominant figure is the lonely pioneer who clears a small farm in the vast, howling wilderness. In these versions, cities appear only after years of rural development as the result of natural, unplanned population growth at certain critical locations.

This myth neglects the fact that some settlers also carried plans for cities into the wilderness. The early Virginians named their first counties "James City County" and "Charles City County." The Puritans immediately set about laying out and developing Boston into a seaport city. Philadelphia's phenomenal success led dozens of other city builders to copy William Penn's straightforward plan for laying out whole cities in a grid pattern years before streets could be built. Cities were not accidents. They were the outgrowth of conscious decisions, and every American frontier attracted men who planned cities as well as those who planted wheat and corn. The settlers who ventured into southwest Ohio in 1788 included those who carried this tradition.

At the end of the War for Independence and the signing of the Peace of Paris in 1783, Americans turned their attention westward to the newly acquired lands of the Northwest Territory. Since 1774 settlers had been streaming across the mountains into Kentucky, and by 1788 it was already home for 70,000 settlers. Few ventured north of the Ohio River, however. This uneven settlement pattern partially reflected more effective British control of the area, but more importantly, it resulted from fierce Indian resistance to white encroachment. Kentucky settlers termed southwest Ohio the "Miami slaughterhouse." Already angry over the loss of their hunting grounds in Kentucky, the Miami, Shawnee, Wyandot and Delaware Indians were determined that they would not be pushed farther west by new waves of white settlers.

The people of the United States and the new government, operating under the Articles of Confederation, were equally determined that these new lands would become an integral part of the emerging American empire. Since 1763 British policy had kept the trans-Allegheny West closed to American settlement in an effort to keep peace with the Indian tribes long loyal to the French. But thousands of residents of the seaboard states saw wealth and opportunity in the richness of the West; the impoverished American government saw the opportunity to raise much-needed revenue to cancel its Revolutionary War debts.

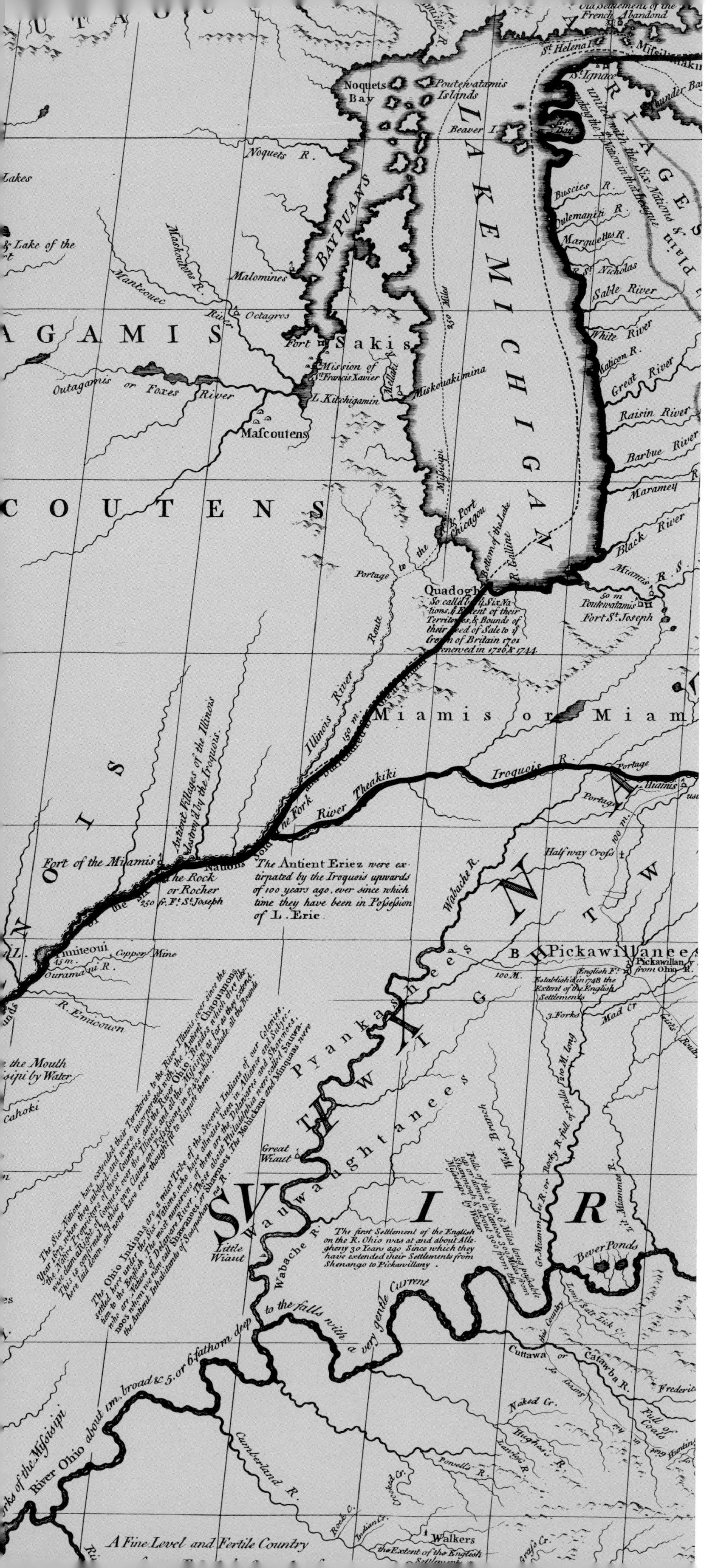

The equal determination of white Americans to settle the West and of native Americans to protect their hunting and home lands propelled the nation into yet another chapter of what had already become a familiar and tragic story. At first the United States government attempted to dictate to the Indian tribes on the grounds that, as allies of the defeated British, they had forfeited all rights to their lands between the Allegheny Mountains and the Mississippi River. The government was willing, however, to allow them to withdraw behind a treaty line that would immediately open most of Ohio to white settlement. Yet, as Pennsylvania Congressman James Duane, serving as chairman of the Committee on Indian Affairs, pointed out, any line was only temporary. It was assumed that the Indians would continue to retreat as white settlements advanced, and that their numbers would decline as they were exposed to new, "white-man" diseases such as cholera and smallpox. But, if the Indians blocked the path west, new treaties would remove them so Americans could settle all the lands to the Mississippi.

Under this harsh policy, three treaties were dictated to the Indians of the Northwest Territory between 1784 and 1786. The refusal of many of the Indians to participate in making these treaties and their immediate, violent resistance soon demonstrated that military action would be necessary to support the policy. To a government burdened with debt and able to field an army of only 700, this was a sobering prospect. In 1787 an alternative policy began to emerge. Its goal of clearing all the land for white settlement remained unchanged, but its methods were different. Abandoning the theory that the Indians had lost their claims to the land through defeat, the government now proposed to pay them for it. In the long run it was presumed that

Cincinnati is at the location of the Bever Ponds on John Mitchell's *Map of the British and French Dominions in North America* (London, 1755), plates 2 and 6. Eugene F. Bliss fund purchase.

No. 1 MIAMI LAND-WARRANT.

THIS entitles Benjamin Stites his Heirs or Aſſigns, to locate one Section, in which the Fee of 640 Acres ſhall paſs, ſubject to the Terms of ſettlement.

Dated the ſeventh Day of December A. D. 1787

Signed by John Cleves Symmes.

Counterſigned by Benjamin Stites

Speshel At the point betwixt the mouth of the little miame and the ohio in the pint

MIAMI LAND-WARRANT.

Miami Land Warrant No. 1.
Issued by John Cleves Symmes to Benjamin Stites on December 17, 1787.
Gift of Mrs. Harold V. Orr.

this policy would be cheaper. This subtle shift in tactics made no impression on the Indians. They would resist.

In the spring of 1786, Benjamin Stites, a Revolutionary War veteran from New Jersey, left Redstone (now Brownsville), Pennsylvania, and floated down the Monongahela and Ohio rivers with a boatload of supplies to the young settlement of Limestone (Maysville), Kentucky, to trade with the settlers. From Limestone he traveled southwest to Washington, where he found the settlers excited after an Indian raid in which they had lost their best horses. Stites formed a posse and chased the thieves across Kentucky, over the Ohio River and up the Little Miami Valley. Nearing the headwaters of the Little Miami, the posse abandoned the chase and proceeded west, crossing the plateau to the Great Miami River. Working its way down the river, the posse reached the Ohio and turned toward home.

Stites was impressed by the rich, fertile lands of southwest Ohio. He soon traveled to New York, where the Continental Congress was in session, to interest land speculators in Ohio. He captured the attention of John Cleves Symmes, a war veteran and member of Congress from New Jersey. In the fall Symmes floated down the Ohio as far as Louisville to see for himself the beautiful Ohio Valley that Stites had described. Symmes returned with a dream of establishing a trade center on the banks of the water highway and of amassing a fortune through the sale of the surrounding land. He immediately set about organizing a land company and negotiating for the purchase of the Miami territory from the government. After opening offices in several eastern cities, he began to advertise the strategically located Ohio land.

Symmes' efforts were timely. Even while a new constitution was being drafted in Philadelphia in July 1787, Congress adopted the Northwest Ordinance that, among other provisions, facilitated the sale and settlement of the lands between the Alleghenies and the Mississippi. People were streaming into the lands bordering the Ohio River in ever larger numbers. Between February and June 1788, almost 5,000 people came down the Ohio in search of new land. In April of that year, the Ohio Company brought 58 settlers to the site of Marietta, where they established the first permanent settlement north of the Ohio River. On October 15, 1788, Congress granted Symmes a charter to develop the tract of land referred to as the Miami Purchase. It lay between the Great and Little

John Cleves Symmes (1742-1814)
John Cleves Symmes was born in Southold, Long Island. An ambitious person, he quickly rose through the ranks of colonial society. He served with the New Jersey militia in the Revolutionary War, as associate judge of the Supreme Court of New Jersey and as a member of the Continental Congress. In 1788 Symmes was appointed a judge for the Northwest Territory and began negotiations to buy one million acres of land between the Great and Little Miami rivers north from the Ohio River. In his haste to settle the purchase, Symmes often sold land before establishing legal claim. Most of his personal property was eventually sold to satisfy suits filed over disputed titles. He died penniless and disillusioned.

John Cleves Symmes after a portrait by Charles Willson Peale. Oil on canvas. Permanent loan from Hamilton County.

Frontiersmen

The adventures and dangers of frontier life intrigued people living in more established communities along the east coast and in Europe. In 1832 Karl Bodmer, a young Swiss artist who later became well known for his etchings and treatment of natural life, visited the United States with Maximilian of Neuwied. During their tour Bodmer sketched scenes depicting stories he heard of Ohio and Kentucky frontier life.

Among the most famous of the frontiersmen was Simon Kenton (1755-1836) who fled west in 1771 from his native Virginia believing he had killed a rival in a love affair. He used the name Simon Butler and worked as a scout for more than 10 years before learning that his boyhood antagonist was living. Bodmer sketched an adventure in Kenton's life while he was still using the name of Butler. It depicts Kenton's

Karl Bodmer, *Simon Butler* Lithograph (1852). Eugene F. Bliss fund purchase.

Simon Kenton. Oil on canvas. Gift of Robert Clarke.

Young Girls Fleeing From Indians (after Karl Bodmer). Oil on canvas. Gift of Peter G. Thomson.

capture, in 1778, by the Indians for stealing their horses. As part of his torture, Kenton was strapped, facing backward, on an unbroken horse. The Indians freed the horse, which then raced through heavy underbrush trying to dislodge its rider.

In another sketch Bodmer illustrated the story of the capture of Elizabeth and Frances Callaway (daughters of Richard Callaway) and Jemima Boone (daughter of Daniel Boone) on July 14, 1776. Together with Jean Francois Millet, Bodmer prepared a lithograph of the sketch for publication in an edition of *The Last of the Mohicans.* The creators of the lithograph were French. Hence, the foliage and clothing of the girls were not authentic. An unknown American artist based his painting, *Young Girls Fleeing From Indians,* on the Millet-Bodmer lithograph.

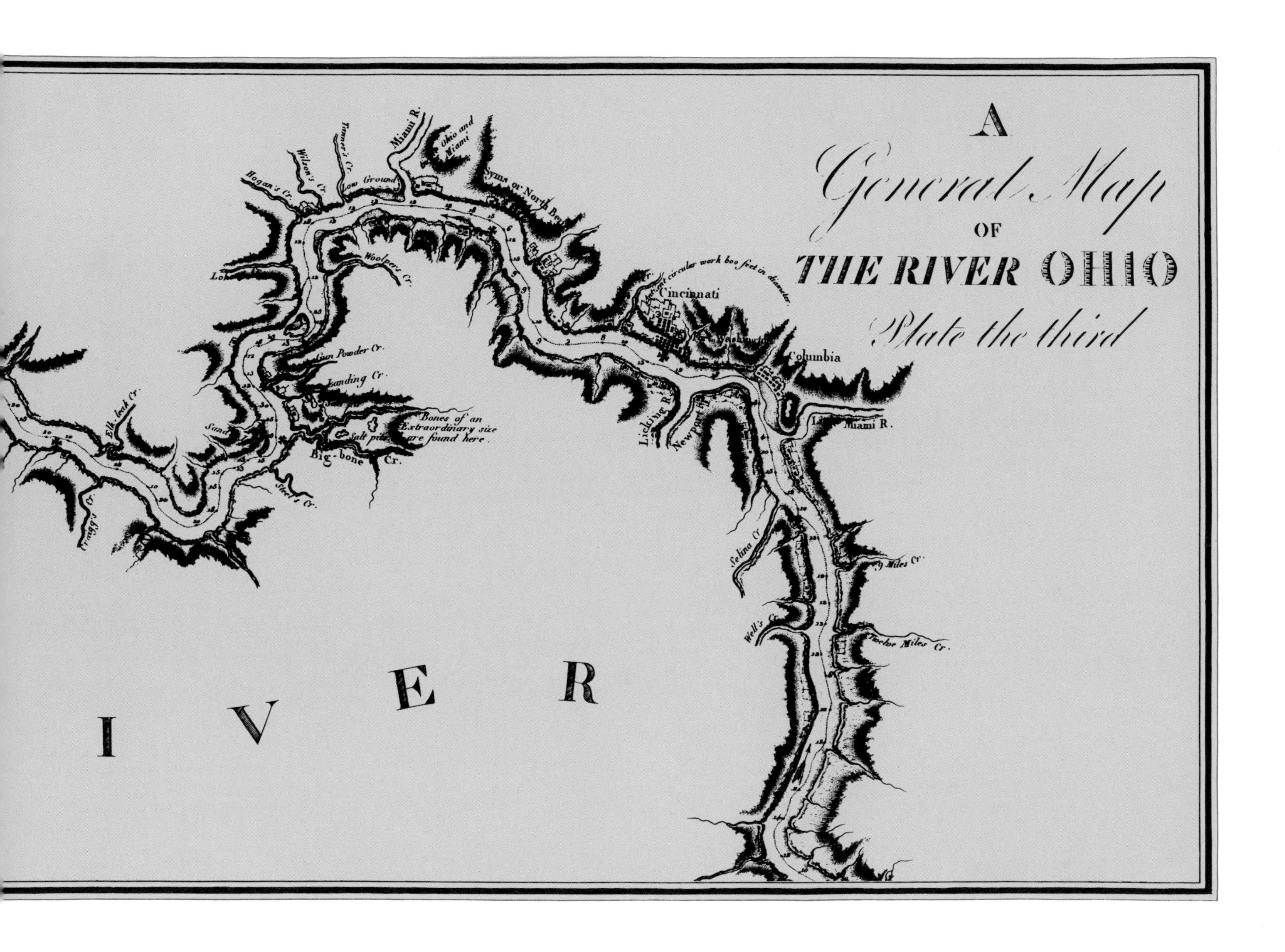

A General Map of the River Ohio from Victor Collot's *A Journey in North America ...Atlas.* (Paris, 1826), plate 10. Eugene F. Bliss fund purchase.

An American Log-house from Victor Collot's *A Journey in North America ...Atlas.* (Paris, 1826), plate 16.

Miami rivers, bounded on the south by the Ohio River and a yet to be determined line between the rivers on the north. Symmes immediately began selling pieces of the tract, which he erroneously believed would encompass one million acres, to other investors—including 20,000 acres along the Ohio and Little Miami rivers to Benjamin Stites.

Stites organized a party of 26 settlers from New Jersey and Pennsylvania and led them west. On November 18, 1788, they stopped at a site about one mile west of the mouth of the Little Miami River near present-day Lunken Airport where the settlers hastily built a blockhouse and several log cabins. They named this first settlement in the Miami country "Columbia."

A second settlement in the territory was organized by Matthias Denman, Colonel Robert Patterson (the founder of Lexington, Kentucky) and John Filson (a surveyor and historian). Denman was a New Jersey speculator who had been interested for years in the Northwest Territory. Based only on what he could learn from a map, Denman selected a tract of 747 acres directly across from the mouth of the Licking River that flowed north out of Kentucky into the Ohio River. After making an initial survey and contributing the name "Losantiville" to the site, Filson disappeared into the wilderness and was never seen again. Israel Ludlow replaced Filson both as surveyor and partner in the venture.

On December 28, 1788, a party of 11 families and 24 men led by Patterson arrived at Losantiville. Israel Ludlow, in an effort to bring an element of eastern order to the frontier town, laid out streets on the Philadelphia grid plan. He drew up lots for houses, vegetable gardens and cornfields, and the settlers began the hard and hazardous business of carving a town out of the Ohio frontier.

Little more than a month later, the party of John Cleves Symmes pulled ashore at a spot east of the mouth of the Great Miami River. By this time cold weather had arrived in earnest. Symmes and his family spent an uncomfortable winter living in a shed that opened to the south and faced a continuously burning fire. During these months Symmes laid out the town of North Bend at the site of his landing.

TO THE

RESPECTABLE

PUBLIC.

WHEREAS the honourable the Congreſs, by their act of the 3d of October, 1787, authorized the honourable the commiſſioners of the treaſury board, to enter into a contract with the ſubſcriber, for the tract of land hereafter deſcribed, and upon the following conditions: the boundaries of the land are—viz. Beginning at the mouth of the Great Miami river, thence running up the Ohio to the mouth of the Little Miami river, thence up the Little Miami to the place where a due weſt line, to be continued from the weſtern termination of the northern boundary line of the grant to Meſſrs. Sarjeant, Cutler, and company, ſhall interſect the ſaid Little Miami river, thence due weſt, continuing the ſaid weſtern line to the place where the ſaid line ſhall interſect the main branch or ſtream of the Great Miami river, thence down the Great Miami to the place of beginning.

The conditions are, that the tract ſhall be ſurveyed, and its contents aſcertained by the

In the "Trenton Circular" John Cleves Symmes advertised land for sale in Ohio prior to congressional approval of his purchase. John Cleves Symmes, *To the Respectable Public* (Trenton, N.J., 1787), p. 1.

The lives of the early settlers in these three villages revolved around the basic tasks of clearing land and providing food and shelter for their families. From the beginning, too, protection against the Indians was a primary concern. Although no concerted attack came that first year, sporadic raids kept the threat alive. Symmes described the effect on the settlers: "I am mortified to see people running away from these settlements, merely because no care is taken by their superiors to save them and their families from the rage of the savages—they feel themselves abandoned to destruction."

The backers of each settlement shared another common concern: they wanted to establish the supremacy of their village over the other two. At first Columbia grew faster than Losantiville or North Bend. Based on the ample yields of the fertile lands of Turkey Bottom, Columbia became the granary and trading center of the area. Columbia, however, had a fatal flaw—it lay on such low ground that it flooded regularly. Many of its settlers soon abandoned the settlement.

Symmes harbored grand visions for North Bend. He believed that its closeness to the Great Miami would enable it to control the trade of the rich farmland of the interior, which Symmes

Fort Washington Garrison. The selection of Losantiville as the site for a fort helped the settlement eclipse those nearby. Initially built in 1789 and garrisoned with 300 soldiers, the fort was the site of training of soldiers for Indian battles. Following the Treaty of Greenville in 1795, the security provided by the fort was a less significant factor in the community's growth. The garrison was moved across the river in 1804 and the fort itself was dismantled in 1809. Oil on canvas. Gift of Clifford A. Wiltsee.

considered the "Egypt on the Miami." Symmes attempted to gain control of the trade of both the Great Miami and the Ohio rivers by laying out a second town, Miami, that would connect North Bend across a 1½-mile strip of land to the banks of the Great Miami River. Like Columbia, natural limitations checked North Bend's potential. The hilly character of the town site prevented easy expansion.

Losantiville, the middle village, had certain advantages over the others. As in Columbia and North Bend, the riverfront offered the hope for controlling the trade of the Ohio. Losantiville, however, was like a giant amphitheater. The flatland along the river, the "bottom," stretched back 800 feet to approximately where Third Street in downtown Cincinnati is today. At that point, the ground rose sharply to the "hill," a 4.5-square-mile, semi-circular plateau above the flood plains. Losantiville also sat immediately across from the mouth of the Licking River, an important artery flowing out from the more developed territory of Kentucky. It was this strategic location that persuaded the government late in 1789 to erect Fort Washington at Losantiville. The fort was obviously important in providing security, but even more importantly, during the next six years of warfare with the Indians, it stimulated trade in the village.

On January 2, 1790, General Arthur St. Clair, governor of the Northwest Territory, arrived to inspect Fort Washington. Although he approved of the fort and the village surrounding it, he did not like the name Losantiville. He soon changed it to Cincinnati in honor of the Society of the Cincinnati, an organization of Revolutionary War officers to which he belonged.

General Arthur St. Clair, the first governor of the Northwest Territory, came to inspect Ft. Washington and the settlement of Losantiville one year after the town was established. He objected to the odd name that John Filson, a partner and surveyor for the development, had given to the town. Losantiville was a pedantic compilation of Latin and French syllables. From Latin, Filson drew os meaning "mouth" and anti meaning "across from." From French he drew ville meaning "town." L represented either the French definite article or the first letter of the Licking River. The composite name meant "town opposite the mouth of the Licking."

General St. Clair renamed the settlement "Cincinnati" in honor of the Society of the Cincinnati, a newly established association of Revolutionary War officers. He was a founding member of the society and the current president of the state society of Pennsylvania. The society had taken its name from Cincinnatus, the citizen-soldier whom the idealistic and peace-loving officers adopted as a role model.

Lucius Quinctius Cincinnatus was a patrician farmer of ancient Rome who was pressed into military leadership to save the republic upon two occasions. Both times, he refused to continue as dictator at the war's end, returning instead to civilian life.

The image of Cincinnatus at the plow appears frequently as a symbol for the city in civic and commercial art of the 19th century. The name was adopted in 1920 by the Cincinnatus Association, the voluntary organization of "Cincinnati's Citizen Crusaders," which was formed to analyze and recommend possible solutions to significant civic problems. The Society of the Cincinnati continues as an organization in the state and nation. Its members are descendants of Revolutionary War officers.

Victor Zappenfeld, *Cincinnatus At His Plow.* Oil on canvas. Gift of the Cincinnatus Association.

Revolutionary War Scene: Soldier Calling a Farmer from His Plow (c. 1876). Strobridge and Company chromolithograph. Gift of Mrs. Gilbert Bettman.

Arthur St. Clair (1734-1818), major general in the Continental Army during the Revolutionary War, delegate from Pennsylvania to the Continental Congress and President of Congress in 1787, was appointed governor of the Northwest Territory in 1787. In 1790 he came to Ft. Washington and in 1791 was recommissioned in the army to lead an attack on the Indians. The battle, held near the Maumee River in November 1791, ended in the worst defeat suffered by the army against the Indians. When he was removed as governor of the territory in 1802, St. Clair returned to Pennsylvania disgraced and financially ruined.

Between 1790 and 1795, Fort Washington provided the operational base for campaigns against the Indian tribes of the Northwest Territory. During the first three years, these campaigns were disastrous. Both in numbers and training, the armies that operated out of Fort Washington were inadequate for the task. In addition, their commanders were not equal to the leader of the Indians, the Miami chief, Little Turtle. In the span of 13 months—from October 1790 to November 1791—Little Turtle won two major battles against his white foes.

In the fall of 1790, General Josiah Harmar set out from Fort Washington with 320 army regulars and 1,133 Kentucky volunteers. The army marched to the headwaters of the Maumee River and burned several deserted Indian villages and the surrounding fields of nearly ripe corn. Believing that the Indians outnumbered his forces, Harmar began a retreat to Cincinnati. However, he permitted Colonel John Hardin with 400 men to pursue the Indians. The Indians attacked and defeated Hardin's forces before they could rejoin Harmar for the retreat south.

The following fall, St. Clair set out with a force of 2,700 men. By the time the army reached the headwaters of the Wabash River, desertions had reduced its ranks to 1,400. On November 4, 1791, Little Turtle attacked and killed 613 whites and wounded 237 others. This was the heaviest level of casualties ever inflicted on a U.S. army by Indians. The Indians remember this victory as "the Battle of a Thousand Slain." The defeat shook the leadership of the Miami Purchase and the United States government. On January 12, 1792, in reporting the news of the defeat, Symmes wrote Elias Boudinot, his business partner:

I had no Idea that our army would have been destroyed in the course of three hours, for it was impossible for anyone to suppose that the army was at any time to be crowded together on a few acres of ground and liable to be surrounded by half their number of Indians, whose every shot could not fail of killing or wounding three or four of our men; while our platoons in returning their fire, three times in four, saw not an Indian they being hid behind trees, but still our men fired on mechanically at they knew not what.

After this defeat, St. Clair was replaced as commander of the army by General "Mad Anthony" Wayne. Wayne, convinced that another defeat would be disastrous, insisted that the army be thoroughly prepared before again engaging the Indians. For 18 months Wayne trained his troops, bolstered the size of the army, laid in supplies and planned strategy. It was during this time of preparation that William Henry Harrison, a young ensign and heir to one of the leading families of Virginia, who had joined the army, was assigned to Wayne's command. He quickly rose to the rank of lieutenant and became an aide-de-camp.

Finally, in October 1793, Wayne marched his troops from Fort Washington. He built Fort Greenville, 75 miles north of Cincinnati, where the army spent the winter. After building additional forts to protect his supply lines, Wayne marched north on July 28, 1794. On August 20 he met and defeated the Indians, led by the Shawnee chief, Blue Jacket, at the Battle of Fallen Timbers near the present site of Toledo. He then pulled back to his base camp at Fort Greenville. Over the next several months he brought in all of the major Indian chiefs to sign the Treaty of Greenville. The document drew a line of demarcation that opened most of Ohio and southern Indiana to white settlement. The Indians were given restricted lands, paid for their losses and allowed to retain their right to hunt

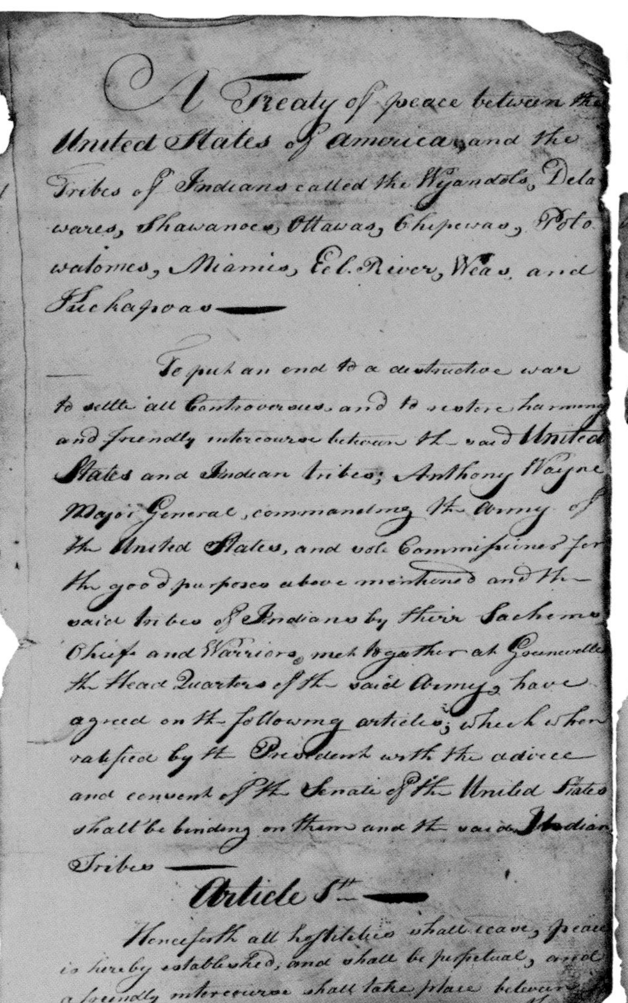

A Treaty of peace between the United States of America, and the Tribes of Indians called the Wyandots, Delawares, Shawanoes, Ottawas, Chipewas, Potowatomes, Miamis, Eel River, Weas, and Kickapoos —

To put an end to a destructive war to settle all Controversies, and to restore harmony and friendly intercourse between the said United States and Indian tribes; Anthony Wayne Major General, commanding the Army of the United States, and sole Commissioner for the good purposes above mentioned and the said tribes of Indians by their Sachems Chiefs and Warriors, met together at Greeneville the Head Quarters of the said Army, have agreed on the following articles, which when ratified by the President with the advice and consent of the Senate of the United States shall be binding on them and the said Indian Tribes —

Article 1st.

Henceforth all hostilities shall cease; peace is hereby established, and shall be perpetual, and a friendly intercourse shall take place between the

north of the Ohio River. However, the federal government now proposed that the Indians be taught to farm, since farming took less land than hunting. The government reasoned that the Indians would benefit through civilization and the whites would benefit by purchasing from the Indians all the "excess" land. Meanwhile, the close contact with white society would continue the process of reducing the Indian population through diseases.

The peace achieved at Greenville could not solve the Indian question permanently. The land policy of the white settlers and the government, particularly as it was administered under Harrison as territorial governor of Indiana, constantly pushed the Indians farther west. This pressure would lead, in 1811, to a new round of Indian wars.

For southwest Ohio, however, the Treaty of Greenville provided a lasting resolution of the Indian problem. In 1804 the garrison moved from Fort Washington across the Ohio to Newport, Kentucky. In 1809 Fort Washington was torn down.

Treaty of Greenville, August 3, 1795, from the Dandridge Papers. Gift of Mary Dandridge.

Anthony Wayne (1745-1796) succeeded St. Clair as commander of the western army with the rank of major general. He began his distinguished military service in the Revolutionary War where he won the sobriquet "Mad Anthony." Wayne came to Ft. Washington in 1792 and prepared for a campaign against the Indians. He remained commander of the army after the successful Battle of Fallen Timbers and died in Erie, Pennsylvania.

THE
CENTINEL
of the *North-Western TERRITORY.*

Open to all parties—but influenced by none.

PUBLIC NOTICE

WHEREAS many good Citizens of this Territory, with a design to check the incursions of the hostile Indians, now at war with the people of the United States, have voluntarily entered into, and subscribed their names to certain articles; each name having a sum annexed thereto, and have severally bound themselves their heirs &c. to pay the same, as in the said articles is mentioned.

We the subscribers therefore, being nominated and appointed to superintend the business of collecting and paying the money thus subscribed; hereby give notice, that the following arrangment is made, for the reward to be given for Indian scalps taken and produced within the period of the eighteenth of April last past, and the twenty fifth of December next ensuing, and within the boundaries following, to wit, begining on the Ohio ten miles above the mouth of the little Miami, on a direct line thence northwardly, the same distance from the said Miami, until it shall extend twenty five miles above where *Harmar's trace* first crosses the said Miami, thence due west, crossing the said little Miami, until it shall extend ten miles west of the great Miami, thence southwardly, keeping the distance of ten miles from the said great Miami, to the Ohio, thence up the middle of the said river Ohio, to the begining; that for every scalp, having the right ear appendant, for the first ten Indians who shall be killed within the time and limits aforesaid, by those who are subscribers, to the said articles, shall, whenever collected, be paid the sum of *one hundred and thirty six dollars*; and for every scalp of the like number of Indians, having the right ear appendant who shall be killed, within the time and limits aforesaid; by those who are not subscribers, the *federal troop* excepted, shall, whenever collected, be paid the sum of *one hundred dollars*; and for every scalp, having the right ear appendant, of the second ten Indians who shall be killed within the time and limits aforesaid, by those who are subscribers to the said articles, shall whenever collected as aforesaid, be paid the sum of *one hundred and seventeen dollars*; and for every scalp having the right ear appendant of the said second ten Indians who shall be killed within the time and limits aforesaid, by those who are not subscribers to the said articles, except before excepted, shall whenever collected, be paid the sum of *ninety five dollars.*

Cincinnati.	Levi Woodward, Darius C. Orcutt, James Lyons	Committee.
Columbia	Wm. Brown, Ignatius Ross, John Reily,	

In the May 17, 1794 issue of *The Centinel of the North-Western Territory* an ad appeared which offered bounties for Indian scalps, (Vol. 1, No. 27, p. 3). Purchase.

William Henry Harrison
(1773-1841)

The center picture of this 1840 presidential Campaign Handkerchief shows William Henry Harrison on horseback surrounded by vignettes depicting his career. Fabric. Gift of Fannie Mae Scovill.

William Henry Harrison (1773-1841), the ninth president of the United States and the first candidate to campaign actively for the office, rose to national prominence because of his role in the development of the Northwest Territory.

Born on a Virginia plantation, young Harrison came to Fort Washington in 1791. Here he served as commandant of the fort and as aide-de-camp to Gen. Anthony Wayne. In 1795 Harrison married Anna Symmes, daughter of John Cleves Symmes, resigned from the army and moved to the village of North Bend near the Ohio-Indiana border. He became involved in important Cincinnati business enterprises including the Miami Exporting Company, Branch Bank of the United States, a distillery and a foundry.

Harrison embarked upon a long and successful political career in 1798 when President John Adams appointed him secretary of the Northwest Territory and subsequently governor of the Indiana Territory. As governor, Harrison worked aggressively to remove Indians through treaties and wars. His 1809 Treaty of Fort Wayne met with unrelenting opposition from Tecumseh and the Prophet, Shawnee warriors and brothers. Assembling an army of 800 men, Harrison defeated the Indian forces at Tippecanoe in 1811. In 1813, as commander of the Army of the Northwest during the War of 1812, Harrison defeated the Indians and their British allies in the Battle of the Thames. Tecumseh was killed, and the dream of a great Indian confederacy died with him.

Leaving the military once again, Harrison returned to the Cincinnati area in 1814 to settle his father-in-law's complicated estate. He reestablished business and social ties to the city and accepted prestigious volunteer assignments, serving as vestryman of Christ Church, trustee

of Cincinnati College and president of the Hamilton County Agricultural Society.

In the next two decades, the "Farmer of North Bend" ran for various political offices, winning some, losing others. He served briefly in the state legislature, House of Representatives and U.S. Senate. During the Jacksonian era, he was forced to accept the comparatively humble office of clerk of court for Hamilton County.

Cincinnati was political headquarters for Harrison's five-year campaign for the presidency. He was the compromise candidate for the Whigs in 1840, engaging in a campaign which brought a new, carnival-like style to American politics. Although Harrison was manor-born, incumbent president Martin Van Buren's aristocratic affectations allowed Old Tippecanoe to appear the homespun candidate of the common man.

The Panic of 1837, the continued depression and a tactical error by a Democratic newspaper set the stage for Harrison's victory. The opposition press had sneered that if one were to give the candidate "a barrel of hard cider, and settle a pension of $2,000 a year on him... he will sit the remainder of his days in his log cabin." Whig propagandists gleefully turned this characterization to their candidate's advantage. The Log Cabin and Hard Cider campaign produced a wealth of political mementos based on these motifs. They are remarkable examples of early 19th century advertising art, and in their numbers and variety attest to the extent to which this campaign captured the popular imagination.

James Henry Beard (attr.), *William Henry Harrison* (c. 1840). Oil on canvas. Loaned by Mrs. Dudley V. Sutphin.

Campaign ribbon. William Henry Harrison Papers.

William Woodruff, *North Bend and residence of the late President Harrison* from the *Ladies' Repository*, (July 1841), p. 193. Engraving. Eugene F. Bliss fund purchase.

113. All the lots on the East side of the fort, formerly belonged to Judge Symmes; on the west, to Denman, Ludlow & Paterson. Few or none of the lots remain the prop of the original owners, settlers, who have sit down upon them & improved them very generally, have gained their occupancy by purch from the proprietors, or from persons in possession.
Deer Creek
Lands purchased by sundry persons, chiefly Military officers
Purchasers unknown
Fort Washington
Dr. Allison
Judge Turner
Capt. Strong
Genl. Harmar
Judge Turner
Capt. Kelly
T Brady
Capital of the Western Territory
1792
CINCINNATI
OF
Military line
Public use
New military line
Genl. St. Clair's order
On a Scale of 200 feet to 1 Inch
THE OHIO

Cincinnati turned its energies to its internal development. As one of its leading citizens, Jacob Burnet, wrote many years later, there was much to do: "Prior to the Treaty of Greenville, which established the permanent peace between the United States and the Indians, but few improvements had been made, of any description, and scarcely one of a permanent character." Although Ludlow had given the village an orderly beginning, in 1795 Cincinnati was a mere collection of rude log structures. For its first several years it had been a garrison town. The presence of the military introduced the chaos of soldiers on the frontier but also stimulated the local economy. In fact, between the demands of the armies and the new settlers, little agricultural surplus remained for commerce beyond the region.

The end of the Indian wars brought more settlers who produced ever larger, more marketable surpluses. Still, for several years the economy remained primitive. It depended largely on barter or credit arranged through millers and merchants for the exchange of produce and goods.

Despite the unsophisticated level of economic exchange, from the beginning producers and settlers recognized that the key to the development of the Miami Purchase lay in learning to exploit the commercial advantages offered by Cincinnati's strategic location along the Ohio River—the most important water route connecting seaboard cities and states with the interior of the new nation.

In the late 18th and early 19th centuries, the cheapest and most common means of transportation on the Ohio was the flatboat, or Kentucky boat. The flatboat was simply a raft with sides. For the settlers entering the area, it became a floating homestead and provided some of the lumber necessary for a first house.

Israel Ludlow, one of the original proprietors of Cincinnati, planned the town of Cincinnati and surveyed the Miami Purchase. Israel Ludlow (attr.), *The Town of Cincinnati, capital of the Western Territory* (c. 1792). Manuscript.

Sketch of a Flat bottom Boat; such as are used to descend the Ohio and the Mississipi [sic] from Victor Collot's *A Journey in North America...Atlas* (Paris, 1826), plate 7.

Flatboat. Model built by Charles E. Mappes, 1972. Gift of Charles E. Mappes.

Boatmen

You hear the boatmen extolling their prowess in pushing a pole, and you learn the received opinion, that a "Kentuck" is the best man at a pole, and a Frenchman at the oar... You are told when you embark, to bring your "plunder" aboard, and you hear about moving "fernenst" the stream... The manners of the boatmen are as strange as their language. Their peculiar way of life has given origin not only to an appropriate dialect, but to new modes of enjoyment, riot, and fighting. Almost every boat, while it lies in the harbour has one or more fiddles scraping continually aboard, to which you often see the boatmen dancing. There is no wonder that the way of life which the boatmen lead... generally plentiful as it respects food, and always so as it regards whiskey, should always have seductions that prove irresistible to the young people that live near the banks of the river.

Timothy Flint (1826)

For the established farmer, the flatboat was easy to construct and could carry between 40 and 50 tons of produce downstream to market. Although the flatboat served well for travel downstream, it could not go upstream. When the farmer reached market, the boat could be sold for lumber or fuel, but the farmer had to walk home. If his trip had taken him all the way to New Orleans, the return trek could take months.

The keelboat was a slight improvement over the flatboat. With a shallower draft and a four-inch keel to protect its bottom, a keelboat could be poled upstream by a crew of men, although the work was difficult. By 1815 keelboats provided regular service between Cincinnati and Pittsburgh, with the round trip taking a month.

River Scene Showing Flatboat and Two Keelboats from Leland D. Baldwin's *The Keelboat Age on Western Waters* (Pittsburgh, 1941). Reprinted, by permission of the University of Pittsburgh Press.

Timothy Flint, *Recollections of the Last Ten Years...* (Boston: 1826), p. 15.

The arrival of the steamboat *Orleans* on October 27, 1811, transformed Cincinnati's future. Since 1803 Robert Livingston and Robert Fulton had been experimenting with and introducing steamboats onto America's inland waterways. They decided that the Ohio River was suited for this use, and they had the *Orleans* built. After leaving Cincinnati the *Orleans* proceeded to Louisville and then returned. The distance of 180 miles took only 45 hours against the current, a feat that caused a great stir among the residents of the city. For the next few days, the *Orleans* gave people short trips up and down the river. For the first time, travel upstream had become as easy as traveling downstream.

The steamboat's impact on commerce was immediate and dramatic. In 1815 it cost approximately $1.50 to ship a barrel of flour from Cincinnati to New Orleans. By 1821 the rate had fallen to $1 a barrel, and then to about 50 cents by 1831. Upstream shipping rates declined even more rapidly so that by 1826 they equalled downstream rates.

The steamboat did not instantly drive earlier forms of transportation off the river. The flatboat continued to be popular, and the number constructed increased each year. It remained cheaper for farmers to float with their goods downriver on a flatboat, dispose of them and return via steamboat, thus avoiding the long walk.

The steamboat was important to Cincinnati's growth not only because it facilitated trade, but also because it provided the city one of its earliest industries. Cincinnati became the second most important center for steamboat construction. The first steamboat built in Cincinnati was the *Vesta,* launched in 1816. Over the next 10 years, Cincinnati dockyards contributed 48 of the 143 steamboats built for the Ohio River trade at that time.

Because it lay at the midpoint of the most important water artery of the American West, by 1820 it was clear that Cincinnati was fortuitously situated. The city boasted a population of nearly 10,000. But even more remarkably, Cincinnati was surrounded by excellent farmland that already supported 150,000 settlers.

Cincinnati was established at the same time settlers were pouring into the Northwest Territory and into the future states of Mississippi, Alabama and Louisiana. The northern settlers demanded goods from the merchants of the city and provided produce from the rich Miami Valley. The Southerners, feverishly establishing cotton plantations built on slave labor, provided rapidly expanding markets for the produce of the north. With the development of the steamboat, Cincinnatians could exploit the river more efficiently and completely than could have been imagined at the time of its founding in 1788.

The *New World,* built in Cincinnati, was used on the Ohio River in the 1840s and 1850s. Broadside. Gift of Mrs. Frank Callahan.

First Boat Built on the Western Waters, 1812 from James T. Lloyd's *Lloyd's Steamboat Directory* (Cincinnati, 1856), p. 42.

Jacob Burnet (1770-1853) Born in Newark, New Jersey, Jacob Burnet moved to Cincinnati in 1796 where he practiced law. He served as judge of the Northwest Territory and of the Ohio Supreme Court, and was an author of the state's first constitution. Burnet was a cultural booster who served as president of such diverse institutions as the Cincinnati College, Colonization Society, Astronomical Society and the Society for the Cultivation of Sacred Music. An account of his frontier experience, Notes on the Early Settlement of the Northwestern Territory, *was published in 1847.*

These natural and historical advantages—one might even say "accidents"—provided only the potential for making Cincinnati a great metropolis. It remained for men, individually and cooperatively, to transform these opportunities into achievements. For those with vision and a keen sense of public responsibility, it became necessary to cooperate with like-minded people on an array of public projects that would develop the city and would benefit everyone. These men were urban "boomers" or "boosters."

Every 19th-century city had its boomers who devised, sponsored and directed a host of projects to move their city forward. At the root of their ideology was an assumption of the need for constant growth. They perceived the great and potentially great cities of America as being in a fierce conflict for urban empire. The failure of any city to press its advantages and grow rapidly meant stagnation and decline. In a country that seemed to possess no geographical limits, these visionaries perceived all limits as signs of weakness and decay.

Young Cincinnati was blessed with an array of boomers as fruitful in their ideas and as energetic in their pursuit of those ideas as any city in the United States. Timothy Walker, a young Harvard-educated lawyer and recent arrival in the city, described the outlook of Cincinnati's boomers by ascribing to them the motto *Possunt quia posse videntur*—"they can prevail because they think they can." Cincinnati became a "hotbed of projects." To one observer, it seemed that "three citizens never meet but one or other immediately offers a book and a pen for subscription to some new project."

The goal of the Cincinnati boomers was to make the city the urban center of a rich and heavily populated Miami Valley. To accomplish this, an effort was made to develop the area in a balanced fashion by keeping in mind the needs of farmers, merchants and manufacturers.

Agriculture was the first and most important reason for the area's health. The first generation of farmers in the Miami Valley produced a variety of products for sale including flour, bacon, lard, pork, whiskey, butter, beef, wool, feathers, beeswax and linseed oil. The boomers attempted to attract farmers to Cincinnati through such projects as building a series of city-owned marketplaces.

Ephraim Cutler, *View of Cincinnati in 1809.* Woodcut.

Timothy Walker (1802-1856) Born in Wilmington, Massachusetts, Timothy Walker arrived in Cincinnati in 1830 with a Harvard degree and training in its law school. In 1833 he helped establish the Cincinnati Law School, and in 1843 he became the first editor of the Western Law Journal. *One of the city's most prominent lawyers, he contributed to making Cincinnati a center for legal reform in the West. Walker's* Introduction to American Law *was initially published in 1837 and quickly became the standard text for beginning law students across the United States continuing through an eleventh edition in 1905, fifty years after his death.*

Glimpse on the Little Miami (from a painting by J. H. Hine). Engraving. Gift from the estate of Elizabeth Williams.

Chester Harding, *Timothy Walker*. Oil on canvas. Gift of Annie Walker.

Daniel Drake
(1785-1852)
Dr. Daniel Drake was born in New Jersey but migrated to Mayslick, Kentucky, near Maysville in 1788. In 1800 his family sent him to Cincinnati to study medicine with Dr. William Goforth. He supplemented his training by attending the University of Pennsylvania. In 1819 he obtained a charter and founded the Ohio Medical College (now the Medical College of the University of Cincinnati). During his adult life he lived intermittently in Cincinnati and was among the city's major promoters. He helped found a circulating library, museum, debating club, hospital, medical journal, lunatic asylum, grocery store and apothecary shop. Drake's Pictures of Cincinnati, *published in 1815, illustrated his enthusiasm for furthering the commercial, intellectual and cultural growth of the city.*

Micajah Terrell Williams
(1792-1844)
Micajah Terrell Williams, a native of North Carolina, came to Cincinnati in 1812 where he reportedly became one of the city's "greatest ornaments." He was editor of the Western Spy *newspaper and served as Cincinnati township trustee, 1817-21, at which time he entered the state legislature. A boomer for physical and cultural improvements, Williams authored the report that led to construction of the Miami Canal. In 1828, along with Nathan Guilford and Samuel Lewis, he engineered the amendment to the city charter that provided tax revenue to establish and maintain a public school system. Williams was regarded as one of the most influential and reliable politicians in the state.*

Francis D'Avignon, *Daniel Drake* (c. 1850). Lithograph from a daguerreotype by Philip Haas.

Micajah Terrell Williams (1819). Oil on canvas. Gift of Mrs. Terrell Thomas and Mrs. A. F. Perry.

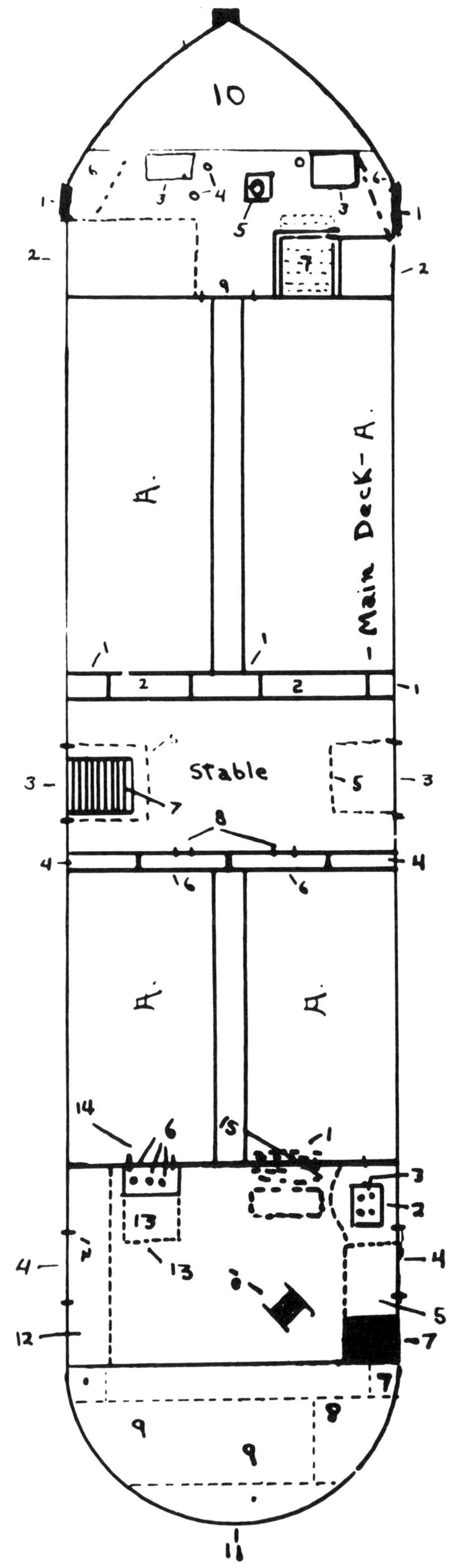

Ohio Canal Boat.
12 by 80 ft. . . . 80 Ton Capacity

Bow Cabin.
1. *Windows.*
2. *Closet-Wardrobe.*
3. *Table.*
4. *Stools—Under table also.*
5. *Stove.*
6. *Lockers for storage and often for beds.*
7. *Steps and Hatch—Entrance from deck.*
8. *Double Beds—One above other.*
9. *Bulkhead—Slide door, used only when boat was empty, or light.*
10. *Often used for Storage.*

Stable.
1. *Feed Boxes.*
2. *Mangers.*
3. *Doors.*
4. *Harness Closets.*
5. *Hatches.*
6. *Granary.*
7. *Portable bridge—For inside only.*
8. *Granary Doors.*

Stern Cabin.
1. *Hatch and Steps.*
2. *Cook Room—Most are enclosed.*
3. *Stove.*
4. *Windows.*
5. *Cupboard.*
6. *Stools—Chairs would not do.*
7. *Flour Bin.*
8. *Wardrobe.*
9. *Double Beds—Same as in Bow Cabin.*
10. *Rocking Chair.*
11. *Stern.*
12. *Double Top locker—Often used as beds.*
13. *Table leaf—Stools under table when not used.*
14. *Upper Bulkhead Door.*
15. *Lower Bulkhead Door.*

Canal Boat. Model built by
Charles E. Mappes, 1971.
Gift of Charles E. Mappes.

But even more important than marketplaces, the boomers pushed a host of transportation schemes to allow the farmers of the Miami Valley to move their goods cheaply and efficiently to Cincinnati where their produce could be processed and shipped to the South and to other markets. The building of more and better roads was one manifestation of this drive for better transportation. Six main roads radiated from Cincinnati to Columbia, Lebanon, Dayton, Hamilton, Lawrenceburg and North Bend. Even though federal law returned 3% of the money raised from the sale of land to the state for road building, the resulting $343,000 yielded between 1804 and 1830 proved inadequate. The boomers therefore promoted the organization of private turnpike companies.

The real energy of the boomers, however, was directed at developing better water transportation routes to the interior of the state. The Great and Little Miami rivers were navigable for only short distances. Moreover, they encouraged farmers to bypass Cincinnati. The solution was both ancient and common to many growing cities in the nation: building canals to augment the Ohio's tributaries and to concentrate the shipment of goods on Cincinnati.

One of the earliest efforts at building canals focused not on Cincinnati but, rather, on a canal around the falls of the Ohio at Louisville. Although steamboats could go over the falls when the river was high, a portage around the falls was required most of the time. The falls tended to make Louisville, rather than Cincinnati, the commercial focus of the Ohio Valley. Cincinnati's merchants and boomers were determined to remove this advantage of their rival city.

Beginning as early as 1804, the Indiana and Kentucky legislatures began chartering companies to build a canal at Louisville. In every instance Cincinnatians strongly supported the efforts. Lack of capital, construction difficulties, and state and urban rivalries all delayed the project. Finally, in 1825 the Louisville and Portland Canal Company renewed its charter and began construction. The project cost $1 million (of which about $230,000 came from the federal government) and was completed in 1831.

Meanwhile, Cincinnatians promoted the most ambitious of all the internal improvement projects, a canal system linking the Ohio River to the Great Lakes. Popular enthusiasm during the early 1820s forced the Ohio legislature to order surveys of possible canal routes. In 1825 it authorized the building of the Ohio Canal from Portsmouth to Cleveland and the Miami Canal from Cincinnati to Dayton. Extension of the Miami Canal from Dayton to Toledo was discussed, but it was not authorized until 1831.

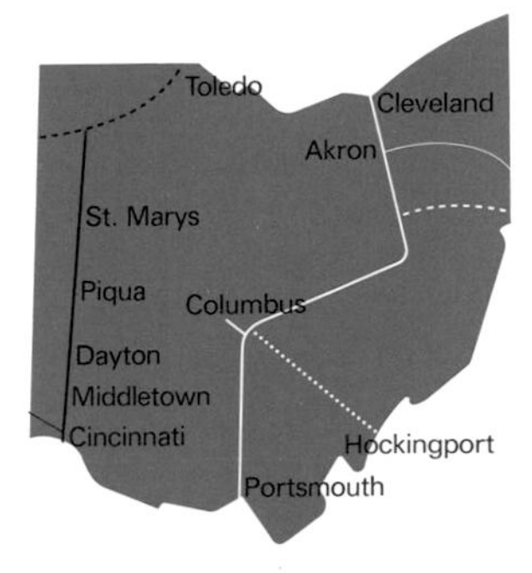

Ohio Canal System

Miami-Erie Canal

White Water Canal to Hagerstown

Wabash-Erie Canal

Ohio-Erie Canal

Hocking Canal

Sandy-Beaver Canal

Pennsylvania-Ohio Canal

Martin Baum (1765-1831)
A Maryland resident of German ancestry, Martin Baum arrived in Cincinnati in 1795. He established the city's first bank, iron foundry and steam mill, and recruited German craftsmen from eastern cities to work in the new manufactories. He was perhaps the first to comprehend the extent to which the development of local industries would benefit the city. Baum suffered financial reverses in the Panic of 1818-19, and could not afford to move into the mansion, now the Taft Museum, which he had constructed to be his home.

Martin Baum. Oil on wood. Purchase.

Cincinnati (c. 1835) with the Steam Flour Mill at the extreme right. Gift of Philip Hinkle.

Predictably, the state representative from Hamilton County, Micajah T. Williams, and other civic leaders lobbied strongly for building canals. Promoters viewed canals principally as transportation links that would provide a way for Cincinnati to get raw materials from the agrarian interior of the state. Initially they would bolster the city's importance as a commercial center where agricultural and eastern manufactured products would be exchanged. More gradually the agricultural products and commercial activity would fuel Cincinnati's growth as a manufacturing center as well.

In July 1825 groundbreaking ceremonies for the Miami Canal were held in Middletown. The canal connecting Cincinnati and Dayton was completed in 3½ years at a cost of $76,582. Soon after it opened in January 1829, newspaper editors declared the canal a success. They pointed out that it had reduced freight rates and increased the volume of produce brought into Cincinnati not only from the immediate vicinity but from the whole Miami Valley. According to one local newspaper, in one week more than 575 tons of produce were brought to the city:

> *The cost of transporting the whole amount for a distance not exceeding 25 miles was $2,800 and it only took 10 boats, 60 men, and 30 boys three days to do the job. By comparison, to bring a similar amount by wagon the same distance, it would take 575 wagons, 2,340 horses, and 575 men. And the cost would have been $7,200.*

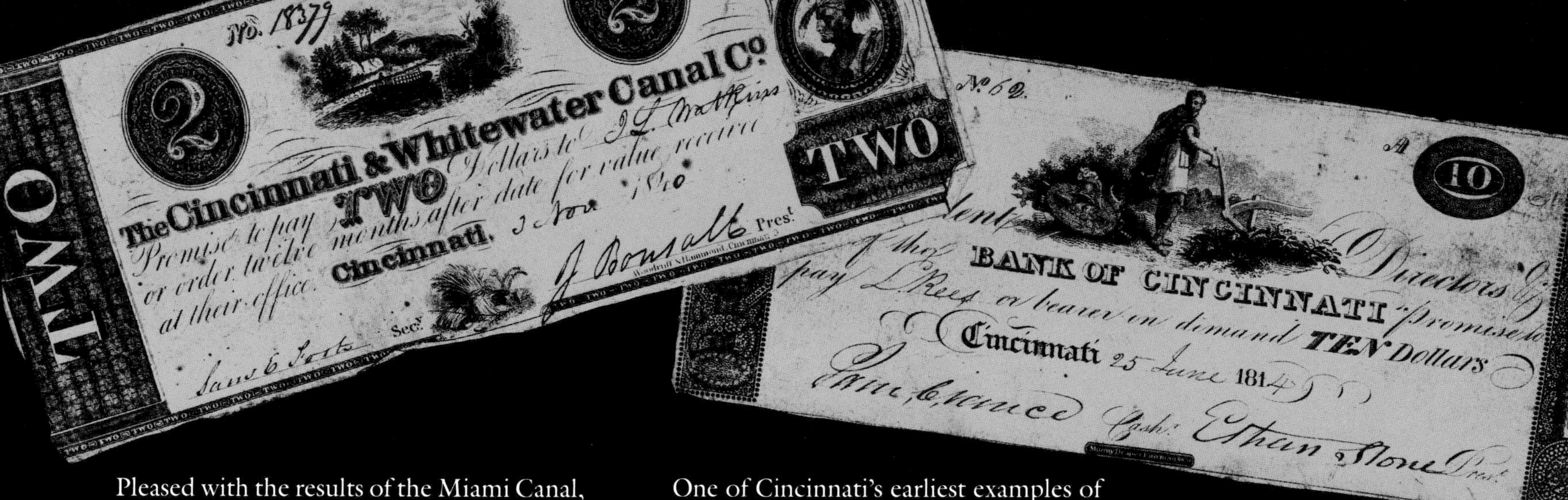

Pleased with the results of the Miami Canal, Cincinnatians sought the construction of a second canal that had not been included in the early transportation proposals. But its purpose was the same—promoting trade with the interior. The Cincinnati Whitewater Canal, chartered in 1837, was 25 miles long and joined Cincinnati to Indiana's Whitewater Canal that ran through the rich agricultural area along the Whitewater Valley from Lawrenceburg to Cambridge. The canal opened in 1843, and farmers used it to ship flour, hams, hogs and grain to Cincinnati. Floods along the Whitewater Valley seriously damaged the canal in 1846 and in 1847. Despite low toll receipts, Cincinnati boosters never doubted that the city would benefit from this trade.

Boomers also promoted the development of manufacturing. Before 1812 the frontier lacked sufficient capital and cheap labor to support the development of industry. Land speculation and trade offered easier and less risky ways of making a profit. The manufacturing that did exist was carried on in small shops by artisans who produced items needed by the new settlers setting up households and farms. By 1806, for example, the 81 artisans working in Cincinnati included tanners, hatters, tailors, shoemakers, blacksmiths, printers, brewers and bricklayers.

The first substantial development of industry in Cincinnati occurred in connection with the chaos caused by the Napoleonic wars raging in Europe from 1807 to 1812. The warfare diverted European manufacturing from traditional goods to the supply of the troops. President Thomas Jefferson's desire to remain clear of the war resulted in an embargo on American shipping that encouraged Americans to produce for themselves.

One of Cincinnati's earliest examples of manufacturing capability was its steam mill. This massive stone structure rose out of the Ohio River nine stories to a height of 110 feet on Front Street between Ludlow and Broadway. The mill, powered by a 70-horsepower Evans steam engine, was capable of producing 20,000 barrels of flour, 500 barrels of whiskey and 1,000 pieces of cloth annually. The mill burned in 1823, was rebuilt in 1826, but was finally destroyed by fire in 1835.

The development of early banking services also facilitated Cincinnati's industrial growth. By 1807 the Miami Exporting Company, which had been founded by Martin Baum, was operating exclusively as a bank. Others soon followed: the Farmers and Mechanics Bank was founded in 1812, the Bank of Cincinnati in 1814, and a private bank run by John H. Piatt in 1815. With the chartering of the Second Bank of the United States in 1816, a group of local merchants lobbied for a Cincinnati branch. Early in 1817 it was organized with a board of directors composed of the town's leading citizens. Jacob Burnet was elected president and Gorham Worth came to Cincinnati from New York to administer the bank as cashier.

The Second Bank of the United States became notorious for unsound banking practices that allowed the irresponsible expansion of credit. Its foolish practices and the economic contractions after the War of 1812 led to the collapse of the nation's economy in the Panic of 1819. Many of Cincinnati's leading men were ruined financially, at least temporarily. Martin Baum, William Henry Harrison, John Piatt and Jacob Burnet were among those who had to sell most of their land in order to satisfy the bank's claims.

Bank Notes issued by the Miami Exporting Company and the Cincinnati and Whitewater Canal Company. Engravings. Gifts of the Ohio Mechanics' Institute.

Bank Note issued by the Bank of Cincinnati, the third bank organized in Cincinnati. It began operation in 1814 and went into liquidation in 1820. Bank President Ethan Stone also was a bank director, a vice-president of the Sunday School Society of the Episcopal Church and of the Agricultural Society and a Justice of the Peace for Hamilton County. Engraving. John J. Rowe Collection.

Nicholas Longworth
(1782-1863)

Nicholas Longworth provided the antebellum West one of its most spectacular rags-to-riches stories. He came to the city about 1803 with little more than the clothes on his back. He built a law practice and, engaging heavily in real-estate speculation, became a leading landowner in Cincinnati at a time when property values were destined to rise dramatically. He was one of the wealthiest men in the United States while still in his 40s paying the second highest property taxes in the nation.

Longworth was one of the early boomers who believed that cultural growth was as important to a city as material growth. In the years before the Civil War, his name and fortune were associated with nearly every arts and educational institution that appeared.

Longworth was exceptionally supportive of individual artists. A contemporary noted that "there was never a young artist of talent who appeared in Cincinnati and was poor and needed help, that Mr. Longworth, if asked did not willingly assist him." His most famous protégés were Robert Duncanson and Hiram Powers. Duncanson, a fine landscape and genre painter, was commissioned to do a series of classical landscape murals in the entrance hall of Longworth's home, "Belmont." Duncanson was black and his success as an artist was extolled by members of the anti-slavery movement.

Hiram Powers was working at the Western Museum in the 1820s when Nicholas Longworth discovered his exceptional talents. He financed the young sculptor's residency in Washington, D.C., and together with fellow boosters, Jacob Burnet and William Henry Harrison, put Powers in contact with members of the political elite. President Andrew Jackson, John Marshall, Martin Van Buren and John Quincy Adams all commissioned portraits by Powers. Executed in the trenchant realism that typlified his American years, they created a sensation in Washington.

In 1837 Longworth and several eastern backers sent Powers to Florence, Italy, to study and work. Powers' ability to capture a likeness was tempered by the classicizing influence of his environment. He became one of the most famous American artists of the age. For the next three decades, Cincinnati was one of the principal markets for his work. He never returned to Cincinnati, but some years later his son came at the urging of Nicholas Longworth's granddaughter to instruct a class for the Women's Art Museum Association.

Nicholas Longworth (1782-1863) from Charles Cists's *Sketches and Statistics of Cincinnati in 1851* (Cincinnati, 1851), facing page 333.

Hiram Powers, right, with William Cullen Bryant in Florence (c. 1870). Photograph. Gift of Annie Walker.

Hiram Powers (1805-1873), *Robert Todd Lytle* (1833). Lawyer and political leader Robert Todd Lytle was born in 1804. After serving in the Ohio Legislature he was elected to the U.S. Congress in 1832. When he was defeated for re-election in 1834, Andrew Jackson appointed him Surveyor-General of the Northwest Territory. His political career was cut short by his death in 1839. Marble. Gift of the Lytle family.

Hiram Powers, *George Washington* (1834-35). Marble. Gift of the estate of Peter G. Thomson.

Cincinnati in 1826

The first thing that strikes an observer in Cincinnati, after having become acquainted with its **relative** *locality, is the comparatively little attention which has been paid to the erection of Manufactures. Commanding the trade of a district of country, which extends at least one hundred miles, in* **every** *direction, and much farther in* **some,** *it would seem to be destined to occupy a prominent stand, amongst the manufacturing cities of the Union; and yet, for years past, this fact has been as little noticed as if "the queen of the West" had been located in a desert, and held no intercourse with the rest of mankind.*

Benjamin Drake and Edward D. Mansfield

Cincinnati's economy stagnated in the aftermath of the bank's closing in 1820. But it recovered rapidly. After the worst of the crises had passed in 1820-1821, production began to expand. For example, pork packing increased so that by 1825 bacon production was up 400% over 1819 and land production doubled. Moreover, the city's traditional industries of flour milling and pork packing were joined in these years by the production of cotton cloth, machine tools and engines. By 1826 Cincinnati's factories produced almost $1,850,000 worth of goods and its population had reached 16,230—up 68% from 1820.

By 1830 Cincinnati had reached a benchmark in its development. It was no longer a frontier settlement in the wilderness but had become an important western river town with a great deal of promise. The concerns of the first settlers—basic survival against the elements and the threat of Indians—had long since passed. Now, the efforts of the city's leaders were directed at establishing Cincinnati not merely as the leading city of the Miami country but of the Ohio Valley and the entire West. The land was cleared and was being populated rapidly; the steamboat dominated the river; the canals threaded the produce of the hinterland to markets along and beyond the Ohio River through the hands of Cincinnati merchants; and a primary industrial foundation had been established. Cincinnati was already being called "Queen of the West."

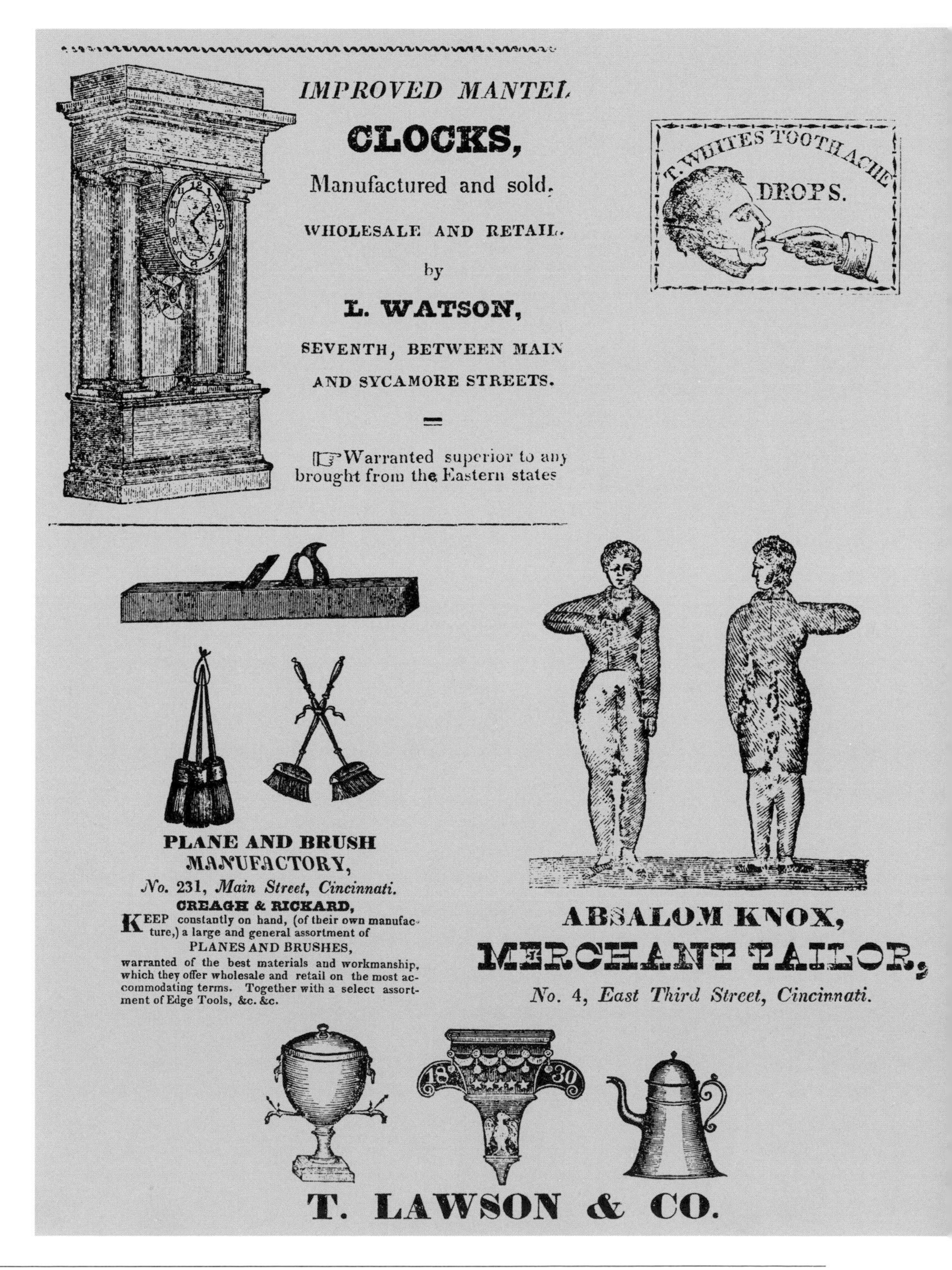

Benjamin Drake and Edward D. Mansfield, made the first reference to Cincinnati as the "Queen of the West" thus far documented. *Cincinnati in 1826* (Cincinnati, 1827), p. 67.

Improved Mantel Clocks,... by L. Watson, Plane and Brush Factory and *Absalom Knox, Merchant Tailor.* From *The Cincinnati Annual Advertiser, Annexed to the Cincinnati Directory, for the year 1829* (Cincinnati, 1829).

T. White's Toothache Drops. From the *Liberty Hall and Cincinnati Gazette,* December 31, 1829, p. 4.

T. Lawson & Co. From *The Cincinnati Directory for the year 1831* (Cincinnati, 1831).

The inhabitants are already consulting as to where the capitol shall stand whenever the nation shall decree the removal of the general government beyond the mountains. If it were not for the noble building at Washington, this removal would probably take place soon, perhaps after the opening of the great Southern Railroad.

Harriet Martineau (1838)

Chapter 2

Of Visions and Dreams

1830-1880

The first four decades of Cincinnati's history brought spectacular development that, in turn, generated a sense of pride in the residents. Beginning in the mid-1820s, observers began to refer to Cincinnati as the "Queen City of the West." In the minds of the city's many visitors and boosters, however, what had occurred prior to 1830 was simply prelude. Steamboats on the river and the opening of canals provided the foundation upon which a truly great city could be built. Cincinnati had become a good city for people with big dreams, and some already envisioned Cincinnati in terms of world leadership. In 1841 one Cincinnati booster, Jacob Scott, predicted "that within one hundred years from this time, Cincinnati will be the greatest city in America; and by the year of our Lord two thousand, the greatest city in the world."

For most of Cincinnati's residents, the dreams were more personal. Cincinnati's expansive economy offered plenty of opportunity for those with limited means. It was a place to get rich. Such dreams held particular meaning for the thousands of immigrants who streamed to America between 1830 and 1860. And while the newcomers quickly discovered that Cincinnati was not utopia, many found the reality was an acceptable substitute.

Harriet Martineau, *Retrospect of Western Travel* (London, 1838), v. 2, p. 49.

John Caspar Wild (d. 1846). *Public Landing*(1835) and *View of Cincinnati from Covington, Kentucky* (1835). Swiss artist, John Caspar Wild, came from Paris to Philadelphia in the early 1830s where he established a reputation as a landscape painter and lithographer. Coming to Cincinnati in 1835, Wild painted two views of the city from Kentucky, the Public Landing and four scenes along residential Third and Fourth Streets. He stayed no longer than two years, returning to Philadelphia. Later he traveled to St. Louis and, finally, to Davenport, Iowa. Gouache on paper. Gifts of Mrs. Charles Graham.

Milward and Oldershaw (1851). In 1850 this large pork and beef house, located in Covington, Kentucky, packed 11,746 hogs and 3,000 heads of cattle primarily for European markets. Hogs were driven up a ramp, visible at the right of the illustration, to pens on the roof. Otto Onken lithograph. Gift from the estate of Clifford M. Stegner.

The most ambitious visions of Cincinnati's boosters would never be realized. For the first 20 years of this period, between 1830 and 1850, the dreams seemed to be coming true. Cincinnati was America's boom town. Her population grew faster than any other American city. She became the country's second largest industrial center and the recognized leader of the world in certain categories. Then, just as Cincinnatians were becoming accustomed to believing that their city was destined for unparalleled greatness, the world shifted. The city's rate of growth slowed while other cities spurted ahead, overtaking Cincinnati. In the 1860s the source of her strength, the Ohio River with its tributaries and canals, seemingly became her weakness as railroads transformed the nation's transportation routes. The new conditions facing Cincinnati challenged her leaders during the 1870s and 1880s. Cincinnatians had to reformulate their sense of who they were and where their city fit in the world.

In the early 19th century, Cincinnati was a city built on commerce. The Ohio River and the steamboat were the bases of her greatness. During the 1820s industry had begun to develop, but initially this was perceived as secondary to and supportive of trade. From 1830 to 1860 Cincinnati's industrial development accelerated and redefined the character of the city.

The industry most responsible for bringing about this change during the second quarter of the century was pork packing. It grew naturally out of the city's close relationship with the rich agricultural region surrounding Cincinnati. From its earliest days, Cincinnati served as one of many local centers for hog slaughtering and packing. But it was not until the 1820s that it was possible to transport pork products rapidly and in large quantities to consumer markets and to acquire a regular supply of salt—primarily from the Kanawha Valley of Virginia—for the packing process. In addition, an important shift towards crop and livestock specialization in the region provided a large supply of hogs. Early farming in the area was diversified and generally for subsistence. Many farmers raised a few hogs because they could be left to roam freely in the local forests and required little care. In the 1820s farmers in the Scioto and Miami valleys grew larger amounts of corn which they fed to hogs. This increased the number of hogs raised, and by feeding corn to the hogs, farmers produced fatter animals with a higher quality of meat.

Each fall drovers from all over southwestern Ohio and eastern Indiana herded thousands of hogs over roads—and others were transported on canal boats—to Cincinnati. By 1835 Cincinnati had become the nation's chief packing center. Ten years later it surpassed Cork and Belfast in Ireland for the leadership of the world by slaughtering and processing a quarter-million hogs. The lack of artificial means of refrigeration confined slaughtering and packing to the period of November to mid-March; still, by 1854 this work provided seasonal employment for 2,450 workers.

As the pork-packing industry rapidly expanded, it received a good deal of comment by the city's boosters. One of them, George Jones of the Cincinnati branch of the Second Bank of the United States, wrote so enthusiastically to a Liverpool correspondent about the prospects of the industry that he was sent two papier-mache models of hogs with the inscription: "To George Jones, as the worthy representative of Porkopolis."

The thorough bred Short Horned

DURHAM BULL,

Five years old, will be kept the present season at the farm of the subscriber, on Walnut Hills, near Cincinnati, until the 1st of September, at $10 the season, except full bloods, which will be $25.

STEUBEN is considered, by all who have seen him, one of the finest Bulls now in the United States, and cannot be exceeded in size or form by any of his age.

STEUBEN was bred by the late Jeptha D. Garrard, Esq., and at one year old took the highest premium offered by the Hamilton County Agricultural Society. At two years old he was not exhibited, and at the last exhibition of the Society, Oct. 17, 1837, the highest premium was again awarded to the BARON.

BARON STEUBEN

Was got by Sam Patch, out of Hyacith; she by the imported Bull Tecumseh, out of Tulip; Tulip by Miranda, out of Lady Monday; Lady Monday by imported Bull Sam Martin, out of the imported Cow Mrs. Mott.

N. B.—Good accommodation can be had on the farm for all cows from a distance. In all cases the fees must be paid as soon as cows are brought to the farm.

JOHN H. KEMPER.

April 2nd, 1839.

Lard Oil Manufacturers.

Anchor Lard Oil Works, J. L. Mitchener, w. s. Plum at elbow of M. Canal.
Barkalow Wm. T. & Co. Poplar b. John & Linn, office 215 Main
Burckhardt & Co. 12 Hammond.
Conkling J. L., 109 e. 5th St.
Cronin Jeremiah & Son, w. s. Culvert be. 7th and 8th.
Emery Thomas, 33 and 35 Water.
Ford William & Son, s. s. Front op. T. P. 12 F'n.
Glenn & Co. Water st. n. side, bet. Walnut and Vine.
Globe Lard Oil Factory, G. & P. Bogen, Harrison Pike near Brighton House.
James & Brother, e. s. M. Canal n. of Liberty.
Ohio Lard Oil Works, Kellum C. B. 17 Walnut.
Peebles & Brother, s. s. M. Canal bet. Elm and Plum.
Queen City Lard Oil Factory, F. Franks, 10 e. Front.
Work M. & Co. 11 Main.
Whetstone Richard A. n. s. 8th e. of Broadway.
Wiedemer F. X. & Co. 17 w. Front.

ANCHOR LARD OIL WORKS.
OFFICE AND MANUFACTORY,
COR. OF PLUM AND CANAL STREETS.
(Elbow of the Canal.)
J. L. MITCHENER & CO.,
MANUFACTURERS.

GEO. CLARK,
LARD OIL MANUFACTURER,
No. 15 Buckeye St., bet. Main and Walnut Sts, Cincinnati.

A. G. CHEEVER & CO.,
Lock Street, between Fourth & Fifth Streets, Cincinnati,
Manufacturers of Star Candles and Lard Oil, a complete Stock always on hand.

D. W. WRIGHT,
LARD OIL MANUFACTURER,
No. 13 Canal, bet. Main & Walnut Sts., Cincinati.
☞Cash paid for Lard. Cash prices, by the Barrel.

Durham Bull (1839). Miami Valley farmers also bred and raised cattle for sale to meat packing firms. Broadside. Gift from the estates of Mr. and Mrs. Charles Amory Blinn.

Advertisements for lard oil, a by-product of pork packing. From the *Cincinnati Business Directory* (1853).

Robert S. Duncanson, *Cincinnati From Covington, Kentucky* (1848-1850). By mid-century Cincinnati had grown to a population of over 115,000 and was the nation's sixth largest city. Duncanson (1817-22 to 1872) was Cincinnati's first notable black artist. Born in New York and raised in Canada, from the early 1840s he spent most of his time in Cincinnati. He also worked in Detroit and traveled extensively, including several trips to Europe. Oil on canvas. Chalmers Hadley memorial fund purchase.

J. W. Hill, *Cincinnati, Covington & Newport* (1853). Harrison P. Diehl began manufacturing fireworks in the early 1850s and built a wooden structure on Mt. Adams from which to display them. The Pyro Garden lasted only a few years but Diehl's company was in business in Cincinnati, and later Reading, Ohio, until 1890. Lithograph. Gift of Robert Clarke.

Prior to 1850 the slaughtering and packing processes were functionally and geographically divided. Draymen transported carcasses from slaughterhouses in the Deer Creek Valley on the eastern edge of the city to packing houses located near the riverfront. After 1850 companies combined these functions into the same buildings as the industry relocated along the Miami-Erie Canal. These new slaughterhouses became world famous for their efficient use of labor in the "disassemblage process." The hogs were first driven up ramps to the top floor of the slaughterhouses, many of which were three or four stories high. As they entered the building, the pigs were knocked unconscious with a sledgehammer and suspended from a moving hook. As they passed down the line, the hogs were bled, scalded, the hair scraped from their hides, then gutted and cleaned before being sent to cooling chambers. The butchering, rendering and salting processes were performed later but with equal efficiency.

Pork packing fostered other industries. Economical Cincinnatians utilized every part of the animal. The bristles were used as binding in plaster, in the manufacture of brushes and in the furniture industry. The city's tanneries used the hides. Two by-products of rendering lard were the bases for several important Cincinnati firms—sterine was used in the manufacture of lamp oil and candles, while cracklings were used for producing soap.

Cincinnati's identification as "Porkopolis" became so strong that many commentators subsequently have given the impression that pork packing and its related industries dominated local manufacturing. Actually, in 1855 meat packing accounted for only 15% of the total value of goods produced in the city. By this time Cincinnati had developed a manufacturing base much broader than pork packing.

Arrival of Hogs at Cincinnati. From *Harper's Weekly* (February 4, 1860), p. 72. Engraving. Elizabeth Haven Appleton fund purchase.

FIVE THOUSAND HOGS WANTED!!

5,000 WELL corn fatted Hogs, for which the highest market price will be paid in cash, on delivery. Apply at SAMUEL LANGTON'S Pork House, on Main street, north of the Canal. Nov. 24, 1835. 6td&w1t

I am sure I should have liked Cincinnati much better if the people had not dealt so very largely in hogs. The immense quantity of business done in this line would hardly be believed by those who had not witnessed it. I never saw a newspaper without remarking such advertisements as the following:

"Wanted, immediately, 4,000 fat hogs."

"For sale, 2,000 barrels of prime pork."

But the annoyance came nearer than this; if I determined upon a walk up Main-street, the chances were five hundred to one against my reaching the shady side without brushing by a snout fresh dripping from the kennel; when we had screwed our courage to the enterprise of mounting a certain noble-looking sugar-loaf hill, that promised pure air and a fine view, we found the brook we had to cross, at its foot, red with the stream from a pig slaughter-house; while our noses, instead of meeting "the thyme that loves the green hill's breast," were greeted by odours that I will not describe, and which I heartily hope my readers cannot imagine; our feet, that on leaving the city had expected to press the flowery sod, literally got entangled in pigs'-tails and jaw bones: and thus the prettiest walk in the neighbourhood was interdicted for ever.

Frances Trollope (1832)

Frances Trollope came to the United States in 1827 to make a fortune. Soon after her arrival in Cincinnati in 1828, she built a "Bazaar" on Third Street which contained a shop, a ballroom and exhibition gallery. Her Bazaar was a failure and Mrs. Trollope returned to England in 1831.

Five Thousand Hogs Wanted!! From *The Daily Cincinnati Republican, and Commercial Register,* November 28, 1835, p. 3.

Frances Trollope (1780-1863), from *The Domestic Manners of the Americans* (London, 1832), p. 85.

Journey to the Slaughter-House from *Harper's Weekly* (February 4, 1860), p. 72. Engraving.

We entered an immense low-ceiled room and followed a vista of dead swine, upon their backs, their paws stretching mutely toward heaven. Walking down to the vanishing point, we found there a sort of human chopping-machine where the hogs were converted into commercial pork. A plank table, two men to lift and turn, two to wield the cleavers, were its component parts. No iron cog-wheels could work with more regular motion. Plump falls the hog upon the table, chop, chop; chop, chop; chop, chop, fall the cleavers. All is over. But, before you can say so, plump, chop, chop; chop, chop; chop, chop, sounds again. There is no pause for admiration. By a skilled sleight of hand, hams, shoulders, clear, mess, and prime fly off, each squarely cut to its own place, where attendants, aided by trucks and dumbwaiters, dis-

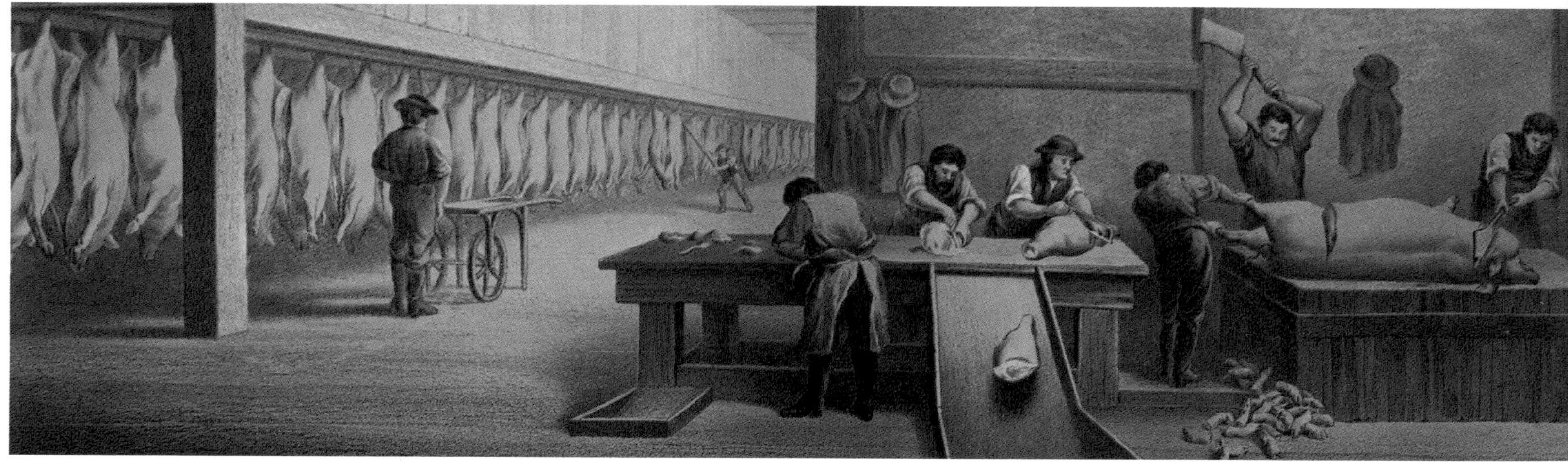

Henry Farny, *The Disassembly Line.* Among the first places that assembly-line principles were applied was the meat-packing industry. Lithograph. Gift of Mr. and Mrs. Fred Heinz.

Frederick Law Olmsted, writing about his visit to Cincinnati in *A Journey Through Texas...* (New York, 1857), p. 9.

patch each to its separate destiny—the ham for Mexico, its loin for Bordeaux. Amazed beyond all expectation at the celerity, we took out our watches and counted thirty-five seconds, from the moment when one hog touched the table until the next occupied its place. The number of blows required I regret we did not count.

Frederick Law Olmsted (1857)

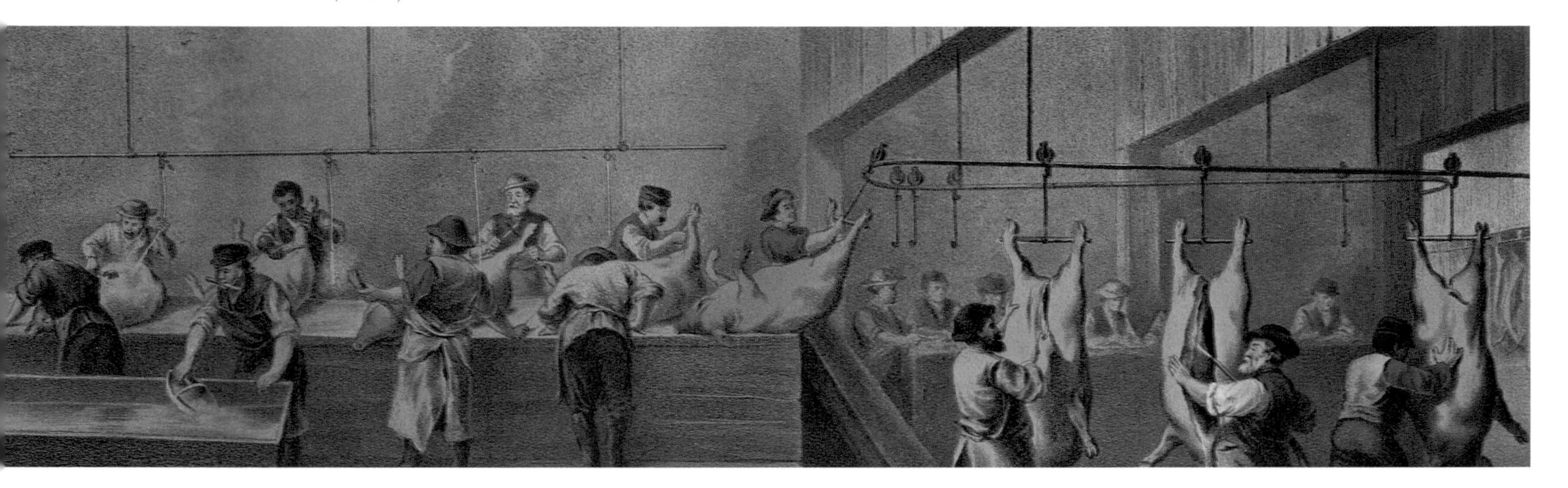

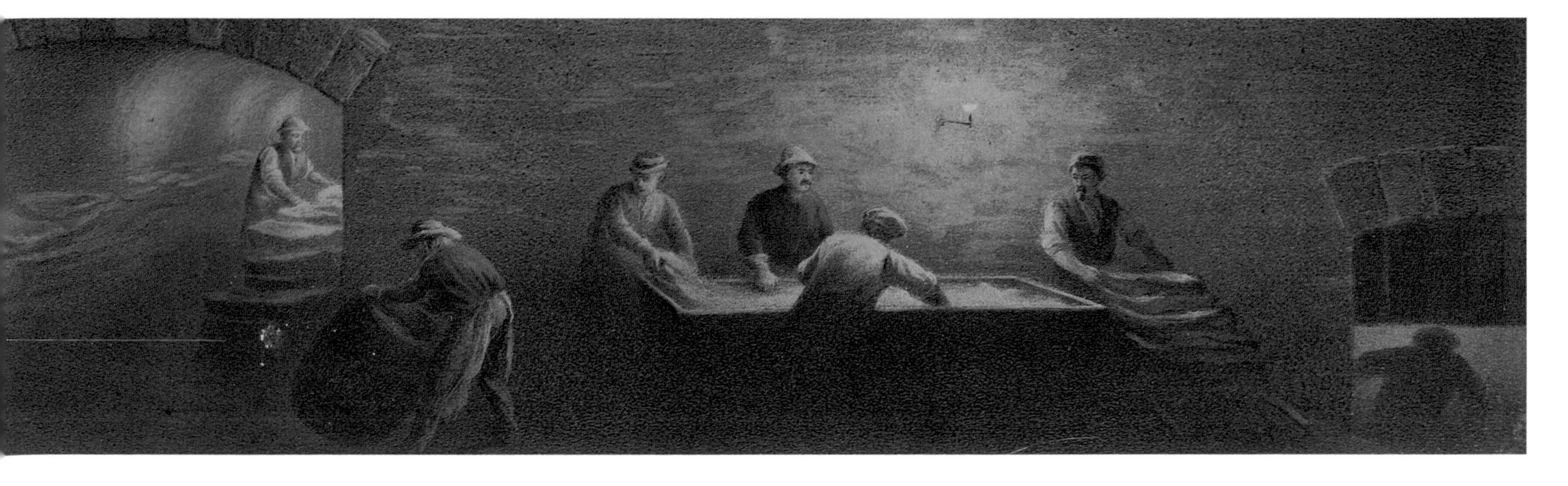

Niles and Company, founded in 1834, manufactured sugar mills, stationary engines, machine tools and rolling mills for southern markets. Production of locomotive engines began in 1851 and continued in their new shop on Congress Street near Butler from 1852 until 1858. Lithograph. From Charles Cist's *Sketches and Statistics of Cincinnati in 1851* (Cincinnati, 1851), facing p. 193.

The iron- and metalworking industries were second in importance to pork packing. By 1850 Cincinnati had 44 foundries, one-third of which concentrated on the production of stoves. Other products included iron railings, mantels, burial cases, castings, steam engines and boilers. Miles Greenwood settled in Cincinnati in 1829, later bought the Eagle Iron Works and built the company into the second largest iron manufactory in the West. It made heavy machine castings as well as an array of items for the home—pulleys, shutter lifts and catches, sash weights, spittoons, teakettles and tailor shears.

The production of steamboat engines was one of the most important branches of the metalworking industry. By 1841 five shipbuilding yards employed 306 workers, making Cincinnati second only to Pittsburgh as a western steamboat manufacturing and repair center. This industry trained Cincinnati workers with skills that would later be employed in the machine-tool industry.

The availability of fine woods spurred the development of an important furniture-manufacturing industry in the Queen City. From surrounding forests came cherry, walnut, maple, sycamore and poplar; pine came from Pittsburgh and mahogany from New Orleans. The industry boomed with the introduction of steam power, which allowed manufacturers to cut prices by a third compared to the costs of handwork. By 1841 census taker Charles Cist reported 48 cabinetware factories and 11 chair manufacturers producing $515,600 worth of goods. A decade later he counted 136 shops employing 1,158 workers who were producing $1,660,000 worth of furniture. As the market for Cincinnati furniture expanded throughout the Mississippi Valley,

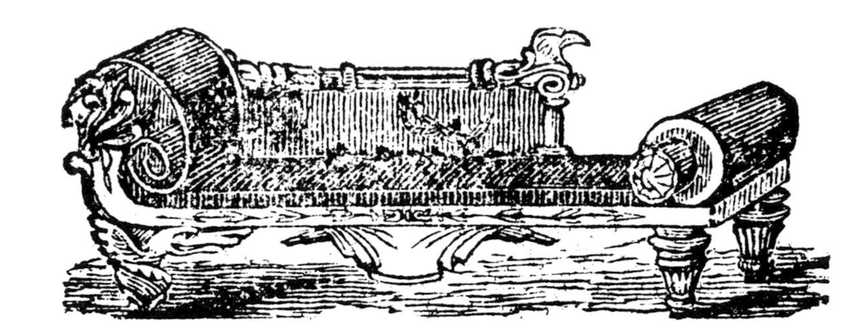

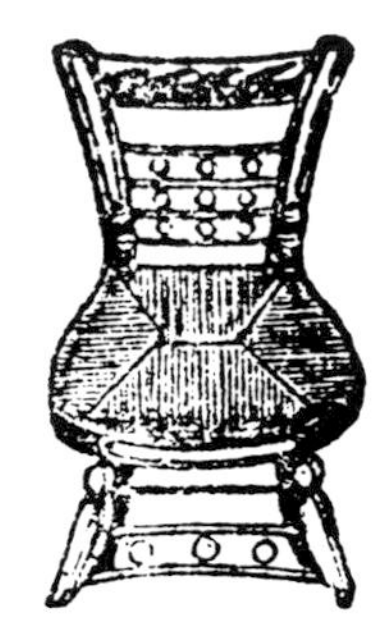

manufacturers discovered it was more economical to ship their wares in pieces for assembly on location. By mid-century Cincinnati furniture graced homes and hotels throughout the Midwest and South.

The manufacture of clothing was a fourth important industry in Cincinnati. During the 1850s the value of locally produced clothing jumped from approximately $2 million to approximately $15 million. In 1860 Cincinnati produced one-half of all the ready-made clothing available in the western markets. The industry also illustrated the city's close ties with the South, which supplied the cotton and bought much of the finished work. In the mid-1850s, between 5,000 and 6,000 seamstresses worked in miserable conditions for extremely low wages in the clothing industry. When they attemped to organize, even the *Cincinnati Enquirer,* which normally opposed worker causes, editorialized in the women's favor. Technology more than agitation produced the increase in wages that followed the introduction of sewing machines in the late 1850s.

In an amazingly short amount of time, Cincinnati had become a major manufacturing center. This could not have occurred had Cincinnati not built excellent transportation facilities, developed thriving commerce and generated sufficient capital to finance new growth. Nor could Cincinnati have built industries so rapidly without an ample labor supply. Traditionally, American labor was scarce and, therefore, expensive. Between 1830 and 1850, however, Cincinnati's booming economy attracted thousands of newcomers who made the Queen City the fastest growing urban center in the United States. These people not only transformed the size and appearance of Cincinnati, they fundamentally changed its religious and ethnic composition.

HENRY BOYD,

MANUFACTURER OF

PATENT

Right and Left Wood Screw and Swelled Railed

BEDSTEADS,

NORTHWEST CORNER BROADWAY & EIGHTH STREETS,

CINCINNATI.

Persons wishing to purchase Bedsteads, would do well to call and examine for themselves, as this Bedstead is warranted superior to any other ever offered in the West; they can be put up or taken apart in one fourth of the time usually required, are more firm, less apt to become loose and worthless, and without a single harbour for vermin.

CERTIFICATES.

The undersigned, having used the above named Patent Bedsteads, feel no hesitation in recommending them to be the best now in use.

Hon. N. C. Read,
J. G. Burnet,
D. L. Rusk,
P. Evans,
P. Grandin, Esq.
Samuel L'Hommedieu,
Samuel Berresford,
William Holmes,
Wm. Marsh, Galt House,

Hon. Henry Morse,
M. Allen,
S. B. Hunt,
Isaiah Wing,
B. Tappan,
Milton McLean, Esq.
Wm.H. Henrie, Henrie H.
J. W. Mason. Fourth st. House.

Hon. Richard Ayres,
Rev. L. G. Bingham,
Wm. D. Gallagher,
J. B. Russell,
Daniel Burritt,
G.W.H.Evans, Cin. Hotel.
James Eshelby,
T. M. Cockrell, Pearl st House.

From 1836 to 1863 black furniture-maker Henry Boyd produced superior bedsteads made of sycamore, maple, cherry, black walnut and mahogany for local, southern and southwestern markets. Robinson and Jones' *Cincinnati Directory for 1846.* (Cincinnati, 1846), p. 466.

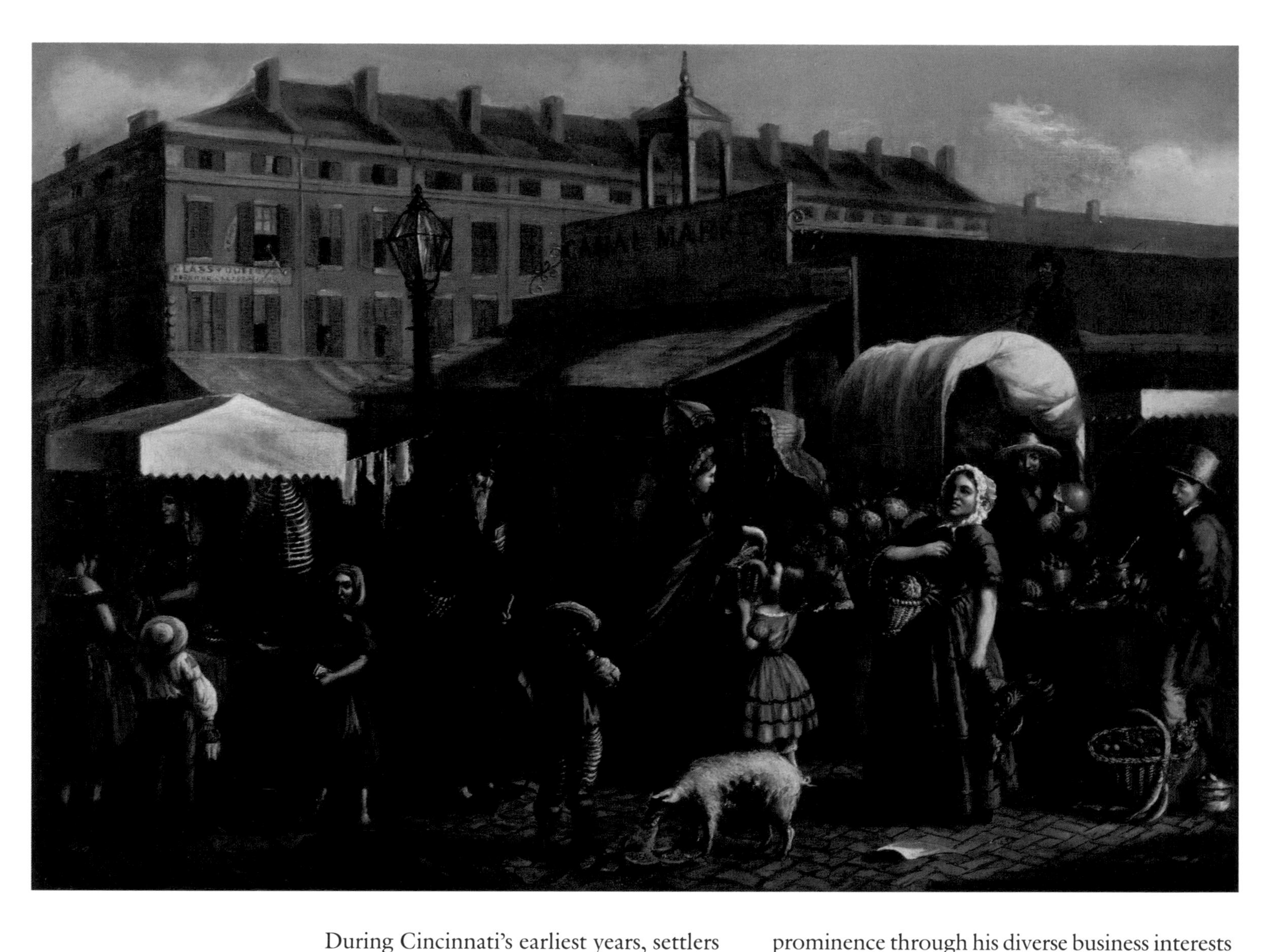

During Cincinnati's earliest years, settlers came from many places, but the vast majority were native-born Americans of English and Scottish ancestry. In the 1830s and 1840s the bulk of the new arrivals came from Germany. A few Germans had lived in Cincinnati since its founding, and some had risen to positions of prominence and influence. David Ziegler, for example, was born in 1748 in Heidelberg, Germany, immigrated to Pennsylvania before the Revolution and came to Fort Washington in 1790. When Cincinnati was incorporated as a village in 1802, Ziegler was elected president of council and served two terms. Similarly, Martin Baum, who was of German parentage, rose to great prominence through his diverse business interests and was elected mayor in 1807 and 1812. In 1825 the German community consisted of only 64 persons, and in 1830 amounted to only 5% of the city's populace. Ten years later Germans constituted 30% of Cincinnati's population, prompting the city council to publish ordinances in German as well as in English. Although the German-born population more than doubled between 1840 and 1850, Irish immigration during the same years reduced the German proportion to approximately one-fourth—but of a city whose numbers had exploded from 46,382 to 115,435 in that decade.

Henry Mosler, *Canal Street Market* (1860). The Canal Street Market, located between Vine and Walnut at present day Court Street, was typical of several that operated in mid-19th century Cincinnati. Oil on canvas. Eugene F. Bliss fund purchase.

In Cincinnati, as in other mid-19th century cities, the poorer people and the new arrivals tended to live on the periphery, while the wealthier and more prominent residents occupied the center. Thus, the thousands of Germans who flooded into Cincinnati settled away from the center of the city in an area north and east of the Miami-Erie Canal. This area was never exclusively German, but their predominance gave the region such a Germanic flavor that it became known as "Over-the-Rhine." The district evolved into a web of streets and alleys lined with closely built, neat rows of residences and shops.

Like immigrants in any time, these Germans faced an array of problems. Many suffered extreme hardships, especially in their early years while establishing themselves and looking for jobs. Collectively, however, German immigrants possessed advantages over other groups. Many of them were skilled tradesmen and craftsmen who could find work as bakers or tailors, or in the rapidly developing industries. Their mechanical skills and the training some brought with them established the foundation for Cincinnati's development as a printing and machine-tool center.

Based in Over-the-Rhine, the Cincinnati Germans developed a rich subculture. They founded organizations and institutions which helped cushion the impact of the American environment for themselves and others from the "Fatherland" while making lasting contributions to the quality of life in Cincinnati. Churches, schools, breweries and beer gardens sprang up throughout the area. The immigrants preserved their language in their homes, churches and schools. In 1836 the *Cincinnati Volksblatt* began publication. By 1850 Cincinnati had four German-language newspapers.

The Germans also formed special-interest societies. Between 1836 and 1860, four German militia units were formed, which became the basis for the Ohio Ninth Regiment during the Civil War. Numerous savings societies were organized to help with financial needs. Cincinnati also became the home of the first American Turnverein. Organized by Frederick Hecker, a hero of the ill-fated 1848 revolutions in Europe, the Turnverein sought to develop a "refined humanity" in its membership through physical exercise and intellectual pursuits. Perhaps the organizations that had the most enduring impact on Cincinnati life were the German singing societies. In 1838 the first German male chorus was formed, and by mid-century there were dozens of bands, orchestras and singing societies. In 1849 many of them joined to hold the first German music festival in the city, the Saengerfest.

Cincinnati Germans represented many different backgrounds and outlooks. One of the most important subgroups was the large number of German Jews who immigrated to Cincinnati. Prior to 1830 no more than 150 Jews, mostly English in background, lived in the city. Over the next three decades, between 8,000 and 10,000 new Jews, mostly from Germany, streamed into Cincinnati.

Jewish residents before 1830 worshipped in an orthodox fashion in two synagogues. The arrival of the German Jews brought new influences. The German Jewish leadership that came to Cincinnati pressed for "modernization" of Jewish laws and ritual to conform them to the larger American culture. Under the leadership of rabbis Max Lilienthal and Isaac M. Wise, who arrived in Cincinnati in the mid-1850s, the Cincinnati Jewish community became a prominent center for the reform movement in America. Reforms included the dropping of certain holy

U. S. Agricultural Fair. The Hamilton County Agricultural Society began holding fairs near Carthage in 1853. Their fair was supplemented in 1860 by another, the eighth annual fair of the United States Agricultural Society, held September 12-20 at the Queen City Trotting Park near Winton Place. Lithograph. Gift from the estate of Grace F. Spiegel.

Major David Ziegler, from Henry Howe's *Historical Collections of Ohio . . .* (Cincinnati, 1908), v. 1, p. 846.

Isaac Mayer Wise (1819-1900)
In the 1840s German Jews heatedly debated proposals to reform Judaism. Isaac M. Wise came to America from Bohemia in 1846 convinced of the need for reform and hoping that American society would foster the necessary experimentation. After a stormy eight years in Albany, New York, Wise came to Cincinnati in 1854 to begin a lifelong collaboration with the K. K. Bene Yeshurun (Children of God) synagogue. Over the next 46 years, Wise refined and promoted his ideas about reform and developed institutions to support them. A new prayerbook, the Minhag America, *a conference of reform Jewish congregations and a Hebrew College to train an indigenous rabbinate were the principal elements of his plan. Through Wise's influence Cincinnati became known, and remains, the center of reform Judaism.*

days, the introduction of organ music and choirs with men and women, an end to the custom of wearing hats during services and, most importantly, the reform of the prayer book. The ideas of these men and their collaborators were communicated through the *Israelite,* which began publishing in Cincinnati in 1854, and through rabbinical training at Hebrew Union College, founded in 1876.

Beginning in 1846 a potato blight drove thousands of Irish from their homeland. Many of them comprised the second group of immigrants to reach Cincinnati. Like the Germans, the Irish organized to meet their needs. They formed several militia units, which became the core of the Ohio 10th Regiment in the Civil War, and, in 1849, the Hibernian Society to assist the Irish here and those left behind. Unlike the Germans, the Irish were mostly of peasant backgrounds. They did not bring the skills and experience that would allow them rapid adjustment to American and urban life. Consequently, the Irish were poorer and less secure than the Germans.

The native-born residents watched this influx of new people closely and fearfully, with newspapers regularly reporting immigration statistics. These foreign people seemed to carry the threat of labor unrest, intemperance, illiteracy, pauperism and crime. The response of the immigrants to their new surroundings often fed such suspicion. German and Irish customs sometimes conflicted with those of the Americans. Native-born Cincinnatians found the way immigrants observed the Sabbath particularly aggravating. Yet, the newcomers thought the American Protestant Sunday—with no entertainment, no saloons and no theaters—was drab and oppressive. Americans mistakenly concluded that the complex of ethnic societies showed that the immigrants wanted to share in the wealth of America without becoming "American."

Many Americans also viewed as dangerous the loyalties of the immigrants to their homeland and to European institutions—especially the Roman Catholic Church. This distrust was expressed in several ways. Judge Bellamy Storer required Irish Catholics who were applying for citizenship to swear on and kiss the Protestant Bible. Officeholders routinely gave native-born Americans preference when hiring for publicly financed construction jobs. Individual immigrants regularly found themselves the objects of violence.

Such anti-foreign sentiment reached its peak in the early 1850s, poisoning the city's political climate. In 1854 one newspaper ridiculed the Democratic Party with a mock "Holy Church Democratic State Ticket" slating Pope Pius IX for "Supreme Judge" and Bishop John Baptist Purcell for the board of public works. In April 1855 an effort to elect city officials resulted in three days of violence. The nativists imported 300 Kentucky toughs to "protect the polls." These men seized the ballot boxes in the predominantly German 11th Ward and tried to do the same in the Ninth. Violence continued into the following day when German militias barricaded the bridges into Over-the-Rhine. The nativists stormed the barricades at night yelling such rallying cries as "Kill the Dutch," but the trained militia easily repulsed them. The anti-Catholic and anti-foreign sentiment—which had surfaced in many American communities at the same time—soon subsided in the face of the rising national controversy with the South over the extension of slavery.

Isaac Mayer Wise. Reprinted with permission. From *Cincinnati in Bronze* (Cincinnati, c1959), p. 14.

Citizenship certificate issued to Gerhard Jacobs.

UNITED STATES OF AMERICA.

The State of Ohio, } ss.
Hamilton County,

Be it Remembered, *That on the* tenth *day of* October *eighteen hundred and* forty three *at a term of the Court of Common Pleas, holden within and for the county of Hamilton, aforesaid, personally came* Gerhard Jacobs a native of Oldenburg who arrived in the United States on the 2 June 1838 now proves residence and character by the oath of Henry Strong a citizen — — *of the state and county aforesaid, and the said* Gerhard Jacobs *to be naturalized and become a citizen of the United States of America, did make application to* the Superior Court of Cincinnati on the 5th day of September AD 1840 — — —

and the said Gerhard Jacobs — *on being admitted by this court, took the oath to support the Constitution of the United States of America, and that he then did absolutely and entirely, renounce and abjure all allegiance and fidelity to every foreign Prince, Potentate, State, and Sovereignty whatsoever, and particularly to the* Grand Duke of Oldenburg — —

This is therefore to Certify, *That the said* Gerhard Jacobs *has complied with the laws of the United States in such case made and provided, and is, therefore, admited a* **CITIZEN** *of the United States.*

In Testimony Whereof, *I have hereunto set my hand, and affixed the Seal of the Court of Common Pleas at Cincinnati, this* 10th *day of* October *A. D. 18*43

J. W. Piatt, *Clerk H. C.*

by [illegible] Warden Depy.

The Underground Railroad

Charles T. Webber (1825-1911), *Slave Auction.* Oil on canvas. Purchase.

20 *Dollars Reward.*

RAN AWAY from the ſubſcriber, living in Woodford county Kentucky, a YELLOW NEGRO MAN, named JEFFREY, between the age of twenty-five and twenty ſix years, tho' he dont appear ſo old, about five feet eight or nine inches high, rather ſlim than otherwiſe, a little knock-kneed, wears his hair in plats on his head. Any perſon who will apprehend ſaid negro, and bring him to me, or ſecure him in the moſt convenient jail to the place where he is taken, and give information to me, ſhall receive the above reward.

WILLIAM BUFORD.

AUGUST 22, 1810. 3‡*

Owners advertised in local newspapers for the return of runaway slaves. *Liberty Hall,* (September 26, 1810), suppl. p. 2. Eugene F. Bliss fund purchase.

In the years after the Civil War, stories of the underground railroad that helped runaway slaves travel north to safety and freedom came to rank among the most popular elements of local legend. They were also among the most exaggerated, misunderstood and difficult to document.

Contrary to legend, no tunnels burrowed under the Ohio River and no highly organized institution existed to spirit runaways northward. Most importantly, the idea that runaways were helpless cargo in the caring hands of highly principled and fearless whites distorted reality.

Runaways found assistance principally from fellow blacks, who rarely trusted even well-known abolitionists with news that a new group of slaves was passing through. In 1837 James G. Birney, publisher of the abolitionist newspaper *The Philanthropist,* speaking of runaways passing through Cincinnati, commented that "I know nothing of them generally till they are past." Certainly some whites in Cincinnati assisted escaping slaves, such as Levi Coffin, the reputed "president" of the underground railroad. While probably more developed in Cincinnati than in most northern cities, the underground railroad remained an informal network primarily by blacks, for blacks.

The Beechers and the Antislavery Movement

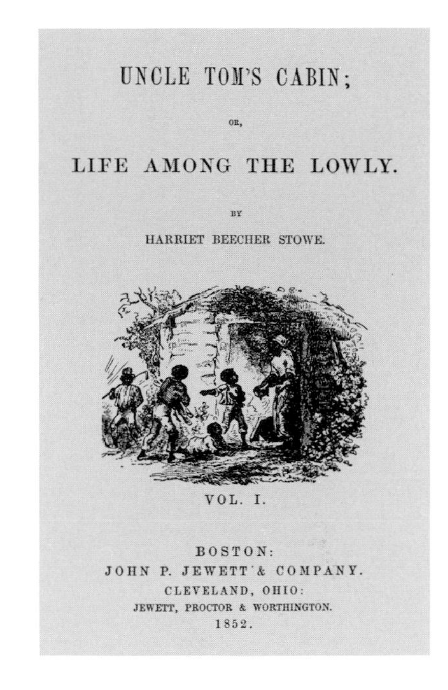
UNCLE TOM'S CABIN;

OR,

LIFE AMONG THE LOWLY.

BY

HARRIET BEECHER STOWE.

VOL. I.

BOSTON:
JOHN P. JEWETT & COMPANY.
CLEVELAND, OHIO:
JEWETT, PROCTOR & WORTHINGTON.
1852.

Cincinnati was the birthplace of an antislavery movement with nationwide repercussions. In the 1830s the Rev. Lyman Beecher, the most powerful preacher of his day, was persuaded to come to the city to head Lane Theological Seminary and several of his talented children accompanied him.

In this border city, the issue of slavery was subject to ongoing debate. While Lyman Beecher was opposed to slavery, he favored gradual emancipation and colonization over immediate abolition. Nonetheless, for a time he allowed Lane to serve as a center for antislavery agitation and uplift programs for free blacks living in Cincinnati.

Rev. Lyman Beecher's reform-minded daughters, Harriet and Catharine, participated fully in the intellectual and cultural life of the city, moving in circles which included Daniel Drake and Salmon P. Chase. They were knowledgeable of the latest thinking on such diverse topics as theology, geography and home economics, and they were particularly interested in efforts to improve the conditions of women and children.

In Cincinnati, Harriet Beecher married Calvin Stowe, a Lane Seminary theology professor, and bore six children. When her youngest baby fell victim to the cholera epidemic of 1849, she was struck by the similiar sorrow experienced by slave women who had their children torn from them. Inspired to write a novel of life in slavery, in 1852 she produced *Uncle Tom's Cabin,* one of the most effective propaganda pieces for the antislavery movement. Although it was written and published shortly after she left the city for Maryland, *Uncle Tom's Cabin* was based upon her Cincinnati experience.

Professors at Lane Seminary, 1840-1850. Left to right: Calvin E. Stowe, Lyman Beecher, Diarca Howe Allen. Photograph. Gift of the Reverend James C. White.

Harriet Beecher Stowe (1811-1896). Engraving.

C. Foster, *Lane Theological Seminary, Walnut Hills.* Lithograph. From Charles Cist's *Cincinnati in 1841: Its Early Annals and Future Prospects.* (Cincinnati, 1841), following p. 120.

The first edition of the controversial *Uncle Tom's Cabin,* published in 1852, was later printed in numerous English and foreign language editions. Gift of Mr. and Mrs. John J. Emery.

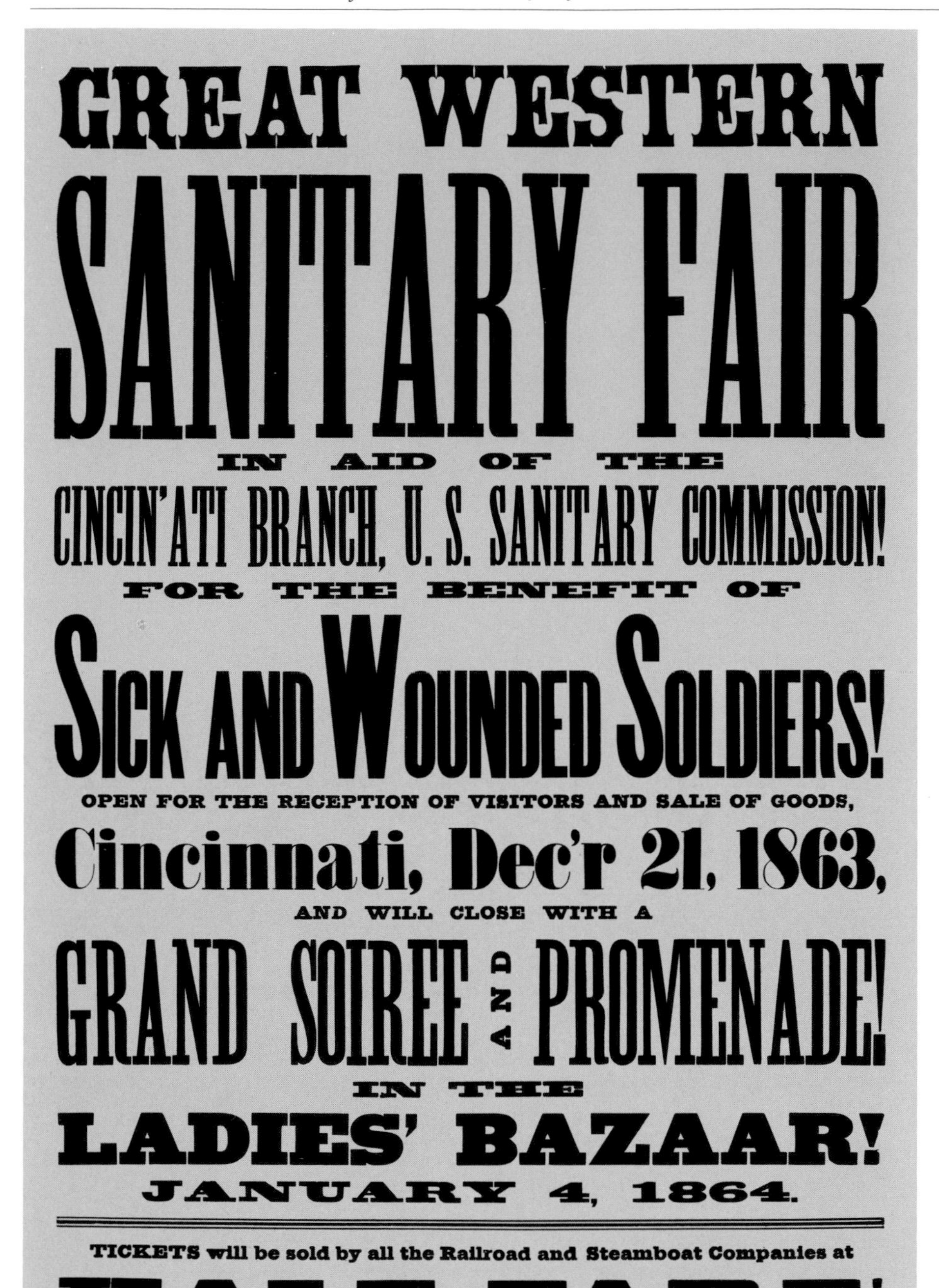
GREAT WESTERN
SANITARY FAIR
IN AID OF THE
CINCIN'ATI BRANCH, U. S. SANITARY COMMISSION!
FOR THE BENEFIT OF
SICK AND WOUNDED SOLDIERS!
OPEN FOR THE RECEPTION OF VISITORS AND SALE OF GOODS,
Cincinnati, Dec'r 21, 1863,
AND WILL CLOSE WITH A
GRAND SOIREE AND PROMENADE!
IN THE
LADIES' BAZAAR!
JANUARY 4, 1864.
TICKETS will be sold by all the Railroad and Steamboat Companies at
HALF FARE!
ONE DAY IN EACH WEEK, to those who purpose visiting the Fair.

The United States Sanitary Commission, a citizens' group devoted to preventing disease and alleviating suffering among Union soldiers and sailors, carried out its mission by acquiring goods and funds through contributions and fairs. The Cincinnati branch, formed in 1861, aided in establishing a soldiers' home, eight hospitals in Cincinnati and Covington, one at Camp Dennison and a burial ground in Spring Grove Cemetery. Its Great Western Sanitary Fair, *December 22, 1863-January 6, 1864, took place at the Fifth and Sixth street markets and Mozart and Greenwood halls. The "Refreshment Saloon" was at the Palace Garden on Vine Street. Citizens sponsored exhibits of relics, war memorabilia and a tour of the Niles Works where two gunboats were being constructed. The sale of handmade articles, produce, flowers, as well as paintings, prints, original letters and poems donated by artists, politicians and authors netted nearly $250,000 for the relief fund.*

Cincinnati During the Civil War

In the early 1860s, Cincinnati was in the middle of the United States' great fratricidal struggle. As the nation drifted towards civil war, Cincinnatians realized they had much to lose. Although direct rail ties to the East had weakened its traditional economic link to the South, Cincinnati merchants still looked primarily to the river and their southern markets. Also, as a prosperous northern city on the border of the slave South, Cincinnatians knew their city could become a prized pawn in a full-scale military confrontation. In the frantic days following Abraham Lincoln's election to the presidency, Cincinnati's politicians searched for an acceptable compromise.

The attack on Fort Sumter, South Carolina, on April 12, 1861, transformed the mood of the city. Militia companies that already existed quickly became the core of fighting regiments. The Rover Guards, Zouave Guards and Lafayette Guards became companies of the Ohio Second Regiment. Over 1,000 Cincinnati Germans rallied around the Turner unit to form the Ohio Ninth Regiment, while the city's Irish residents became the backbone of the Ohio 10th Regiment. Those who did not join active fighting units formed home guards to protect the city. In this same spirit, the black community attempted to form a unit called the "Attucks Blues" in honor of the ex-slave who became the first American killed in the Revolution during the Boston Massacre in 1770. However, they were forcibly stopped and informed that they were to keep out of this "white man's war."

The first 18 months of the Civil War hit Cincinnati hard. The river trade collapsed, banks failed, and farm surpluses glutted the markets. According to one visitor, "The trade of Cincinnati was paralyzed for a time...and there was much poverty, I was told, among the working classes." In addition, the war went badly for the

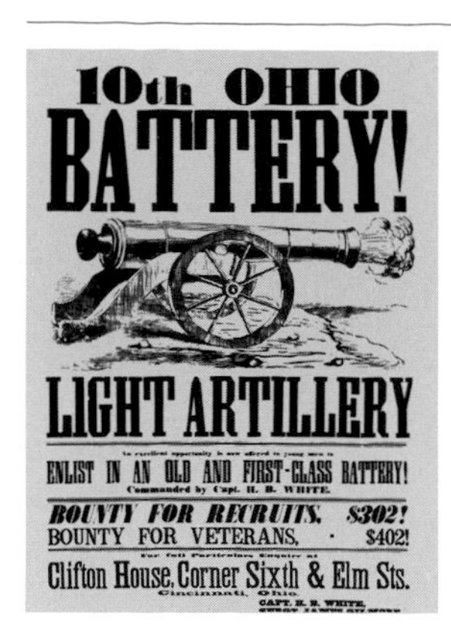

Union. It seemed Confederate troops could move at will. On August 30, 1862, at Richmond, Kentucky, seasoned Confederate troops under Gen. Kirby Smith routed an inexperienced Union army. Suddenly Cincinnati was exposed to direct attack and was all but defenseless. Although the Confederacy could not have held the city for an extended period of time, its capture would have given the South massive supplies—boots and shoes alone filled 12 warehouses—and an awesome psychological victory.

In early September 1862, Cincinnatians rallied to protect their city. Gen. Lew Wallace raised a force of 72,000 that included men from the city and "squirrel hunters" from the surrounding countryside. This huge force moved across the Ohio River on a hastily constructed pontoon bridge and marched to positions about three miles south. The men hastily completed earthwork defenses centered on Fort Mitchell while officers attempted to give orders to the citizen-defenders. In the face of this formidable force, Gen. Henry Heth withdrew his 10,000 men without a fight.

Although the next summer brought a flying raid by Gen. John Hunt Morgan through the northern fringes of the city, Cincinnati was never again in serious military danger. Economic conditions improved as factories filled military orders and merchants won contracts to supply the army. Through army enlistments and holding such home-front functions as "The Great Western Sanitary Fair," Cincinnatians supported the war.

Yet the desire to end the bloodshed through compromise never disappeared. In elections during the war years, Cincinnati voters consistently favored those Democrats known as Copperheads who supported compromise with the Confederacy. George H. Pendleton, who represented Ohio's First Congressional District, became the vice presidential nominee of the Democratic Party in 1864. Second District Congressman Alexander Long's outspoken support of peace-at-any-price led to his censure by the House of Representatives.

The nation's agony finally ended with Lee's surrender at Appomattox Court House on April 9, 1865. When news of the surrender reached Cincinnati at 9:30 that night, huge bonfires and fireworks lit the sky. Despite pouring rain Cincinnatians by the thousands filled the streets and were described as "perfectly mad with joy." Five days later the city was again plunged into anger and despair when news of President Lincoln's assassination reached Cincinnati. The assassin's brother, Julius Brutus Booth, was then performing at Pike's Opera House in Cincinnati and had to leave town quickly.

10th Ohio Battery! The 10th Ohio Volunteer Infantry, recruited under the command of Colonel William Haines Lytle, was mustered into three years' service in 1861. The regiment campaigned in West Virginia, Kentucky and Tennessee, taking part in the Battle of Chickamauga in which Lytle lost his life. Gift of Mrs. LeRoy Saunders.

Alfred E. Mathews, *The 73rd Reg't. Illinois Vol., Crossing the Pontoon Bridge, at Cincinnati, Friday Sept. 12, 1862.* When Cincinnati seemed threatened by General Kirby Smith's Confederate forces, Major General Lew Wallace organized the defense of the city and northern Kentucky. To reach Kentucky, a pontoon bridge was hastily constructed. Middleton, Strobridge and Company lithograph.

View of Camp Dennison, 16 miles northeast of Cincinnati, Ohio (1865). A vast tract near Madisonville was arranged for military instruction. Middleton, Strobridge and Company lithograph. Gift of Henry M. Pinkvoss.

Peter H. Clark (1829-1926) Peter Clark gained a national reputation for his three decades of leadership in organizing black education in Cincinnati. Clark's interests, however, were not limited to the schoolroom. Throughout his life Clark struggled to discover the right political road for American blacks. Although most blacks embraced the Republican Party, Clark experimented with socialism out of principle and with the Democratic Party hoping that a divided black constituency would force each party to compete for the black vote. His political unpredictability angered whites and unsettled blacks, but few disagreed with Wendell P. Dabney's assessment that Clark was "Cincinnati's greatest colored product from the standpoint of intellectuality, courage, and racial loyalty."

Peter H. Clark, Cincinnati's Most Famous Colored Citizen. Photograph. From Wendell P. Dabney, *Cincinnati's Colored Citizens* (Cincinnati, 1926), p. 104.

The Ohio River formed the border between the slave South and the free North. Cincinnati lay along the path for thousands of freed blacks and runaway slaves escaping the South before the Civil War. Most blacks traveled farther north, possibly as far as Canada, but some settled in Cincinnati. Generally, between 1820 and 1870, the black proportion of the city's population amounted to only a modest 2½%. On several occasions, however, that percentage increased significantly. At the end of the 1820s it rose to 9.6% and in 1840 to 4.8%.

This third stream of "outsiders" troubled the native white citizens of Cincinnati. The problems that confronted the foreign immigrants were compounded for blacks. They were forced to occupy the worst housing, particularly in the infamous "Bucktown" (or "Little Africa") area that lay between Sixth and Seventh streets from Broadway to Culvert. Conditions were appalling. Visitors spoke of courtyards filled with garbage, one water hydrant to serve 300 people, and several open sewers. The area drew the poorest and most disreputable elements of the city's population, including some poor whites—mostly Irish. The predominance of blacks in the area led many Cincinnatians to associate the reputation of Bucktown with that of the black community. Bucktown became a code word for vice and crime, and this reputation affected all blacks in the city.

Blacks faced difficulties in securing jobs as well. Although a few blacks amassed small fortunes, most were forced into menial, low-paying positions. Before 1840 black women found work easier to obtain than did black men. Jobs as chambermaids, washerwomen and domestic servants were open to them. After 1840, however, labor shortages caused by the economic boom became serious enough to open the mainstream of Cincinnati's economy to black men—particularly on the riverfront, where many found work as roustabouts and stevedores.

The Civil War disrupted even these modest gains. The loss of southern markets and the closing of the river trade markedly reduced the availability of work on the river. Keen competition for the remaining positions resulted, particularly between the blacks and the Irish. The growing tension came to a head in July 1862. Lexington, Kentucky, faced a possible invasion by Confederate troops under John Hunt Morgan. The danger prompted Cincinnati to send a contingent of 120 of the city police force to Lexington, leaving too few policemen to deter lawlessness in Cincinnati. Violence broke out on July 10 and continued for a week. Blacks on the riverfront or in Bucktown were in the path of the mobs, whose numbers swelled each night. Many blacks left the city for the safety of the surrounding hills, while others armed and barricaded themselves in Bucktown.

The city's history had been punctuated by earlier race riots in 1829, 1836 and 1841—all coinciding with peaks of black residency. But the 1862 riot marked an important turning point. The advances in employment which black men had achieved over the preceding 20 years were steadily reversed. In 1860 employment of blacks in the mainstream of the commercial and industrial activity of Cincinnati had reached 33% of the Negro labor force. By 1870, this figure had dropped in half.

Classification and Course of Study for the Colored Schools of the City of Cincinnati.

Session.	Years.	Age.	Classes.	Subjects.	Text-Books.	Ground to be passed over.	Oral and General Exercises.
PRIMARY DEPARTMENT.							
First.	1	6	**G.**	Elements of Reading.	Cards, Black-Board, and Slate.	Alphabet and Cards Nos. 1, 2, 3.	Spelling from Cards, Sounds of Letters, Elements of Words, Oral Defining, The Bible (used throughout the course,) Music.
Second.	1	6½	**F.**	Elements of Reading.	Cards, Black-Board, and Slate.	Cards completed.	Spelling from Cards, Oral Defining, counting as far as one hundred, vowel sounds, formation of letters and words, Music.
First.	2	7	**E.**	Elements of Reading.	McGuffey's First Reader, and Slate.	Reader completed.	Formation of Letters and Figures, Defining, Counting, Vowel Sounds joined to Consonants (as *la*, *ma*, *gra*, etc.,) Music.
Second.	2	7½	**D.**	Reading and Spelling.	McGuffey's Second Reader, and McGuffey's Speller.	Reader 101 pages, Speller 36 pages.	Writing Numbers as far as one hundred, Analysis of Words, Defining, Consonant Sounds, Music.
First.	3	8	**C.**	Reading and Spelling.	Second Reader, and Speller, Duntonian System of Penmanship.	Reader completed, Speller 72 pages.	Writing numbers as far as one thousand, Analysis, Elementary Sounds with action, Defining, Penmanship, Music.
Second.	3	8½	**B.**	Reading, Spelling, and Mental Arithmetic.	McGuffey's Third Reader, Speller. Ray's Second Arithmetic.	Reader 113 pages, Speller 108 pages, Arithmetic 35 pages.	Writing Numbers to one million, Defining, Geography, Tables in combination, Spelling by sounds, Penmanship, Music.
First.	4	9	**A.**	The same continued, Geography,	The same continued, Cornel's Geography.	Reader completed, Arithmetic 84 pages, Speller completed.	Reading with *action*, Spelling, Definitions, Arithmetic through Addition, Penmanship.
INTERMEDIATE DEPARTMENT.							
Second.	4	9½	**D.**	Reading, Spelling, Arithmetic, Geography.	McGuffey's Fourth Reader, Ray's Second Arithmetic, Spell r, Dictionary.	Reader 73 pages, Arithmetic completed, Speller continued.	Reading with action, Primary Rules finished, Reduction Tables, Definitions, Grammar, Penmanship, Music.
First.	5	10	**C.**	Reading, Written Arithmetic, Geography.	Fourth Reader, Ray's Third Arithmetic, Intermediate Geography, Speller.	Reader 150 pages, Arithmetic to Compound Numbers, Geography Western Continent.	Reading with action, Defining, Grammar, Map Drawing, Penmanship, Music.
Second.	5	10½	**B.**	Reading, Arithmetic, Geography, Grammar.	Fourth Reader, Arithmetic, Geography, Pinneo's Primary Grammar.	Reader 224 pages, Arithmetic to Fractions, Geography of Europe, Grammar 64 pages.	Principles of Elocution, Defining, Out-Line Maps, Map Drawing, Penmanship, Music.
First.	6	11	**A.**	Reading, Arithmetic, Geography, Grammar, U. S. History.	Fourth Reader, Arithmetic, Geography, Grammar, U. S. History (C. A. Goodrich, or Guernsey.)	Reader completed, Geography completed, Arithmetic through Fractions, Grammar completed, History 80 pages.	Elocution continued, Exercises on the Maps, Defining, Map Drawing, Recitations, Penmanship, Music.
PRINCIPAL DEPARTMENT.							
Second.	6	11½	**I.**	Reading, Arithmetic, Geography, Grammar, History, Algebra.	McGuffey's Fifth Reader, Geographical questions, History of U. S., Arithmetic, Ray's Algebra pt. 1st, Pinneo's Analyt. Grammar.	Reader 120 pages, Arithmetic to Partial Payments, Algebra to Equations, History to Revolution, Grammar 82 pages.	Declamation, Elements of Composition, Map Drawing, Penmanship, Music.
First.	7	12	**H.**	Reading, Arithmetic, Algebra, Grammar, History.	Fifth Reader, Arithmetic, Algebra, Grammar, History.	Reader 239 pages, Arithmetic completed, Algebra to Radicals, Grammar 150 pages, History completed and reviewed.	Declamation, Composition, Use of Globes, Map Drawing, Penmanship, Music.
Second.	7	12½	**G.**	Reading, Algebra, Grammar, History.	Fifth Reader, Algebra, Grammar, History of England.	Reader 352 pages, Algebra completed, History —— pages, Grammar completed.	The same continued, and "*Familiar Science*."
First.	8	13	**F.**	Reading, Algebra, Geometry, History, Analysis.	Fifth Reader, Second Part Algebra, Davie's Elements of Geometry, English History, Green's Analysis.	Reader completed, Algebra through Simple Equations, Analysis —— pages, History —— pages, Geometry to Book 4.	Book Keeping, and the same subjects continued as before,
Second.	8	13½	**E.**	Algebra, Geometry, History, Analysis, Ancient Geography, Aids to Composition.	Algebra, Geometry, Ancient Geography, Aids to Composition, Green's Analysis.	Algebra completed, Geometry completed, History completed, Analysis completed, Geography completed.	The same subjects continued, Commercial Arithmetic.
First.	9	14	**D.**	History, Geometry, Composition, Philosophy, Physical Geography.	General History, Higher Geometry, Gray's Philosophy, Physical Geography.	History —— pages, Geometry 3 books, Philosophy —— pages, Geography completed.	Reading, Experiments, and the same continued as before.
Second.	9	14½	**C.**	History, Geometry, Philosophy, Astronomy, Physiology, Constitutional Law.	History, Geometry, Philosophy, Astronomy, Cutter's Physiology, Mansfield's Constitutional Law.	History completed, Geometry completed, Physiology —— pages, Philosophy completed, Astronomy —— pages.	The same subjects Teaching.
First.	10	15	**B.**	Trigonometry and its applications, Chemistry, Astronomy, Physiology, Moral Science.	Davie's Trigonometry, Gray's Chemistry, Astronomy, Wayland's Moral Science, Cutter's Physiology.	Trigonometry completed, Astronomy completed, Physiology completed, Chemistry —— pages, Moral Science —— pages.	The same subjects
Second.	10	15½	**A.**	Continued as above, Mensuration, Logic, Science of Government,	The same as above, Young's Science of Government, Whateley's Logic.	All subjects completed, and a general review.	The same continue

REMARKS.—1. In carrying out the above system of Classification and Course of Study, the teachers should endeavor to impress upon the minds of their pupils such moral principles as will tend to elevate their position in society, and give them character as men and women.

2. Teachers should qualify themselves thoroughly for their profession, so as to be prepared at all times to give such oral instruction upon the subject-matter of the text-books as will fully illustrate its practical utility, and never allow a pupil to think he understands a subject until he can give a full and clear explanation of it to others. One of the best means of accomplishing this is to have frequent *reviews*.

3. Pupils will be advanced from one class to another wl stand all the subjects of study belonging to that class, and their claims to promotion, their application to study, re general deportment, will all be taken into account.

4. Accurate registers should be kept of the character of the deportment of each pupil—habitual deficiencies wi grounds for placing a pupil in a lower class. Pupils who sickness or other causes, must satisfy their teachers tha regularly studied, before they will be permitted to take th

FIRST ANNUAL REPORT

OF THE

BOARD OF TRUSTEES,

FOR THE

COLORED PUBLIC SCHOOLS

OF CINCINNATI,

For the School Year, ending June 30, 1855;

WITH ADDITIONAL DOCUMENTS, EXHIBITING THE CONDITION OF THE COLORED SCHOOLS.

Printed by Order of the Board.

CINCINNATI:
MOORE, WILSTACH, KEYS & CO.,
NO. 25 WEST FOURTH STREET.
1855.

Classification and Course of Study for the Colored Schools of the City of Cincinnati from *First Annual Report of the... Colored Public Schools...* (Cincinnati, 1855), pp. 20-21.

First Annual Report of the ... Colored Public Schools ... (Cincinnati, 1855).

It requires no keenness of observation to perceive that Cincinnati is destined to become the focus and mart for the grandest circle of manufacturing thrift on this continent. Her delightful climate; her unequaled and ever-increasing facilities for cheap and rapid commercial intercourse with all parts of the country and the world; her enterprising and energetic population; her own elastic and exulting youth; are all elements which predict and insure her electric progress to giant greatness. I doubt if there is another spot on the earth where food, fuel, cotton, timber, iron, can all be concentrated so cheaply—that is, at so moderate a cost of human labor in producing and bringing them together—as here. Such fatness of soil, such a wealth of mineral treasure—coal, iron, salt, and the finest clays for all purposes of use—and all cropping out from the steep, facile banks of placid, though not sluggish navigable rivers. How many Californias could equal, in permanent worth, this valley of the Ohio!

Horace Greeley (1850)

From Charles Cist's *Sketches and Statistics of Cincinnati in 1851* (Cincinnati, 1851), p. 257.

Despite these hardships, blacks in Cincinnati achieved something unique in the United States before the Civil War. In 1852 they won from the state legislature the right to organize and operate the Independent Colored School System. The proceeds from taxes on black property financed the system, and a black school board elected by the black community administered it. This institution had a far-reaching impact. The black community gained political experience and developed leadership far superior to almost any other place in the country. The more than 60 graduates of Gaines High School in the 10 years after it opened in 1866 provided a base for the emerging black middle class, as well as winning a reputation for Cincinnati wherever the graduates taught. The independent black school board was abolished in 1874, weakening the power base of the black politicians. Yet the success of the black community in running the system helped to undermine the racial stereotypes held by whites and helped build pride and confidence.

Cincinnati's burgeoning population and its expanding industries made the city not only bigger but more complex. Municipal government was inadequate to cope with the changes. When Cincinnati—with fewer than 10,000 people—was chartered as a city in 1819, governmental responsibilities were confined to two general areas. First, it regulated aspects of commercial activity by building and maintaining markethouses, docks, wharves and streets and by licensing and regulating carts, wagons, drays, taverns and theaters. Second, the city government stepped in during emergencies that were beyond the control of individuals, such as fires, riots, epidemics and unemployment resulting from natural disasters.

Miles Greenwood (1807-1885)
Miles Greenwood was a machinery and iron products manufacturer. His Eagle Iron Works became an important munitions center during the Civil War. In the 1850s Greenwood was a principal proponent for the establishment of a paid fire department to replace volunteer organizations. He subsequently served the new department as its first Chief Engineer.

After 1830, with the influx of immigrants, this limited view of the role of city government became inadequate. Thus, it grew in size and in functions that reflected the massive social and economic changes occurring in the city. In 1820 city government included 47 officials; by 1860 that number had jumped to 1,139, serving a city of 161,044 people. In 1820 approximately 7% of the city government's spending paid for all of the social services it provided; by 1860 about 60% of the city budget went for such services that now included education, health, poor relief, police and fire protection. Part of this expansion occurred as the city absorbed services that private groups had initiated. For example, through an endowment first established in 1826 by William and Abigail Woodward and another by Thomas Hughes in 1824, secondary education was made available to children. As the common school system became well established, it became logical for the city to take over its operation. In July 1851 the boards of trustees of the two independent high schools were dissolved and a new Union School Board began the direction of the schools.

In other instances the transformation of government resulted from the modernization of an established public function. Fire protection had rested on a gradually evolving system of volunteer fire companies throughout the first half of the 19th century. By mid-century these volunteer fire companies reflected the ethnic and social fragmentation of Cincinnati's population. Rivalry and jealousy between the companies increasingly led to violence. Such competition also hurt the ability to fight fires. The older members of the Independents No. 3 company formed a committee to study reforms. Headed by Miles Greenwood, the committee surveyed methods of firefighting from throughout the United States. In New York they found that firefighters experimented with steam fire engines; in Boston they discovered that the city paid their firemen; in New Orleans companies used horses to pull their equipment. By combining these elements, Cincinnati created the model for American urban fire companies for the next 50 years.

Eighteen fifty-three marked the establishment of Cincinnati's paid fire department and completion of A. B. Latta's innovative steam fire engine, "Uncle Joe Ross." After the 5-ton prototype proved too heavy for regular use, lighter horse-drawn engines were acquired by the city. This is the first photograph of a Cincinnati fire company with its equipment, 1860.

John Aubrey, *Miles Greenwood.* Oil on canvas. Gift of Mrs. Franklin Greenwood.

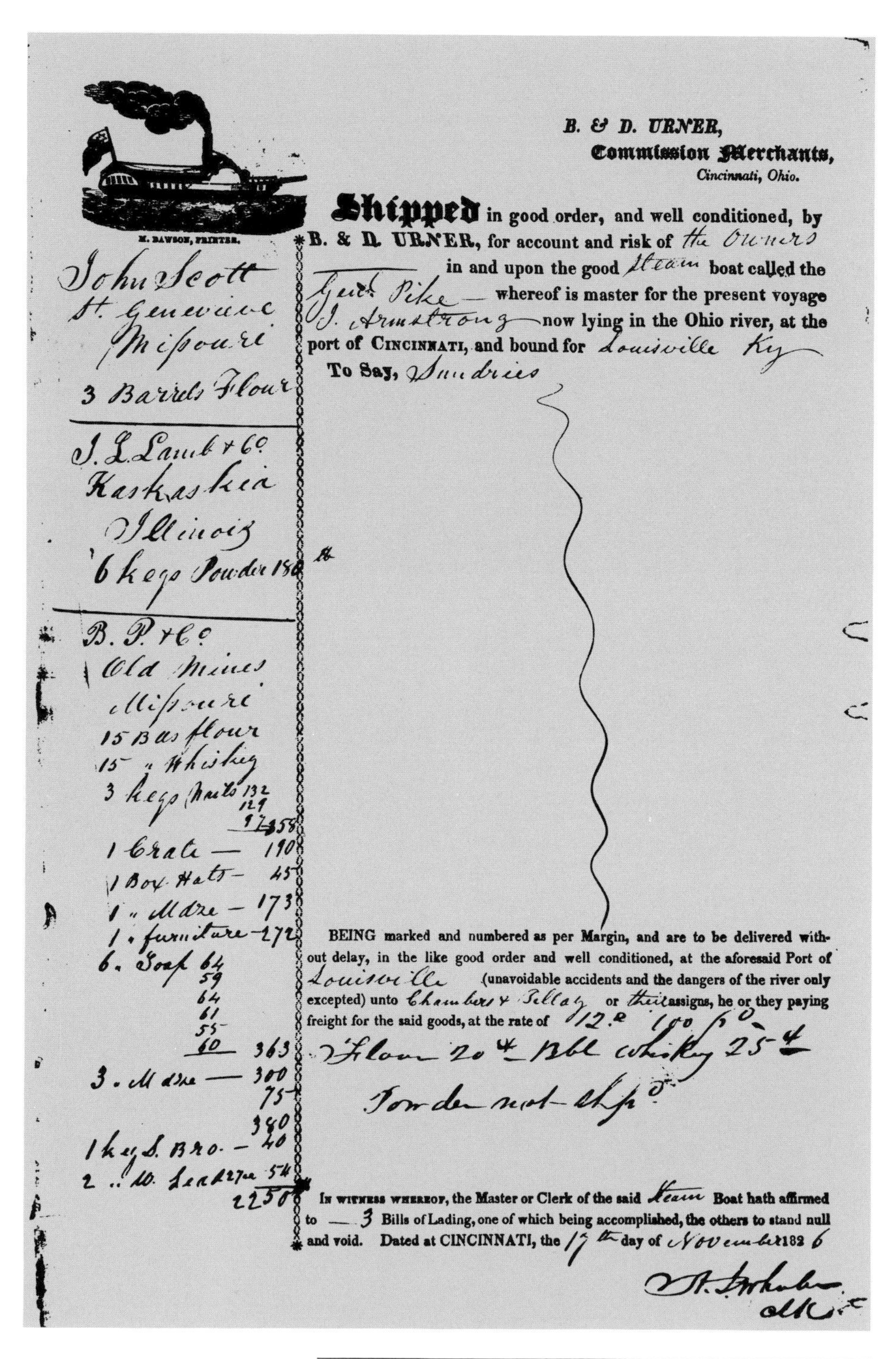

B. & D. URNER,
Commission Merchants,
Cincinnati, Ohio.

M. DAWSON, PRINTER.

Shipped in good order, and well conditioned, by B. & D. URNER, for account and risk of the Owners in and upon the good Steam boat called the Genl. Pike whereof is master for the present voyage J. Armstrong now lying in the Ohio river, at the port of CINCINNATI, and bound for Louisville Ky

To Say, Sundries

John Scott
St. Genevieve
Missouri
3 Barrels Flour

J. L. Lamb & Co
Kaskaskia
Illinois
6 kegs Powder

B. P. & Co
Old Mines
Missouri
15 Bas flour
15 " Whiskey

BEING marked and numbered as per Margin, and are to be delivered without delay, in the like good order and well conditioned, at the aforesaid Port of Louisville (unavoidable accidents and the dangers of the river only excepted) unto Chambers & Pellat or their assigns, he or they paying freight for the said goods, at the rate of 12 ½ 100 lbs
Flour 20¢ Bbl whisky 25¢
Powder not shipd.

IN WITNESS WHEREOF, the Master or Clerk of the said Steam Boat hath affirmed to 3 Bills of Lading, one of which being accomplished, the others to stand null and void. Dated at CINCINNATI, the 17th day of November 1826

Clk.

Bill of Lading, issued by B. & D. Urner, commission merchants, for goods to be shipped on the steamboat General Pike. Engraving. John J. Rowe Collection.

At mid-century, as Cincinnatians worked to modernize their governmental apparatus and to accommodate increasing numbers of immigrants, the city reached its zenith. The 1850 census revealed that the Queen City had become the sixth largest city in the United States, the third largest manufacturing center and America's fastest growing urban center. Cincinnati appeared to be fulfilling the dreams of her most ardent boosters.

But never again would purely quantitative measurements rank Cincinnati so high among American cities. During the 1850s, Cincinnati grew by 40%, adding 45,000 people but, the momentum had passed to others. St. Louis added 83,000 residents to catch up with Cincinnati's 161,000. Chicago exploded from a town of 30,000 to a city of 109,260—and was just taking off.

What happened to Cincinnati's fortunes? Did Cincinnati's decline relative to the growth of others result from a failure of vision by the city's leadership, or from a failure to modernize its transportation system? Or did the city become complacent and self-satisfied, cutting short its own potential for greatness?

By 1860 many observers had begun to focus on Cincinnati's lack of rail connections as the chief cause of its "decline". They tended to blame Cincinnati's business community for having failed to invest enough at a critical time to make the city the center of the nation's rail system. In this judgment boosters failed to evaluate realistically the extent to which the economic and financial decisions that shaped rail construction in the United States during the 19th century could have been controlled by Cincinnatians on behalf of their city. Had they examined the forces that produced Cincinnati's economic and population boom in the years

Jacob Strader (1795-1860)
Jacob Strader was born in New Jersey. He came to Cincinnati in 1816 and soon began to learn about riverboating. He became engaged in boat building in 1824 and over the next 20 years built 23 boats. In the 1840s Captain Strader shifted much of his interest to railroads and banking. He became president of the Little Miami Railroad in 1846 and served as president of the Commercial Bank for many years.

before 1850, they might have understood more fully why the boom faded.

Cincinnati largely became the Queen City of the West because the steam engine revolutionized transportation at the same time that settlers were pouring into the Ohio Valley. The development of the steamboat allowed Cincinnati to exploit the commercial opportunities of the Ohio River. Thanks to the steam engine and the productivity of the agricultural region in the watershed of the Ohio River, Cincinnati emerged as a commercial-industrial city with a diversified economy. But if Cincinnati initially benefited from the impact of the steam revolution on transportation and from bringing thousands of acres of rich land under cultivation, the continuation of these same processes would, in time, cause her decline. As the energy of steam was adapted to travel on land and as the vast regions of the Mississippi Valley came under the plow, Cincinnati's era of boundless growth ended.

Railroad service was introduced in the United States in 1828. Until that time, land travel had always been slower, less predictable and more expensive than water travel. Railroads' potential to change that situation was perceived quickly, but most people assumed that oceans, rivers and lakes were the "natural arteries" and would remain dominant. They believed that railroads were "artificial arteries" that would complement the water routes: railroads would carry people and goods to the waterways, thus enhancing, not displacing, the steamboat and canalboat.

The first successful Cincinnati-based railroad company was the Little Miami Railroad, chartered in 1836. The line linked Cincinnati and Springfield, where it connected with another line extending to Lake Erie and gave Cincinnati direct access to the Great Lakes. Early financial troubles, aggravated by the Panic of 1837, were only overcome by investing $200,000 of public money and the private investment of Cincinnati businessman John G. Kilgour.

In the 1840s one other railroad was begun from Cincinnati. The Cincinnati and Hamilton Railroad was chartered in 1846 and expanded in 1847 into the Cincinnati, Hamilton and Dayton Railroad. Built entirely with private funds, the line reached Hamilton in 1846 and Dayton in 1851, where it joined a rail line to the north.

During the second quarter of the century, railroad mileage grew rapidly in Ohio despite little help from the state itself. In the 1820s and 1830s, Ohio had encouraged and helped finance the development of a progressive transportation system that included turnpikes and canals. When railroads came along, the state sought to protect

Public Landing, Cincinnati (c. 1855). At mid-century the public landing was the busiest in its history. Middleton, Wallace and Company lithograph. Gift of Watson Smith.

Joseph Oriel Eaton (attr.), *Jacob Strader.* Oil on canvas. Gift of Mr. and Mrs. John J. Strader.

Cincinnati, Hamilton and Dayton Railroad. The railroad constructed a new depot in 1864 in the West End. F. Tuchfarber and Company. Oil on iron. Eugene F. Bliss fund purchase.

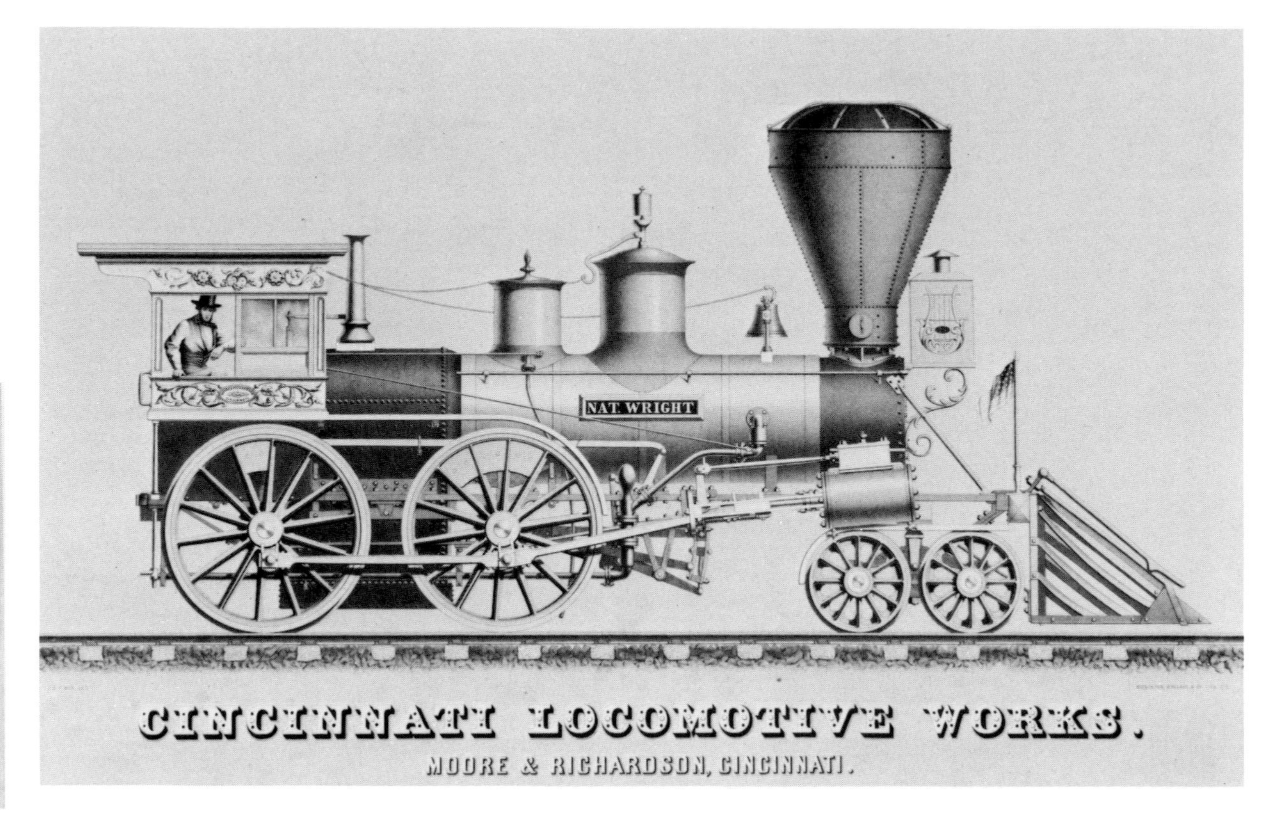

Cincinnati Locomotive Works. Founded in 1853 when Robert Moore and John G. Richardson leased Anthony Harkness & Son's buildings and grounds, the Cincinnati Locomotive Works manufactured locomotives for the Little Miami Railroad as well as other railroads serving the city. Middleton, Wallace and Company lithograph.

its heavy investment in canals, and several early railroad charters provided for compensating the state for any loss of canal revenues. Then the mood of the public changed regarding the role of state government in promoting and financing transportation projects. Many western states, including Ohio and Indiana, had over-extended public funds by promoting development schemes. In Ohio this shift culminated in a new constitution in 1851 which made it illegal for the state or the cities to invest in such projects. Delegates from Hamilton County saw these changes as ways to protect Cincinnati's river and canal advantages against competition from railroads.

Such actions, however, failed to discourage railroad building in Ohio. Between 1850 and 1860, more than $100 million was spent in building rail lines. Track mileage increased from 575 to 2,946, giving Ohio the most track of any state in the country. People both within and without Ohio invested heavily in building railroads even though the lines generally failed to yield great profits. Some, such as the Little Miami Railroad, showed modest profit, but they were exceptions: by 1860 three-quarters of the railroads in the state were insolvent and paid no dividends.

Even so, this great effort to construct railroads in the Midwest began to affect Cincinnati. First, railroads enabled the Queen City's rivals to expand their own lines of trade, sometimes at the expense of Cincinnati. For example, Louisville built a rail line to Lexington earlier than a line connecting Covington to Lexington was completed. Thus, central Kentucky began to funnel its goods through Louisville rather than Cincinnati. Landlocked Indianapolis had failed to become more than a sleepy government center of 4,000 by 1846. But in September of that year, a rail line opened that connected Indianapolis to the Ohio River at Madison, Indiana. This line gave farmers of central Indiana direct access to the Ohio River without going through Cincinnati. Indianapolis enjoyed a boomlet. Its population grew to 10,800 by 1852 and to 18,611 by 1860.

Second, as railroads demonstrated their advantages over water routes, people ceased to view railroads primarily as a means of connecting inland towns to terminals located on water routes. Ohio's first railroad lines had been built along north-south routes to connect the Ohio River and Lake Erie, just as canals had done. But by the 1850s, railroads had demonstrated certain advantages over water transportation: they were not idled for weeks or months at a time during the winter as canals and rivers were by freezing weather; they could move people and freight at lower costs than canals; they were faster than steamboats; and they could connect cities by shorter routes. For example, by river, the route between Pittsburgh and Cincinnati was 470 miles and took three days. By rail, the trip was reduced to 316 miles and 15 hours. Similarly, the route from Cincinnati to New Orleans was reduced from 1,484 miles and eight days to 922 miles and 2½ days. If railroads could challenge traffic between river cities, their greater advantage was that they could carry people and products between cities not connected by rivers and canals. Increasingly, rail lines reached out from eastern cities into the nation's rich agricultural heartland passing east-west through central and northern Ohio. Midwestern producers whose goods were ultimately bound for eastern markets soon were able to ship directly east and avoid the circuitous route down the Ohio and Mississippi rivers through New Orleans.

In 1848 William Bebb, governor of Ohio, addressed the Young Men's Mercantile Library Association in Cincinnati on the importance of railroads to the city's future:

The railroad has made the land as subservient to commerce as the water. Railroads are to be the ***artificial rivers*** *of these latter days, and wo to that commercial city that suffers these rivers to be diverted from it. Cincinnati may, by these instrumentalities, if she will, command the Mississippi valley. Her present greatness is already attracting them and it will require a good deal of neglect and repulsion from her to drive them off,* ***yet she may do it, and thus dash her golden hopes.***

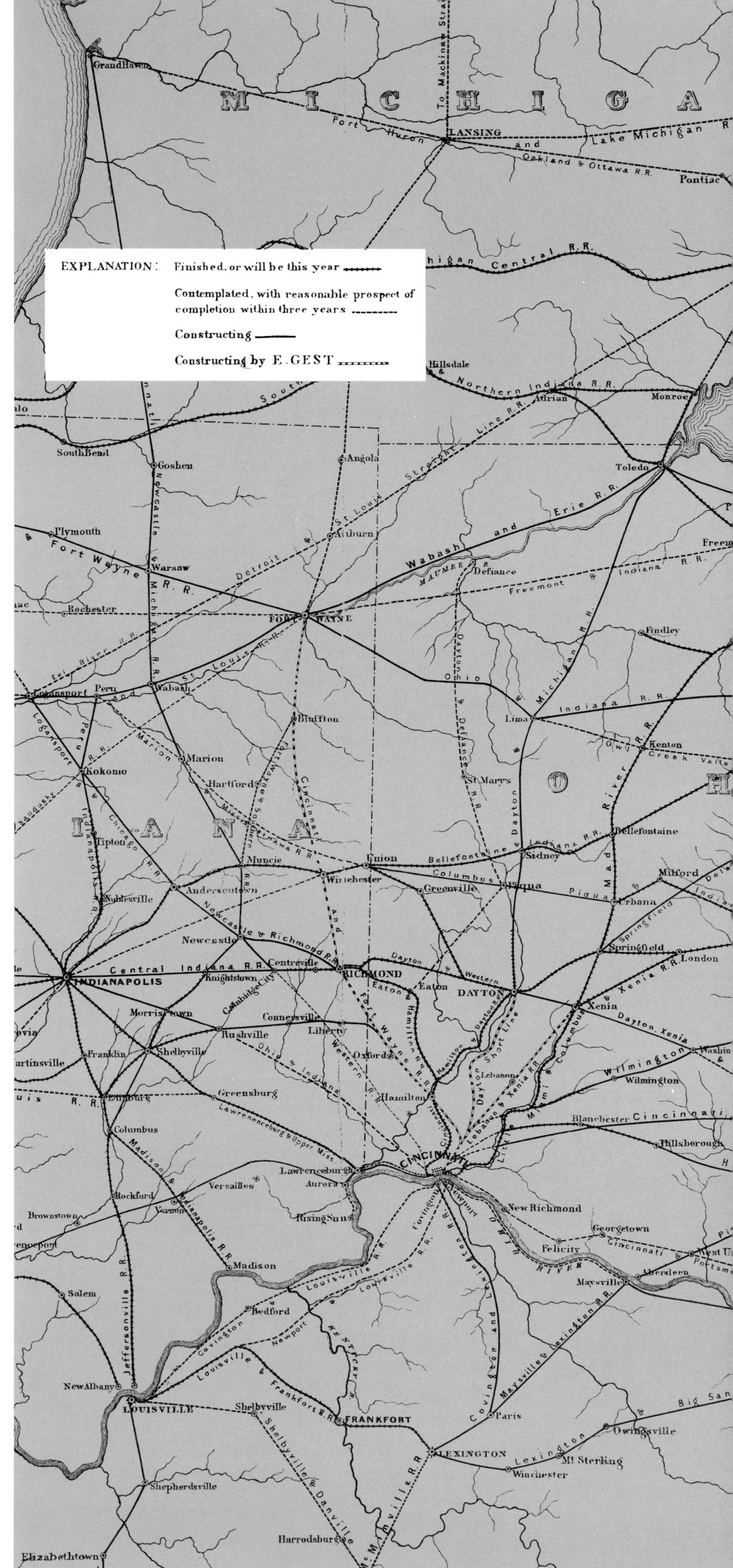

Erasmus Gest (1820-1908), *Gest's Map of Railways Centering at Cincinnati with their Tributary Lines in Adjoining States and Canada West* (1853). Gift of the Cincinnati Art Museum.

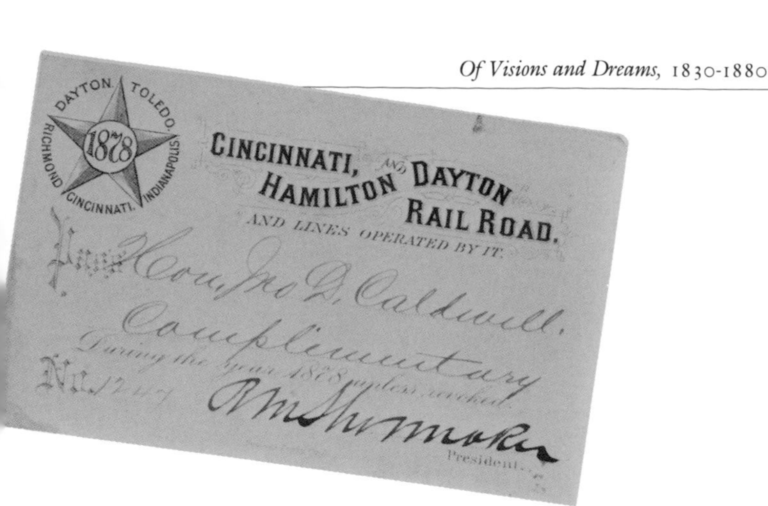

Bebb's remarks may have overestimated Cincinnati's capacity to shape her future, but the city appeared to lack its earlier vigor in completing several development projects that affected her economic well-being. The enlargement of the canal at the Falls of the Ohio in Louisville, the building of a bridge across the Ohio River, the rail lines to connect Cincinnati with Lexington and with Indianapolis were all pursued with conspicuous deliberateness and frequently over the opposition of business interests tied to the river.

Still, at mid-century, Cincinnati controlled the trade of the upper Ohio, and that trade was flourishing. From 1848 to 1851, an average of 3,649 steamboats docked at Cincinnati each year. The yearly average dropped to 2,961 in the 1856-1859 period. A depression and a prolonged drought in the late 1850s that restricted river travel blurred the impact railroads may have had on this decline. And Cincinnati did respond by building enough rail lines to supplement its existing transportation system. Most importantly, Cincinnati's economy had reached a stage of development that afforded a wide range of investment opportunities. Cincinnatians perceived their city more as a manufacturing center than as a trading center. Its leaders did not generally believe that railroads would substantially affect that status. Cincinnati investment capital had become important throughout the Ohio and Mississippi valleys in developing factories and commercial facilities, even in rival cities like Chicago.

As the pace of Cincinnati's growth slowed during the 1850s, people became aware that Chicago had emerged as Cincinnati's primary challenger. In 1854 the value of Chicago's export and import trade was about one-half of Cincinnati's, but by 1858 parity had been achieved. Some Cincinnatians did not find such statistics alarming, for Cincinnati's industrial output was four times larger than Chicago's. Even Stephen Douglas observed in 1859, "There is no better place than Cincinnati for manufacturers, and no better place to distribute than Chicago." Other observers were not comforted, noting that Chicago was pushing out railroad enterprises in all directions. But more fundamental forces were at work: railroads were effects as well as causes. Chicago benefited from railroads just as Cincinnati had benefited from steamboats, and Chicago was building its trade on the agricultural productivity of the Mississippi Valley, just as Cincinnati had earlier profited from the productivity of its surrounding region.

A comparison of the pork-packing industries in the two cities illustrated the remarkable ascendancy of Chicago in the 1850s. In 1845 Cincinnati was world-famous as "Porkopolis" for processing more than 250,000 hogs. By 1858 that figure had risen to 414,752, while Chicago packed 135,474. Just eight years later, however, Chicago had become, in Carl Sandburg's phrase, the new "hog butcher of the world" by packing 573,344 head, while Cincinnati remained constant at 408,345. Cincinnati's pork-packing industry did not decline noticeably—it remained the second largest center for another 20 years. In this and other areas of economic activity, Cincinnati's development leveled out and grew more slowly.

Cincinnati's loss of leadership in the West deeply disturbed its boosters. Some vehemently condemned the city's leaders, as did William M. Corry in 1860, when he contended that Cincinnati had "long been laboring under bad advisers, careless agents, and small officers. Her citizens have put their trust in themselves too little, and in schemers and charlatans too much, and her widow weeds and discrowned head

To encourage riders and attendance at community events, railroad companies offered reduced fares. *Marietta and Cincinnati Railroad Employee's Ticket,* gift of Sarah A. Thomas; *Cincinnati, Hamilton and Dayton Railroad* ticket, gift of the Ohio Mechanics' Institute.

Governor Morrow, built in 1841 by Thomas Rogers of Patterson, New Jersey, was the first locomotive of the Little Miami Railroad. Model built by John H. White, Jr., 1974. Gift of John H. White, Jr.

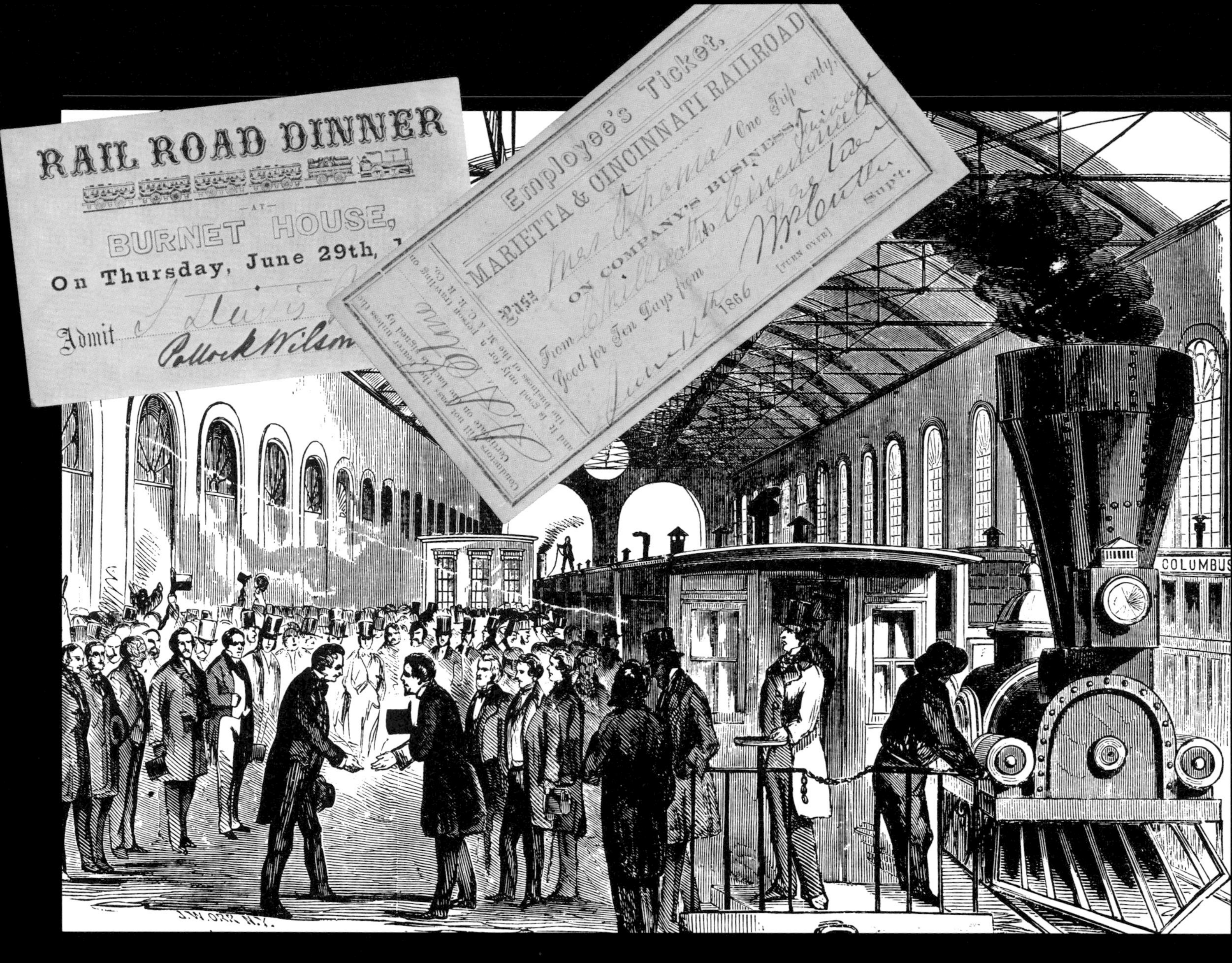

attest their errors and her sorrows." The frustration was, perhaps, understandable, but the hyperbole was misleading. Cincinnati continued to grow for the remainder of the century, reaching a population of 255,139 by 1880 and 325,902 by 1900. Yet, Corry touched upon an essential reality about the city. In 1850 Cincinnati had been self-confident, energetic and at center stage. By 1860 the city seemed adrift and disoriented as it adjusted to its destiny of playing only a supporting role among western cities.

The convolutions surrounding the Civil War further distressed Cincinnati. Its trade had been almost equally divided between that going east and that going downriver. Its people had developed close economic and personal ties with Southerners. At first the loss of river traffic caused severe economic problems, but after 1863 a rising number of war contracts and renewed river trade reduced the economic impact.

Following the war Cincinnati businessmen embarked on several projects to re-establish southern trade based on Cincinnati's manufacturing and the South's mineral resources. The boldest such enterprise involved building a rail line into the upper South similar to a concept that Daniel Drake had promoted 30 years earlier. Now, because of Chicago's growth and that of other Great Lakes cities, Cincinnati embraced the scheme. Its business leaders felt that such a rail line would help Cincinnati exchange its manufactured products for raw materials. They chose Chattanooga as the terminus for the Cincinnati Southern Railroad because it rested at the edge of the central Appalachian coal and iron deposits. Although the project was undertaken in 1869, construction was not begun until 1873 or completed until 1880.

Depot of the Little Miami Railroad, located between Front Street and the Ohio River near present day Dan Beard Bridge (I-471). Clipping. Gift of Mrs. Russell Wilson.

While the Cincinnati Southern Railroad was under construction, Cincinnati's boosters forged a new identity for themselves and the Queen City. They worked to create a city of culture and tradition, of beauty and pageantry. Whether the boosters, having given up on making Cincinnati the nation's largest city, turned inward and built an artistic tradition for its own sake or whether they consciously chose a path that would distinguish Cincinnati among the sprawling, rambunctious cities of the West, they may not have known themselves. The cultural development accomplished in the next 20 years was as awesome in its way as the phenomenal growth had been a generation earlier. Parks and playgrounds, a music hall and an "art palace," festivals and expositions, and even a baseball team built civic pride among Cincinnatians.

Music Hall, March 18, 1880, Commemorating the Completion of the Cincinnati Southern Railway. Construction of the railway began in 1873, and in 1880 the first passenger train ran from Chattanooga to Cincinnati. A banquet to celebrate the event was given by the citizens of Cincinnati for their southern visitors. M. P. Levyeau and Company lithograph. Gift of W. W. Taylor.

The Cincinnati Red Stockings of 1869

During the early 19th century, American baseball slowly emerged from the English game of rounders. Wealthy gentlemen organized the first teams in New York in the early 1840s. By the early 1860s, when the first teams were assembled in Cincinnati, there was increasing pressure to pay talented players recruited from the lower classes. A pretense of amateurism was maintained by finding jobs for these men with local establishments, but expecting no work from them.

In 1866 several young Cincinnati lawyers and businessmen interested in playing baseball as amateurs formed the Cincinnati Red Stockings. Under the influence of Englishman Harry Wright, who came to Cincinnati in 1866 as a professional cricket player with the Union Cricket Club, the Red Stockings moved towards revolutionizing the game.

Beginning in 1869 the Red Stockings took the controversial step of forming an entire team of openly paid players. Salaries ranged from $600 to $1,400. These new Reds soon established themselves as the dominant team in the West and then undertook a tour of the East. By defeating the New York City Mutuals and the Brooklyn Atlantics, the Red Stockings captured the attention and admiration of the country. When the team returned triumphantly to the Queen City, they were presented a 27-foot "champion" bat. By the end of this first season, the team had outscored their opponents 2,395 runs to 575, winning 64 games and tying one.

At the opening of the 1870 season, the team reeled off another 27 victories. Then, on June 14, they fell to the Brooklyn Atlantics by the score of eight to seven in 11 innings. Nine thousand partisan Atlantics fans viewed the game, and newspapers across the country reported the loss. The Reds dropped only four more games during the remainder of the season.

At the end of the 1870 season, the combination of waning fan support and increased salary demands that threatened to push the payroll above $8,000 caused the team president, Arnold Champion, to announce the suspension of the team. Although the city was without professional baseball for the next six years, the example of Cincinnati's professional team spurred the formation of similar, professional baseball clubs across the country.

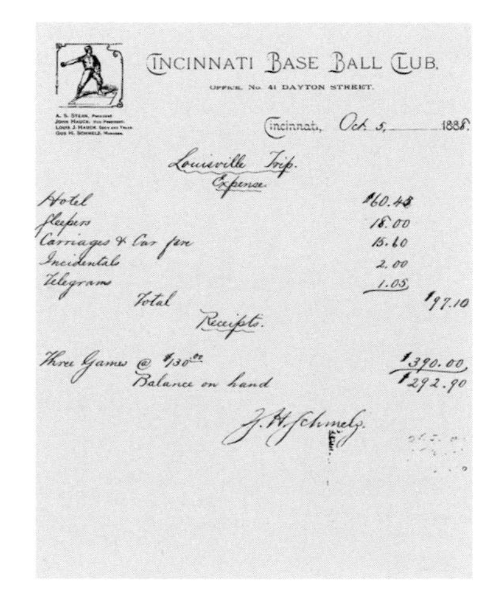

Cincinnati Base Ball Club.
Office No. 41 Dayton Street.

Cincinnati, Oct. 5, 1888.

Louisville Trip.
Expense.

Hotel	$60.45
Sleepers	18.00
Carriages & Car fare	15.60
Incidentals	2.00
Telegrams	1.05
Total	$97.10

Receipts.

Three Games @ $130.00	$390.00
Balance on hand	$292.90

J. H. Schmelz

To the Ladies of Cincinnati, The Red Stockings. Cover of sheet music illustrating the 1869 Red Stockings. Oliver Ditson and Company (Boston) lithograph.

Baseball—the Match Between the "Red Stockings" and the "Atlantics." Harper's Weekly (July 2, 1870), p. 424-25.

Presentation of the championship bat to the Red Stockings on their return to Cincinnati from their triumphal tour of 1869 from *Harper's Weekly* (June 24, 1869), p. 477.

Expense account for the Cincinnati Reds' 1888 trip to Louisville to play a series with the Eclipse Club. From the Cincinnati Base Ball Club Records, 1882-1888.

FIFTH STREET.

WALNUT STREET.

VINE STREET.

FIFTH STREET.

One of the first developments in rekindling pride came about unintentionally. Successful businessman Henry Probasco sought only to give the city a fountain in honor of his deceased business partner and brother-in-law, Tyler Davidson. While touring Europe he visited several foundries in search of a fountain free from conventional mythological symbolism. His search ended at the Royal Bronze Foundry of Bavaria, headed by Ferdinand von Miller. The fountain's design had been developed around 1840 by August von Kreling, the nucleus of a group of young artists who strove for realism in their work. The fountain Kreling had designed and which so pleased Probasco portrayed the blessings of water. It was headed by the "Genius of Water." Water fell from her fingers onto sculpted figures depicting the importance of water in quenching thirst and fire, for bathing and for growing crops. The city tore down a market house in the middle of Fifth Street and, in 1871, erected the fountain that quickly became Cincinnati's symbol.

The city's appearance needed attention. Cincinnati had become seriously overcrowded with its people working and living in the smoky basin. Prior to the Civil War, Cincinnati's officials, like those in most other American cities, did not appreciate the need for parks. On various occasions Cincinnati had turned down offers for the sale of land well below market value by such men as Nicholas Longworth and Jacob Burnet.

Plan of Esplanade. 1871. Ink on paper. Tyler Davidson Fountain Collection, 1866-1900. Gift of William S. Rowe.

Esplanade from William F. Poole's *The Tyler Davidson Fountain Given by Mr. Henry Probasco to the City of Cincinnati* (Cincinnati, 1872), facing p. 4. Gift of Thomas Lampertz.

Davidson Fountain—(Front View.), from Poole's *The Tyler Davidson Fountain*, facing p. 1.

Plaster models of the front and rear figures (September 1869). Photographs. Tyler Davidson Fountain Collection.

Designs for drinking cups of white tin plate, ornamented of the same metal bronze as the fountain itself (1870). Signed Fritz Miller. Tyler Davidson Fountain Collection.

LIST OF ANIMALS DONATED TO THE ZOOLOGICAL GARDEN.

Two European horned owls.......Henry Schneider, Esq., Cincinnati.
Two magpies, one raven, two alligators, one wood owl, two little screech owls, one coot, one golden eagle, two buzzards, and one Muscovy duck.......Peter Schwan, Esq., Cincinnati.
One American buzzard.......Peter Dilg, Esq., Cincinnati.
Two Cashmere goats.......Albert Fischer, Esq., Cincinnati.
One Virginian deer (doe).......Herman Alms, Esq., Cincinnati.
One horned owl.......John Twachtmann, Esq., Cincinnati.
One rattlesnake.......A. Fennel, Esq., Cincinnati.
Three Virginian deer (two bucks and one doe) and two peacock.......W. S. Munson, Esq., Cincinnati.
One raccoon.......A. Sunderbruch, Esq., Cincinnati.
One peacock, one pea-hen, and two pairs of turtle doves, Frank Louck, Esq., St. Bernard, O.
One Muscovy duck.......Chas. Reid, Esq., Avondale, O.
One black bear.......Miss Annie Sanborn, Cincinnati.
Two rattlesnakes and one little screech owl...C. Terne, Esq., Cincinnati.
One horned owl.......Geo. C. Smith, Esq., Clifton, O.
One opossum.......J. Kaiser, Esq., Cincinnati.
Two horned and two little screech owls...A. Strauch, Esq., Spring Grove.
One raccoon.......C. Moerlein, Esq., Cincinnati.
One North American porcupine.......———, Xenia, O.
One American crow.......Miss Lulu Dunnavant, Cincinnati.
One raccoon.......F. Gruneberg, Esq., Cincinnati.
Two Capuchin apes.......K. Gams, Esq., Cincinnati.
One Makako monkey.......Jos. Graff, Esq., Cincinnati.
One buzzard.......A. H. Smith, Esq., Burg Hill, Trumbull County, O.
One pair Jacchus monkeys.......Chas. Espich, Esq., Cincinnati.
One little screech owl.......Robert Hosea, Esq., Clifton, O.
One golden eagle.......Board of Park Commissioners, Cincinnati.

The earliest efforts in America to create planned green spaces began in eastern cities in the 1830s and focused on developing cemeteries in countrylike settings. Mt. Auburn in Boston (1831), Laurel Hill in Philadelphia (1836) and Greenwood Cemetery in New York (1838) became models for this new type of cemetery. Rural cemeteries were designed to preserve the sense of informality, simplicity and openness of the natural setting, enhanced by careful improvements through plantings and the construction of ponds and lakes. Adolph Strauch, a German-trained landscape gardener, had settled in Cincinnati to develop and care for the hilltop estates of people like Probasco. In the 1850s he applied the rural cemetery concept at Spring Grove in the Millcreek Valley on the northern edge of the city.

Strauch also shaped the city's first parks outside the basin. The need for a better supply of water prompted the acquisition of property on Mt. Adams from Joseph Longworth in 1869. His father, Nicholas Longworth, had once maintained vineyards there in his "Garden of Eden." From the beginning it was decided that any land the waterworks did not require would

Eldridge Derry Grafton, *Adolph Strauch* (1822-1883), "In Compliment to Adolph Strauch, The Pioneer Landscape Gardener of the West." Watercolor (1883). Gift of Otto Strauch.

Spring Grove Cemetery (1858). The original development plan was made by John Notman, designer of Philadelphia's Laurel Hill Cemetery. Adolph Strauch's landscaping plan was adopted soon after he became superintendent in 1855. Middleton, Strobridge and Company lithograph. Gift from the estate of Grace F. Spiegel.

List of Animals Donated to the Zoological Gardens, from the *First Annual Report of the Zoological Society of Cincinnati, for the Year 1874* (Cincinnati, 1875), p. 32.

Listening to the Beautiful Song Birds at Cincinnati Zoo (c. 1908). Post Card. Gift of Dorothy Hermanies.

be developed as a park. Here and in Burnet Woods, Strauch directed the planting of trees and greenery, the development of lakes and ponds and the careful maintenance of the grounds in such a way that nature would be enhanced but not altered.

The creation of the Cincinnati Zoological Gardens provided Cincinnatians with yet another type of open space. Led by Andrew Erkenbrecher and others, the Zoo was incorporated on July 11, 1873. Rejected as a tenant for Burnet Woods, which was then being developed as a park, the Zoological Society purchased land of its own and opened on September 18, 1875, with a curious menagerie that included an old circus elephant and a blind hyena. The collections grew rapidly in size, scope and popularity. In succeeding years the institution faced numerous financial problems, from which businesses and philanthropists rescued it, until 1932 when the city purchased it.

Cincinnati Music Hall and Exposition Buildings (1879). Russell, Morgan and Company lithograph.

From the Metropolis to the Porkopolis. When Theodore Thomas became a resident of Cincinnati in 1878, *Puck* magazine publicized his move on the cover of its October 9th issue.

Alfred Traber Goshorn (1833-1902)
One of Cincinnati's leading citizens of the 1860s and 1870s, Alfred T. Goshorn earned a reputation as the "father" of the Cincinnati Industrial Expositions and achieved international prominence as Director-General of the U.S. Centennial Exposition held in Philadelphia in 1876. According to one early biographer, his exceptional managerial ability and wide-ranging participation in civic affairs led to Cincinnati's "advancement in every phase."

A. T. Goshorn held many offices of importance and served as one of two early mayors of Clifton. His contributions as originator and three term president of the Cincinnati Industrial Expositions earned him such wide acclaim that he was asked to direct the U.S. Centennial Exposition in Philadelphia, a post he held from 1873 to 1877. He received awards and decorations from many foreign countries to commemorate his service.

Alfred Traber Goshorn
From Harry Ellard's *Baseball in Cincinnati* (Cincinnati, 1907), p. 136.

A series of festivals and expositions begun in the 1870s demonstrated how the city combined commerce and culture in this period. From 1838 to 1860, the Ohio Mechanics' Institute had sponsored a series of 18 trade fairs, which ceased in Civil War years. Under the leadership of Major Alfred T. Goshorn and Miles Greenwood, and with the cooperation of the Ohio Mechanics' Institute, the Chamber of Commerce and the Board of Trade, Cincinnati prepared a fair for the fall of 1870 that was larger than any held before the war. That year Saengerfest Hall was built in time for the spring festival of German singing societies, and in the fall it became the nucleus of a fair that attracted visitors from outside the Cincinnati area. This and succeeding fairs had certain common features, including machinery, much of it manufactured in Cincinnati, displayed in a "Power Hall," plus horticultural and art exhibits. The expositions proved so popular and successful in the early 1870s that Goshorn became the director-general of the nation's Centennial Exposition held in Philadelphia in 1876.

As years passed, the expositions changed. Less attention was given to the business purposes that had largely inspired them. They became increasingly elaborate with greater emphasis on pageantry. These expositions culminated in the Centennial Exposition of the Ohio Valley and Central States that ran from July 4 through October 27, 1888, celebrating the settlement of the city. The exposition succeeded in every respect except financial, but that critical measure ended the annual fairs until the early 1900s, when they were revived for several years.

The festivals provided an important symbol of how the city now worked to attract visitors and businessmen while also promoting its cultural life. Every spring, about the time the grapes bloomed, the city's German singing societies would assemble for a saengerfest. Out of this tradition Cincinnati held its first May Festival in 1873. Theodore Thomas, a prominent New York conductor, was persuaded to coordinate all of the singing societies into a grand festival. After the second festival in 1875 proved as successful as the first, Reuben Springer offered $125,000 to build a better facility to house both musical performances and the industrial expositions. His gift was conditioned upon the citizens matching it and the city granting the land in perpetual exemption from municipal taxation. The city and the public met his challenge, and between 1875 and 1878 Music Hall was built between Elm Street and the Miami-Erie Canal in time for the 1878 festival. The building gave Cincinnati a facility that attracted the Democratic national political convention to the city in 1880.

Centennial Exposition Bridge (1880). James Landy photograph. Gift of Justin Behle.

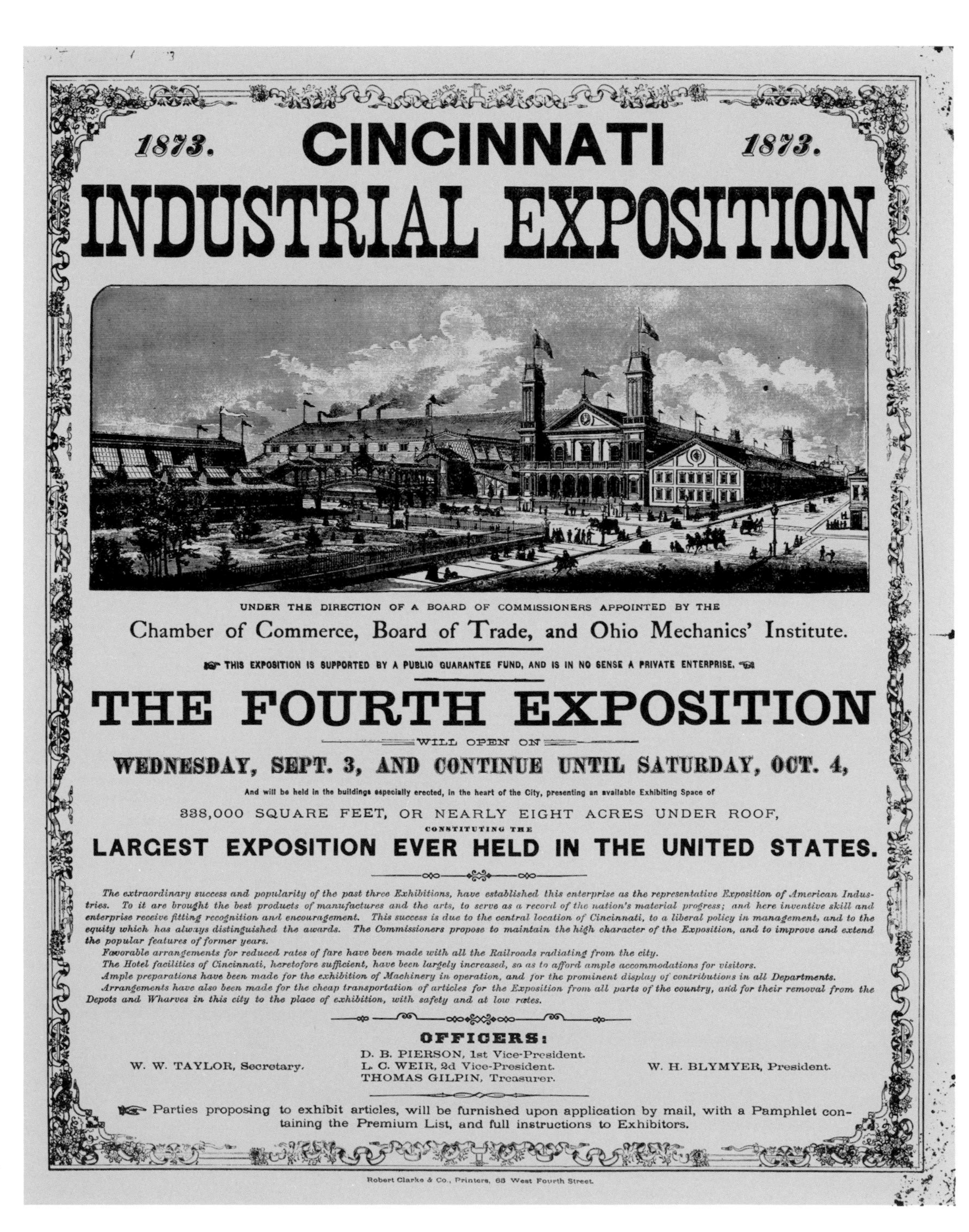

The Seventh Industrial Exposition of Cincinnati in the Grand Permanent Buildings, September 10th to October 10th—View of the Exhibits Displayed in the Music Hall, from *Frank Leslie's Illustrated Newspaper* (September 20, 1879). From the Cincinnati Musical Festival Association Records, 1875-1962. Gifts of John Warrington, Cornelius J. Hauck, Samuel Pogue, Mrs. Louis Nippert and Ted Gardner.

An advertisement printed by Robert Clarke for the Cincinnati Industrial Exposition (1873). Broadside.

Many of the same people instrumental in establishing Cincinnati's parks and expositions, its Zoo and May Festival also helped found the Cincinnati Art Museum. A group of Cincinnati women organized to prepare an exhibit of women's art for the nation's Centennial Exposition. After the exposition the committee transformed itself into the Women's Art Museum Association of Cincinnati for the purpose of founding a museum.

Cincinnati modeled its venture on the South Kensington Museum in England. Inspired by the 1857 "Crystal Palace" exposition with its emphasis on the decorative arts, the South Kensington Museum stressed the importance of the arts to industrial development. In 1878 the Women's Art Museum Association sponsored a lecture series that explored this relationship. The speakers and their topics said much about Cincinnati at the time: the president of the Chamber of Commerce, Sidney Maxwell, gave the inaugural lecture on "The Manufacturers of Cincinnati and Their Relation to the Future Progress of the City." George Ward Nichols spoke on "Those Branches of Manufacture Which Would Be Especially Benefited by Trained Designers and Workmen from the Art Schools." The series concluded with Charles P. Taft explaining "The South Kensington Museum: What It Is; How It Originated; What It Has Done and Is Now Doing for the World." Through formal training at the School of Design and inspiring exhibits at the museum, these cultured women and businessmen hoped that workers would learn not only their narrow skills but also pride in workmanship, thrift, industry and respectability.

Fest-Halle (1870). In the 1870s music reigned supreme in Cincinnati's cultural life. For the Saengerfest of 1870, a great auditorium 110 ft. by 250 ft. was constructed on Elm at 14th Street, opposite Washington Park. On the first evening 12,000 people, sitting and standing, packed the hall. Charles F. Wilstach and Company lithograph. Gift of the College of Music.

Paul Jones, *Cincinnati Fall Festival, The Magnificent Venetian Spectacle Marco Polo, Sept. 7 to 19, 1903* (1903). Strobridge Lithographing Company watercolor.

Strobridge Lithographing Company, *The Cincinnati Fall Festival, Aug. 28 to Sept. 22* (1906). Lithograph.

In 1900 another series of industrial pageants began under the sponsorship of the Cincinnati Business Men's Club, the Fall Festival Association and the Chamber of Commerce. The sixth in this series, in 1910, was known as the Ohio Valley Exposition featuring the produce, resources and products of the South. It also celebrated the completion of the Fernbank Dam on the Ohio River and the success of the Ohio Valley Improvement Association, established in 1895, to promote the canalization of the Ohio River to make it navigable the year around from Pittsburgh to Cairo.

Strobridge Lithographing Company, *The Cincinnati Fall Festival, Aug. 28 to Sept. 22* (1906). Watercolor.

Valentine Bonhajo, Artwork for an exposition poster (1886). Watercolor.

Women's Work

Maria Longworth Nichols Storer (1849-1932)
Maria Nichols was bright, bold and affluent; and she was perhaps the most powerful woman in Cincinnati in the late 19th century. Rookwood Pottery, which she started in 1880, is reputed to be the first major American industry owned and operated by a woman. What's more, by the turn of the century, it was the most prestigious art pottery in the United States, and among the most highly regarded in the western world.

Maria, her father, Joseph Longworth, and her husband, Col. George Ward Nichols continued the tradition of cultural boosterism begun in the 1820s by her grandfather, Nicholas. They were instrumental in the founding of the May Festival (1873), the College of Music (1878), and the Cincinnati Art Museum (1881), and the transfer of the School of Design from the university to the Art Academy.

Following the death of Col. Nichols, Maria married the Cincinnati attorney and politician, Bellamy Storer.

Finding suitable employment for women was not posed as a problem in antebellum society. In frontier Cincinnati spinsters were a rarity, and married or widowed women whose families needed their income "took in" sewing, laundry and boarders. Mechanization, industrialization, and a slow-down in economic and population growth diminished demands for these traditional cottage industries. From about mid-century many women who needed income were obliged to work long hours under deplorable factory conditions for substandard wages.

Finding more suitable "women's work" became a favorite cause of America's genteel reformers who feared that prevailing conditions jeopardized the health and morals of the mothers and future mothers of the nation. Cincinnati reformers pioneered in the concept that education in applied design would enable women to find suitable, profitable work in the emerging industrial world, and that the infusion of superior artistic qualities in the city's manufactures would make them more competitive in the national marketplace.

George Ward Nichols, author of *Art Education Applied to Industry* (1877), was the chief propagandist for the movement resulting in the establishment of the Cincinnati Art Museum, Art Academy and Rookwood Pottery patterned after English prototypes at South Kensington and Lambeth.

The Cincinnati experiment in art education and art applied to industry enjoyed a considerable success. The academy graduated an exceptional number of young men and women whose achievements in fine and commercial art have brought fame to the city. And local industries such as Rookwood Pottery and Gibson Art Company which provided "women's work" shared in the glory as well as the profit. Wages for women remained woefully inadequate but working conditions for artists were good, and the jobs carried a measure of prestige.

Cincinnati Art Museum—View from the Southwest (1884). Photograph.

Rookwood Artists at Work (c. 1892). Photograph.

In 1882 the city provided the Art Museum Association with 20 acres in Eden Park. Such a building conflicted directly with the prevailing theories of how the park should be developed, but construction proceeded and the "Art Palace of the West" opened May 17, 1886.

This amazing burst of energy to establish cultural institutions that would enrich lives and enhance the reputation of Cincinnati marked the city's coming of age. By the 1870s Cincinnati had reached a stage of economic and social maturity sufficient to create and support a rich cultural life. These efforts were never purely esoteric, they also focused on the material needs of the city. By providing places of beauty and retreat for the inhabitants of the overcrowded basin, by providing avenues through which citizens could experience music and art, Cincinnati's leaders sought to make the city livable and, perhaps, make better people out of the tens of thousands who lived and worked here.

Looking beyond the impact of these projects on Cincinnati's citizens, the city's boosters hoped they would maintain the city's national place. In 1878 Murat Halsted, the editor of the *Cincinnati Commercial*, declared with some justification and even more hope that "Cincinnati is the central city of the Nation. It is one of the cosmopolitan places...There is no other American city that is like Cincinnati...Washington will remain our political and New York our commercial capital, but Cincinnati will be the city of national conventions and the social center and musical metropolis of America."

Eden Park Bandstand. Free concerts, popular in Eden Park since 1872, were held in this tile-roofed bandstand from 1914 until the Seasongood Pavilion replaced it in 1960. Photograph. Gift of the Mt. Adams Gazette.

Eden Park Spring House. The thatched-roofed spring house was built in 1900 over a spring which, according to local legend, provided medicinal benefits. When the spring was found to be impure it was covered by an arched gazebo completed in 1904. Photograph. Gift of Albert O. Kraemer.

Chapter 3

Scramble Up the Hills

1870-1914

During the last third of the 19th century, Cincinnati grew in population and in area. A revolution in urban transportation made it possible for large numbers of people to escape the dirty, crowded basin and live some distance from their work. As inclined planes, trolley and railroad lines were built, people sorted themselves out along economic, religious and ethnic lines and formed new communities on Cincinnati's hilltops. This reorganization of the city transformed the basin. Offices and retail stores were concentrated in the central business district occupying ever taller buildings, while poor people still living in the basin were pushed to its fringes.

Rapid changes in where people lived were compounded by revolutionary changes in the way they worked. The combination of these sweeping changes precipitated a social and political upheaval that exploded in the 1880s in the greatest riot and labor strike in the city's history. Out of that chaos emerged a talented politician, George B. Cox, who proved able to impose some order and stability on the rapidly developing city. In time, Cincinnatians grew tired of Cox's methods and brought an end to boss rule, but for more than 30 years Cincinnati was dominated by one of the nation's greatest political bosses.

Louis Charles Vogt, *Mt. Adams Incline.* Oil on canvas. Gift of the Ohio Mechanics' Institute.

South Side of Fourth Street Between Walnut and Vine, Cincinnati, Ohio (c. 1871). Ehrgott, Forbriger and Company lithograph. Gift of P. W. Schath.

Lafcadio Hearn (1850-1904)

The density of the population [in Bucktown] is proportionately greater than in an other part of the city, although it is mostly a floating population—floating between the work-house or the penitentiary, and the dens in the filthy hollow. Ten, twelve, or even twenty inhabitants in one two-story underground den is common enough. At night even the roofs are occupied by sleepers, the balconies are crowded, and the dumps are frequently the scenes of wholesale debauchery the most degrading...
In the alley which runs by the old Allen Church, on Fifth and Culvert, some twenty feet below the fill, is a long stagnant pool of execrable stench, which has become a horrible nuisance, and which never dries up. Insect life, the foulest and most monstrous, lurks in the dark underground shanties near by; and wriggling things, the most horrible, abound in the mud without.

From Cincinnati's incorporation as a town in 1802 until the middle of the 19th century, its boundaries were fixed to the 3.88 square miles of the basin. Between 1849 and 1855, 1.5 square miles were annexed, but by 1860, with a population of 161,044, an average of 30,000 people lived in each square mile, making Cincinnati one of the most densely populated cities in America. Between 1869 and 1918, however, Cincinnati reached out and annexed more than 65 square miles as the population of the area approached a half-million people.

The change was not confined to numbers. Annexation transformed the structure and quality of life in Cincinnati. In 1870 Cincinnati was still fundamentally a "walking city" in which everyone, rich and poor, German and Irish, black and white, lived in the close confines of the basin.

In the mid-19th century, all American cities were walking cities. Everyone had to live within walking distance—one or two miles—of work, shops and church. In Cincinnati topography aggravated this normally congested situation. Steep hills to the north, east and west and the Ohio River on the south impeded expansion. The resulting jumble of housing, factories, warehouses and shops, combined with the widespread use of coal and lack of proper means for disposal of waste, gave Cincinnati a less-than-pleasant environment.

The structure of Cincinnati as a walking city was different from the 20th century city. The most desired residential location was near the center of the city, particularly along Fourth Street. Pockets of upper-class residences were also found farther from the center—including the area around Garfield Place and later near Dayton Street in the "West End" of the basin.

The least desirable locations were around the edge of the basin, such as along the riverfront and the Deer Creek Valley on the eastern edge of the city. Only those too poor to escape tolerated living near the jumble of warehouses, slaughterhouses and factories on land with poor drainage or vulnerable to floods. East of Broadway near the Deer Creek was Bucktown, largely populated by blacks and many poor Irish. Bucktown's saloons, coffeehouses and brothels attracted crowds of rowdy dockworkers, boatmen and factory hands. In areas along the riverfront known as Rat Row and Sausage Row, conditions were similar. Most Cincinnatians avoided these frightening areas.

Over-the-Rhine was another district on the periphery. Unlike Bucktown and the riverfront, Over-the-Rhine had become the primary district for German immigrants to settle in when they reached the city. By 1860 the statistical dominance of the Germans had given way to those of native-born stock, many of whom were born to immigrant German parents. Socially, the district remained the center of laboring-class residents.

Prior to the 1870s, only a few of the wealthiest citizens were able to afford horse-drawn vehicles and maintain the flexible schedules necessary to live away from the core of the city. Living outside the basin was impractical for just about everyone else until several developments revolutionized Cincinnati's internal transportation system and, consequently, the structure of the city. A bridge across the Ohio River between Cincinnati and Covington had been discussed seriously since the 1820s, but it was not until 1846 and 1847 that the Ohio and Kentucky legislatures issued charters to undertake its construction. Legal challenges, economic depression, the Civil War and labor disputes

Lafcadio Hearn, quoted from *Cincinnati Commercial* (August 22, 1875), p. 3:3. Hearn was a reporter for the *Cincinnati Enquirer* (1874-1875) and the *Cincinnati Commercial* (1875-1877). He wrote sensational accounts of murders and poverty and chronicled riverfront life.

Panoramic View of the City (1866). Looking from the roof of the Ohio Mechanics' Institute building at the southwest corner of Sixth and Vine streets. Photograph. Gift of Judge Charles W. Hoffman.

Panoramic View—City of Cincinnati (1900). Henderson Lithographing Company engraving. Eugene F. Bliss fund purchase.

Mt. Adams Incline (c. 1902). The best views of the Ohio River and its bridges were from the Mt. Adams Incline. Photograph.

Cincinnati and Covington Suspension Bridge (1866). Strobridge and Company lithograph.

prevented completion of the project until 1867. Designed by John A. Roebling, an innovative engineer, the Suspension Bridge opened in December 1866 as the world's longest and first truly modern suspension span.

Beginning in the 1840s, horse-drawn buses, or omnibuses, operated in Cincinnati. They were the city's first effort to establish regular fares and routes for moving people about the basin. However, their high fares and limited capacity restricted their impact. In 1859 city council passed an ordinance to provide for the development and regulation of horse-drawn street-railway lines. Streetcar lines soon sprang up all over the basin with little coherence or order. In 1875, 14 lines provided 45 miles of track and employed 550 men and 1,000 horses. By 1880 John Kilgour had become the dominant figure in local transportation by creating the Cincinnati Street Railway Company through a series of mergers, which reduced the confusion. The streetcars were a significant improvement over omnibuses, but they too were limited. Horses were expensive to purchase and maintain: they cost an average of $100 to buy; they required the services of blacksmiths and veterinarians; they consumed large amounts of feed; and, on the average, they lasted only four years. More importantly, the steep hills surrounding the basin required the use of so many extra horses that the horsecar lines were limited to use in the basin and in the Millcreek Valley.

Price Hill Incline (c. 1914). The only incline to use a double set of tracks—one for passenger service, the other for freight. Photograph.

Omnibuses, the only form of public transportation before iron rails for horsecars were laid in downtown streets in 1859, continued to make trips to the suburbs until the 1880s.

The destinations and connections were listed on this horsecar which ran between the Little Miami Railroad Depot and downtown.

Mt. Lookout Steam Dummy at Delta Avenue and Linwood Road (c. 1890). Because steam locomotives frightened horses, they were disguised as horse cars and popularly called "dummies."

High water cars, with their bodies and motors raised above the tracks, were used from 1901 to 1940 to go through water as deep as four feet.

Santiago (1908). Summer parlor cars were in use in Cincinnati by 1898. The Santiago was built by the Cincinnati Car Company.

The real breakthrough in scaling the hills came in 1872 when the Main Street, or Mt. Auburn, Incline opened. People had employed inclines for centuries, but they became popular modes of urban transportation in the 1870s both in Pittsburgh and Cincinnati. Using steam power generated in a powerhouse on top of the hill, horse-drawn streetcars and other vehicles drove onto a platform. The incline used a cable to raise or lower the platform with its cargo. Three more inclines were built during the four years after the opening of the Mt. Auburn Incline: the Price Hill Incline opened in 1874 and the Bellevue and Mount Adams inclines in 1876. Cincinnati's fifth incline, the Fairview, was constructed 14 years later to provide crosstown connections. Inclines provided Cincinnati cheap and convenient access between the basin and hilltops for the first time. Very quickly the horsecar lines met the inclines at the base of the hills and expanded outward from the summits into the surrounding areas.

Several other experiments were tried to provide better access to outlying districts. Established villages used commuter steam railways to provide links to the city. The Kilgours employed a steam "dummy" to promote the development of their real-estate holdings in Mt. Lookout. In addition, during the 1880s several cable-car lines were constructed, challenging the inclines for traffic. Finally, beginning in June 1888 with the electrification of the street railway from the top of Gilbert Avenue, trolleys quickly displaced the horsecars, commuter steam railways and cable lines.

The College Hill Omnibus (1870s). Photograph.

Post Office 24. Photograph. (c. 1885). Gift of Mrs. Anthony D. Bullock.

Mt. Lookout Steam Dummy. Photograph. Gift of John H. White, Jr.

High Water Car on Ludlow Avenue. Photograph. Gift of the Cincinnati Transit Company.

Santiago. Photograph.

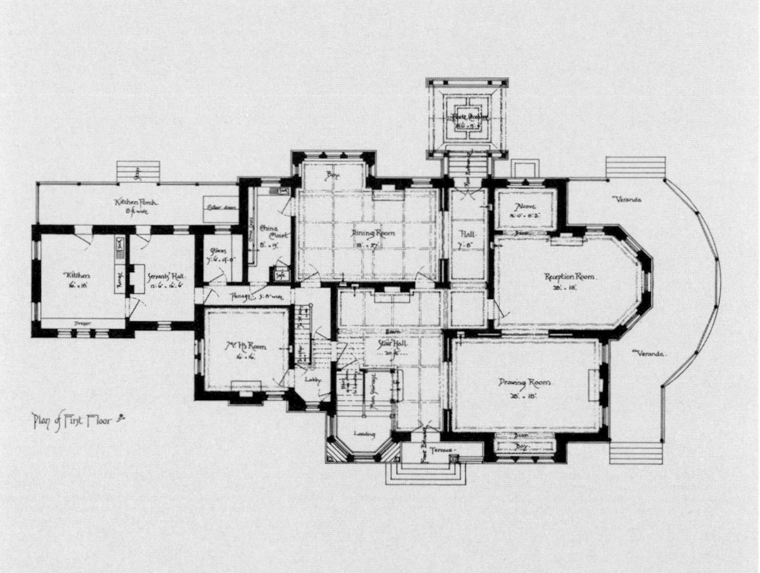

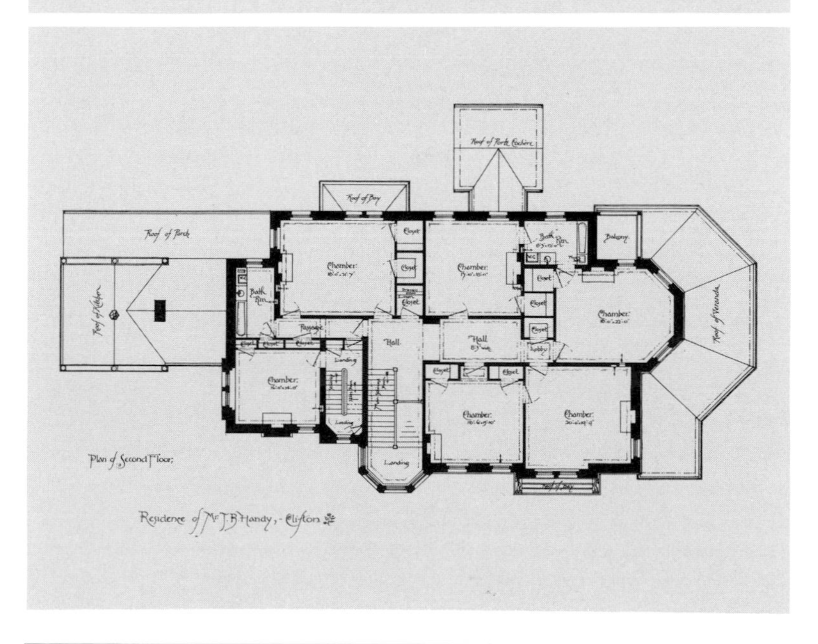

RESIDENCE OF HENRY PROBASCO, ESQ.

RESIDENCE OF MRS. MARY SHILLITO.

RESIDENCE OF GEO. K. SHOENBERGER, ESQ.

James W. McLaughlin, *Residence of Mr. T. B. Handy, Clifton* (c. 1880). Ink on paper. James W. McLaughlin Architectural Record Collection.

Residence of Henry Probasco, Esq. from D. J. Kenny's *Illustrated Cincinnati...* (Cincinnati, 1875), p. 309; *Residence of Mrs. Mary Shillito* from Kenny (1893), p. 236; and *Residence of Geo. K. Shoenberger, Esq.* from Kenny (1875), p. 310.

"The geographical location of Price Hill is most fortunate, as the prevailing west winds waft the smoke, gases and impurities which arise from the city proper away from it. The hygiene is unexcelled. The oxygen of the fresh, pure atmosphere brings the roses to the cheeks and elasticity to the step. What could be more beneficial than to reside in this perpetual health resort and still have such easy access to one's business?"

These developments had a dramatic impact on the structure of Cincinnati. The city pressed outward from the basin in a series of concentric rings. The exact path of development reflected the course and extent of the mass-transit system. By 1890 more than 100,000 people lived in dozens of communities in Hamilton County and northern Kentucky surrounding the basin. The hills were no longer insurmountable. As people, especially from the middle class, began to scramble up the hills, they formed new communities where only farms had been and transformed outlying autonomous villages into suburbs.

The wealthy had not waited for the development of mass transportation to begin moving from the basin. Upper-class Cincinnatians began as early as the 1830s and 1840s to search out retreats away from the noise and crowdedness of the city. In their search for solitude and beauty, they constructed homes on Mt. Auburn, Clifton, Walnut Hills, in Wallace Woods south of Covington and in Fernbank along the river. Along Lafayette Avenue in Clifton in the 1860s, the merchant princes of the city erected castle-like mansions and surrounded their palaces with gardens. Their homes had views of the Millcreek Valley that inspired those looking out and awed those looking up. The magnificence of the Clifton estates won for it and for Cincinnati international fame. *Lippincott's Magazine* commented that "the incomparable mountain suburb of Clifton" had only one rival in America or Europe, the "mountain paradise of Wilkemolke, which the Elector of Hesse adorned at the expense of a hundred ill gotten millions."

Although the wealthy led the way in populating new suburban areas, the bulk of the people fleeing to the hilltops after 1870 were from the middle class. Many of these new suburbs were based on long-established farming villages that were transformed by the arrival of commuter transportation. The small village of Pleasant Ridge, at the crossroads of Montgomery Pike and Columbia (later Ridge) Road, had served nearby farms since the 1820s. The arrival of the Cincinnati Northern Railroad in 1881 brought a wave of newcomers, doubling the population in a decade. Among the newcomers were truck farmers of German stock from Wooden Shoe Hollow near Winton Place who continued the farming traditions of the area. In greater numbers came families headed by middle-class business and professional men who commuted daily to Cincinnati.

College Hill developed as an even more specialized autonomous village within the orbit of Cincinnati during the 1840s and 1850s. The presence of the Farmers' College and the Ohio Female College gave College Hill a unique character and atmosphere. The opening of the College Hill Railroad in 1876, however, set in motion the transformation of the village into a commuter suburb of Cincinnati.

In the case of some suburbs, the ethnic or racial identity of the new inhabitants was more important than their economic and social status in establishing the character of the community. From the middle of the 19th century, Avondale attracted some of Cincinnati's leading industrialists. In the 1870s and 1880s, less affluent middle-class homeowners joined them. Then, in the 1890s, Avondale became the primary destination for German Jews seeking to move out of the crowded West End. With the addition of southern and eastern European Jews, by 1920 Avondale had become the home for three-quarters of the city's Jewish population.

The Millcreek Valley

The lands west of [Spring Grove Avenue]... are a succession of gardens and hot houses; what beds of onions, and rows of beets and parsnips and carrots; what peaches and cucumbers and melons; what multitudinous heads of cabbage and cauliflower and lettuce, and hills of succulent young corn, one passes, are not to be reckoned by any process of mental arithmetic.

Cincinnati Commercial (1866)

View of Glendale, Near Cincinnati (c. 1860). Middleton, Strobridge and Company lithograph.

While most towns near Cincinnati had begun as autonomous villages and became suburbs only as the city expanded, Glendale was planned as a community in a rural setting whose residents would work in Cincinnati. In 1851, 30 people formed the Glendale Association and purchased 600 acres, once the farms of John Riddle and Edmund R. Glenn (from whom the village name was obtained), along the line of the Cincinnati, Hamilton and Dayton Railroad. Robert C. Phillips planned the town, lots were sold and by 1852 the first house was built.

Ohio Female College (1859). Located on the grounds of the present Emerson A. North Hospital, the college offered courses in literature and the arts from 1849 until 1872. Middleton, Strobridge and Company lithograph. Purchase.

In the late 19th century some manufacturers subscribed to the philosophy that good working conditions were synonymous with good business. Architects suggested that well-planned factories in pleasant surroundings would encourage increased production and pride in workmanship. Often new factory buildings were located on landscaped grounds or in industrial parks which served as buffers between the plants and adjacent residential areas.

From the mid-19th century, some Cincinnati suburbs, including Avondale and Walnut Hills, had small settlements of blacks. Although the vast majority of Cincinnati's blacks were concentrated in the West End after 1870, several outlying black communities sprang up during the process of suburbanization. For example, beginning in 1893 Charles M. Steele developed a subdivision of small lots just north of College Hill, which he sold to black migrants primarily from Nicholas County, Kentucky. The black residents who moved to "Steele Sub" found jobs on nearby farms, in the rail yards and factories in Cincinnati, and as domestics and day laborers all over the area. Most had to build their own homes in stages as they saved enough for materials. As these people sought to reconstruct the best of the life they had left behind, "Steele Sub" became, in effect, a rural southern black village on the fringe of Cincinnati.

Neighborhoods in the Millcreek Valley and the "Norwood Trough" developed differently than the more prestigious hilltop communities. In the mid-19th century the Millcreek Valley was a beautiful truck-farming area. But this rural character disappeared between 1870 and 1890 as factories moved there and stimulated the development of housing for workers in Camp Washington, Cumminsville and St. Bernard. Norwood became Cincinnati's most important industrial suburb. Known as Sharpsburg until 1869, the area was occupied primarily by farmers, especially dairy farmers. During the 1870s Norwood could not compete with hilltop communities for residents, even though a rail line had passed through in the 1850s. Then, just before the turn of the century as the Millcreek Valley became filled, Norwood began to develop as a manufacturing center. It offered industries cheap land, room for expansion, excellent rail connections and access to a plentiful supply of labor. By 1910 Norwood was home for 49 manufacturing concerns that employed almost 10,000 workers—nearly half of whom commuted daily from Cincinnati. Increasingly, however, workers sought convenient housing in Norwood itself. Its popu-

United States Playing Card Company, Norwood, Ohio (c. 1900). Photograph of an architectural rendering. Gift of Thomas H. Landis and Samuel Hannaford and Sons.

lation soon had a higher proportion of factory workers than other Cincinnati suburbs.

Life in these emerging suburbs differed in many respects from life in Cincinnati before 1870. Certain members of the family were much more mobile than they had once been. The daily commute for those with full-time jobs or those attending high school in the city became a regular feature of life accompanied by all the frustrations of mass transit. One commuter line had such a terrible reputation for accidents and delays that a newspaper commented sarcastically that the railroad's management felt compelled to place Bibles in the coaches. For those who did not travel to town each day, the neighborhood, with its stores and traveling vendors, became a world of its own. In dozens of communities the main street supported scores of small shops and businesses that depended primarily on the trade of the immediate community. In addition, the iceman, locksmith, scissors sharpener and umbrella repairman, the traveling butcher and baker, and assorted vegetable and fruit vendors brought services door-to-door.

A few neighborhoods developed business districts that served whole areas of town. Particularly important were Peebles Corner in Walnut Hills and Knowlton's Corner in Cumminsville. Situated at the crossroads of numerous streetcar lines, both of these shopping districts were convenient for commuters to shop in while making transfers. Going shopping in Knowlton's Corner on Saturday evening became as much a social event as an economic event.

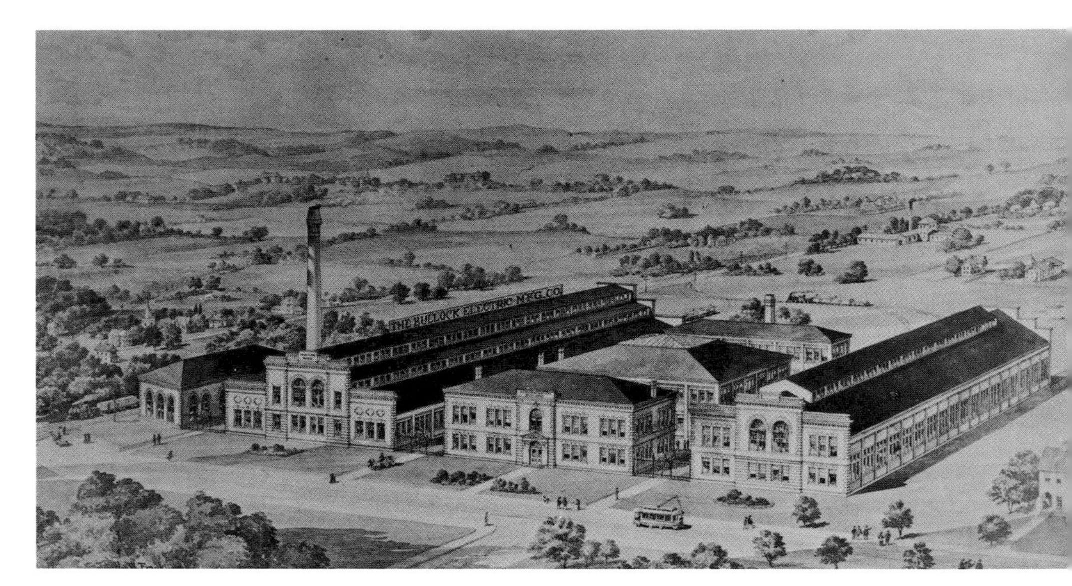

Bullock Electric Manufacturing Company, Norwood Works, 1898-1904. Photograph. Gift of James W. Bullock.

Bullock Electric Manufacturing Company. Architectural rendering.

The Procter & Gamble Company Factories (c. 1920). Photograph. Gift of Milton J. Niederlehner.

Suburbanization involved more than laying out streets and building new houses. It also meant creating a sense of community. Many institutions and organizations facilitated this purpose. The newly arrived German farmers in Pleasant Ridge organized the Pleasant Ridge Evangelical Lutheran Church, which has remained an important influence on neighborhood life. After 1905 the new Jewish residents of Avondale moved most of their synagogues from the basin to the hilltop. In addition to churches, fraternal and social organizations flourished everywhere. The growth of neighborhoods stimulated the development of a new type of organization variously termed "improvement associations," "civic leagues" or "welfare leagues," depending on the neighborhood. Regardless of the name, each organization took on a variety of tasks for its neighborhood and the city.

The Pleasant Ridge Welfare Association, formed in 1908, worked to extend sewer lines and street lighting, to guarantee adequate fresh water and to improve services on the interurban line that served the community. Residents complained continually about poor ventilation, inadequate heat, malfunctioning brakes and the lack of taillights on the train cars. Twenty years later the Fairview Civic Association, concerned with the impact of automobiles on the neighborhood, proposed parking restrictions and worked to widen the streets.

In addition to such bread-and-butter issues, the early organizations undertook projects to build a sense of pride among the residents of their communities. The Pleasant Ridge Welfare Association published a monthly newsletter, sponsored a neighborhood baseball team and Fourth of July parades and promoted community gardens for the children. The Fairview Heights Civic Association held annual summer festivals and produced such noteworthy plays as *The Womanless Wedding* and *Doctor of Alcantara.*

The community organizations worked to coordinate their efforts with the activities of similar groups across the city. In 1907 seven neighborhood associations formed the Federated Civic Association, which by 1911 expanded to include 31 affiliated organizations. As people grew familar with one another and as the city extended basic services as part of annexation, many of the original neighborhood associations became primarily social clubs. By the 1920s many had died out.

The diffusion of the city's population into new communities across the river and onto the hilltops, together with the concentration of manufacturing in the Millcreek Valley and Norwood Trough, freed the basin for a new type of specialization. Offices, department stores and banks became concentrated in the city's center. Factories, warehouses and railroad facilities absorbed much of the land around the fringe, forcing the people left in the basin into ever more compact residential areas. As the traditional center of black residence on the east edge of the basin was taken over for factories, the blacks moved into the housing in the West End that the middle class was abandoning. By 1900, 85% of Cincinnati's black population was concentrated there—segregated in fact if not by law.

Pleasant Ridge Hotel (1876). Built in 1853 by William Scudder, the hotel is at the northwest corner of Montgomery Road and Ridge Avenue. Photograph.

Fourth Street

Between 1830 and 1860, Fourth Street was the most prestigous residential address in the city. Like most of the old "walking city," it was devoted to a mixture of uses. Churches, educational institutions, hotels, groceries and specialty shops were interspersed among townhouses occupied by the urban elite.

As transportation improvements allowed people to move outward from the core during the 1870s, the physicial pattern of the walking city, which placed the most desirable and expensive residential areas close to business and shopping, began breaking down. From the 1880s, when Thomas Emery's Sons built such fashionable flats as the San Rafael and the Lombardy, apartment buildings replaced single-family residences on West Fourth Street. In the Lytle Park area, the Sinton-Taft family preserved a residential enclave by retaining their own home (the future Taft Museum) and by owning the Lytle and Lincoln apartment buildings. The St. Nicholas Hotel (1859-1911) at the corner of Race Street and the Grand Hotel (1874-1933) at Central Avenue were favorite spots for meetings, business luncheons and banquets.

While Fourth Street declined in importance as a place to live in the late 19th century, it held its own as a place to shop for quality goods, earning the title of Cincinnati's "Fifth Avenue." After 1900 it became the city's "Wall Street" as well when most of the major banks began to move their headquarters up from Third Street. During the first decade of the 20th century, Fourth Street became the skyscraper district of the city with the construction of the Union Savings Bank and Trust Company (Fourth and Walnut Building) and First National Bank (Clopay Tower) buildings both designed by famed Chicago architect Daniel Burnham and the Ingalls Building (ACI Building) designed by Cincinnati architect Alfred O. Elzner.

Southeast Corner, Fourth and Race Streets (c. 1890). Looking east, the St. Nicholas Hotel on the right.

Northwest Corner, Fourth and Main Streets (1903). Background, the Mercantile Library Building under construction. Photograph. Gift of Eugene W. Nickerson, III.

The Union

NO PEOPLE CAN BECOME GREAT WITHOUT BEING UNITED, FOR "IN UNION THERE IS STRENGTH"

Entered as second-class matter, February 13, 1907, at the Post Office at Cincinnati, Ohio, under the act of Congress of March 3, 1879

The Union, June 9, 1932. From the Wendell Phillips Dabney Papers.

Jennie D. Porter. Photograph in George W. Hays' *Reminiscences... 1890 to 1929* (Cincinnati, c1929) from the Records of the Urban League of Greater Cincinnati, 1921-1975. Gift of the League.

The handling of public schools showed the growing pattern of segregation in the city. After blacks were enfranchised with the passage of the 15th Amendment, Cincinnati's white power structure moved to undermine the most important black political power base in the city, the Independent Colored School System. Blacks lost control of the system in 1873 and gradually saw the system dismantled. In a decade, all that remained was the Elm Street School in Walnut Hills, which became Douglass School in 1910. The destruction of the segregated school system was not a move toward integration; in fact, it was a way to deprive black teachers of jobs and to squeeze black students out of the public schools. In 1870, 87 blacks were employed in Cincinnati teaching almost 3,800 students. By 1912 only seven black teachers remained, and less than 300 black students were enrolled.

In 1914 a young black teacher, Jennie D. Porter, convinced the school board to allow her to organize an all-black staff and student body in the old Hughes High School building in the West End, which she renamed the Harriet Beecher Stowe School. Porter was a follower of Booker T. Washington and attempted to apply his "accommodationist" policies to education in Cincinnati. She believed that segregated schools would offer greater job opportunities for black teachers, greater inspiration for black youth and better preparation of black students for the world. In 1923 a modern Stowe School was opened. It had facilities for a full range of vocational training programs, which Porter believed were better suited for black children, given the limited job opportunities available to them. She soon made Stowe the center of much of West End community life as well. By 1927 she was supervising the work of 180 teachers and 3,020 students.

Office of The Union—Dabney Building, 420 McAllister (1925). Photograph. From the Wendell Phillips Dabney Papers.

Porter succeeded at building this segregated subsystem. Her proposals played on the prejudices and desires of the white board and the people they represented. She was a master at public relations and institutional politics. One of the methods she used was to organize her students into various choral and musical groups which were available to entertain at functions all over the city. She also had her teachers and students prepare meals for the school board as a way to demonstrate their achievements.

Although successful, Porter drew the fire of the black leaders who felt her acceptance of segregation doomed blacks to inferior status. The most outspoken of these leaders was Wendell Phillips Dabney. He was the recognized leader of the city's black Republicans—organized in the Douglass League—and the publisher of Cincinnati's most important black newspaper, *The Union,* from 1907 until his death in 1952. Dabney spoke out in favor of true integration and attacked Porter as "Jubilee Jennie" for her willingness to use her students as entertainers to patronize the white community.

Just as the scramble up the hills changed the structure of the city, the Industrial Revolution revolutionized the work place, and subsequently life in the city. The industrialization process was more than simply the introduction of power-driven machinery or the application of a new technology to the manufacturing process. It reorganized work and changed the status of the worker. In the traditional, small artisan shop, each worker became skilled at performing all of the tasks involved in producing a particular item. But in a modern factory, each worker performs only a few tasks and a product comes from the contributions of many different workers. Industrialization particularly affected artisans. Those who moved from the small shop to the large factory found that the new environment transformed their role and identity. Inside the large factory the shoemaker did not exist, only cutters, lasters, bottomers, trimmers, heelers, edgesetters and machine operators. Iron molders became floor molders or core molders. Narrowly focused training programs replaced apprenticeships.

For the owners and managers of the factories, industrialization meant greatly reduced labor costs. In 1865 the cost of labor in building a carriage was approximately $45.67. After the reorganization of carriage making along industrial lines, labor costs were reduced to $8.10. Although each industry followed its own path, the advantages of industrial reorganization increased during the depression that followed the Panic of 1873. As the factory system replaced artisan shops during the 1870s, the number of Cincinnati industries employing over 100 workers increased from 59 to 109.

For the worker these changes generally meant a reduction of wages and loss of status. An increasing number of women and children were forced to work to help their families get enough money on which to live. By 1890 women dominated the labor force in the manufacture of furs, regalia and society banners, clothing, textiles, boxes and bags. They generally earned about one-half to one-quarter of the wages men received for factory work.

In response, labor organizations gained support. Strikes became more frequent, particularly in areas that were industrializing, such as iron molding and printing. They were increasingly concerned with apprenticeships, regulation of machinery and the role of the foreman in the shop as well as with wages and hours.

Globe Carriage Company, manufacturers of buggies and phaetons (c. 1885). Photograph. Gift of Charles M. Williams.

Bench Workers and Machinists at L. Schreiber and Sons Company (c. 1889). Photograph.

Those living through the changes taking place in the 1870s felt a need for order that heightened their awareness of lawlessness in Cincinnati. The city seemed to be overrun with tramps and vagabonds. In 1884, T. S. Matthews, a resident of the Garfield Park area, wrote that the benches in the park "now serve only as a loafing place for the most disreputable and worthless vagabonds of both sexes... the door of our house is not only latched and bolted at night, but has a chain, a precaution against sneak thieves... Every night the parlor maids have to draw the curtains of all the windows opening on the street and shut and latch the shutters... This nightly battening down of the house increases our sense of siege." In 1878 alone the police arrested more than 1,300 prostitutes and 2,000 drunks. Criminal activity was not confined to the basin area. Throughout the last part of the 19th century, newspapers chronicled surges of criminal activity in various suburban communities. During a week in December 1875, the *Cincinnati Gazette* reported four burglaries in Avondale. In 1878 the community learned that thieves had been robbing the Colored Cemetery regularly for 10 years and selling the bodies to medical schools. In late 1883 a series of brutal crimes plagued the city, including the murders of an Avondale couple for the $15 each the sale of their bodies would bring from a medical school. By January 1, 1884, the jail contained 23 men accused of murder.

James Landy photographs of the 1884 Flood:

Main Street, East Side, looking South from Second Street.

Public Landing, looking up Sycamore Street.

Flood of 1884
The Flood of 1884 was one of the worst in Cincinnati history—second only to the Great Flood of 1937. On February 6, 1884, when it became apparent that the Ohio River would rage out of control, a relief committee was organized to plan for the impending disaster. On February 14, the river crested at 71.1 feet; two weeks passed before the waters subsided. Ten people were killed and thousands were left homeless. More than $200,000 was raised from entertainment benefits and contributions from people and organizations all over the country. The relief committee supplied rescue boats, rubber boots for police and cots for displaced persons in temporary quarters. Carloads of food donations came from as far away as Kansas. The relief work continued until April 1884.

Suspension Bridge, from Covington.

Fourth Street, looking West from Mill Street.

MAYOR'S OFFICE,
Cincinnati, March 30, 1884.

PROCLAMATION
OF THE
MAYOR.

Misguided men, alleging indignation that the criminal laws are not properly executed, have themselves been led into the crime of assaulting the public officers of the peace and destroying public and private property.

I, therefore, the Mayor of Cincinnati, do hereby command all such persons to desist from this lawlessness and obey the constituted authorities.

I call upon all good citizens to rally for the preservation of the public peace. Such as are willing to enroll themselves as special police during the emergency will please report themselves at the police station nearest their homes, where the officer in charge is hereby directed to enroll them and provide means of assembling.

The members of the Grand Army of the Republic are requested to assemble with their officers at their posts and report themselves by messenger to me for similar duty.

Citizens are warned to keep the boys and youth of their families at home, and all to remain quietly in their homes, except those organized and enrolled as above directed.

All persons found on the street after 7 o'clock this evening will be required to show good cause for being abroad. The authorities of the city and of the State are determined that order shall be immediately and permanently restored, and the consequences of disobedience to this proclamation will be upon those who fail to regard it.

THOS J. STEPHENS, Mayor.

Proclamation of the Mayor, March 30, 1884. Broadside. Gift of Isaac Anderson Loeb.

Against this backdrop, the murder of liveryman William Kirk on December 24, 1883, set in motion a series of events that shook the foundation of Cincinnati. Two of Kirk's young employees, William Berner, an 18-year-old German, and Joseph Palmer, a 19-year-old mulatto, beat Kirk to death with hammers, robbed him of $285 and dumped his body in some brush along the Millcreek in Cumminsville. Within a few days the men were arrested and soon confessed. Berner's father hired the city's most skillful defense attorney, Thomas C. Campbell, who, recognizing that racial prejudice doomed Palmer, quickly separated the trials of the two men. After a highly publicized trial, the jury found Berner guilty not of murder but only of manslaughter.

The verdict enraged Cincinnati. Political cartoons caricaturing everyone connected with the trial, especially Campbell and the jury, and satirizing the entire criminal-justice system appeared in saloons. On Friday, March 28, Judge Samuel R. Matthews sentenced Berner to 20 years in prison, the stiffest punishment allowed for manslaughter. That evening a crowd estimated at between 6,000 and 8,000 assembled at Music Hall to protest the verdict. The *Cincinnati Gazette* described the "stupendous gathering" as a "cosmopolitan audience" made up of a cross-section of the entire city. Though of diverse backgrounds, "every man seen looked honest and determined; every man seemed ready for the work."

A series of prominent Cincinnatians addressed the audience. Andrew Kemper, a physician, made the principal speech. He compared the Berner verdict to other recent miscarriages of justice in Pennsylvania and Kentucky. Although Kemper and other speakers called for the citizens to respond within the law, Kemper asserted that at the foundation of the American system lay the principle that "the people make the laws, and the people see that they are enforced." The crowd repeatedly interrupted the speech with applause for his references to lynchings in other cities. They cried out for a "vigilance committee." The meeting broke up after the adoption of a series of resolutions, which included a call for the jurors in the Berner case to leave the city.

As the crowd filed out of Music Hall, it had no leadership and no goal. But quickly and, apparently, spontaneously, certain elements in the crowd turned into a mob and headed for the jail on Sycamore Street behind the courthouse. Part of the mob forced its way into the jail shouting, "Hang Berner." But Berner had already been sent to Columbus. Sheriff Morton Hawkins, hoping to avoid full-scale rioting, instructed his 13 deputies not to fire. After the intruders ran through the jail and realized that Berner had already been removed, the deputies, now reinforced by a detachment of the militia, were able to clear the jail temporarily. By this time, however, a crowd of 20,000 swirled around outside the jail, calling for blood and throwing stones. The rioters rushed all of the entrances a second time. Through the determined use of a battering ram, they gained entrance. This time the police seized and arrested 25 rioters. As the jail was being cleared, shots rang out and several rioters were killed. Finally, the militia cleared the street.

All day Saturday small groups clustered on street corners. Handbills urged citizens to organize. The authorities reinforced the defenses at the jail. Barricades went up blocking access to the jail from across the canal, east and west on Court Street, and from Main Street to the south. Sixty militiamen were placed behind each

Scenes from the Cincinnati Riot, March 1884. Achert and Company lithograph. Gift of Mrs. Albert L. Russel.

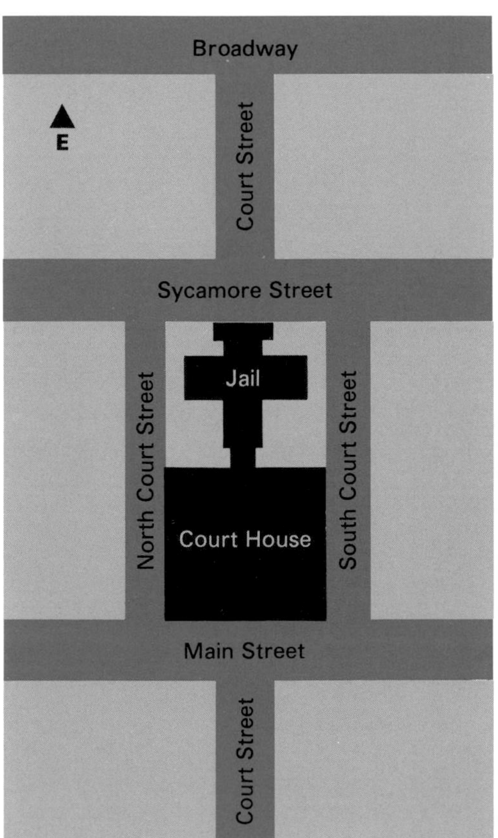

Court Street, looking west from Broadway. Rombach and Groene photograph.

Court Street, looking west from the Court House. Photograph.

Court House Front, looking East, Gattling [sic] Gun and Battery in Foreground. James Landy photograph.

Interior of the Court House After the Riot. Photograph.

barricade. The police were dispatched ahead of these defenses. By dusk the mob formed again and now focused its attention on the very symbol of justice, the Hamilton County Courthouse. After several hours of hurling bricks and shouting angry slogans, the crowd surged forward past the defenders and gained entrance to the courthouse. The rioters set fires in offices throughout the building and, despite the efforts of the militia and police, the building became engulfed in flames. As Captain John J. Desmond moved across the front of the building with his Lytle Greys, he was shot and killed, and two of his soldiers were wounded. Soon, detachments of the Ohio National Guard arrived in the city, marched to the courthouse and ruthlessly cleared the streets.

By Sunday morning the fire had reduced the courthouse to a smoldering pile of rubble. Fifty-four rioters lay dead along with Desmond and three policemen; more than 200 on both sides were injured. The depth of Cincinnati's torment was laid open.

In the aftermath of the courthouse riots, elements of the city's elite organized a variety of committees to bring the city back under control. They unleashed a stream of law-and-order oratory and proposed an array of reforms. But the rift in Cincinnati society, in American urban society, went much deeper. In May 1886 the labor elements of the city, led by factory artisans in industries undergoing the most rapid changes, organized a general strike. The strikers claimed they were joining the quest for law and order because their strike aimed at securing the promises vaguely held out by a new, but flawed, law reducing the workday to eight hours. In conjunction with general strikes in cities across America, 12,000 Cincinnati workers paraded through the streets on May 3. By May 8 no freight moved in or out of the city; garbage went uncollected; laundresses, streetcar conductors, waitresses and machinists cooperated in shutting down the city. Municipal leaders called out the militia. By the end of the month, 32,000 had walked off their jobs. Cincinnati was on the edge of a violent abyss for the second time in two years. Gradually, agreements were struck, usually favorable to the workers, and the strike dissipated.

Although Cincinnati escaped a second conflagration, the Courthouse Riots of March 1884 and the General Strike of May 1886 revealed the city was out of control. No person stood above the conflicting interests to pull the scattered elements of the city together. Out of the chaos of the mid-1880s, however, a new system gradually emerged with a new leader who brought order.

Since the Civil War Cincinnati politics had been reduced to a factional struggle. Each faction represented the narrow interests of a group or individual, but none was strong enough to remain in power for any length of time and organize the badly fragmented city government. At the heart of this system was the ward boss, who controlled a block of votes. Lacking any coherent view of the needs of the city, most of the bosses became "bummers" willing to trade their block of votes for the most enticing favors offered.

Saloons were the real centers of political life in Cincinnati. It was from a saloon at the corner of Longworth and Central avenues, "Dead Man's Corner," that a young politician emerged who would transform Cincinnati's political system—George B. Cox. He was born in 1853 to an English immigrant father and Canadian mother. After Cox's father died when George was eight, the boy was on the

Child Labor at L. Schreiber and Sons Company (c. 1889). Photograph.

streets earning a living. He worked as a bootblack, newsboy, delivery boy for a market, tobacco salesman and bartender before purchasing a saloon.

Cox was active in politics from the age of 18 and showed an ability to challenge weak political figures successfully. He might have become just another petty ward boss, but ambition and vision took him well beyond that. Cox accepted the political practices of his day and rewove them into a fundamentally different system. From the beginning Cox seized opportunities and turned them into long-range assets. In 1884 he fought for the right to head the local presidential campaign of James G. Blaine against the wishes of the established party leadership. Although Blaine lost nationally, he carried Hamilton County. Cox emerged with a reputation as a good organizer and in control of the newly formed Young Men's Blaine Clubs, which served as his political base for 30 years.

In 1887 Cox formed an alliance with Joseph Foraker, who had become governor the previous year. Foraker oversaw from Columbus the passage of legislation which reorganized municipal government in a way that provided greater opportunities for patronage; he entrusted this power in Hamilton County to George Cox.

Dispensing political jobs and favors became a high art under Cox and his lieutenants, Rudolph "Rud" Hynicka, who handled City Hall, and August "Garry" Herrmann, who directed affairs at the county courthouse. Jobs were parceled out to the ward chairmen, to the precinct captains and to the faithful. In exchange, those receiving government jobs contributed 10% of their first year's salary and 2½% thereafter to Cox's campaign fund. Even more important, those receiving jobs were expected to monitor the pulses of their areas. They sent information

Over-the-Rhine saloons and beer gardens were social and political centers of this German community in the 19th century. Waiters carried 10 to 12 beer steins at a time. The sausage man made his rounds from early morning until after midnight. The Wiener Wurst man sold sausages from a large tin while a boy accompanied him with the bread, salt and pepper.

Henry Farny, *The Transrhenane Waiter, The Wiener Wurst Man,* and *The Sausage Man.* Engravings from D. J. Kenny's *Illustrated Cincinnati...* (Cincinnati, 1875), pp. 134-5.

Henry Farny, *Wielert's Saloon.* Engraving from D. J. Kenny's *Illustrated Cincinnati...* (Cincinnati, 1875), p. 133.

about voters to Hynicka and Herrmann, who kept extensive card files on voters in the city and county.

The most famous and successful of the ward bosses was Mike Mullen in the Eighth Ward. His area included much of the "bottoms" along the riverfront on the east side of the downtown as well as the more exclusive residential sections on East Fourth Street. For the thousands of poor people in the ward, Mullen became a saint because of his concern about their daily needs. Mullen saw that coal was distributed to the needy in the winter, food got to the hungry, and jobs were provided to the unemployed. He oversaw the creation of Lytle Park with a playground in 1905. Beginning in 1903 Mullen sponsored annual picnics at Coney Island—10 miles upriver. For weeks ahead of time, he passed out tickets to the families in his own ward and to children from all over the city. Each family received tickets for free rides, ice cream and lemonade as well as a round trip on the *Island Queen.*

Mullen's motivations were political as well as altruistic. Mixed with these rather pleasant favors for his constituents were reports of outright vote buying and transporting Kentuckians into his ward to build majorities on election day. Mullen's influence on his ward was demonstrated in 1897 when he switched from the Democratic Party to the Republican Party and took the ward with him. Within a few years, Mullen was Cox's personal representative on city council, where the mere announcement by Mullen that "I trust the resolution will not pass" was enough to doom any bill.

Through a series of political maneuvers from 1884 to 1897, Cox emerged as the leading figure in the Republican Party. After 1897 he was the master of the political scene, regardless

Fred's Place, Race Street and West Canal (north side). A saloon that served the neighborhood, Fred's Place had a "sitting room," or women's section. Photograph. Gift of Eugene W. Nickerson, III.

Campaign broadside for Michael Mullen (1907). Gift of William A. Baughin.

Foucar's Cafe (c. 1898), at 426 Walnut Street, was a popular meeting place during the late 19th and early 20th centuries. "Siesta," the pastel by Frank Duveneck opposite the mahogany bar now is in the collection of the Cincinnati Art Museum. Photograph from the Foucar Collection. Gift of Ted Eberle.

of party. Yet Cox held political office only once, when he served on city council while still in his 20s. He ran twice for county clerk but was defeated. Cox's leadership rested on personal influence that was exercised through an unofficial but well-understood system. He was the "central brain" coordinating all of the competing interests and balancing all of the factions. During the day Cox received a steady stream of visitors at his office above The Mecca, a saloon. In the evening, he shifted his headquarters to Wielert's Cafe or another Over-the-Rhine establishment. In both settings Cox was a listener. An observer reported:

He never talked; he sat like a graven image with menacing and considering eyes, slowly chewing tobacco, posing a reflective cigar before his face, and regularly consuming a tall glass of lager every 12 to 15 minutes. On either side of him at a large circular table where he sat, lounged members of his cabinet. And every now and then the men with cocked derby hats arrived from different wards, sat down at his table, and talked, and talked, and talked.

Increasingly, an entire range of political reformers and journalists assailed Cox. Perhaps the most famous was written by muckraker Lincoln Steffens in *McClure's Magazine* in 1905 entitled, "Ohio: A Tale of Two Cities." According to Steffens, recent Ohio politics was best understood as a tale of the state's two leading cities, "Cleveland, the best governed city in the United States, Cincinnati, the worst." Steffens visited Cox one morning in his dark and dreary office above The Mecca to question him about his political methods. When Steffens rhetorically raised the question of whether Cincinnati had a mayor, council, and judges, Cox responded, "Yes, but–." He pointed with his thumb back over his shoulder to the desk, "I have a telephone, too." Other critics referred to Cox as the "dictator of Cincinnati and Hamilton County" and "Cincinnati's uncrowned king."

Cox, not surprisingly, had a different view of his role. In 1911 he wrote a defense of his career. He was unapologetic about the term "boss," for "this is the age of the boss." Cox understood his role as a "product of evolution–a natural product of American political life" in the late 19th and early 20th centuries. Although he had no ambition to become a boss when he entered politics, he evolved into a boss "because of my peculiar fitness." In direct response to Steffens' charges, Cox asserted that he and his organization had made "Cincinnati the best governed city in the United States... there is less dishonesty among the officeholders than in any of the large cities in the country. The gambling houses were driven out many years ago and the social evil is regulated as much as possible... Cincinnati is not a wide open city in the popular sense of that term, but it is possible to get a drink on Sunday–our Germans demand that privilege and it was through my efforts that Cincinnati obtained its new waterworks, but my chief work has been in seeing that Cincinnati has the right men to serve it... the people do the voting, I simply see that the right candidates are selected."

"DEPOSE THE BOSS!"
"ENTHRONE THE PEOPLE."

EXECUTIVE COMMITTEE.
LEWIS VOIGHT, President.
S. W. BARD, Vice-President.
EVAN EVANS, Secretary.
J. B. WILSON, Treasurer.
E. E. GREENWALD,
DR. H. W. ALBERS.
ROBERT W. WISE,
ADOLPH GEIGER,
FRED. BELCHER,
W. H. CAMPBELL,
J. B. S. EVANS.

HEADQUARTERS
+ C·I·T·I·Z·E·N·S +
Republican · Association
ROOM No.
PIKE BUILDING,
Cincinnati, March 19th, 1892.

DEAR SIR:

A careful perusal of the following letter from SENATOR JOHN SHERMAN, on "Political Bossism in Hamilton County," is requested of you by the above Association:

United States Senate,

WASHINGTON, D. C., Feb. 29, 1892.

MESSRS. LEWIS VOIGHT, Chairman;
EVAN EVANS, Secretary, and others.

GENTLEMEN:–

Your note of the 22nd inst. is received. You state that you were appointed by a Republican meeting held at the Lincoln Club, that had "for its object the overthrow of a gang in Hamilton County who have seized and degraded the Republican organization." You enclose the circular of your Executive Committee to the Republicans of Hamilton County, proposing an organization of the Citizens' Republican Association "with a view of rebuking corruption and purifying our party

"Depose the Boss! Enthrone the People" (1892). Leaflet. Gift of Mrs. Donald C. McGraw.

In the late 19th century, Cincinnatians took their beer-drinking seriously. Whether they carried it home in "growlers" or drank it at the neighborhood saloon, on the average, every man, woman and child consumed 40 gallons a year—24 more than the national average.

Saloons abounded everywhere. In 1890 the city directory identified 1,810, with 136 along Vine Street alone. Saloons near the river served a rough clientele while elegant establishments, like Foucar's Cafe, were clustered at the center of the downtown. Hundreds of Over-the-Rhine saloons run by Germans were favorite places for conducting business, settling political disputes and holding regular meetings of social clubs.

The beginning of Prohibition on January 16, 1920, was more than an economic disaster. It destroyed long-established social patterns as well.

The Christian Moerlein Brewing Co. Moerlein's Old Jug-Lager Krug Bier. Exhilarating, Stimulating, Re-Juvenating, Wholesome, Delicious & Pure. Pottery. Cornelius J. Hauck Collection.

The Mecca Cafe. Located at 431 Walnut Street, R. W. Gruber's and Fred. B. Salmar's famous saloon was in business from 1893 to the beginning of Prohibition. Photograph. Gift of Mrs. Anthony D. Bullock.

Henry Mosler, *George B. Cox.* Oil on canvas. Gift of the Shubert-Cox Theaters.

Cox's self-serving and one-sided statement provided some balance to the simplistically negative pictures painted of him by the reformers and muckrakers of his day. In addition to the municipal waterworks that Cox cited, city officeholders and administrators who served under Cox's direction improved the police and fire departments, paved hundreds of miles of city streets, built sewer lines, tried to reduce the smoke problem in the basin, brought some order to the development of utilities by awarding publicly regulated monopolies, and maintained low taxes. For all its political improprieties, Cox's organization accepted the secret ballot and voter registration. But most importantly, Cox and the organization he built provided a center that was strong enough and enduring enough to hold the city together through a period of rapid change and growth.

Louis J. Porr, *The Bellevue Brewing Co., Cincinnati, O.* The Bellevue Brewing Company was formed about 1878 and continued until Prohibition. Lithograph. Purchase.

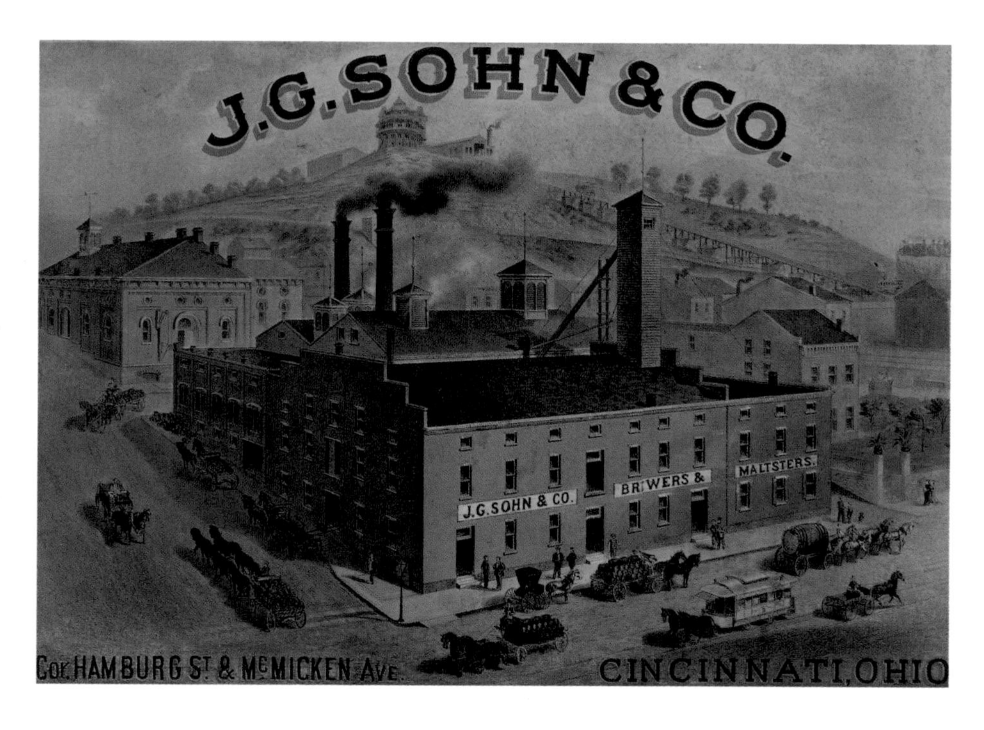

J. G. Sohn & Co.—Brewers and Maltsters (c. 1894). Typical of the many small to medium-sized breweries in Cincinnati during the late 19th and early 20th centuries, Sohn, later the Mohawk Brewing Company, brewed lager and Bohemian beer from 1866 to 1935. Show Card. Oil on iron. F. Tuchfarber and Company. Gift of Robert D. McCarron.

The Cox organization was determined to incorporate suburbs that were "of the city, but not in it." Cincinnati sought to annex these areas for their tax base and to increase the status and size of the city. In 1892 Mayor John Mosby declared that "if it [is] your desire that Cincinnati should grow, that it should be prosperous in the future, then we must consider the question of annexation above all others." Cincinnati held out the promise of water, sewer and other utilities to small villages and towns. These supposedly idyllic communities were increasingly hard pressed to meet the demands of their residents for sidewalks, pure water, sewerage and natural gas. Despite these problems and the debts that accompanied their solution, the question of annexation deeply divided every community. In a few cases, such as Kennedy Heights, local government was so inept and inadequate that a clear majority of the residents favored annexation. In most instances, however, only the passage of the Lillard Law in 1893 made expansion possible for Ohio cities. Under this law a majority of the ballots cast in both the city and suburb combined accomplished annexation. The law enabled Cincinnati to

swallow suburbs as it expanded. Only because changes were made in the law was the highly coveted industrial suburb of St. Bernard saved. Norwood escaped by becoming a city itself.

As important as the policy of annexation was to the Cox organization, within the policy lay the seeds of the organization's demise. New territory brought with it thousands of new middle-class voters. To them, Cincinnati's politics under Cox was an embarrassment and an affront. It seemed outdated in light of the work of progressive reformers in other cities. Cox was a master of the old methods. Although he improved the delivery of a variety of services, his approach was always piecemeal and dictated by politics. Progressive reformers, on the other hand, advocated an entirely new approach to municipal administration. They sought to apply methods of scientific management through the work of professionally trained city managers.

The difference in the two approaches was reflected in the way each side approached the need for an improved water supply and sewer system. Under Cox, there was no coherent and orderly plan; rather, the city built individual lines—often as ploys to communities targeted for annexation. In the most blatant case of self-interested decision making, an isolated line was run in 1895 to the section of Clifton where Cox had recently built a house. By contrast, under the one-term reform administration of Gustav Tafel in 1896, engineers evaluated the water and sewer situation and developed plans for improving service for the entire city. Although Tafel was not in office long enough to implement the plan, the Cox-backed administration of Julius Fleischmann picked up the highly popular section that called for building a new waterworks at California, upriver from the points where the city dumped its sewage into the river.

Efforts to clean up and reform Cincinnati politics were as old as the Cox organization itself. Because Cox co-opted much of the Democratic Party into his organization by splitting patronage on a 60-40 ratio, these efforts had difficulty getting a foothold. They depended upon fragile alliances between reform Democrats and Republicans and non-partisan independents. But the reformers could not survive more than one term in office.

The most important of the reform administrations was that of Henry Hunt in 1911-1912. Hunt was the son of a wealthy Clifton couple. He was educated at Yale and the University of Cincinnati Law School. Hunt allied himself with the voices of reform, and, by appealing to the suburban voters, he was elected as county prosecutor in 1908. Hunt could not move against Cox until after the election of 1910, when a reform judge presided over the grand jury room. Hunt charged Cox with perjury in testimony Cox had given in 1906 to a committee of the state legislature. Cox had sworn that he had never personally received any interest on public funds deposited in local banks. Hunt found two former bank treasurers who testified they had delivered such money to Cox. Eventually, a Cox-appointed judge dismissed the case on the grounds that Cox's constitutional rights had been violated in 1906. Technically, Cox won, but the trial had shattered his spirit. Soon after, Cox announced his retirement from politics. Cox had used the ploy of "retirement" twice previously to deflect criticism. Although he became less active, on election eve in 1910 Cox stood outside Wielert's Cafe to review the parade of the faithful. Twenty-four hours later, however, Cox's demise was tabulated. The victory denied Hunt in court was gained at the polls when Cincinnati elected him mayor.

Henry Thomas Hunt
(c. 1910). Photograph. Gift from the estate of Charles Ludwig.

Hyde Park Square
(c. 1900). Postcard.

Hunt was determined to place Cincinnati's government on a sound foundation. He turned to professional managers to evaluate the needs of the city and develop scientifically sound proposals for meeting its challenges. Hunt and the managers understood the size and complexity of the problems Cincinnati faced. Hunt determined that the primary challenge to improving the quality of life in Cincinnati was in relocating working-class and poor people out of the decaying residences of the basin and into newer and more sanitary suburban settings. He identified the lack of cheap, rapid and adequate transportation facilities as the biggest obstacle to reaching this goal and set about making plans to convert the old Miami-Erie Canal bed into a rapid-transit loop. It would provide quick access to commuters who used nine existing interurban lines to reach the edge of the city and then had to poke along street railways into the center of the city. Hunt's rapid-transit line would operate as a subway downtown in the old canal bed and run above ground to Cumminsville, east to Norwood and Oakley and then back south through the Deer Creek Valley to the downtown. Hunt believed the rapid-transit system would be "of greater value to the city than the Cincinnati Southern Railroad and will aid immensely in improving municipal health." With the creation of the transit loop, Hunt predicted that "the housing problem would solve itself, the commerical well-being of the city would be stimulated and our economic situation would be benefited."

Many Cincinnatians recognized that Hunt's proposals responded to real needs of the city and found his management methods to be clear advances over those of the Cox organization. But Hunt was defeated for re-election in 1913 and was unable to carry through with his programs for the same reason that earlier reform administrations had been turned out after one term. It would be costly to clean up the city and undertake the major improvements needed, and Cincinnati seemed to value low taxes more than modern government. The rapid-transit plan became a political orphan. Although later city administrations spent $6.2 million developing about one-third of the system, the subway was doomed. It lacked the necessary political support. World War I caused construction costs to soar, and the automobile's growing popularity after the war killed the interurban system that was to feed the subway.

Republicans returned to political power in 1913, but for the first time since 1884, they were without Cox. His organization continued to dominate city affairs for another 11 years under the weakened rule of Rud Hynicka. But an era was over. Cox remained out of the public view until he died of a stroke on May 20, 1916.

Cox was a product of the rough-and-tumble politics of the late 19th century. Because he mastered the limited tools available to the politician of his day, Cox was able to guide Cincinnati through a period of fundamental social and economic change. His methods could not put Cincinnati onto a fully modern footing. Hunt and his reformers pointed in that direction, but in 1912 the people were not yet prepared for the hard task involved. Disgusted with the city's unwillingness to face up to its needs, Hunt left Cincinnati after his defeat and returned only once later in his life.

Subway tube under construction (1920s). Excavating for Cincinnati's subway system began in 1920. Using the Miami-Erie canal bed to the present Norwood lateral, the route originally was planned to follow a 16-mile loop from downtown through the suburbs. When construction prices soared, the route was modified. The project was finally abandoned in 1927 after two miles of tunnel and seven miles of surface route, except track, had been completed. Financed by a bond issue passed in 1916, the city's subway debt was not paid until 1966 at a total cost of $13 million. Photograph.

EXIT

Chapter 4

New Ways to Cope

1914-1945

On August 1, 1914, the *Deutscher Staats-Verband* (German Alliance) assembled for its annual picnic at Chester Park. This day was different from earlier picnics, and a sense of foreboding filled the air. Europe was plunging toward war. On July 28 Austria had declared war on Serbia in response to the assassination of Archduke Francis Ferdinand. The next day Russia mobilized in defense of the Serbs, and on July 31 Germany ordered Russia to back down or face war. The Cincinnati German-American community followed these developments with special concern. Austrian and German immigrants who were still citizens of their home countries waited anxiously for orders for them to return to Europe.

The German-American leaders in Cincinnati wanted the picnic to "become a patriotic demonstration as a testimonial to the old *Vaterland*." To accommodate the group, I. M. Martin, the park manager, arranged to receive telegraph messages regarding European developments. No news had arrived by evening when many assembled to hear speeches from the leaders. Word finally arrived during a seemingly endless anti-prohibition speech. Judge John Schwaab, president of the *Staats-Verband*, rose and declared, "The die is cast; Germany has declared war on Russia; it has been forced to do so." Schwaab called on everyone to rise and sing *"Die Wacht am Rhein,"* a German national song. The anthem spread throughout the park and was concluded with three mighty "hurrahs."

Murals portraying Cincinnati workers installed in Union Terminal in 1933 were created by Weinold Reiss from photographs taken in local industries such as the Baldwin Piano Company factory.

In making a mural, grid patterns were drawn on the photograph, which was then enlarged to full size. A watercolor sketch was made to indicate the colors to be used. Glass mosaics were pasted onto two-foot sections of tracing paper. At the terminal the glass sides of the sections were pressed into wet concrete and the tracing paper was peeled away.

Photographs and watercolor sketch from the Gregory Thorp Collection.

Chester Park (c. 1905) began in the mid-1870s as a driving club and later headquartered the Queen City Jockey Club. From the turn of the century until the 1930s it was a popular picnic and amusement park. Photograph.

William Harry Gothard, *Cincinnati Industries* (1934). Oil on canvas. Gift of Walter A. Draper.

Tägliches Cincinnatier Volksblatt.

Herausgegeben von der Cincinnati Volksblatt Compagnie, No. 127 Ost Siebente Straße, nahe der Main Straße.

81. Jahrgang. | Cincinnati, Samstag, den 7. April 1917. | Preis 2 Cents. | No. 84.

Eine Proklamation

In welcher das Bestehen des Kriegszustandes angekündigt wird,

Wurde sofort, nachdem er die Kriegsresolution unterzeichnet,

Von dem Präsidenten Wilson erlassen.

Die Bürger des Landes werden darin aufgefordert, alle Gesetze des Lan-

Die Kriegs-Resolution von dem Präsidenten Wilson unterzeichnet.

Mit den Vorbereitungen für den Krieg wurde sofort an

ges wird die Ausgaben verdoppeln, da die Mobilisation der nöthigen Reservevorräthe mit der Entwicklung der Armee Schritt halten muß. Die Gesammtausgaben für die Million Mann für das erste Jahr würde sich demgemäß auf $6,000,000,000 stellen.

Von den verlangten $3,000,000,000 Millionen wird ungefähr die Hälfte vom General-Quartiermeisters-Departement für die Unterbringung der Truppen in den Trainirungs-Centren etc. ausgegeben werden; weitere $500,-

Wetterbericht.

Für Ohio: Schönes und wärmeres Wetter am Samstag; wahrscheinlich Regen während der Nacht und am Sonntag.

County-Gefängniß und $500 Geldstrafe verurtheilt.

Die chemische Zusammensetzung der Brandbomben war derart, daß das Feuer erst ausgebrochen wäre, wenn die Schiffe sich vier oder fünf Tage

Since the mid-1830s Germans had constituted the largest group of immigrants settling in Cincinnati. By 1870 roughly 23 percent of the city's 200,000 residents were German-born. All eastern and mid-western American cities had received thousands of Europeans searching for a new life during these years, but the continued concentration of German immigrants set Cincinnati apart from most. In the first half of the 19th century, the heavily German and Irish makeup of Cincinnati's immigrant population was fairly typical. In the last half of the 19th century, the origins of the bulk of European immigration shifted away from the northwestern sections of Europe. Rapidly growing cities such as Cleveland and Chicago attracted a great number of immigrants, and a majority of them came from central, southern and eastern Europe. Cincinnati grew much more slowly in this period, and only one-third of its immigrant population came from these parts of Europe. As a result, Cincinnati retained its strong German identity.

Long before the early decades of the 20th century, people of German extraction had become successful in Cincinnati. They ran three banks and more than 200 savings and loan associations. They supplied over 200 doctors and 167 lawyers, and dominated the skilled and semi-skilled trades in brewing, machine tools, cabinetmaking and baking. The German community supported two daily newspapers and 31 periodicals and a host of organizations and institutions. Beneath all of the numbers, however, lay a different reality. The lengthy presence of the Germans in Cincinnati and their success meant that the city had thoroughly assimilated most of the German-Americans. As the city expanded out of the basin, Cincinnati's German-Americans joined the exodus to the surrounding hilltop communities. By 1910 fewer than a third of the residents of Over-the-Rhine were first- or second-generation Germans.

As in other cities, differences developed between the more established, better assimilated German-Americans and immigrants who arrived in Cincinnati after 1890. Not only did the two groups maintain separate organizations, their views of Germany differed. The earlier immigrants retained a great respect for German culture but grew critical of political developments in Germany; the newer immigrants chauvinistically defended the German Empire and its policies.

When World War I erupted in August 1914, some German-Americans saw the war as an opportunity to rekindle unity in their community. They formed relief organizations such as the German-Austrian-Hungarian Aid Society, which collected money under the motto of "Gold gave I for iron." The German-language press attacked the course of United States policy towards Germany. Even though President Wilson had declared American neutrality in thought and action, his own sympathies toward England complicated his efforts to treat Britain and Germany impartially. Convinced that Wilson's policies favored the British, the *Freie Presse* declared in June 1915 that "if Wilson would be as conscientious in protecting German soldiers from American bullets as he is English ships from German torpedoes, we would be celebrating victory now." Such strident criticism of U.S. policies sometimes embarrassed Cincinnati's German community, but rarely was its loyalty questioned. As America's relations with Germany deteriorated and Germany resumed submarine warfare on January 31, 1917, Cincinnati's German-American spokesmen joined the nation's outcry. Leaders reaffirmed their loyalty to the United States, yet expressed again their determination to prevent open conflict between the countries they loved.

The *Tagliches Cincinnatier Volksblatt,* April 7, 1917, announces that the resolution of war against Germany was signed by President Wilson on April 6 and that German ships in U.S. harbors will be confiscated for supply transport to Europe.

"Nasty Corner," the southwest corner of Fifth and Vine Streets (c. 1890), became respectable when the Carew Building was constructed on this site in 1890. Photograph. Gift of the Ohio Mechanics' Institute.

NEW FIRST GERMAN READER.

Lesebuch

für

amerikanische Volksschulen.

Erster Theil.

Bearbeitet von

Mitgliedern des „deutschen Lehrer-Vereins"

in Cincinnati.

Cincinnati:

Verlag von A. E. Wilde & Co.,

256 Vine Straße.

Lesebuch für Amerikanische Volksschulen (Cincinnati, c. 1863). A German-language text intended for use in the public schools. Compiled by the members of the German Teachers Club in Cincinnati.

Finally, the dam broke. On April 6, 1917, the United States declared war on Germany. A flood of anti-German sentiment poured forth across the country expressed in thousands of individual remarks and small acts of violence. On April 9 Cincinnati anglicized the names of 13 streets. German Street became English Street, Bremen became Republic, and Berlin became Woodrow. The public library removed German books and periodicals from circulation. On October 10 federal agents raided the offices of the *Volksblatt.* Soon German-language papers had to submit their copy to censors. Most devastating of all, the Cincinnati Board of Education eliminated German-language instruction in the elementary grades of the public schools. During the 1914-1915 school year, 15,008 students were enrolled in German classes taught by 73 full-time and 84 part-time teachers. After war broke out in Europe, the board restricted the content of the German-language courses and instructed teachers to avoid all "debatable passages" referring to German political institutions, rulers and military leaders. With United States' entry into the war, Superintendent Randall Condon wrote that it had been "shortsighted" to allow "large numbers of people from foreign lands to come to us and make their homes within our borders without becoming an integral part of our local and national life." He expressed regret that "we have been content to allow them to live in segregated groups, keep alive their love for the country from which they came... and continue the use of their native language to the exclusion of English through which there might grow up mutual understanding and a community of feeling." In June 1918 the school board voted to stop teaching German in elementary schools.

Before radio and television, posters played a major role in mass communication, and World War I saw their first large-scale use for political purposes. To persuade people that a total commitment to the war effort was needed, psychological techniques were used. Appeals on a personal basis were meant to induce feelings of guilt for not doing one's part. Slogans, symbols, personifications, and messages from national leaders were used to invoke patriotism. The United States and England depicted the enemy as villainous or monstrous more often than did other countries. Women, initially portrayed in their traditional roles as wives and mothers, were pictured in their new jobs in industry as more men went to war and labor became scarce. As many as 3,000 poster designs were executed by artists—at no charge—for U.S. government and civilian agencies, and it was not unusual to have a printing of 100,000.

With few exceptions the World War I posters in the Society's collection were given by Joseph Sagmaster.

Ellsworth Young, *Remember Belgium,* United States Printing and Lithography Company.

F. Strothmann, *Beat back the Hun with Liberty Bonds.* Lithograph.

Zoo Fete for the Fatherless Children of France, Thursday, July 11 (1918).

For Every Fighter a Woman Worker. American Lithographic Company.

Shortly after the United States entered the war, President Wilson established the Committee on Public Information. Through pamphlets, news releases, posters, motion pictures and other media of propaganda, the committee intensified wartime hysteria, portraying German soldiers as barbaric Huns. The results were especially noticeable in heavily German Cincinnati, where the pressure to conform to the American way of life became overwhelming. Many German families anglicized their last names; hundreds of German organizations changed theirs as well. The German Mutual Insurance Company became the Hamilton County Fire Insurance Company, and its statue,"Germania," was hastily retitled "Columbia." The North Cincinnati Turners became the North Cincinnati Gymnasium. The *Staats-Verband* became the American Citizens League. Cincinnati's German community also threw its effort into organizing a Liberty Bond Crusade and raised $95,300 by 1918.

World War I destroyed Cincinnati's German community. The intensely anti-German feelings generated during the war made it uncomfortable for German-Americans openly to claim and nurture their heritage for many years. With German instruction eliminated from the public schools, the German-American societies were weakened; the *Volksblatt* went out of business at the end of 1919 and the *Freie Presse* closed in 1924. Prohibition, which had initially been adopted as a wartime measure to conserve grain, became "permanent" in 1920 with the adoption of the 18th Amendment. This act not only closed more than two dozen breweries that had operated in Cincinnati before the war, it also affected hundreds of bars and saloons that had important economic and social significance for the German community.

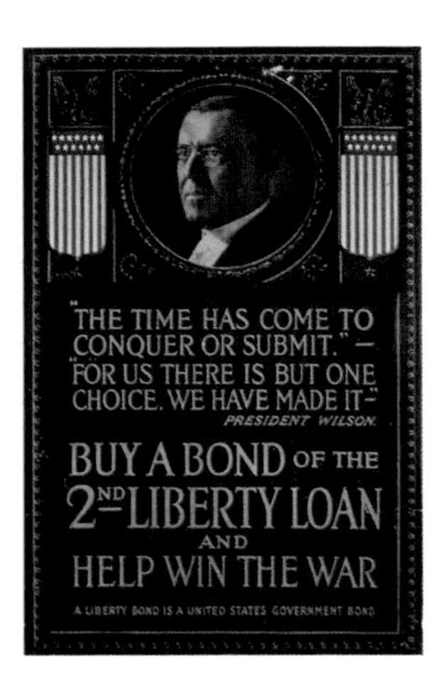

"The Time Has Come to Conquer or Submit..." American Lithographic Company.

Jacob Godfrey Schmidlapp **(1849-1919). Portrait from the Schmidlapp Report, May 1943 in the Cincinnati Model Homes Company Records.**

The war was a particularly traumatic experience for Cincinnatians, but the city itself was not greatly affected. The war had neither generated new industries nor, except for brewing, distilling and barkeeping, harmed existing ones. Cincinnati's most distinguishing feature in 1920 was its stability. Other Ohio cities of Columbus, Dayton, Cleveland and Toledo grew rapidly and were three-quarters larger in 1920 than they had been in 1900. Youngstown and Akron had more than doubled. Cincinnati, however, grew only 20% in 20 years. While the other cities all had large numbers of new immigrants among their residents, only 10% of Cincinnati's population were foreign-born, and half of them were German. Cincinnati's greatest change was geographic. Through annexation the city expanded from 35.27 square miles in 1900 to 72 square miles in 1918. As the migration from the basin to suburban communities continued, Cincinnati's most intractable problem concerned the living conditions of its working-class residents still trapped in the basin.

About 100,000 of Cincinnati's 401,247 residents in 1920 lived in tenement housing in the basin. Improvement in their living and working conditions depended primarily on the initiatives of individuals and private groups. Before 1910 reformers had concentrated on controlling tenement housing through laws governing the availability of toilets and accessibility to light and air. These reformers also promoted tenant and landlord education and even the establishment of a "model tenement" by the Associated Charities. After 1910 reformers shifted their efforts by attempting to accelerate the pace at which all housing in the basin would be abandoned. They tried to assist the move of working-class people to new suburban communities.

Jacob Schmidlapp, who made a fortune in distilling and banking, undertook the first effort at building good housing for the poor away from the basin. He began in 1911 by constructing 96 apartments in Norwood in the hope of providing factory workers there the chance to live closer to their jobs. Norwood harassed Schmidlapp by overcharging for building permits and overvaluing land for tax purposes, but his construction went forward. Schmidlapp intended not only to provide decent, low-cost housing, but to convince other wealthy people to join him or follow his example. Thus, Schmidlapp set up his homes to return a 5% profit on his investment, an approach he termed "philanthropy plus 5%." Following the Norwood success, in 1914 Schmidlapp organized the Cincinnati Model Homes Company and built units at Washington Terrace on Kemper Lane in Walnut Hills. Each apartment had a bath, indoor toilet and gas heat. To emphasize a sense of community, Schmidlapp abandoned the high-density tenement in favor of buildings that housed just four families. By providing recreational facilities and community-oriented activities, the company attempted to provide a "neighborhood" environment for its tenants. In projects in Norwood, Oakley and Walnut Hills, Model Homes accommodated 107 white families and 337 black families. After Schmidlapp's death in 1919, the company's momentum faltered. Neither philanthropists nor businesses followed in Schmidlapp's footsteps. The Better Housing League continued to decry the deteriorating housing situation for poor people. The league pointed out that as industries and commercial centers expanded in the basin and as more blacks migrated to the city, the tenements became increasingly overcrowded and unsanitary.

Children playing behind early 20th century tenement. Photograph. Paul Briol Collection.

The Cincinnati Model Homes Company's *Lincoln Terrace Apartments* in Walnut Hills. Photograph. From the Southwestern Ohio Lung Association Records.

Mary M. Emery (1844-1927). Photograph. Gift of Lee Shepard.

Built in 1913, *the Union Central Building* at the southwest corner of Fourth and Vine streets was Cincinnati's tallest building until the Carew Tower was completed in 1930. The 34-story structure now is the Central Trust Tower. Lithograph. Gift of Julia F. Carder.

The most notable effort to develop model housing in the early 1920s was directed not at the immigrants and blacks but at a different class of urban poor. In 1922 Mary Emery, the widow of wealthy Cincinnati industrialist Thomas Emery, hired a Cambridge, Massachusetts, firm to design a new town that would provide good housing in a community setting for a projected 5,000 people from every level of society. The plan proposed for her town of Mariemont attempted to capture the environment of an English garden city. Within the village, clusters of group homes opening onto protected courtyards were meant to rent cheaply to lower-income people. There were also streets of modest cottages and sites for larger and more expensive single-family homes. The plans included schools, recreational facilities, a shopping district with a theater, inn, library, shops, a town hall and a community church. Housing reformers quickly declared Mariemont a "national exemplar," and it was written about in magazines and professional journals. For all of its success, Mariemont failed to address the need of the working class for inexpensive housing. Construction costs drove rents much higher than anticipated. The average rent for a four-room apartment in Cincinnati in 1923 was $24.20 per month; the lowest rent in Mariemont was $35.

Lincoln Terrace Apartments. Artist's rendering. From the Cincinnati Model Homes Company Records.

In 1926, before the Inn was used as a hotel, the Mariemont Company's rental and sales office occupied the lobby area. Photograph. Gift of J. P. Northcutt.

Mariemont a New Town "A National Exemplar..." From a prospectus for Mariemont (Cincinnati, c. 1925). Front cover illustration.

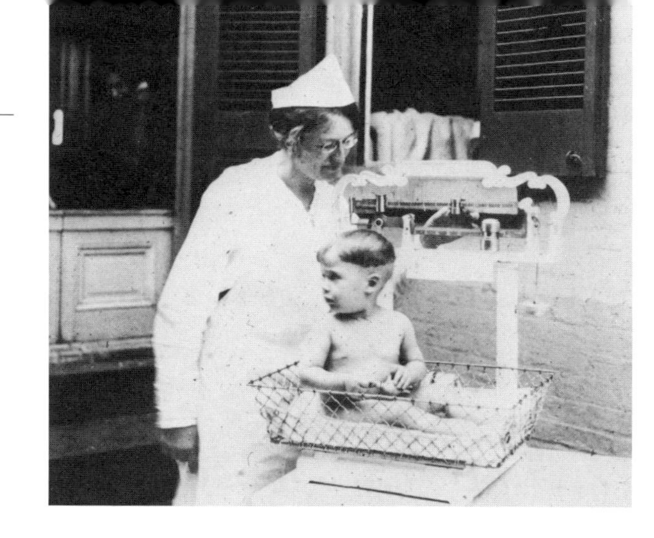

Reformers also strived to improve health-care services for thousands of poor in the basin. In 1916 the National Social Unit Organization chose the Mohawk-Brighton area for a three-year experiment to provide health care through a democratic model. The National Social Unit was the inspiration of Wilbur C. Phillips, who earlier had served as the secretary of the New York Milk Committee and as the director of the Milwaukee Child Welfare Commission during its socialist administration. The National Social Unit believed that health care could not be isolated from a complete effort at improving the lives of a group of people. The Mohawk-Brighton community was organized into 31 block clubs, each of which elected a block worker, a news carrier, a social-data collector and a street organizer. Through study, discussion and democratic decision-making, the residents of the neighborhood were to identify their needs and then discuss with doctors, nurses and social workers the best way to meet those needs. Between 1917 and 1919 the organization established a child health-care program, prenatal and postnatal care, medical examinations for all preschool children and supervision of all local tuberculosis cases. When influenza began to spread in eastern cities, the social unit initiated a neighborhood education program that taught ways to prevent and treat the disease. During the last four months of 1918, the death rate from influenza in Cincinnati was 4.10 per thousand, while in Mohawk-Brighton it was about half that rate at 2.26 per thousand. Despite its success in delivering health care and social services, the participation of the residents in formulating programs made it different from other social-reform organizations. In a postwar America in the throes of a "Red Scare" following the Russian Revolution, those suspicious of the

Social Unit nurse visiting family with amputee child. Photograph. Gift of the Southwestern Ohio Lung Association.

Making His Weight illustrates the National Social Unit Organization's child health-care program (1918). Photograph. From the Southwestern Ohio Lung Association Records.

social unit attacked it as "but one step away from Bolshevism." They claimed it was trying to create a second government within Cincinnati. Mayor John Galvin led the attack and, ignoring a vote of confidence by the residents of Mohawk-Brighton, withdrew the city's support of the program. It closed in November 1920.

In addition to addressing the housing and welfare needs of the poor, social reformers wanted to make the city more healthy and attractive than the Cincinnati that, like Topsy, "just growed" during the 19th century. They joined forces with business-oriented professionals who were developing the still-novel science of urban planning to create a modern, efficient Cincinnati during the 20th century. The first manifestation of planning in Cincinnati occurred when George Kessler of Kansas City was commissioned to plan a system of parks and parkways for the city. The resulting Kessler Plan of 1907 recommended that Cincinnati develop several parks scattered throughout the city that took advantage of the natural hillside vistas of the basin and the Ohio River. It suggested that a system of parkways link the hilltop parks. The plan was only partially realized, but many of Cincinnati's existing parks and Victory, Central and Columbia parkways were included in the plan.

By 1914 the Chamber of Commerce, the Federated Improvement Association and the Business Men's Club advocated a broader type of city planning. Other volunteer groups included the City Planning Committee of the Woman's City Club and the United City Planning Committee, which by 1921 represented 32 civic organizations. In 1918 the City Planning Committee was formed to act as the coordinating body for the development of the Cincinnati area. These efforts resulted in an official city plan, adopted and published in 1925. The first

By the late 19th century, Cincinnati's air was infamous. The steep hills, the large number of factories and the universal use of bituminous coal for industrial and residential heat produced a serious air-pollution problem. Doctors spoke of "Cincinnati lung." Merchants tried in vain to keep the gritty, greasy residue from ruining dry goods. Housewives had to wipe off tabletops and windowsills daily.

In 1903 the city created the position of smoke inspector, but the office was never sufficiently staffed. A broad cross-section of citizen groups took up the cause of smoke abatement to supplement the governmental effort. The most important such group was the Smoke Abatement League, formed in 1908, which took responsibility for monitoring the downtown area. From offices on the 30th floor of the Union Central (Central Trust) Tower, inspectors watched for problems, discussed corrective procedures with violators and brought persistent offenders to court.

Reformers initially concentrated on large manufacturers, who quickly recognized economic as well as the environmental advantages of improved furnaces, automatic stokers and higher-grade coke. Small manufacturers found it more difficult to make these costly improvements. Other inspectors concentrated their efforts on locomotives and steamboats, both highly concentrated in the basin area.

The Smoke Abatement League lost much of its funding during the depression when privately financed charities gave their full resources to helping the unemployed. By the late 1930s, however, stiffer municipal legislation was adopted. The city increased the number of its inspectors to 15 and forced coal suppliers to grade and inform customers of the cleanliness of their fuel.

The substitution of natural gas and fuel oil for coal in factories and homes after World War II helped solve Cincinnati's smoke problem. But, the proliferation of automobiles in the same years brought new clean-air challenges.

View of the smoke-filled basin from the Monastery on top of Mt. Adams with the Rookwood Pottery Building in the foreground (c. 1915). Photograph.

of its kind for a city the size of Cincinnati, the plan strived to "foresee and make provision for... the public health, safety, convenience, comfort, prosperity, beauty and general welfare of Cincinnati as a home for its citizens." The plan acknowledged the stable, slow growth of the city's population, took pride in its high percentage of American-born residents, worried about the modest increase in the black population, stressed the importance of its diversified economy and praised its moderate climate:

Cincinnati is fortunate in having no very hot or no very cold spells... The thermometer gets below zero not oftener than once a year. There is little snow, and no deep snow... The climate is not damp... Cincinnati is also remarkably free from fogs.

Eighth Street Spires.
Photograph. Paul Briol
Collection.

The planners tried to establish an agenda for developing a city that would be more attractive and more livable for its people yet remain economically stable and prosperous. The most important recommendation of the plan was its support for comprehensive zoning, an innovative idea at the time. Specifically designed to give city officials control over undeveloped land, zoning was also intended to protect Cincinnati's suburbs from the evils of the basin by providing building guidelines, parks, playgrounds, community centers and open spaces. For the downtown, the plan proposed developing a civic center stretching from City Hall to Music Hall where major public buildings, such as the post office and the public library, would be located. Little was said about the Ohio River except for its flooding and recreational potential, but the plan endorsed the building of a union railroad terminal. Indeed, the plan gave great attention to the transportation needs of the city and recommended a variety of policies concerning a proposed rapid-transit loop and the construction of thoroughfares. Ideas from raised roadways to elevated walkways, from one way streets to "left turn eliminations" were explored as means to cope with the new problems created by automobiles.

Ironically, the plan, developed under the auspices of the city government, dealt in great depth with streets and thoroughfares at the same time the disastrous condition of the city's streets played a critical role in reforming that government. The Republican machine was not the same without Cox. Following Cox's death in 1916, "Rud" Hynicka took control of the organization. Garry Herrmann withdrew from active politics, and Mike Mullen died in 1921. To replace them, Hynicka made Fred Schneller the Number Two man and Froome Morris the

spokesman for the organization, which remained fundamentally unchanged. The Republican machine continued in power through control of a bloated patronage list and the timing of primary elections. The Hynicka organization made almost 6,800 political appointments, all of whom were expected to work to turn out the vote when the party needed it. Primary elections for city offices were held in the late summer of odd years when few people voted, enhancing the machine's ability to control the outcome.

The efficiency of government continued to decline. The symbol of the organization's inability to manage the city in the early 1920s became the potholes and the ruts in the city's streets. All over the city, roads deteriorated to the point that they became impassable. Al Segal wrote a front-page column in the *Cincinnati Post* under the heading of "Cincinnatus" in which he satirized the condition of the streets. On June 8, 1923, Segal recounted a drive he had taken with a photographer during which they concluded that the potholes of Cincinnati were living organisms in a great Darwinian struggle in which width and depth were the measures of fitness. In another column Segal wrote that the city caused an international incident when two Cincinnatians fell through a pothole on Linwood Avenue and ended up in Bombay, India. The residents of Bombay threatened to attack for fear that all of Cincinnati would plunge through the earth as well. Although Mayor George P. Carrel and Hynicka armed the citizenry against a threatened attack, Segal wrote, peace was restored when invading savages taught Cincinnatians the art of pothole repair.

Several factors were responsible for the condition of Cincinnati's streets and the level of municipal services. A rural-dominated legislature unreasonably restricted the amount of tax revenue a city could raise for general operations. Between 1910 and 1923 general operating costs in Cincinnati rose 21.9% while revenues increased only 11.3%. To circumvent these restrictions, many cities called anything they could a capital-improvement project and issued bonds to carry out the work. As a result Cincinnati's bonded indebtedness grew so large by 1921 that one-half of the city's taxes went to service the debt. The machine was forced to retrench in the early 1920s. Municipal departments reduced wages, lengthened working hours and laid off employees. At times the city halted street repairs, stopped collecting ashes and cut city-owned horses from three meals to two meals a day.

Despite the image of frugality the organization wanted to project, Cincinnatians witnessed the reality of inefficiency and corruption. The administration cut street-cleaning and repair crews but let jobs without competitive bidding to contractors who used expensive granite blocks rather than asphalt to repair streets. Cincinnati's per capita cost of government was the fourth highest in the nation and the highest in Ohio.

Yet the Cincinnati political machine limped on without effective challenge longer than any other city machine in early 20th century America. Reform movements had swept urban America in the years before World War I, including an especially successful one in Cleveland led by Tom Johnson that earned it the reputation of the best-governed city in America. Cincinnati's stable population growth and economic diversity generated comparative peace, where rapid growth produced problems that brought reformers to power in other cities. Cincinnati was in a state of grumbling apathy in need of leaders who could convince its citizens that things could be different. This leadership

View of the intersection of Erie Avenue and Madison Road looking north (1928). Photograph. Gift of the Cincinnati Transit Company.

Murray Seasongood (1878-1983)
Murray Seasongood advocated and worked for good government long after he retired from elective office in 1930. For 34 years he taught courses on municipal corporations at the University of Cincinnati Law School. He lectured widely and published many of his essays on government. As a trustee of the Hamilton County Good Government League, the National Legal Aid Association, the National Municipal League and dozens of other organizations, he supported reform on many fronts. Seasongood remained active well into his 90s in the law firm that he had joined in 1903, just after graduating from Harvard Law School.

Murray Seasongood (c. 1928). Photograph. Gift of Murray Seasongood.

Keep Cincinnati the Best Governed City, Vote for the Charter Committee Candidates (1929). Pamphlet.

SAMPLE BALLOT

We Need a Change—Help Us! Help Yourselves!
Put Your Cross (X) Under The Liberty Bell

CITY OF CINCINNATI REPUBLICAN TICKET	CITY OF CINCINNATI DEMOCRATIC TICKET	CITY OF CINCINNATI FARMER-LABOR TICKET	CITY OF CINCINNATI INDEPENDENT TICKET
For a Straight Ticket Mark Within This Circle.	For a Straight Ticket Mark Within This Circle.	For a Straight Ticket Mark Within This Circle.	For a Straight Ticket Mark Within This Circle. X
For Mayor GEORGE P. CARREL	For Mayor CHAS. L. BONIFIELD	For Mayor CHARLES HERBST	For Mayor JOSEPH B. KELLEY
For Vice-Mayor GILBERT BETTMAN	For Vice-Mayor THOS. H. MORROW	For Vice-Mayor MARY D. BRITE	For Vice-Mayor THOMAS H. MORROW
For Clerk of the Municipal Court J. A. CLINE	For Clerk of the Municipal Court WILLIAM MARSCHHEUSER	For Clerk of the Municipal Court CHAS. J. W. SCHROEDER	For Clerk of the Municipal Court WILLIAM L. NIMMO
For Members of Council at Large (Vote for not more than six) OTTO K. FRANCIS	For Members of Council at Large (Vote for not more than six) RUTH M. BUDDEKE	For Members of Council at Large (Vote for not more than six) CHAS. BRYSON	For Members of Council at Large (Vote for not more than six) JULIUS LUCHSINGER
WM. E. HESS	JOHN C. DEMPSEY	HUBERT C. CARPENTER	JOHN SAUER
BERTHA C. LIETZE	LILLIE H. GORMAN	GEORGE FRIEDRICH	JOHN W. SHORTEN
CORINNE F. McCLOSKEY	PHILIP E. LAWWILL	GEORGE RECH	MARGARET WELSH
ANDREW J. MURPHY	JULIUS R. SAMUELS	JACOB E. WAGNER	ADOLPH G. WULFF
CHAS. A. RAGOR	BETTIE WILSON	WALTER J. WEISMAN	ANNA W. WURST
For Member of Council JESSE MACDONALD	For Member of Council B. A. LEONARD	For Member of Council	For Member of Council B. A. LEONARD
For Assessor WALLACE W. KLINGELHOFFER	For Assessor EDW. ELZENHOEFER	For Assessor	For Assessor EDWARD ELZENHOEFER

WARD 25 46

Reformers wanted symbols removed from ballots (1921). Broadside. From the Resor Papers. Gift of Chase Shafer.

emerged from the Cincinnatus Association, an organization formed in 1920 largely by veterans coming home from military service. Victor Heintz, a former congressman who had resigned to join the war effort, returned to Cincinnati as a political organizer for Warren Harding. Heintz called together business and professional men who were committed to improving Cincinnati. The organization was consciously bipartisan, but most of the leadership, including John Hollister and Robert Taft, were loyal Republicans reluctant to do anything that might bring down the machine. For a couple of years, the membership pondered and debated important issues in the sort of quiet way that did not stir popular attention or embarrass the machine.

In October 1923 Cincinnatus unintentionally became the platform for new leadership. The impetus was a three-mill special operating levy similar to those voters had rejected the two preceding years. Although the members of Cincinnatus had spent many meetings detailing the failures of the city administration in providing proper street repair and garbage collection, the pressing shortage of funds seemed compelling. Then, Murray Seasongood, a lawyer and member of the organization's program committee, challenged the group's inclination to endorse the levy and announced his willingness to debate the issue. A week later, on October 9, Seasongood debated a fellow Cincinnatus member, Leonard Smith, who spoke for its passage. Seasongood attacked the "gang" for its misuse of tax money and its failure to deliver services. He argued that the damage of the machine went beyond anything tangible to include the psychological effects on the citizens that had "drugged them into a state of political lethargy that is fast making the city a laughing-stock... The whole history of the organization has been a blot on the city," Seasongood charged.

As effective as Seasongood's presentation was in persuading Cincinnatus to call for the defeat of the levy, his impact would have been minimal had not two newspapers reported the debate to the community, making it "the shot heard round the wards." The organization ineptly responded by attacking Seasongood's motives. The levy was defeated, but that was not surprising. Similar levies had been turned back even without any clear opposition leadership. The campaign's importance was that the public discovered a spokesman for reform who was willing to grab at the opportunities offered.

Counting the votes in a Cincinnati Proportional Representation election. Photograph. Paul Briol Collection.

Events moved quickly after the November election. Immediately after the levy defeat, Seasongood called for a thorough investigation of the city administration. Hynicka appointed a large committee, which included a wary Seasongood, and hired Lent D. Upson of the Detroit Bureau of Government Research. The resulting Upson Report detailed numerous failings of the organization but also balanced its findings with sympathetic comments about the limits imposed by the inadequate tax structure. Seasongood felt the report had pulled its punches and refused to sign it, but the report officially chronicled the failings of the Republican organization in managing the city.

Other reformers emerged and coordinated their efforts. Henry Bentley, a grassroots politician, proposed a Birdless Ballot League to push for the removal of partisan symbols from ballots, hoping to undermine the machine's ability to control uninformed voters. By early spring in 1924, a loose confederation had focused on reorganizing the structure of city government by means of a new charter. Ed Alexander, who was allied with the national Progressive campaign of Robert M. LaFollette, prepared an initial draft of the charter. The draft was debated and refined during April and May by Alexander; Bentley; Seasongood; Guy Mallon, a prominent lawyer who had sponsored the Australian ballot reform in Ohio; Charles Taft; Ralph Holterhoff, also involved in the Birdless Ballot League; Agnes Hilton of the League of Women Voters and pioneer suffragette; and Marietta Tawney of the Woman's City Club.

The draft charter proposed running the city by modern managerial principles popularized through the work of Fred Taylor, an efficiency engineer and the father of scientific management. The charter proposed shifting power away from elected politicians to a professional, trained specifically to manage a municipal bureaucracy. Administrators were to be chosen on the basis of training and competence rather than politics. With the day-to-day responsibilities for the city in the hands of professionals, it was possible to redefine the role of elected officials. In place of a large council representing fragmented ward interests, the charter proposed a small council of nine chosen at large. Voters would elect council through an elaborate system of balloting termed "proportional representation."

The Charter Committee was formed to take the charter before the people. Bentley labored to coordinate the entire effort and build an effective organization in time for the November elections. Seasongood's oratory complemented Bentley's organizational skills. Seasongood provided the spark, he personalized the fight. On election day the charter was approved, 92,510 to 41,105.

To secure the promised benefits of the new charter, the reformers transformed the Charter Committee into a permanent organization. They nominated nine candidates for city council in elections set for November 1925. Seasongood headed the slate comprised of a mixture of Democrats, reform-minded Republicans, and even one sitting Republican councilman, Charles O. Rose, who had grown increasingly independent of the organization. The Republicans fielded a short slate of six candidates; 24 independents also entered the race. The campaign was lively. It was highlighted by a "debate" between Seasongood and an empty chair before a meeting of the Madisonville Welfare Association when the Republican spokesman failed to appear. In the end, the Charter Committee elected six to council; Republicans won three seats.

Take this Card to the Polls and Vote as explained below.

THE CITY CHARTER COMMITTEE SELECTED AND ENDORSED THESE CANDIDATES

1	ASA V. BUTTERFIELD
	ALBERT D. CASH
	ANSON C. FRY
	CHARLES P. TAFT
	CHARLES H. TOBIAS
	EDWARD N. WALDVOGEL
	RUSSELL WILSON
	W. L. ANDERSON
	WALTER BECKER

Mark the figure 1 in front of your favorite.

Mark 2, 3, 4, 5, 6, 7, 8, 9, in front of the other eight candidates IN THE ORDER OF YOUR PREFERENCE.

Be sure to give each a number.

Do NOT use an X.

Names of candidates will be rotated on the ballots. [OVER]

A "birdless ballot." Under Proportional Representation voters selected candidates in order of preference (1939). Broadside. From the records of the Charter Committee of Greater Cincinnati.

The Taft Family

The Tafts of Cincinnati make up one of the nation's greatest political families. Patriarch Alphonso Taft (1810-1891) set the pattern which many of his descendants would follow. Born in Vermont he moved to Cincinnati in 1839 to practice law. During his career he was judge of the Superior Court of Cincinnati, Secretary of War and Attorney General in President Grant's cabinet and minister to Austria and Russia.

Alphonso had five sons: Peter Rawson and Charles Phelps by his first wife, Fanny Phelps, and Horace, William Howard and Harry by his second wife, Louise Torrey.

William Howard Taft (1857-1930) was born at the family home on Mt. Auburn. A graduate of the Cincinnati Law School, which he later served as dean, his first public office was assistant prosecutor of Hamilton County. He gained national recognition as governor of the Philippines and as Secretary of War in Theodore Roosevelt's administration. At the urging of his family and President Roosevelt, Taft reluctantly agreed to run for president in 1908. He received the official notification of his nomination at his brother's Pike Street mansion. He defeated William Jennings Bryan and became the 27th President of the United States. Taft lost his bid for a second term in a three-party race which Woodrow Wilson won. In 1921 President Warren G. Harding named Taft Chief Justice of the Supreme Court, a position he had wanted more than the presidency, and where he served until several months prior to his death in 1930.

Taft—Head and Shoulders Above Them All (1908). A campaign post card. Gift of Anita Fenton.

William Howard's older half-brother, Charles Phelps Taft (1843-1929) was trained as a lawyer and a scholar. He served in the Ohio House (1871) and the U.S. Congress (1895), but was best known in Cincinnati as a publisher and philanthropist. In 1873 he married Anna Sinton, daughter of iron magnate David Sinton. In 1879 and 1880, Taft and his father-in-law acquired two Cincinnati daily newspapers to form the *Cincinnati Times-Star.* Mr. and Mrs. Charles Phelps Taft worked systematically to endow institutions that would promote the intellectual and cultural development of Cincinnati's citizenry. They created the Cincinnati Institute of Fine Arts to endow the Cincinnati Symphony Orchestra and to establish their home with its priceless art collection as the Taft Museum. In 1930, Mrs. Taft created a $2 million Charles Phelps Taft Memorial Fund at the University of Cincinnati to be used for teaching and study of the humanities. It was supplemented in 1961 by a $3 million bequest from her daughter, Louise Taft Semple, that was designed to make the Classics Department, which her husband, Dr. William T. Semple headed for 40 years, the best in the country.

Senator Robert A. Taft (1889-1953), the eldest son of William Howard, served in the U.S. Senate from 1939 until his death. Generally considered one of the ablest political leaders of his time, Robert Taft was a serious but unsuccessful contender for the Republican

presidential nomination in 1940, 1948 and 1952. Known as "Mr. Republican," the senator was a champion of individual liberty and conservative fiscal policies. He sponsored federal welfare programs, however, particularly in the area of education, and co-sponsored the public housing law of 1949. His son, Robert Taft, Jr. (1917-) went to Washington as congressman-at-large from Ohio in 1963 and in 1970 was elected to a term in the senate.

Charles P. Taft II (1897-1983), the youngest son of the president, became one of Cincinnati's most popular public figures. He was an original member of the Charter Committee, was elected county prosecutor in 1926 and to city council in 1937. Although Taft was a Charterite in local politics, he ran for governor as a Republican in 1952 and served in various federal posts in Washington during the Franklin Roosevelt administration. Taft was mayor in 1956-1957 when Cincinnati received *Fortune Magazine's* designation as the nation's "best-governed" city. He retired from city council in 1977 after 30 years of service.

Hulbert Taft (1877-1959), the son of Peter Rawson and Matilda Taft, was editor or publisher of the *Times-Star* for more than 50 years. Under his guidance this staunchly Republican newspaper allegedly endorsed none but Republican political candidates. His son, Hulbert Taft, Jr. (1917-1967) founded the Taft Broadcasting Company.

Other members of the family were active in political and cultural circles. Mrs. William Howard Taft, for example, was a founder and first president of the Cincinnati Symphony Orchestra. Mrs. Robert A. Taft was active in the women's suffrage movement, helped organize a local chapter of the League of Women Voters and was its first president.

The Alphonso Taft House at 2038 Auburn Avenue was the birthplace of William Howard Taft. Photograph (c. 1867). Gift of the William Howard Taft National Historic Site.

The home of Charles Phelps and Anna Sinton Taft, Pike Street, now the Taft Museum. Photograph. Gift of Milton Niederlehner.

Charles Phelps Taft, II (1897-1983). Photograph. Gift of Julia Warren.

Charles Phelps Taft (1843-1929). Photograph. Gift from the estate of Hulbert Taft.

Hulbert Taft (1877-1959). Photograph.

Anna Sinton Taft (1852-1931). Photograph.

Robert A. Taft, Sr. (1889-1953). Photograph. Gift from the estate of Hulbert Taft.

The victories of 1924 and 1925 brought the reformers to power. The victories in themselves neither improved the administration of the city nor united the reformers. Seasongood and Bentley soon split over the future role of the Charter Committee and over candidates for mayor and city manager. Seasongood was an individualist who saw himself as the leader of a diverse and growing reform movement larger than any single organization. Bentley believed that building the Charter Committee into a permanent organization was necessary if this reform effort was to last longer than earlier ones. Bentley's candidate for mayor lost to Seasongood's—Seasongood himself. Seasongood soon resigned from all organizations, including Charter. He also won approval of his choice for city manager, C. O. Sherrill, superintendent of buildings and grounds in Washington, D.C., over Bentley's candidate, C. A. Dykstra from Los Angeles. Over the next four years, Sherrill supervised the smooth reform of Cincinnati government. He hired professionally trained administrators, initiated a program to repave the streets, improve lighting and install traffic signals and street signs. The work was made possible by new taxes approved in 1925.

Cincinnati shared in the nation's prosperity and boom spirit of the 1920s, but its growth was moderate compared to other cities. Between 1900 and 1930, Cincinnati dropped from the ninth-largest city in the United States to 17th with a population of 451,296. As in other cities, business prosperity was reflected in numerous construction projects in the downtown area. In Cincinnati most of the new buildings were financed by established families and their businesses. The Charles P. Tafts built the Dixie Terminal (1921), the Phelps apartments (1926) and the Masonic Temple (1928). Businessmen

The Cincinnati and Suburban Bell Telephone Company building, southwest corner of Seventh and Elm streets, was designed by Harry Hake with a decorative border of French telephones and headphones above the second story (c. 1931). From the records of Harry Hake and Partners, Inc. Gift of Harry Hake III.

The Times Star Building, designed by Samuel Hannaford and Sons and completed in 1933, features statues and bas-relief sculpture of printing and literary greats. Photograph of an architectural rendering.

built the Queen City Club (1927) and a new Chamber of Commerce building (1927) on Fourth Street, plus the Cincinnati Club (1924) opposite the Doctors' Building (1923) on Garfield Place. In addition, the Cincinnati Enquirer (1926) and the Cincinnati Gas and Electric Company (1929) constructed new office facilities.

Perhaps more revealing about Cincinnati's economy and the financial stability of its leading families and businesses were the construction projects begun in 1929 and extending into the early 1930s, uninterrupted by the stock-market crash and the onset of the Great Depression. Early in 1929 the Cincinnati and Suburban Bell Telephone Company, whose principal owner was the Kilgour family, began a new building at Seventh and Elm streets that was not completed until 1931. Even more dramatic was the project of John J. Emery, heir to an industrial-chemical and real-estate fortune. On August 24, 1929, Emery announced plans to build a 48-story office tower with a department store, restaurants, a 1,000-room hotel, a 25-story automated parking garage and an arcade of shops. This city-within-a-city at the corner of Fifth and Vine would occupy the site of the Carew Building and the Emery Hotel. It also would re-create the Emery Arcade that had run between Vine and Race streets since the 19th century. Despite the stock-market crash, construction of the tower began in January 1930 and was completed that October. The hotel portion of the complex opened in 1932, the same year the Rockefeller Center, employing similar architectural styles and mixed-use concepts, opened in New York City.

CAREW TOWER
CINCINNATI

Carew Tower, Cincinnati and the *Netherland Hotel* from the Frederick A. Schmidt Company's rental brochure. Gift of Ashley L. Ford.

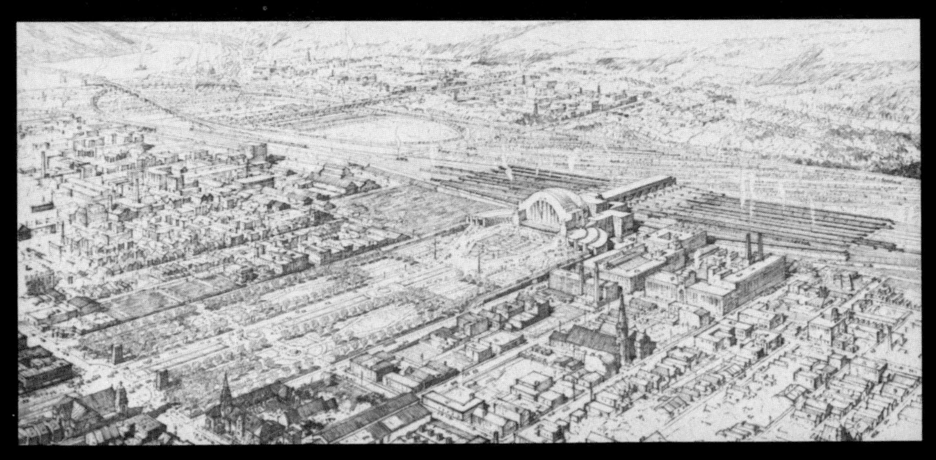

At virtually the same time Emery announced the Carew Tower project, work began on the construction of a new railroad facility. Its $41 million cost included the acquisition of property and the construction of switching yards, roundhouses, viaducts over the Millcreek and a new Union Terminal building. The project had been discussed for years, but in 1929 seven railroads serving Cincinnati began to build a consolidated facility on the site recommended in the 1925 city plan. The New York architectural firm of Fellheimer and Wagner proposed a daring Art Deco design for the $8 million Union Terminal that caught the imagination of Cincinnatians and seemed to reflect their renewed sense of pride.

To decorate the large walls in the concourse, the architects planned murals dedicated to Cincinnati workers. Two artists, Frenchman Pierre Bourdelle and German immigrant Winold Reiss, submitted designs. Reiss won the principal contract. He developed 14 mosiac and frescoed murals derived from a series of photographs taken in factories around Cincinnati. The murals focused on the workers themselves, not on the machinery and technology or on the owners of the businesses. These bold and beautiful works conveyed pride and confidence. They stood in sharp contrast to the economic realities emerging across America during the terminal's construction, completed early in 1933.

Privately financed construction projects such as the Carew Tower, Union Terminal and the Taft family's Times-Star Building, which also opened in 1933, temporarily cushioned Cincinnati from the full impact of the Great Depression. In 1930 construction in Cincinnati was only 6% below its peak in 1928, while the national average was one-third below the 1928 level. Even in 1932 Cincinnati stood sixth in

Louis Conrad Rosenberg (1890-) was commissioned by the Cincinnati Union Terminal Company to execute a series of illustrations showing the construction of the terminal. Working from photographs and architectural renderings, Rosenberg produced eight dry points between 1930 and 1932. Gifts of the Cincinnati Union Terminal Company.

Station Steel Arches, December 1931 (1932).

Cincinnati Union Terminal, Perspective from East—from architect's drawings (1930).

Cincinnati Union Terminal From Air Perspective (1930).

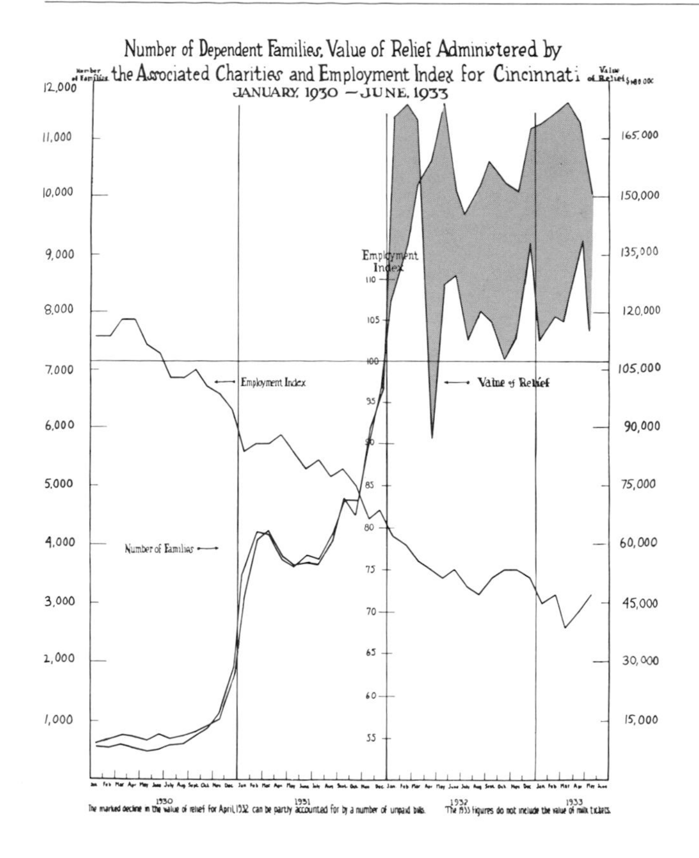

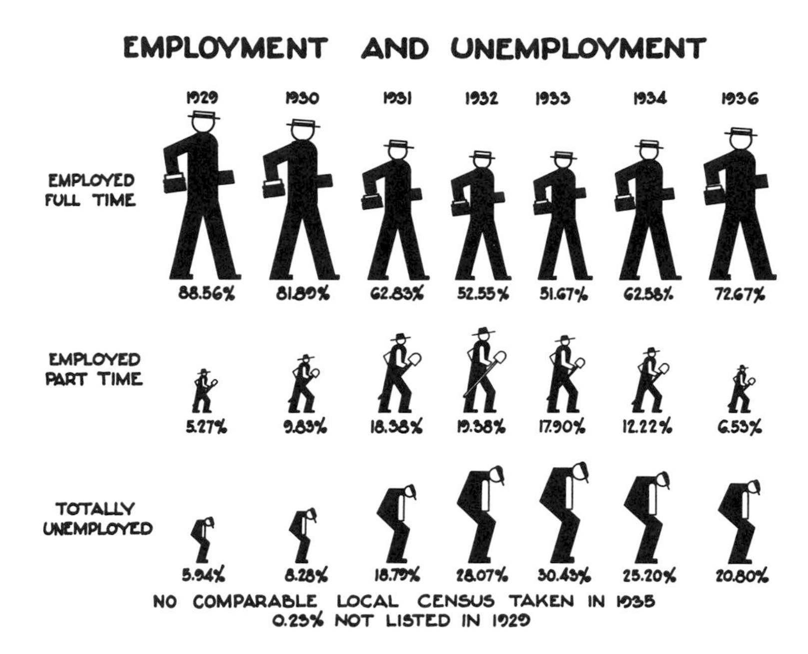

the value of construction among the nation's cities. Yet, the depression hit Cincinnati as it did the rest of the nation. Unemployment jumped from 5.9% in 1929 to 18.8% in 1931 and 28.1% in 1932. In the spring of 1933, with unemployment at 30.4%, only 52% of Cincinnati's labor force had full-time jobs. Among blacks, who made up 10% of the city's population, the numbers were much worse. Only one-third had full-time jobs; more than 54% were totally unemployed.

The magnitude of the problem overwhelmed the traditional relief agencies. One of the principal relief organizations, Associated Charities, assisted 3,721 families and individuals in 1929. In 1930 the number of families seeking aid jumped to 6,000 and by 1932 rose to 23,188. In addition to the efforts of organized charities, hundreds of individuals and companies also did what they could to help the poor and the unemployed. An especially notable example was Leah Weiss, who organized a relief kitchen in 1929. Throughout the 1930s she cared for the needs of hundreds of children, families without heat, light or food and drifters who slept under the bridges. Mrs. Weiss collected donations of bread from Rubel's Bakery, bologna from Kroger's, milk from French Bauer and clothing from Shillito's and other department stores.

The city government also saw rising needs and dwindling resources, but it performed remarkably well. The city trimmed expenses in the early 1930s. Only in 1933 was it forced to cut wages, and the cuts were restored in 1934. Throughout the depression decade, Cincinnati generally had the lowest tax rate in the nation for a city of over 300,000. City Manager C. A. Dykstra, who had succeeded C. O. Sherrill in 1930, wrote that "American cities in 1933 found themselves in the most precarious position in their history." But, he added, "We here have been immensely more fortunate than in most cities." That year the city balanced its budget and cut $3 million from its $102.9 million bonded debt. Indeed the city whittled away at its debt, cutting it to $70 million by 1943, and repeatedly retired bonds bearing 4% or 5% or more interest for new ones carrying from 2½% down to 1¼%. Thus, in 1934, in the fifth year of the Great Depression, Dykstra wrote, "The time is here to consider a pay-as-we-go policy." Neither the worst flood in the city's history in 1937 nor the severe business recession of 1938 (which pushed unemployment back over 20%) seriously disturbed the financial well-being of the city government.

Number of Dependent Families, Value of Relief Administered by the Associated Charities... The Shaded portion of the chart shows the gap that developed beginning early in 1932 between the number of people seeking assistance and the available resources. From the records of the Family Service of the Cincinnati Area. Gift of the Service.

Employment and Unemployment statistics, 1929-1936. From *Municipal Activities of the City of Cincinnati, 1936,* p. 26.

The 1937 Flood

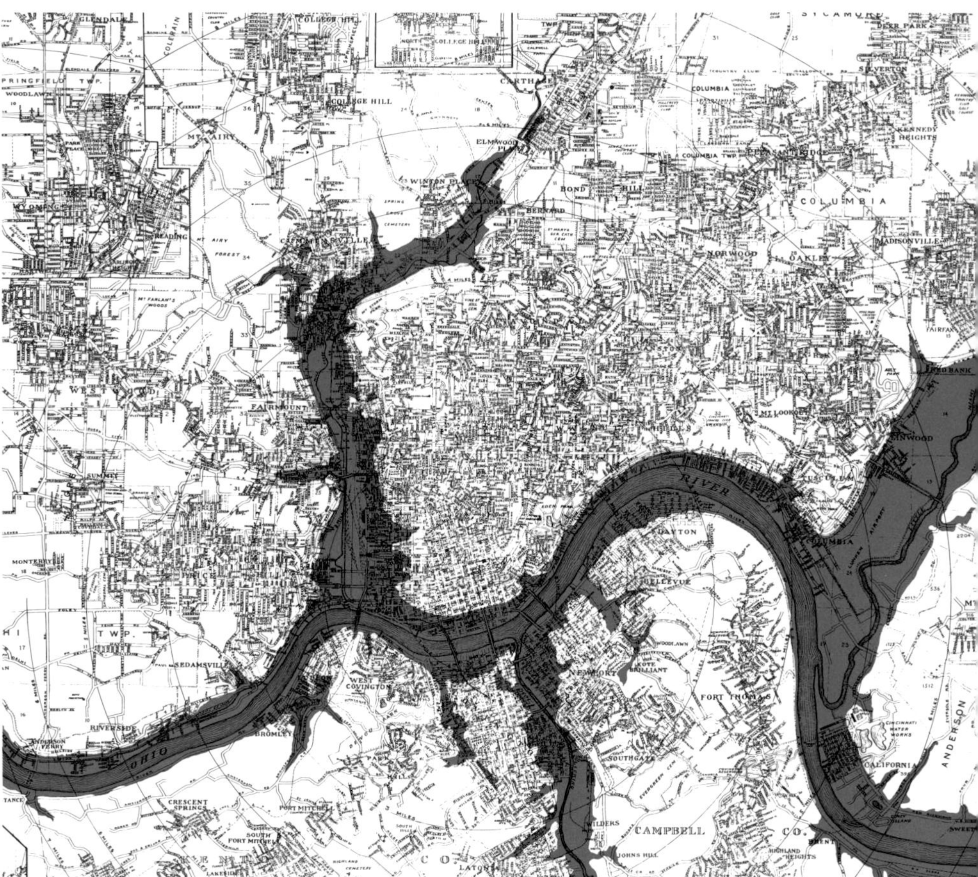

"If we hadn't had so much rain, there wouldn't have been a flood," was the explanation given by a weary Cincinnatian in 1937 for the worst flood in the city's history.

There had been higher than average rainfall during January throughout the 14 states with tributaries feeding the 981-mile Ohio River. In Cincinnati the bottom lands had flooded as usual, and on the morning of January 16, the water stood at 51.55 feet, just short of the 52-foot flood stage. By the following evening, it had dropped to 49.1 feet. Cincinnatians believed that this year's flood was over.

But on January 18 the river began to rise rapidly. Meteorologists explained that the flood was "backing" up the river. Water was rising rapidly at Cairo, Illinois, where the river had been at flood stage for more than a week. Continued rains in southern Illinois created a damming effect, and the flood progressed eastward towards Louisville and Cincinnati.

Relief organizations in the city had been mobilized earlier to care for residents along the Ohio and Little Miami rivers. They were now augmented as the Red Cross, YMCA, YWCA, WPA workers, Boy Scouts and countless citizens rescued thousands made homeless by the rising water. All except the smallest private boats were commandeered, and the Coast Guard sent additional boats and crews from Virginia and Maryland. Music Hall became a giant relief center where clothing was accepted and sorted.

So many sightseers blocked streets adjacent to the river that City Manager C. A. Dykstra restricted access to people having official business. Thomas Emery's Sons advertised that to avoid traffic congestion and help police and rescue workers, people could view the flood from the top of the Carew Tower. The company donated the 25¢ admission fee to the American Red Cross. By January 23 the river had reached 72.8 feet, and between four and five thousand people had seen it from the tower's 48th floor observation deck.

The Transit Company maintained service for another week by using high-water cars, elevated tracks and motor buses instead of

Columbia Avenue looking east from Delta Avenue. When boats were not available for salvaging purposes, two WPA workers built a raft and helped residents evacuate their homes. Photograph. Eugene F. Bliss fund purchase.

Wagner's Complete Map of Cincinnati and the Kentucky Cities, Showing the 1937 Flood Area (A. C. Wagner Company, 1937).

electric trolleys. Railroads with tracks on low ground could not come into the city. Some lines suspended service; others used suburban stations. Only the Chesapeake & Ohio and Southern railroads continued to use Union Terminal, and the C&O ran a shuttle service between Cincinnati and northern Kentucky. The Suspension Bridge was the only bridge open the entire length of the Ohio.

Sunday, January 24, was Black Sunday. At 73.4 feet, the river had surpassed the 1884 and 1913 floods, heavy rain was falling, 38,000 were homeless. And then, a 10-alarm fire broke out in the Millcreek Valley when a snapped trolley wire ignited a pool of gasoline leaking from storage tanks. The flames spread quickly. At its worst the fire covered 3.5 square miles and involved 500 firemen, including 75 from suburban and from Dayton and Columbus companies. That afternoon the rising river closed the water works' East End pumping station and flooded the electric company's generators. The city began doling out water a few hours each day. By Wednesday citizens were getting water from fish and park ponds, hillside springs and streams, breweries' and distilleries' artesian wells, the river and its tributaries and from Norwood and Wyoming. Electrical power came from neighboring cities.

On January 26, the river crested at 80 feet. Forty-five square miles of Hamilton County were under water; 61,600 Cincinnatians were homeless. The Millcreek and Little Miami River valleys were lakes; California and Newtown were submerged. Knowlton's Corner and the home plate in Crosley Field were under 20 feet of water. It was not until February 4 that businesses reopened, and on the following day the 1937 flood became history as the river dropped below flood stage 19 days after it left its banks.

Strike Up the Band—a little humor on Eastern Avenue as the water receded. Photograph. Gift of Charles M. Williams.

Aerial view of the basin looking west. M. Parks Watson photograph (c1937). Gift of the Cincinnati Gas and Electric Company.

Clifton Avenue Water Station. By driving a pipe into the hillside, Red Cross and WPA workers provided water for drinking and cooking. Photograph. Gift of Charles M. Williams.

The Depression gave new meaning to organized labor in Greater Cincinnati. Although craft unions dated back to the mid-19th century in the city, they remained relatively weak. Trade unions all over America did not attempt to organize unskilled industrial workers, which was the fastest-growing portion of the work force. In addition trade unions frequently reflected ethnic divisions. In Cincinnati the split between Germans and Irish hampered cooperation and impeded efforts to organize workers. Compounding these internal problems, the fear of socialism manifested in the Red Scare after World War I strengthened conservative, anti-union sentiment in Cincinnati.

In the 1930s Cincinnati workers, particularly in Norwood, organized a different kind of union. In 1922 General Motors had located its Fisher Body and Chevrolet divisions there. During the Depression workers faced threatened layoffs, piece-rate pay and speed-up of the assembly line. Many considered working conditions at Norwood plants to be among the worst in the country. Since a large percentage of the automotive employees in Norwood were migrants from southern Kentucky, many workers were already familiar with the United Mine Workers union and were anxious to organize the labor force at the automotive plants.

After the passage of the National Industrial Recovery Act in 1933, "company" unions were formed at both the Fisher Body and Chevrolet plants. Then, in mid-1934 the leaders of these company unions requested assistance from the American Federation of Labor to form a local chapter of the United Automobile Workers union. Local 19940 (later Local 131) received its charter in February 1935.

Local 19940 played an important role in the development of the national UAW. In 1935 it participated in the first major strike against General Motors and helped pressure the A.F. of L. to charter the UAW as an independent national union. In 1939 the Norwood local supported a successful effort to shift UAW's affiliation from the A.F. of L. to the Congress of Industrial Organizations (CIO).

With the National Labor Relations Act in 1935, it became easier to organize unions. This altered national situation was reflected locally. In 1933 unions claimed 40,000 members. Ten years later there were more than 70,000 union workers in the Greater Cincinnati area.

The Philip Carey Manufacturing Company, maker of asphalt shingles, represented Cincinnati paperworkers in the Union Terminal murals. The United Paperworkers International Union, AFL-CIO, Local 321 contributed to the costs of moving the mural to the Greater Cincinnati Airport in 1973.

Waiting for work: "Clean and Tidy. Dirty Men Will Not Be Sent Out" (1930s). Photograph. Paul Briol Collection.

Cincinnati's government performed well in another respect during the 1930s. Armed with the Official City Plan of 1925 and competent governmental management, the city was capable of using federal dollars effectively when the New Deal began to pump money into the nation's economy. "Of the utmost importance," Dykstra reported at the end of 1933, "through the activity of the Federal Government, Cincinnati has the good fortune to be embarked upon a well-planned civil works program which has put more than 20,000 of our people back to work and gives us more than a million dollars a month in new purchasing power." He added, "We can enter the new year with hope and with relative satisfaction." Using federal money, the city attacked many of the problems reformers had identified and worked at solving in earlier years and implemented many of the plans that had been proposed but never acted upon.

The Works Progress Administration, or WPA, directly touched the lives of more people than any other New Deal agency and became the area's largest employer. Between 1936 and 1939 the WPA employed almost 35,000 men and women in projects ranging from small construction jobs, documented by dozens of stone plates on park walls and concrete slides, to staffing day-care centers and teaching nutrition to slum dwellers. During the depression decade, the city expanded its park acreage by 40% and accomplished a variety of park improvements compatible with the 1907 Kessler Plan. For example, through the WPA's Civilian Conservation Corps, an average of 118 men worked each day from 1935 to 1937 constructing roads, trails, bridges, guardrails, fireplaces and sewer lines in Mount Airy Forest. Through WPA's Federal Writers Program, Cincinnati's best fact book on the city's history and sites, the *Cin-*

cinnati Guide, was compiled. Another New Deal agency, the Public Works Administration, or PWA, made possible long-delayed capital-improvement projects throughout Hamilton County. Between 1933 and 1940, the PWA infused about $27.9 million into the local economy. PWA projects included Columbia Parkway, Laurel Homes, the Millcreek Interceptor Sewer, several buildings and an addition to the stadium at the University of Cincinnati, the Reptile House at the Zoo, schools in Lockland and Madeira and a new post office downtown.

Of all the innovative and daring programs entered into by the federal government during the New Deal, none proved more controversial than public housing. Yet, even in this activity, the New Deal borrowed conspicuously from the experimental ventures of such earlier reformers as Jacob Schmidlapp and Mary Emery. Cincinnati's worst housing problem was in the West End. The area contained some of the city's oldest housing and had absorbed most of the southern blacks who had migrated to Cincinnati during recent decades. To take advantage of newly available federal funds, the Cincinnati Metropolitan Housing Authority was formed in 1930. In cooperation with the city's planning office, the housing authority proposed clearing large areas of the West End slum housing and replacing the tenements with medium-density apartments similar in design to those built by Schmidlapp's Model Homes Company. In addition, vacant land on the outskirts of the city would be developed for those displaced from the West End and for other poor families.

From the beginning, the plan stirred debate. The site chosen for slum clearance was bounded by Lincoln Park Drive (later renamed Ezzard Charles Drive) on the south and Liberty Street on the north between John and Linn streets. The center of the worst housing in the West End, however, lay further south. Many homeowners claimed that the prices offered were based on low, 1931 depression-level appraisals and concluded that the real purpose of the project was to remove blacks from the area surrounding the new Union Terminal. Blacks became even more disturbed when they learned that two proposed developments for outside the basin, Winton Terrace and English Woods, were designed for whites and that the housing authority planned to bar blacks from the new Laurel Homes in the West End as well.

Aerial view of the West End before construction of the Laurel Homes and Lincoln Court housing projects (c. 1935). Photograph. Gift of the Better Housing League of Cincinnati.

Construction of Laurel Homes (1937). Photograph. Looking east, Liberty Street at the left of the project.

Actually, the Cincinnati Metropolitan Housing Authority had requested federal funds to build three separate neighborhood units in the West End, one for blacks and two for whites. Once the amount of funding available was determined, the plan was scaled down dramatically to just one neighborhood unit for white families only. Yet, 61% of those displaced by Laurel Homes were black. White opposition combined with lack of funding killed the housing authority's plans for housing for blacks outside the basin. Under pressure from black leaders and the Better Housing League, the housing authority finally agreed to permit black families to move into Laurel Homes. The development had displaced 769 black families but only made available 30% of the 674 new apartments to blacks. As bold as the project was, the housing authority carefully kept units for black families segregated from apartments for whites. Later, during 1941 and 1942, the housing authority constructed an additional 1,015 units for blacks in the Lincoln Court project just south of Laurel Homes.

In a separate housing program, New Dealers borrowed from the urban planners' thinking that had produced Mariemont in the 1920s. The Resettlement Administration chose Cincinnati, Milwaukee and a tract of land between Washington and Baltimore as sites for new greenbelt towns. Greenhills was planned to be a community for lower- to middle-class families in the midst of a forested area. It was designed on a circular plan that oriented residences inward and away from the street to promote interaction among neighbors. Apartments of different sizes, rowhouses, duplexes and single-family homes were placed close together. A variety of forces bitterly opposed Greenhills, with real-estate companies and savings and loan associations leading the fight. Residents of Mt. Healthy expressed the fear that the project would destroy property values and bring in blacks. Despite early promises to the contrary, blacks were not admitted to Greenhills. Nor could most of Cincinnati's poor whites meet the minimum income and credit requirements to live there. The New Deal's accomplishments both in Laurel Homes and Greenhills were considerable, but the urban housing problems that inspired such projects were far larger than the experimental programs in the 1930s could solve.

As the decade closed, Europe was once again at war. As the United States began to re-arm, military contracts generated jobs beyond the scope of any New Deal program. With the city's unemployment down to 8.3% by May 1941, WPA employment declined. The program finally ended on April 30, 1943. Its last employee, Hazel Weeks, commented, "All of us looked forward to the day when the WPA would no longer be necessary, but we are sorry that it took a war to accomplish that end."

World War II brought Cincinnati's industries back to life. As early as March 1941, nine months before the Japanese attack on Pearl Harbor brought the United States into the war, the federal government awarded over $12.6 million in defense contracts in Cincinnati in addition to the expansion of the giant Wright Aeronautical plant in Lockland.

America swung its industrial capacity fully behind the war effort, and Cincinnati plants adjusted to unprecedented demands. The city's concentration of machine-tool plants made it a vital center in the conversion process. In December 1940 the head of the Advisory Commission to the Council of National Defense urged the LeBlond Machine Tool Company to "forget everything except the welfare of our

The 1,660-foot long Columbia Parkway Viaduct which bridged Fifth Street from Pike to Martin Street was completed in 1938. (1938). Photograph. Gift of T. H. Hite.

country" and pushed it to find ways to speed up the delivery of machine tools. By 1942 Cincinnati Milling Machine Company, which had greatly enlarged its plant between 1938 and 1940, was shipping seven times more equipment than during its peak peacetime year. Other Cincinnati companies also found ways to support the war effort. Cambridge Tile used the machinery with which it compressed clays before the war to produce "granola"-type cereal bars for K rations. Procter & Gamble applied its soap-manufacturing experience to produce glycerine, used in high explosives and as a base for newly developed sulfa drugs. The United States Playing Card Company produced parachutes.

As Cincinnatians met the demands of yet a second world war, much had changed during the brief span of a single generation since World War I. The German community, which had been one of Cincinnati's distinguishing characteristics through most of the 19th century, had ceased to exist. People, no longer content to cope with the problems that haphazard growth, slum tenements or preventable fires and diseases caused, increasingly looked to government to make their lives better. Generally they believed that municipal government could, in the words of the Official City Plan of 1925, "foresee and make provision for... the public health, safety, convenience, comfort, prosperity, beauty and general welfare of Cincinnati as a home for its citizens." The people established a new municipal government, one better able to manage the city's business efficiently; one that proved remarkably capable of managing the problems and the federal money that came with the Great Depression. Cincinnatians had largely accepted the vision of her reformers and planners and empowered their government to analyze the city's needs and to implement new ways to cope.

Soldiers gaze at World War II banner in Union Terminal which reads, "Strong in the strength of the Lord we who fight in the people's cause will never stop until that cause is won." Photograph. Paul Briol Collection.

He's Watching You (1942). World War II, relying on civilians and combatants, stressed logistics, troop transportation, and secret development of new weapons. Posters cautioned against "careless talk" to prevent espionage and sabotage as well as repeating the patriotic themes of World War I. Division of Information, Office for Emergency Management. Gift of the War Production Board.

Coney Island Swimming Pool, Cincinnati, Ohio
36
Photo by Myron Benson
35
Coney Island Mall, Cincinnati, Ohio
Photo by Myron Benson

Coney Island, Cincinnati, Ohio

Chapter 5

My Neighborhood and Our City

1945-1988

The years following World War II brought rapid changes to Cincinnati. Some, like the spread of people into more distant suburbs and the influx of new people, continued established patterns. Other changes, such as the construction of expressways and the rebuilding of the downtown business district, were consciously planned. Still other developments, including the civil rights movement and the preservation of historic buildings, reflected changing national values. One change, the revival of neighborhood organizations, in 1981 earned Cincinnati an "All American City" designation from the National Municipal League. Despite delays, miscalculations and unforeseen developments Cincinnati accommodated the forces of change well enough that the city gained a national reputation. Observers characterized Cincinnati as a dynamic, thriving city whose citizens cared deeply about its survival and who believed that their caring made a difference in shaping Cincinnati's future.

Cincinnati, more than many cities, was committed to planning. This commitment extended back at least as far as 1920, when the city created a planning commission with a professional staff. In 1925 it officially adopted a city plan and during the 1930s used New Deal dollars to implement some of its housing, recreation and transportation concepts. The city also noted that following the 1937 flood warehouses and other buildings along the riverfront were decaying rapidly. By 1939 planners proposed clearing the area along Third Street for a boulevard similar to Central Parkway and developing a park-like area extending towards the river. World War II prevented implementation of the plan, but the planning process continued.

At the urging of Cincinnati's civic and business leaders, on February 16, 1944, city council authorized the planning commission to prepare a new and comprehensive city plan. The 1925 plan had become obsolete. Not only had the plan failed to provide adequately for some new developments, like the automobile, it had not addressed issues urban planners now incorporated into their thinking. The Director of Master Planning, Sherwood Reeder, explained that "a city cannot plan efficiently by considering only the things that we can see, such as highways, parks, buildings and the like" but must also examine the underlying social and economic factors. In addition, possibly influenced by the war, planners increasingly recognized that urban planning must be done in terms of the entire metropolitan area and not just the city itself.

Coney Island, famous for its landscaped Mall, 200-foot by 400-foot Sunlite Pool with a white sand beach and Moonlite Gardens where the big bands played, began in the 1880s when James H. Parker rented his apple orchard to picnickers. By 1886 investors had purchased Parker's farm, located 10 miles east of downtown on the Ohio River, named it "Ohio Grove — the Coney Island of the West," and founded the amusement park that remained the largest in southwestern Ohio until Kings Island opened in 1972. From 1925 to 1947 the favored way to travel to Coney was aboard the 5-decked sidewheeler Island Queen, *the last of 19 steamboats that made four trips each day from the wharf on the public landing.*

Postcard scenes, all 1940s: *Coney Island Mall* and *Coney Island Swimming Pool*, gifts of Rosalind Baer; *Coney Island*, aerial view, Eugene F. Bliss fund purchase.

The Cincinnati Riverfront (c. 1945) Photograph. Paul Briol Collection.

While the city planning staff began working on a new master plan, business and civic leaders formed the Citizens Planning Association to promote discussions about the future needs of the city. Frederick V. Geier, president of the Cincinnati Milling Machine Company; Richard R. Deupree, president of the Procter & Gamble Company; Walter Draper, president of the Cincinnati Street Railway Company; and John J. Emery were among those who participated. Their speeches sometimes echoed earlier Cincinnati boosters like Daniel Drake. They saw Cincinnati in a struggle with other urban centers for population, jobs and status. Walter S. Schmidt, a real estate executive, observed: "We are entering an era of competition between cities. Population is not growing as it was. The city which makes itself a convenient one in which to work and live and rear a family will survive and grow because it will be attractive to industry." Business leaders were particularly concerned that because the depression and war had postponed rebuilding and relocating of industries, Cincinnati's factories had become old, ugly, outmoded and poorly situated.

Beginning in 1946 the recommendations of the planners began to appear in a series of volumes addressing such topics as "population," "transportation," "economic development" and "communities." On November 22, 1948, city council adopted the 1948 Master Plan. The planners hoped its goals were farsighted enough to be inspiring, yet practical enough to be attainable.

The plan emphasized highways and communities. After the passage in 1944 of a federal highway act, planners envisioned the building of a new type of highway, the expressway, that would revolutionize regional traffic patterns. Relating their thinking to the federal system, the planners called for four expressways from Columbus, Dayton, Indianapolis and Lexington to converge at Cincinnati. Modifying the boulevard concept, they recommended a Third Street Distributor that would connect all of these routes on the southern edge of the downtown and provide easy access to the heart of the city while keeping through traffic off city streets. The riverfront area south of Third Street, two-thirds of which was either unused or occupied by vacant buildings, would be cleared. To transform the riverfront into an asset, the plan proposed placing there a baseball stadium, a city administration center (including a new city hall), a convention center and several apartment towers, plus ample parking and recreation space. All of this would be developed in ways to minimize potential flood damage and to support the central business district.

Proposed Rehabilitation Plan for the Cincinnati River Front (1939). From the city engineer's *Preliminary Report on a Plan of Redevelopment for the Central River Front* (Cincinnati, 1939). Gift of the Municipal Reference Bureau.

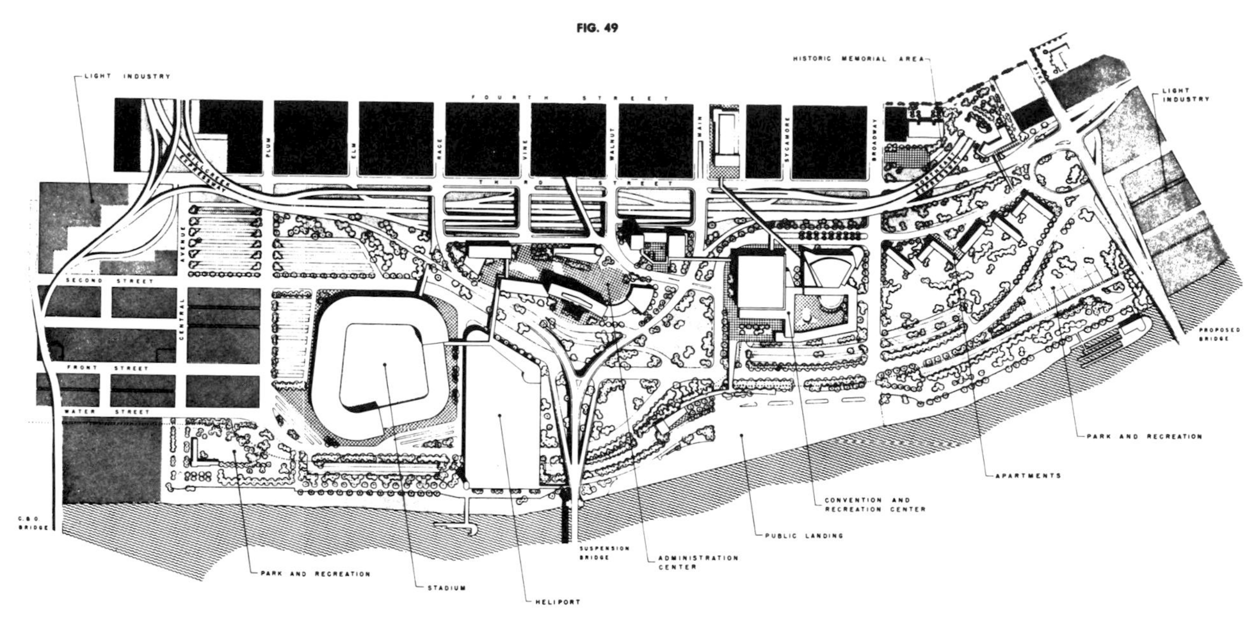

DOWNTOWN RIVERFRONT REDEVELOPMENT PLAN

Although Cincinnati's topography largely dictated the location of the expressways, planners coordinated their proposed routes with other goals. For example, one expressway would pass through the Millcreek Valley, the historic transportation corridor into and out of the city before inclines provided Cincinnatians with alternative routes. Between the basin and the valley lay the West End filled with decrepit, overcrowded tenements. The planners linked their expressway proposal with plans to develop industrial sites near downtown by recommending clearing the West End.

The 1948 plan also anticipated that people would move away from the center of the city. It tried to prepare both for new suburban growth and the adjustment of older city neighborhoods. Professional planners in 1948 viewed the ideally organized city differently from their 1925 counterparts. Earlier planners thought of Cincinnati as a large and complex city, but a single social unit. The 1948 plan assumed that the city was too large to function as a single unit and should be reorganized. It identified 91 distinct neighborhoods in Hamilton County which it clustered into 22 communities. Each community was primarily residential with heavy industry and transportation confined to corridors or "separator belts" running between them. Each neighborhood of 4,000 to 8,000 would have its own elementary school, playground and small business district. Each community of four or five neighborhoods would have a junior high school, community center with library, playfields and meeting facilities and a larger shopping district. By this reorganization planners sought to "recapture the advantages of the medium sized city in each of these communities and at the same time make available those institutions to be found only in a great metropolitan city."

For example, the Millcreek Center community would include Cumminsville, Northside and Winton Place and would house 25,000 people by 1970. The plan noted that land along the north shore of the Millcreek (forming the southern border of these neighborhoods) was prone to flooding, so it recommended gradually eliminating residential properties there and encouraging the development of industrial sites.

One of the largest communities proposed in the plan was called "Northeast Hills." This region included Amberley, Blue Ash, Concord, Deer Park, Silverton, Kennedy Heights, Montgomery and Pleasant Ridge. In 1940 the 15 square-mile area contained 23,300 people; by 1970 it was projected to house 56,000. The plan retained municipal boundaries between cities and towns in the area, but ignored them in recommending where shopping, educational and recreational facilities should be developed.

Downtown Riverfront Redevelopment Plan. From *The Cincinnati Metropolitan Master Plan and The Official City Plan of the City of Cincinnati* (1948), fig. 49. Gift of the City Planning Commission.

Alfred Bettman (1873-1945)
"As long as Cincinnatians love their city and strive for its future greatness; as long as they remain eager to make it the best place in which to live, the spirit and work of Alfred Bettman, member of the City Planning Commission from 1926 and its Chairman from 1930 will live on. Death came to him (January 21, 1945) just as his beloved Cincinnati, for which he had labored because it was his native city, was awakening through the beginning of the Master Plan project to the full practical import of the doctrines he had so long advocated."

Quoted from the dedication of the *Metropolitan Master Plan* (1948).

The Roselawn Valley Shop-In, built in 1949, was the area's first shopping center.

Powel Crosley, Jr. Photograph. George Rosenthal Collection.

The four seater *Super Convertible*, manufactured by Crosley Motors, Inc., had a folding rear seat, roll-down windows, 44 cubic inch engine, got from 35 to 50 miles-per-gallon and cost nearly $1000. Photograph. *From Crosley, a Fine Car.* Gift from the estate of Powel Crosley, Jr.

Powel Crosley, Jr. (1886-1961)
Powel Crosley, Jr. was known as the "man with the Midas touch." To most Cincinnatians he seemed to possess an inexhaustible supply of ideas about what Americans needed. Beginning in 1921 Crosley pioneered in the manufacture of affordable table-top radios as well as the programming that made everyone want to buy one of his new sets. In 1922 he started WLW which for a brief time in the late 1920s had a phenomenal 500,000 watts of power. Though forced to cut back to 50,000 watts, its sole control of the 700 kilocycle frequency made it the first "clear channel" station and won it the nickname, "The nation's station."

From this base the Crosley Corporation expanded into a variety of new products. The "Shelvador" refrigerator caught other manufacturers off guard by utilizing storage space on shelves recessed into the door. Crosley advertised the X-ER-VAC as a mechanical scalp massager which stimulated hair growth and the Taylor-tot as a replacement to the traditional baby carriage.

The Crosley touch reached beyond manufacturing enterprises. After two years as a director, in 1936 Crosley bought the controlling interest in the Cincinnati Reds to guarantee that the club would remain in Cincinnati. He renamed Redland Field "Crosley Field" and introduced night baseball to the major leagues. Attendance increased, and the Reds won a league championship in 1939 and a national championship in 1940.

Crosley's real dream, though, was to manufacture automobiles. As early as 1907 he built prototypes. In 1939 he actually turned out 5,500 Crosley cars before being sidetracked by World War II. In 1945 Crosley sold his broadcasting and manufacturing interests and devoted his energies to developing "America's most needed car." Convinced that Detroit's large, expensive cars left the average American with only a used-car option, Crosley imitated the small, efficient European automobiles. Using an innovative light-weight engine, offering just a few models with only Spartan options, the Crosley sold for only $850 and got between 30 and 50 miles per gallon. Although mildly popular at first, the small Crosley failed in an automobile market increasingly dominated by manufacturers who made their cars longer, heavier and less efficient.

In 1952 Crosley sold his automobile operation and kept only the Reds, which he owned until his death in 1961. The man with the Midas touch failed to convince Americans that they needed the product he cared about most. The day of the small car in America was still 25 years and several gasoline shortages in the future.

Despite the importance planners placed on reorganizing Greater Cincinnati communities, little came of the proposals. As Ernest Pickering, chairman of the Cincinnati Planning Commission, admitted in 1958, the popularity of the automobile was even greater than predicted. For a decade all efforts went into "appeasement of the automobile." The proposals also conflicted with long-standing loyalties of residents to their traditional neighborhoods and communities. Northeast Hills never meant anything to people who were proud of the traditions of the "Ridge" or believed that Montgomery should decide for itself where to place its schools and how to develop its business district. Greater Cincinnatians greeted these proposals with apathy and dismissed them as artificial.

Cincinnati's planners were brave in their attempt to anticipate the postwar world. Few economists or political leaders had a clear idea of what would happen to the nation's economy after the war. Many believed that unemployment would climb again, requiring the government to fund large work-creating projects. Instead, American industry boomed after the war. Military spending remained high as a cold war developed. In addition, Americans who had little money to spend during the depression and who had few opportunities to spend their salaries during the war began to draw upon wartime earnings to pursue long-deferred goals. They wanted to buy houses, cars and consumer goods. Manufacturers converted from wartime production to the manufacture of automobiles, refrigerators, washing machines, toasters—all kinds of products—in record numbers. With the aid of federal programs, new ways were available to finance long-term mortgages. Home ownership was within the reach of more people than ever before. The home-building and automobile industries were essential components of the strong postwar economy. They also greatly changed how Cincinnatians lived.

In the late 1940s and 1950s new suburban developments sprang up all around the city. Thousands of families bought their first homes in subdivisions of small Cape Cod houses and bungalows. Those with greater resources sought ranch-style homes on larger lots equipped with everything from garbage disposals and dishwashers to air conditioning. Like their parents and grandparents who had fled the basin as soon as inclines and their financial resources allowed, these new suburbanites sought a private home with as much land around it as they could afford.

The new suburbs were in fact and in jargon "bedroom suburbs." More than ever before, people separated the place they worked from their home. They also separated home from where they shopped, went to school or attended church. Lost to some extent was the personal involvement among the people living in the neighborhood and with the people who, in earlier neighborhoods, had usually lived near the businesses they operated.

The automobile made it all possible. Suburban housing patterns reflected the new reality that nearly every family owned a car. People no longer walked to the store, to school, or, frequently even to a bus stop. Except for children riding great yellow buses to schools, people drove themselves. The traveling butcher, fruit and vegetable vendor and milkman all became unnecessary. Churches in the suburbs built huge parking lots, and those in the city added them so their parishioners could come from across town for services. Scattered neighborhood shopping districts with "mom and pop" stores gave way to the centrally located shopping center, which soon became the covered shopping

The dream home for the Cincinnati family in the late 19th century was in a hilltop suburb such as Clifton, Avondale or Westwood. It was an ideal that held sway until about 1910 when increased interest in country life prompted a number of affluent city-dwellers to seek properties in semi-rural areas further away from the city. Some already maintained summer cottages in the far eastern and western townships. But living year-round in the country became feasible for downtown businessmen only with the introduction of the family automobile, the construction of paved roads and the availability of reliable water and utility services.

Most who migrated to the country in the early 20th century were characterized by their interest in outdoor activities such as golf, horseback riding and gardening or by their desire to enjoy closer contact with nature. Fresh air and outdoor recreation had been prescribed since the late 19th century for their therapeutic effect on respiratory disease and the "nervous disorders" that supposedly resulted from the conditions of modern, urban life.

Easy access to sports and leisure-time activities was an important enticement to country life. The establishment of country clubs not only provided for golf, tennis, shooting and riding, but it fostered a sense of community among new residents. In many instances housing sites were developed in conjunction with country clubs.

Wynnburne Park, a development bordering the fairways of Western Hills Country Club (chartered 1912), was platted in the 1920s. The developer stressed the advantages of living "only a mashie shot away" from the sporty 18-hole course. Wynnburne homesites were advertised as being "far enough removed from the grind and dust of the city, yet near enough to be only a short drive away."

Almost without exception those families who purchased farm properties in the country were people of means. But those who congregated in the Columbia Township highlands of Indian Hill were among the wealthiest and most influential in Greater Cincinnati. Farms in Indian Hill, as in the Western Hills, were small—usually less than 90 acres. A number of Indian Hill pioneers bought several farms and combined them into huge estates, thus preserving the country environment.

Subdivisions appeared in Indian Hill in 1923 with the platting of the Camargo Realty Co. project on the periphery of the proposed Camargo Country Club (1925); Willow Hills and Burley Hills subdivisions followed in the 1930s. The familes there understood at an early date how legal tools, such as zoning, and political tools, such as incorporation, could enable them to control growth and preserve a semi-rural atmosphere. Indian Hill incorporated as a village in 1941 with approximately 2,000 residents.

By 1980 the 20-square mile area had a population of only 5,521 and no business district. The Village owned 2,200 acres of recreation and "greenbelt" land. This country suburb had acquired a reputation as one of the city's most prestigious residential areas, in part because its leaders worked collectively to preserve their early vision of the idyllic country life.

While Cincinnati homeowners by the 1970s and 1980s had demonstrated renewed interest in city living, adherents of country life remained strong. Many families sought properties in semi-rural Clermont County and Warren County, which postwar expressways had placed within commuting distance of the downtown.

The Baker and Norton Realty Company, builders of *Wynnburne Park,* promised "solid comfort" in English and American Colonial style houses and a "health and happiness-giving environment" in its subdivision eight miles from Fountain Square at Cleves-Warsaw Pike and Neeb Road.

Earth Turned on Swifton Center-- 54 Stores, Parking for 3000 Cars

SILVERTON
SANTA CLAUS NOW! ! !
A present for your family—3-bedroom brick priced right; dead-end street, school bus at corner, perfect for children; living room, full dining room, tile kitchen, breakfast area, GE dishwasher and disposal, plus family room with fireplace on 1st; 3 air-conditioned bedrooms, tile bath on 2nd; storage on 3rd; recreation area, workshop corner, Bendix washer, lavatory and shower in basement; gas heat; garage; level lot.
VIRGINIA BUCHANAN, PL 1-4141
W. L. Readnour BR 1-7600
Office, No. 1 Hotel Mariemont

SILVERTON
(Multiple Listing No. 129)
1-FLOOR-PLAN BRICK
An unusually spacious home. Living room 19x14, dining room, 2 twin-size bedrooms, tiled bath and kitchen with paneled breakfast room, finished 3rd bedroom on second. Many excellent features such as basement recreation room and lavatory, marble sills, lots of closets and beautiful lot, near St. John and bus.
Mrs. Heekin, RE 1-0683
Rob't O. Strong, RE 1-8531

Springfield Township—1 Acre
Secluded Ranch, $13,950
ONLY $2,500 DOWN
See this new home, featuring tremendous living room with log fireplace and adjoining dinette, ultra-modern kitchen with dining area and exceptional cabinet and counter space, tile bath and 2 twin-size bedrooms, full basement, automatic forced-air heat. LEVEL LOT.
MAL Realty Hu 1-0986

SYCAMORE TOWNSHIP—New Area
CUSTOM BRICK RANCH
2-CAR ATTACHED GARAGE
30-ft. living room, wood-burning fireplace, full dining room, 3 generous bedrooms, tile vanitory bath, kitchen with natural cabinets, plus large breakfast nook, paneled game room and full bath in basement; wall-to-wall carpeting; covered rear porch with grill; lot 100x265. FOR QUICK SALE—ONLY $27,900.
M & M Realty TW 1-3773

WESTWOOD—2-bedroom, 1-floor with unfinished 2nd; nearly
NEW BRICK, 5 ROOMS, $16,500
Consider Older Home in Trade
LOCKER CO. HU 1-5800, HU 1-4067

WESTWOOD—EPWORTH AVE.
One-family, five-room brick; modern in every respect; 2-car garage.
GR 1-5041 HU 1-4172
WEBER REALTY SERVICE

WHITE OAK—On Transportation
6-Room Brick—$15,750
4, tile bath, 1st; 2, 2nd; beautiful yard 65x250; exceptionally nice condition. JA 1-3977, KI 1-1275, MU 1-4428, KI 1-4826.
GOLDEY REALTY JA 1-3846

WYOMING
CAPE COD ON FOREST—2 large bedrooms, bath and powder room; screened porch.
MORTON / BRUCE Homes
VA 1-2222 8466 VINE

mall. The Swifton Center opened in 1955 on Reading Road with 60 stores, 60,000 square-feet of retail space and parking for 4,000 cars. It was correctly perceived as a threat to the future of the downtown as a retail center, and it was quickly followed by the Western Hills, Kenwood and Tri-County shopping centers.

As people left the older neighborhoods ringing the basin for new bedroom suburbs, working-class people, the blacks and the poor—many of them new residents of the city—replaced them. Although foreign immigration into Cincinnati was reduced to a trickle by this time, almost 100,000 people moved into the city between 1940 and 1970, principally from the mountain regions of eastern Kentucky and Tennessee. These Appalachians experienced many of the difficulties immigrants had faced. Frequently, they had few resources. First jobs for unskilled and semi-skilled workers were in factories, especially in the automobile plants in Norwood and Sharonville. Appalachians found housing in "port-of-entry" neighborhoods such as Over-the-Rhine, Lower Price Hill and the East End.

The city's older neighborhoods also absorbed people displaced from the West End. The 1948 plan viewed the housing there fit only for demolition. In 1950 the 400-acre area housed 67,520 people including more than 54,000 of the city's 78,685 blacks. By 1959 the city had prepared a detailed plan for preparing sites for light industry, wholesaling and retailing, plus partial replacement of housing stock by constructing about 850 rental units.

Large-scale destruction of residences began in 1960 without an adequate plan for relocating the 40,000 people displaced. The Cincinnati Metropolitan Housing Authority had no more success after the war than it had during the depression in building small-scale housing developments for blacks outside the basin. Wherever it attempted to build, white residents resisted. A 1952 proposal to construct housing for blacks along Kirby Avenue in Northside sparked the formation of a coalition of neighborhood groups from Northside, College Hill and Mt. Airy. The coalition won. The most successful effort to develop a substantial amount of housing for blacks was the opening between 1952 and 1955 of 646 units in Millvale on Beekman Street.

West End blacks who could not find or did not want public housing had few alternatives to moving into older neighborhoods. Both Mt. Auburn and Walnut Hills absorbed thousands of West End blacks between the mid-1950s and mid-1960s. Black residence in Mt. Auburn, for example, increased from 2% in 1950 to 10% in 1960 and 74% by 1970. Many other blacks moved to Avondale. Middle-class Jews were moving to new suburbs, especially Roselawn, Bond Hill, Golf Manor and Amberley Village. Between 1950 and 1960 the white population of Avondale declined nearly 60% from 21,429 to 8,894, while the black population expanded almost sixfold from 3,464 to 19,799. Blacks frequently could not afford to care for the large, one-family homes that had already begun to deteriorate before they moved in, so landlords carved them into multiple-family apartments. As businesses along Reading Road followed their Jewish customers northward, the once-thriving business district began to decline.

Forcing blacks to leave the West End not only displaced people, it also destroyed important black institutions. The Ninth Street YMCA and the Cotton Club, famous for its big-name acts, did not survive the upheaval. Dozens of West End churches moved to the hilltops, but had to assemble substantially new congregations.

When ground was broken for the Swifton Village Shopping Center, Rollman and Sons Company, the prime tenant, expected the suburban store to serve an expanding population without diminishing sales at its downtown store. *Cincinnati Post*, June 10, 1955.

Ads for new Cape Cod and ranch-style homes from the *Cincinnati Times-Star* (July 23, 1955).

Patterns of race relations in all areas came under scrutiny in the 1950s and 1960s. Although Cincinnati's public facilities were not legally segregated, clearly understood prohibitions prevented blacks from entering most hotels, restaurants and amusement sites, including Coney Island. Blacks were also excluded from many employment opportunities. Restrictions on admittance to membership or apprenticeship in the skilled-trade unions kept blacks out of the construction industry. With a surge of public funds for construction projects in the mid-1960s, this restriction became untenable. In June 1963 the National Association for the Advancement of Colored People threatened to picket the construction site of the new Federal Building at Fifth and Main, prompting the Mayor's Friendly Relations Committee to work feverishly to prevent the protest. Although contractors and unions agreed to bring more blacks into the skilled construction trades, by the summer of 1965 there had been no progress. In July the Congress of Racial Equality conducted work stoppages and a sit-in, drawing national television news attention that forced public hearings on race discrimination in the building trades. In 1966 a federally assisted training program was launched to prepare young blacks for union apprenticeship programs, but few were able to secure jobs.

Despite increasing confrontations both nationally and locally, most Cincinnatians were surprised when rioting broke out in Avondale in 1967. It was happening in other cities, but Avondale did not seem comparable to Watts. However, Cincinnati like the rest of the nation, had moved too slowly to accommodate the expectations of people so long treated unequally.

The spark was minor. Posteal Laskey, a black, was convicted of raping and murdering a white Price Hill secretary. Many in the black community felt Laskey was the innocent target of white fear resulting from six unsolved murders in the city. When Laskey was sentenced to death, protestors appeared on the streets. One of these was Laskey's cousin, whom police arrested on June 12 for loitering while he was carrying a sign along Reading Road that called for Laskey's freedom. That evening blacks held a rally on the grounds of Samuel Ach school to demonstrate their right of protest. When the meeting broke up about 9:30 p.m., groups of black youths began roaming the streets, shouting their defiance and breaking windows. Within minutes, half of the Cincinnati police force on duty at the time—285 policemen—arrived at the scene. The young blacks threw rocks and molotov cocktails through store windows, setting half a dozen fires.

The next day city officials called in the National Guard, which deployed about 1,000 men, and met with black leaders. At a special meeting of city council, blacks presented 11 grievances, but the meeting dissolved into angry exchanges. Violence broke out again that evening in Avondale, Walnut Hills, Corryville, the West End and Millvale. Sporadic violence continued the next two nights while leaders in both black and white communities worked to quiet the rioters. By the end of the week, a tense calm was restored and the National Guard left.

National Guard during the 1967 riot. Photograph. From the *Cincinnati Enquirer* Collection.

Boarding up store windows in Walnut Hills (1967). Photograph. From the *Cincinnati Enquirer* Collection.

The week of rioting caused an estimated $2 million in damages and cost an additional $1 million for police and guardsmen. During the week 316 blacks were arrested on riot-related charges—three-quarters of whom were under 25. Compared to the riots in many American cities, Cincinnati's disturbance was relatively small. But Cincinnatians were surprised and confused that it could happen in their city.

Only gradually did some whites come to understand how extensive dislocation and the frustratingly slow pace toward full equality had built up anger and frustration. Blacks attributed the outburst of violence to the lack of jobs, noting that 27.7% of those arrested were unemployed. They also complained of unequal treatment by police and the courts. In the months after the riots, the city and businesses gave increased attention to the importance of finding jobs for unemployed youths and promised assistance to improve conditions in Avondale.

Progress proved difficult to come by, though neither the city and its business leaders nor the black community forgot what had happened or the promises that had been made. For a number of years a variety of federal programs provided employment, especially during the summer months, for large numbers of black youths. As the federal government cut back those programs, the business community took increased responsibility for finding jobs that would help blacks. Efforts to locate businesses along Reading Road in the black area of Avondale proved fruitless until, in 1981, Oscar Robertson, the former basketball star for the University of Cincinnati and the Cincinnati Royals, gained the backing of the city manager and financial institutions to build an Avondale Town Center. Designed to include grocery and other shopping opportunities long absent from the area, the development had enor-

Skywalk design prepared by Garber, Tweddell and Wheeler, architects. From *Cincinnati CBD Plan: Cost Studies* (Cincinnati, 1958), following p. 4. Gift of Young and Klein, Incorporated.

Unveiling the refurbished Tyler Davidson Fountain, October 16, 1971. Photograph.

In 1971 Carl Solway and Jack Bolton sponsored *Urban Walls, Cincinnati,* a project that transformed 10 blank building walls into gigantic works of art. This design is at the southeast corner of Fifth and Plum streets.

mous symbolic as well as economic importance.

By the late 1960s, it had become difficult to find funding for business developments in neighborhoods. The city had turned much of its attention to the aging, grimy, stodgy-looking central business district. The 1948 Master Plan had not devoted much attention to the downtown area beyond providing for the Third Street Distributor and recommending parking facilities. The success of regional suburban shopping centers changed things. Between 1948 and 1958, the central business district's share of the city's retail sales declined from about two-fifths to less than one-third, and the value of its property amounted to only 10% of the city's real estate. To combat this trend Ladislas Segoe, an experienced urban planner, suggested that the downtown should build on its inherent strengths: "its compactness and wide choice of goods." He proposed imitating the accessibility and convenience of suburban shopping centers. Expressways and parking garages would make it easy for people to shop downtown. In addition he suggested creating pedestrian malls by closing selected streets to automobiles. While Cincinnati did not adopt pedestrian malls, an alternative was found: second-level walkways. The skywalk system succeeded splendidly.

By the mid-1960s many business and civic leaders concluded that the lack of new construction downtown demonstrated that Cincinnati had a serious problem. Since the close of the building boom of the 1920s, the only major building completed in the heart of the downtown was the Terrace Hilton (1948). On the edges of the core, the Public Library opened a new facility (1955), Procter & Gamble completed new headquarters (1956) and Kroger finished a new building (1959) praised at the time as a "sky-high symbol of what downtown rejuvenation can mean to the city." Although the sponsor of each project claimed confidence in the future of downtown, they failed to generate a building boom.

The city and the business community recognized the need for a coordinated approach to downtown redevelopment. In 1964 the planning commission released a plan for the central business district. It broke the 12-block area into nine prime development parcels, each designated for office, retail, hotel and convention uses. In 1965, the "Year of the Core," the city abandoned its approach of working with a prime developer in favor of granting development rights for each block independently. It awarded "Block A," Fountain Square, to the Cincinnati Redevelopment Corporation headed by a Columbus developer, John Galbreath, to build an underground garage, a new public square and an office tower. Also in 1965 the city signed a contract for a new Stouffer's motel and the Federal Reserve Bank began a new building.

By 1971 the first fruits of long years of planning for downtown were visible. After six years of disruption to dig the underground garage, construct the DuBois Tower and the Fifth Third Bank Center and to prepare a new setting for a refurbished fountain, the new Fountain Square was dedicated on October 16, 100 years and 10 days following the original dedication. The first segment of the skywalk also opened in 1971. In the decade that followed, the pace of tearing down and building anew increased.

How did Cincinnati's airport end up in Boone County, Kentucky? By 1940 everyone agreed that geography doomed Lunken Airport. Steep hills and short runways made approaches difficult while frequent flooding turned the field into "sunken" Lunken. When Greater Cincinnati Airport in Northern Kentucky was opened in 1947 it was intended to serve only temporarily as the major passenger and cargo airport in the metropolitan area. Planners agreed that a more centrally located passenger facility in Blue Ash would better serve residents in the northern suburbs, especially near Hamilton and Middletown, as well as factories in the Millcreek Valley and near Norwood. After voters turned down a third bond issue in 1955 to finance the proposed facility, efforts shifted to expanding and improving the Greater Cincinnati Airport.

Detail from the Aeronca aircraft factory Union Terminal mural.
Gregory Thorp Collection.

Ruth Lyons
(1907-1988)
In postwar Cincinnati a phenomenon and pioneer emerged in television broadcasting. Ruth Lyons was called "the most influential housewife" in the Midwest.

To seven million viewers who watched her, she was a friend who shared her concerns, ideas, opinions and family from noon to 1:30 five days a week. Miss Lyons began on WLW-TV in 1949 exhibiting the same disregard for conformity that had already made her a popular radio personality. She had no script, no rehearsals and refused to take direction. Instead, with a keen sense of timing, she shared with her audience whatever happened to be on her mind—careful to include the mention of some 100 sponsors each week that had waited up to three years for the opportunity.

To the station, Ruth Lyons was "big business," grossing $2 million annually—unheard of at the time in daytime TV even for network programs.

After more than 30 years in broadcasting, ill-health forced Ruth Lyons' retirement in 1967.

Ruth Lyons Newman (c. 1965). Photograph. Gift of Herman and Ruth Newman.

Simultaneously, the city turned its attention to the riverfront. Memory of the 1937 flood stalled progress on proposals outlined in the 1948 plan until agreement was reached in 1963 that all structures would be raised above flood stage by constructing podiums. Through a $15 million grant from the federal government in 1966, the city purchased property in the central riverfront area. The real breakthrough came later the same year when the city and county agreed on the historic Public Landing as the site for a new sports stadium, and new owners of the Cincinnati Reds agreed to sign a long-term lease to play there. The next year, when the American Football League expanded, Cincinnati obtained one of the new franchises. Construction of Riverfront Stadium began in 1968 and was completed in time for the 1970 All-Star game. With the stadium as an anchor, development of the central riverfront moved ahead quickly. Through private funding the Coliseum opened in 1975, while Yeatman's Cove Park with its massive Serpentine Wall, itself part of the city's flood control system, was ready by 1976. The first phase of development for Sawyer Point Park began in 1978, and in 1980 residential living returned to the riverfront with the opening of One Lytle Place.

Although Cincinnati's downtown and riverfront redevelopment generated pride among residents and impressed visitors, its success generated concerns that gained momentum as several of the city's oldest buildings were destroyed. Many were outdated and uneconomical, but their disappearance collectively prompted concern that in its drive to revitalize the downtown, the city was destroying its most visible link to the past, one that reflected the unique mixture of forces and people that had built Cincinnati.

Such concern was not unique to Cincinnati, as evidenced by the passage in 1966 of the National Historic Preservation Act. Just as the federal government provided funds in unprecedented ways for cities like Cincinnati to engage in redevelopment, the concern that federal dollars would help destroy the nation's sense of its past prompted the legislation. In Cincinnati building by building, block by block, project by project, the issue was debated. In some instances workable compromises were discovered. For example, when construction of the Northeast Expressway (I-71) endangered Lytle Park, a citizens group led by Councilman Charles P. Taft and insurance executive William T. Earls worked from 1958 to 1967 to develop plans to tunnel under the park and put together a financial package to save it. A long struggle took place from 1965 to 1972 between Cincinnati's most important corporation, Procter & Gamble, and people who wanted to save the oldest surviving church in the downtown area, Wesley Chapel, constructed in 1831 on Fifth Street west of Broadway. The company offered several options, including moving the building across the street, but the congregation elected to build a new church in Over-the-Rhine. The building came down in 1972. Preservationists then turned their efforts to saving the Albee, an ornate theater built in 1927. They lost the battle in 1977 so that Fountain Square South, a $111 million hotel-bank-office complex could be constructed.

Though enduring many frustrations, preservationists took pride in several achievements, such as when Music Hall underwent a $5 million renovation in 1969 and 1970. The future of Union Terminal proved more difficult to resolve. Rail traffic dwindled steadily after World War II until the last passenger train pulled out on October 29, 1972. People universally loved the

Construction of Riverfront Stadium. (1969). Photograph.

building, and they proposed a variety of alternative uses for it, including a convention center, a bus garage, an educational center, a museum of science and industry and a shopping mall. When the Southern Railroad razed the concourse to improve its yard facilities, citizens, businesses and unions rescued the giant murals of Cincinnati workers by moving them in 1973 to the Greater Cincinnati Airport. A refurbished terminal gained a new lease on life when it opened in August 1980 as a specialty shopping mall.

During these years the principal voice for preservationists was the Miami Purchase Association for Historic Preservation, organized in 1964. Between 1975 and 1978, the association surveyed historically and architecturally significant buildings throughout the city. Its inventory identified 981 individually important structures as well as another 1,500 buildings in clusters and districts. The extensiveness of the list surprised city officials. Then, in 1980 Miami Purchase nominated all of the surviving work of Samuel Hannaford, Cincinnati's most prominent 19th century architect, for inclusion on the National Register of Historic Places. This nomination included the Workhouse, an aging structure and an obsolete penal institution. City officials felt the nomination was inappropriate. Partially in response to the inventory and the Hannaford nomination, the city created the position of city urban conservator with a professional staff responsible to a nine-member, citizen Historic Conservation Board. This new body assumed responsibility from the Miami Purchase Association for making nominations to the National Register whenever federal money could conceivably be used to destroy eligible buildings. The change also forced the city to give increased attention to historic preservation concerns in its own planning process.

Looking across Fountain Square to the Albee Theater. Photograph. Paul Briol Collection.

Caroline Williams, *Wesley Chapel,* Lithograph.

The high cost of downtown development and the vigor with which the city pursued it ignited another reaction. Residents of the city's older neighborhoods had long felt that their concerns and needs were subordinated to those of the downtown. In the 1950s, for example, the widening of River Road into a "modified expressway" to carry traffic between the western suburbs and the city disrupted the communities of Sedamsville and Riverside. In the early 20th century, Sedamsville, a working-class neighborhood, had supported over 100 businesses. The flood of 1937 drove out many of them, but the business strip along River Road remained the heart of the community until road widening began. Shirley Caine, a resident, recalled: "They said when they put this road through you would have better facilities, your property values would go up and your business would flourish. Well, we haven't had any businesses to flourish at all." Three isolated streets, clustered on a hillside above the road and the river, were all that remained of Sedamsville. Riverside had a similar experience, except that engineering miscalculations in rerouting traffic during road construction destroyed the area's tenuous drainage system and caused landslides. As other communities had done a generation earlier when individual complaints went unheeded, the residents formed the Riverside Civic and Welfare Club to lobby for greater consideration of their needs by the city during the construction of River Road and for repair of damages when it was completed. The battle continued into the 1970s.

All photographs by Michael Isaacs.

Cincinnati Looking East from the Clay Wade Bailey bridge (1982).

The City (1982).

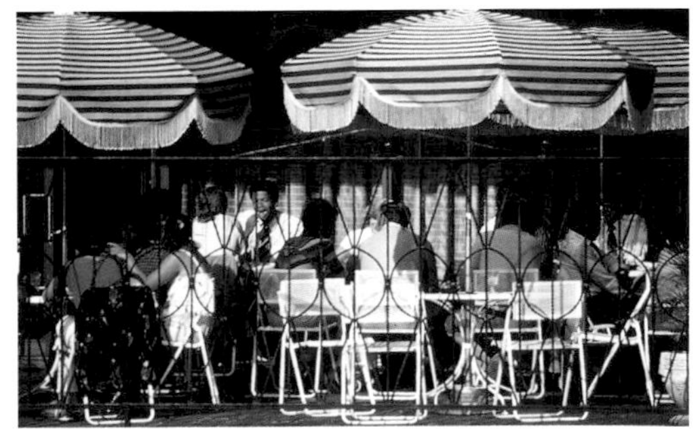

Other communities also organized to gain attention at City Hall for their concerns and to secure some federal community development money for their neighborhoods. The Charter reform of the 1920s had eliminated Cincinnati's ward system of electing city council. This made it more difficult for city government to determine the needs of neighborhoods. To fill this void, residents created neighborhood organizations in the 1960s and 1970s to advise city officials.

Some groups organized to protect their communities against what they feared "the city" or "outsiders" were doing to them. Riverside fit this pattern, as did neighborhood groups in the 1960s that sought to keep blacks out of their communities. Similarly, some neighborhood groups formed to fight to keep open their schools.

Riverfest, 1982. An estimated 550,000 people watched the WEBN-sponsored fireworks display during the Labor Day weekend.

Fountain Square from the Westin Hotel's atrium in Fountain Square South (1982).

Loll Forty Three restaurant's outdoor cafe on Fountain Square Plaza (1982).

Increasingly residents formed neighborhood organizatons in an effort to assert control over their own lives. An early example of this came when blacks were moving into Avondale. Residents of North Avondale saw that in South Avondale "a condition of panic developed, formed by rumor, fear, prejudices and exploited in some instances by unscrupulous and avaricious real-estate interests, thus causing homeowners to list their homes for sale and flee the area." They formed the North Avondale Neighborhood Association in 1960 to fight scare tactics of realtors and to make a functioning, integrated neighborhood. They worked with individual real-estate agents, sympathetic financial institutions and City Hall. By 1970 they had stabilized the neighborhood at 60% white and 40% black. Similar concerns prompted development of community organizations in College Hill, Bond Hill, Paddock Hills and Kennedy Heights. The Clifton Town Meeting was formed in response to worries about spreading black slums, thousands of students attending the University of Cincinnati and Hebrew Union College, and the general confusion created by several hospitals in the area. It worked to preserve the upper-middle-class, suburban lifestyle of the area. Some residents worked through the organization to preserve gaslights along their streets; others fought efforts to widen streets that would increase traffic through the community.

Organizing community councils was not confined to white or to middle-class neighborhoods. Through the Community Action Commission and Model Cities programs, dozens of community organizations were formed in poor and black neighborhoods. Blacks forced from the West End needed to re-create organizations through which they could address their problems. Bailey Turner, working for the Community Action Commission, developed block clubs on Mt. Auburn that fed into its community council. They attacked problems of overcrowding, juvenile delinquency, crime and deteriorated housing. Supported by federal funds, similar efforts were made in Over-the-Rhine, Evanston and Avondale.

The interests of community councils evolved as needs changed, but at one time or another many were concerned about maintaining and developing housing. The availability of federal funds for rehabilitating housing prompted some community councils to form and incorporate neighborhood development corporations. One of the earliest and most effective was the Good Housing Foundation on Mt. Auburn. Led by Carl Westmoreland, the foundation arranged for federally-guaranteed loans through local financial institutions, negotiated city agreements to improve public facilities, such as street lighting, and undertook the purchase and rehabilitation of more than $12 million worth of property. The project gained national attention among preservationists and urban planners interested in restoring vitality to neighborhoods near downtown areas. Other communities, including Bond Hill, Paddock Hills, Walnut Hills, College Hill, Northside and Madisonville, created corporations to stimulate residential and business development.

The growth and effectiveness of neighborhood organizations changed the way city government operated. During the 1960s the city council and administration focused their attention and resources on the redevelopment of the downtown and riverfront. In 1971 a coalition of Democrats and Charterites campaigned for city council with promises that if they were elected, they would give greater attention to the neighborhoods. Their success produced notice-

able changes. A newly appointed city manager, E. Robert Turner, took steps to implement the coalition's promises and established mechanisms for neighborhood participation in making policy.

The city invited community councils to help establish budgetary priorities. By the mid-1970s a regular procedure was developed for neighborhoods to identify needs, assign priorities and communicate them to municipal department heads. Gradually, the city broadened the areas in which community organizations could participate to include overseeing federal block-grant funds and developing long-range plans for neighborhoods. This process culminated in 1981 when the city established a Department of Neighborhood Housing and Conservation. It was for the strength of its neighborhood organizations that the National Municipal League named Cincinnati an "All American City" in 1981.

On May 13, 1893, Mayor John B. Mosby presided over the formal dedication of Cincinnati's new City Hall. This impressive building was six years in the making and cost the citizens of Cincinnati over $1.6 million. A parade, marching bands and speeches by dignitaries, including Ohio Governor William McKinley, were all part of the celebration of the formal opening of the new building.

Designed by Samuel Hannaford, Cincinnati's most prominent 19th-century architect, the building was considered one of the finest structures of its type in the country. Hannaford's proposal was selected from a group of 14 proposals submitted by competing architects from as far away as Washington, D.C., New York and Chicago.

The massive granite building occupies a full city block and includes a 250-foot-tall clock tower. It was built to serve as the center of municipal government and to house all of the city offices, including the Mayor's Office, City Council Chambers and Police Court.

By the time the building had reached its 50th birthday, it was considered too small and too inefficient to continue to serve the purpose for which it was designed. Although many believed that the building should be razed and replaced by a new, larger and more efficient city hall, over the years the city committed its resources to other projects and public improvements, and no new building was ever built.

Gradually many city offices were moved to other sites. At the same time the architectural and historical significance of the building became more widely accepted, and in 1972 City Hall was placed on the National Register of Historic Places. Today it is regarded as the finest example of Richardsonian Romanesque architecture in the city.

Glencoe Place, rehabilitated by the Mt. Auburn Good Housing Foundation (1980). Lisa Koepke photograph.

Samuel Hannaford, *City Hall.* (c. 1887). Presentation drawing from the Samuel Hannaford Architectural Record Collection.

More and more middle-class people became interested in living in neighborhoods where they did not need to drive to work. This combined with an increased respect for older buildings in the 1970s to produce a return to city living. This national trend was first observed in Cincinnati on Mt. Adams. As early as 1951 some middle-class families moved there. The real boom began a decade later when a few young businessmen began "rehabbing" and selling old homes. The Mt. Adams development was an isolated event for several years, but the gasoline crisis of the 1970s and an ever-growing percentage of singles and childless couples generated similar developments in other older neighborhoods and in the downtown business core.

These urban pioneers reversed a century-long trend of living ever further out. Their motivations varied. Some sought imposing views of the basin and the Ohio River from Prospect Hill on Mt. Auburn and from Mt. Adams; others delighted in the architectural gems they found in abundance along streets such as Purcell Avenue in Price Hill or in Tusculum and East Walnut Hills. Many were primarily concerned with finding a house situated in economically and racially mixed communities where they could enjoy greater interaction with their neighbors than they could find in bedroom suburbs. A growing number of people, both young and old, were attracted to the convenience of downtown apartments in the Garfield Park, West Fourth Street and riverfront areas.

Even though the return of middle-class professionals brightened the city's economic picture, it caused a reaction of its own. In low-income areas such as Over-the-Rhine, residents were fearful that if the district were placed on the National Register of Historic Places, they would soon be displaced. By the 1980s "gentrification" was one of the more complex problems facing the city. Ironically, the success of policies to make the city a safe and exciting place for middle-class people to live threatened the security of people who feared that with their limited resources they would soon be unable to afford their houses or to find other, inexpensive alternatives.

By the early 1980s, the primary goals of the 1964 plan for redeveloping the downtown had been achieved, but the city continued to look forward. In 1979 the city planning commission began work on a "Cincinnati 2000 Plan" to guide downtown development through the next two decades. The resulting plan projected nearly doubling the eight million square-feet of office space in the downtown area. In addition, the plan

Model of Cincinnati created by the Cincinnati Department of Economic Development. Although the color coding is complex, generally the lighter colored buildings have either been constructed or proposed since 1964, including some projects under construction in late 1982. Photograph (1982) by Michael Isaacs.

gave new weight to the preservation of older buildings by observing that in certain instances the economic potential of new structures "may be outweighed by the need to retain a sense of the city's past and a human scale." Some of these older buildings could become office space; others might be developed as apartments. The plan projected the need for 6,000 more apartments in the next 20 years, more than tripling the number available downtown.

The Year 2000 Plan for Cincinnati reflected a sense that Cincinnati had become and would remain a vital urban center into the next century. This confidence and pride no longer rested on the same basis 19th century boomers used. According to the 1980 census, Cincinnati's population fell from 453,514 in 1970 to 385,457. While the metropolitan area increased by 5,000 during the decade to reach 1,392,394 people, its ranking dropped from 22nd to 28th in the nation. Cincinnatians took solace in noting that, unlike many northern cities, the region had not lost population during the decade, and, as they had done for more than a century, they continued to work at making the Queen City a better place to live.

In the years after 1960 efforts to improve the quality of life in Cincinnati proceeded along two paths. At the city's center tremendous resources were poured into revitalizing the downtown. From the riverfront to Garfield Park, new buildings were constructed almost everywhere.

In the mid-1980s, a speculative building boom produced a number of impressive office buildings in the core, including Atrium II, Ameritrust Center, Columbia Plaza (later Chiquita Center) and Cincinnati Commerce Center. Two landmark hotels—the Netherland Plaza and the Cincinnatian—were restored and a Hyatt hotel erected. Together with pre-existing hotel rooms

All photographs by Michael Isaacs.

Eden Park's Gazebo and Watertower (1982).

Riverfront Stadium at Night from Mt. Adams (1982).

Mt. Adams and Immaculata Church from the Cincinnati Playhouse (1981).

and an expanded Convention Center, Cincinnati was positioned to be a major player in the contemporary convention and visitors market. Through the bicentennial year, the boom in new construction and restoration of important older buildings continued. And when bicentennial events brought scores of visitors and national press attention to Cincinnati, area residents were pleased and proud of their city.

New jobs came to Greater Cincinnati in the 1980s with the expansion of local service and high-tech industries and the arrival of national companies such as United Brands. At the same time, traditional jobs disappeared with the closing of the General Motors plant and L.S. Ayres stores and the Campeau Corp. takeover of Federated Department Stores.

As the decade drew to a close, area residents were concerned about several problems that defied easy solutions—the hazards posed by the Fernald uranium-processing plant, the failure of county and city government officials to resolve a crisis stemming from the inadequate new jail, the plight of the homeless, the shortage of housing for low-income families and the difficulties of providing adequate local services with diminished federal aid.

Nevertheless, Cincinnatians demonstrated their faith in voluntary solutions and commitment to their community by voting to tax themselves for causes that enhanced the quality of life. In the mid-1980s, county voters created a new Museum Center at Cincinnati Union Terminal, which will house the Cincinnati Historical Society Museum and Library, the Cincinnati Museum of Natural History, and the Robert D. Lindner Family Omnimax Theater when it opens in 1990-1991. And voters also passed critical levies to increase support of Cincinnati Public Schools and to aid repair of the city's aging infrastructure.

Although the needs of the downtown and the neighborhood, and the city and the county, were frequently in conflict during the 1970s and 1980s, by the bicentennial year a more unified view of Greater Cincinnati had emerged. More and more residents spoke with pride about both "my neighborhood" and "our city."

Fountain Square at Night (1982). Michael Isaacs photograph.

Cincinnati Celebrates '88

by Joseph S. Stern Jr.

Chairman, Greater Cincinnati Bicentennial Commission

Birthday parties seldom take six years to plan. But a 200-year-old deserves the best. In 1988 Greater Cincinnati celebrated the 200th anniversary of the landing of the pioneers in the area that was to become metropolitan Cincinnati. Planning for the '88 celebration began in 1982 when City Council established the Greater Cincinnati Bicentennial Commission. Mayor David S. Mann appointed 15 citizens to the Commission; this number was later raised to 38. Joseph S. Stern Jr. was appointed chairman.

City Council gave the Commission three goals: (1) leave a permanent legacy to the community (Cincinnati's centennial celebration in 1888 featured a highly successful national exposition, but no permanent landmark survived); (2) develop a series of events appropriate for the bicentennial year; and (3) involve as many citizens as possible.

Fireworks shot from skyscrapers gave the effect of a giant birthday cake celebrating the Greater Cincinnati Bicentennial. Photograph © Richard Binstadt.

Atop the gateway sculpture, water flows downstream in an Ohio River model, shown here under construction. Photograph © Robert Flischel.

The Commission's first year was an organizational one. In a public competition, the Commission chose Richard J. Greiwe as executive director. Greiwe's energy, enthusiasm and natural bent for orchestrating large events confirmed this selection as a wise one.

At the request of the Commission, individual citizens and groups presented ideas for bicentennial projects that would result in a permanent legacy to the city. After months of review, the Goals and Mission Committee, headed by Sidney Weil, determined that the consensus of the committee favored a riverfront project. The choice made great sense. The Ohio has been inextricably linked with Cincinnati's growth as a major inland commercial and manufacturing center, and more recent developments of the 1960s and 1970s, including Riverfront Coliseum, Yeatman's Cove Park, downtown residential buildings and the riverboat restaurants, have capitalized on the river's recreational and aesthetic appeal. A new riverfront project could guarantee the continuing celebration of the Ohio River, linking the communities of Greater Cincinnati as the region enters its third century.

The task of selecting one specific project was placed in the hands of the Steering Committee, capably guided by William N. Liggett. After much discussion, the committee selected the development of a sprawling recreational facility at Sawyer Point on the banks of the Ohio. A Riverfront Advisory Committee had been promoting the idea for 15 years and had laid the groundwork. The Bicentennial Commission assumed control of the project and brought it to fruition.

The project turned out to be larger than originally planned. There were 22 acres to develop, and all plans had to be approved by the city's Urban Design Review Board. In the early 1980s, the city had received a $6 million federal grant to help construct a recreational facility. These funds

The Greater Cincinnati Bicentennial Commission made the creation and endowment of a grand recreational park at Sawyer Point its permanent legacy project. Photograph © Jeff Friedman.

could be used for the bicentennial project, but additional monies were needed. The Procter & Gamble Company initiated the fund-raising campaign with a $2 million gift to build and maintain a performance pavilion. Liggett's committee contacted corporations, foundations and individuals and raised another $7 million. In two years the $15 million needed for the park was in place.

A portion of an old Cincinnati water works was redesigned as an ampitheater at Bicentennial Commons. Photograph © Maureen France.

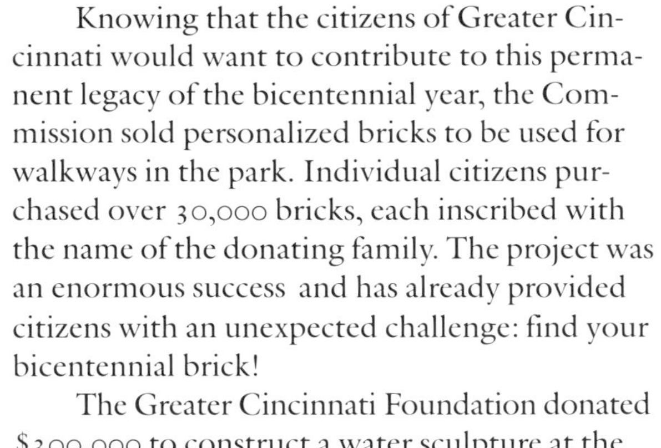

Knowing that the citizens of Greater Cincinnati would want to contribute to this permanent legacy of the bicentennial year, the Commission sold personalized bricks to be used for walkways in the park. Individual citizens purchased over 30,000 bricks, each inscribed with the name of the donating family. The project was an enormous success and has already provided citizens with an unexpected challenge: find your bicentennial brick!

The Greater Cincinnati Foundation donated $300,000 to construct a water sculpture at the park's entrance to portray Cincinnati's historic relationship with the Ohio River. Andrew Leicester won a public competition to design and build the sculpture, which featured 17 historic elements, including a miniature Ohio River complete with water running from Pittsburgh to Cairo, Illinois.

Of all the elements in the sculpture, none attracted so much attention as the infamous "flying pigs." Leicester's design placed bronzed, winged pigs atop four smokestacks at the entryway to the park. The pigs, a whimsical tribute to Cincinnati's early days as "Porkopolis," sparked a tremendous brouhaha over their historical and aesthetic appropriateness, with pro-pig and anti-pig forces exchanging ringing denunciations. The debate culminated at a January 1988 City Council committee meeting when the Commission was summoned to "explain the pigs." At a tumultuous session that generated national press coverage, the pro-piggers carried the day. Flying pig sweatshirts and statuettes soon filled the city's gift shops, and the winged swine themselves now sit proudly atop the sculpture.

Four bronze winged pigs cap steamboat stacks on the gateway sculpture. Photograph © Robert Flischel.

Personalized bricks pave the promenade beyond the main gate to Bicentennial Commons. Photograph © Steven Dulle.

Bicentennial Commons is sited on 22 acres next to the Ohio River, minutes away from downtown Cincinnati and Northern Kentucky. Photograph © Jeff Friedman.

Visitors enter through an environmental sculpture with a local history theme. The fountain masks were inspired by Indian artifacts from the Ohio Valley culture. Photograph © Robert Flischel.

figures and information panels on Ohio River history. The Riverwalk starts with the timeline in the park on the Cincinnati side, crosses the John A. Roebling Suspension Bridge, and continues along Riverside Drive in Covington.

The park, named the Bicentennial Commons at Sawyer Point, was dedicated the weekend of June 3, 1988. Some 350,000 people attended the ribbon-cutting festivities and the musical events of the dedication weekend. They were not disappointed. They enjoyed the beautifully designed promenades and overlooks, the graceful performance pavilion, the imaginative gardens and play areas, the first year-round artificial ice-skating rink in the United States (which doubles as a roller-skating rink), a tennis pavilion and volleyball courts, an amphitheater which incorporates the remains of an early city water works building, and an 18-foot statue of the city's namesake, the Roman citizen-soldier Cincinnatus. The Commons, so named to recognize its appeal to all citizens, is truly an oasis in an urban setting.

As an adjunct to the park project, the Commission funded the development of a two and one-half mile historic Riverwalk, which features a geologic timeline, statues representing historic

Summertime ice and roller skating were made possible with the installation of the nation's first outdoor synthetic ice surface. Photograph © Jeff Friedman.

Small Cincinnatians take delight in the play area, with its maze of inviting equipment. Photograph © Brad Smith.

Although the dedication of the Bicentennial Commons was the focal point of the year-long celebration, it was only one of several grand events. The 1988 Bicentennial celebration commenced on New Year's Eve, 1987, with a downtown "Countdown" that included music and entertainment in the Convention Center and over 20 other locations along the skywalk. Despite a cold, drizzly night (one of the few times a bicentennial event encountered poor weather), over 65,000 people spent New Year's Eve in the city. Just before midnight on Fountain Square, a spectacular laser show ushered in the bicentennial year. The Countdown proved to be so successful that it will be repeated on New Year's Eve, 1988, and may become an annual event.

Celebrating '88 began on Fountain Square, December 31, 1987 with the Countdown. Photograph © Barkan, Keeling, Taggart.

Roy Rogers, movie idol and "King of the Cowboys," received a warm welcome at the Homecoming salute to famous hometown folk on July 9. Photograph © Maureen France.

Procter & Gamble's new international headquarters made a striking backdrop for 200 Years on Parade. Photograph © Barkan, Keeling, Taggart.

In July the city hosted "Homecoming Week" to honor famous Cincinnatians. Over 50 outstanding Cincinnatians, who had earned national attention in fields from medicine to the movies, were feted with a colorful parade and black-tie dinner. Other ceremonies recognized the Cincinnati 200, a group of leading local citizens. Homecoming Week also included the Major League All-Star Game. Held in Cincinnati for the fourth time, the game attracted fans from coast to coast and focused national attention on Cincinnati and the Bicentennial. A giant fireworks display from the tops of the tallest downtown buildings, witnessed by crowds on both sides of the river and from Cincinnati's famous hilltops, capped off an extraordinary week.

Theme floats depicted various periods in local history, from the settlement as birthplace of the Northwest Territory through the 21st century. Photograph © Maureen France.

People donned vintage clothing to fit the historical theme of the parade. Photograph © J. Miles Wolf.

Fireworks showered downtown Cincinnati in a spectacular display on July 10. Photograph © Maureen France.

Pre-game festivities were a highlight of the All-Star game on July 12. Soon-to-be President George Bush made the first pitch. Photograph © J. Miles Wolf.

The grandest event of the year—the "jewel in the crown"—was Tall Stacks weekend, October 14-16. Fourteen riverboats from the Ohio, Mississippi, Missouri and Tennessee rivers docked at the public landing, reviving an era when steamboats ruled the river. Rides on the *President*, the nation's largest inland riverboat, and an old-time steamboat race between the *Delta Queen* and the *Belle of Louisville* provided the highlights of this grand spectacle. Some 56,000 people sailed on special cruises; another 30,000 had passports for boarding only.

Perhaps as many as one million people, from all over the country, came to the riverfront in a holiday mood to enjoy the recreation of the "Sternwheeler Age" in America. Continuous shoreside entertainment added to the festivities. The Toronto *Daily Mail* picked the Tall Stacks as one of the top 10 world events for 1988. Tall Stacks put the spotlight on Cincinnati, and helped stake its claim of being America's greatest inland river city.

Fourteen riverboats arrived at the Port of Cincinnati for Tall Stacks, a unique event that recaptured the spirit of the sternwheeler age. Photograph © Brad Smith.

They came from near and far: the *Mark Twain* from Hannibal, Missouri; the *River Queen* from Jeffersonville, Indiana; and the *Becky Thatcher* from Cincinnati. Photograph © Jeff Friedman.

It was a memorable event. People came for passport tours of ships in port, to take cruises and just to look. Photograph © Richard Binstadt.

The paddlewheel of the *Delta Queen*, one of the last authentic steamboats and a favorite here. Photograph © Barkan, Keeling, Taggart.

Storefronts were built to suggest the way the Public Landing looked in the mid-1800s. Photograph © Robert Flischel.

Riverboats at night. The *Belle of Louisville* is the last original Mississippi River style steamboat. Photograph © Jeff Friedman.

In addition to the opening of the Bicentennial Commons and the other special events, the year featured over 30 special performances, educational programs, and community events, including "River Crossings," a celebration of Cincinnati's black community, commemorative posters, history books for young and old, touring community history panels, a bicentennial quilt and a Cincinnatus mascot who visited area schools.

Fittingly, the final event focused attention on the city's first event: the landing of pioneers at Yeatman's Cove, December 28, 1788. On the eve of the anniversary, a birthday ball was held to recognize the contributions of the 6,000 volunteers who worked at the year's events. The next day, December 28, the landing of the first flatboat at Cincinnati was reenacted, and citizens attended a Bicentennial Birthday Party at the Convention Center.

"River Crossings," a musical drama by Althea Day premiered at Music Hall. Hundreds of volunteers worked on the project. Photograph © Jeff Friedman.

It has been a memorable year, a proud old city remembering its past and encouraging its citizens to invest in its future. The Commission has carried out its mandate.

The bicentennial quilt was a community effort with 8,804 volunteer quilters participating in the stitchery. Photograph courtesy of the Ohio Valley Quilters' Guild.

Cincinnatus, the bicentennial mascot, explains the origin of the city's name to young admirers. Behind him stands the bronze statue of Lucius Quinctius Cincinnatus. Photograph © Tony Walsh.

A Cincinnati Portfolio

Gregory Thorp

Photographs and text by Gregory Thorp. Images selected from work commissioned in 1980-1981 by Strauss, Troy & Ruehlmann Co., LPA. Gift of the law firm.

First there was the river, and at this bend, the mouth of another river... Later, settlements on the banks of both rivers, and ferries and bridges. But first there is a river.

When you navigate up river from New Orleans past Memphis, past Louisville, the excursion has a particularly southern flavor. At Cincinnati the mood changes. The seven bridges of Cincinnati harbor seem to announce the union of North and South. It's your first northern city! You can feel it. It appears dependable, industrious, undefeatable.

And yet a particular charm of Cincinnati is the city's closeness to its neighborhoods. The bend in the river is enlivened by many tensions: southern folkculture/European tradition; family/corporation; neighborhood/tourism.

Aspects of downtown delight the eye and spirit.

The wading pool at Yeatman's Cove is near the site of Griffin Yeatman's tavern of the 1790s.

Building ornamentation atop the Central Trust Tower (1913).

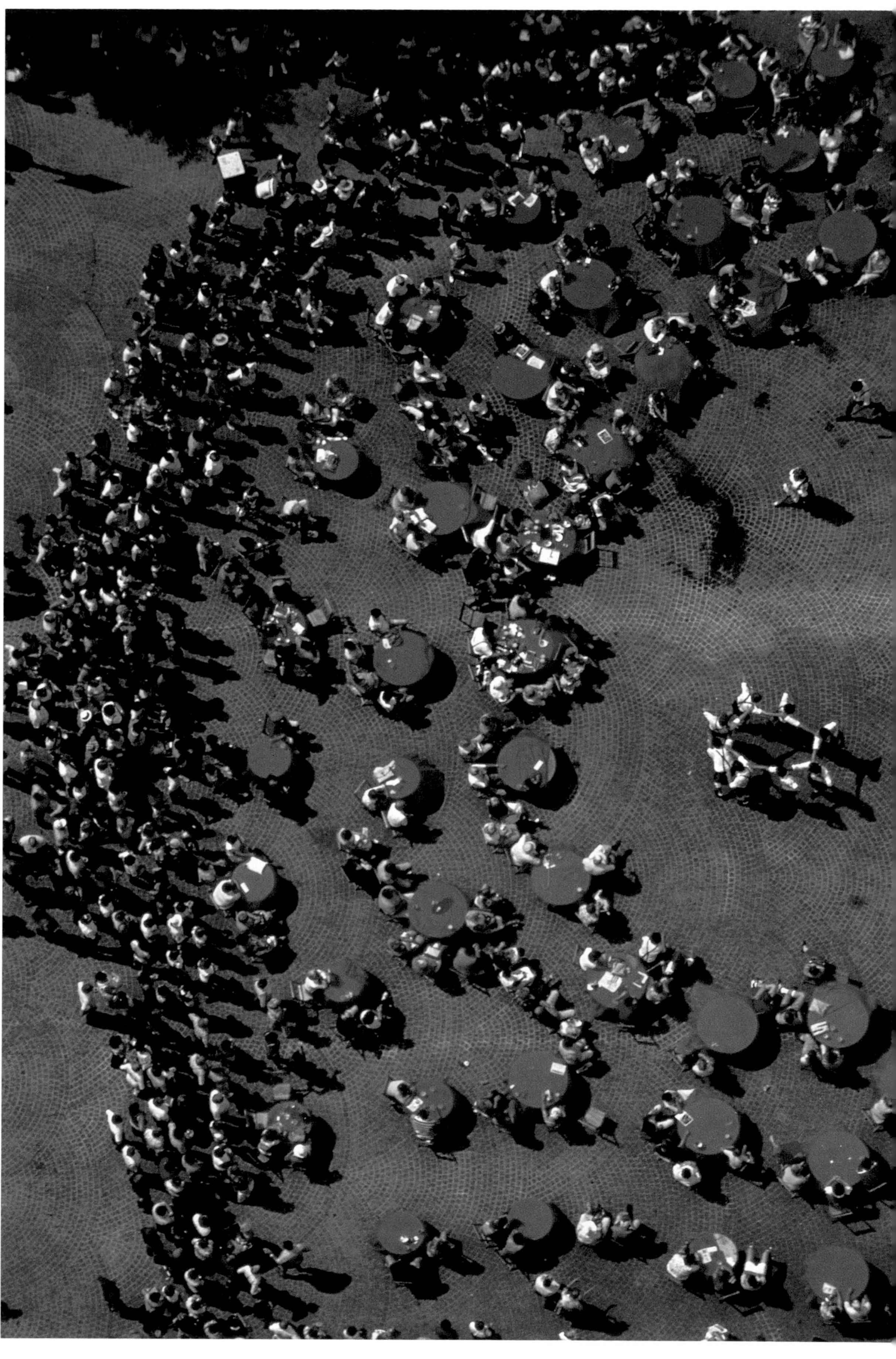

Tyler Davidson Fountain (1871).

Dancing on the square during Oktoberfest.

"Over-the-Rhine" is a neighborhood of many traditions and inevitable flux. One focal point is the Findlay Street Market, symbol of a thriving city's soul: The Marketplace!

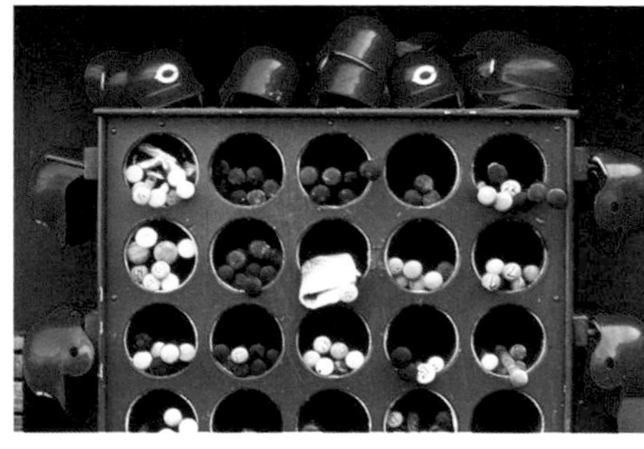

At field level, below the eye of the enthusiastic fans or the commentators' relentless chatter, the Game is serious, matter-of-fact and personal. Baseball **is** *the choice of tools, the crack of the bat, codewords at the batting cage, and the thud of ball into mitt.*

Mother-of-God Church (1871) in Covington, Kentucky watches over the traffic to and from Ohio.

From the earliest white settlements along this bend in the river, there evolved permanent habitations—a nucleus of houses, fortifications, businesses, and places of worship—the village! And livestock, and boat builders, and soap, and architects, and government buildings, and insurance, and culture, and preservation of culture, so that future generations might know something of this evolution and not have to start from scratch.

Corporate and Community Sponsors

The history of Cincinnati's two hundred years of economic growth is both long and complex. The city initially grew by processing and shipping agricultural commodities, but it soon also began manufacturing a wide variety of products. Today Cincinnati's economy increasingly moves from manufacturing to service-related jobs. Growth of banking, insurance, computer, accounting, legal and other professional services has absorbed several million square feet of new office space in the past decade, and several additional office towers are under construction or being planned.

Manufacturing products and providing services each employs about the same number of Cincinnati's workers. Similarly the sponsors included in this section of *Cincinnati: The Queen City* are almost evenly divided between them. It is a diverse accumulation that reflects the variety of Cincinnati's economy. Of the 88 corporations, health care facilities, educational institutions and professional associations described, more than half have roots extending back into the 19th century. Yet several companies are basically post-World War II creations. They demonstrate that Cincinnati's economy can foster new enterprises as well as sustain established firms.

Those unacquainted with Cincinnati are generally surprised to discover the number of companies, long a part of the city's history, whose products are well known. Names such as Ivory soap, Baldwin pianos, Palm Beach clothes, Red Cross shoes, Stearns and Foster mattresses, Jergen's lotion, Drano, Bicycle brand playing cards, Gibson greeting cards, Formica and Kroger's are familiar to many who know little of Cincinnati itself. Many of these companies are represented in this section.

Also represented are several companies whose names and products are unfamiliar to nearly everyone. For a century and more, Cincinnati has been a center for the manufacture of products used by other manufacturers to make consumer goods. From staplers and sifters to grinders and gears, Cincinnati is a machine and tool maker for both the nation and the world.

These individual stories of people and companies are collectively instructive regarding the city's unique history and economy—its pork-packing beginnings, the role of the river, the city's location in the heartland of the nation on the borderline between North and South. They demonstrate, too, that a city never leaves its history behind. Processing and distributing agricultural commodities remain significant sources of employment today. The Ohio River, so fundamentally important to the city's early growth, now handles more tonnage than the Panama Canal. And more livestock is slaughtered annually in Cincinnati today than when the city was widely known as Porkopolis.

Challenged by more rapid growth in southern and western cities, jolted by corporate takeovers and leveraged buyouts, and occasionally perplexed by public companies going private and private companies going public, Cincinnati nonetheless presents a picture of economic stability. It boasts 13 *Fortune* 500 companies, 11 of which are profiled in this section. Also included are about half of the city's 50 largest employers and about half of its 20 fastest-growing public companies. Complementing this picture are biographies of four of the 10 largest law firms, six of its 15 largest hospitals and the two largest universities in the area.

Collectively the corporate and community sponsors of this bicentennial edition of *Cincinnati: The Queen City* provide a reasonable profile of the city's economy that supports a population of 360,000 at the center of an eight-county metropolitan area with a population of 1.69 million. Ranked 27th among the nation's urban centers, Cincinnati is located within 600 miles of two-thirds of the nation's population, purchasing power and manufacturing establishments.

While the city's dream in the 1830s and 1840s of becoming the greatest city in the nation has long since been abandoned, Cincinnatians have succeeded in building one of the country's most livable cities, and one of its most beautiful as well. With a dynamic downtown and rapidly expanding suburbs, an efficient government and a stable, profitable and diversified economy, Cincinnatians take great pride in their city. Its corporate leaders, too, have built a solid reputation of commitment to their city that extends beyond business activities to the quality of Cincinnati's cultural, recreational and human-service institutions.

The celebration of Cincinnati's bicentennial in 1988 reflected these characteristics of the city. Six years of planning and millions of dollars in fund-raising resulted in a wide array of special events in addition to the completion of a new riverfront recreation area. Over the course of the year, hundreds of visitors joined in festivities that frequently attracted national attention. The memories of this year, which has served to deepen the city's pride and strengthen its sense of community, may be the celebration's most enduring legacy, for these qualities are vital resources as Cincinnati faces the challenges of its third century.

The Cincinnati Historical Society expresses its appreciation to 88 corporate and community sponsors for their assistance in publishing this Bicentennial Edition of *Cincinnati: The Queen City*.

Acme Wrecking Company

The Acme Wrecking Company was founded in 1953 by Schuyler J. Smith, who really got into the wrecking business by accident.

Following his discharge from the Army in 1946, Smith established a pony keg in Walnut Hills, employing neighborhood youths. Since the pony keg proved only moderately profitable, he closed down and opened a dry cleaning business at Lincoln and Gilbert avenues instead. Then he expanded next door with a men's clothing store.

As a sideline Smith and a friend took on small wrecking jobs. Profits from their first assignment, demolishing a carriage house in Cincinnati, were so good that Smith decided to enter the demolition business full time.

Acme's first office was a one-room building with a wood stove on Wehrman Avenue near Whittier Street. Preparations for the construction of Interstate 71 forced the company out of that location. However, business increased steadily, and Smith was able to purchase several adjoining lots down the street, at the corner of Syracuse and Wehrman avenues.

Smith's wife Grace typed contracts and prepared company correspondence from a small basement office in their home, simultaneously caring for their three daughters, Stephany, Schuyler Jeanne and Annette, who later would join the family business.

The 1960s brought prosperity to the Acme Wrecking Company. The firm built new offices on the Syracuse property after winning several major contracts, including the demolition of the Globe-Wernicke buildings and the Allis Chalmers plant in Norwood. Soon Procter & Gamble, General Motors and the City of Cincinnati became clients.

These contracts were an integral part of Acme's transition from residential demolition to industrial dismantling, which remains its specialty today.

Thanks to many changes that occurred with the enforcement of affirmative action and Smith's excellent reputation in the business, Acme continued to grow during the 1970s. Smith was a charter member of the National Association of Demolition Contractors, the industry's trade organization, and became its first black director.

By the early 1970s Acme had a dozen full-time employees and a fleet of trucks, cranes, excavating and loading equipment. Contracts included The Crane & Breed Casket Co. on Eighth Street; Longview State Hospital; the downtown Greyhound Bus Terminal; Block D West (Harry's Corner), the future site of Convention Place; renovation of the Cincinnati Convention & Visitors Center; and the removal of tracks and trestles at the Union Terminal for its development into a shopping center.

Acme also demolished the Eastwood Village housing project, now the headquarters site of U.S. Shoe. The Jim Beam Distillery of National Distiller's (now Quantum Corp.) became a steady client when it began a series of mergers and sales in the early 1980s.

Schuyler Jeanne Smith, who joined the company in 1973, was named vice president in 1984. After 10 years in management consulting, the Smiths' youngest daughter, Annette, joined the firm as project manager for field operations. In addition to working in this capacity, she also serves as corporate secretary/treasurer.

With his daughters' help, Smith was able to realize Acme's expansion potential in other areas. Today Schuyler Jeanne is also president of J.M. Harris Contractors, and Annette is president of the Acme Metals Co., both subsidiaries of Acme Wrecking Co. Harris Contractors is housed next door to the Syracuse Street headquarters, and Acme Metals occupies the old Modern Laundry building which burned during during the 1968 race riots.

The major contracts that the Acme Wrecking Company won during the 1960s changed its focus from residential to industrial dismantling. Photograph courtesy of Acme Wrecking.

American Financial Corporation

Whatever your scenario for the American Dream might be, it surely is a rags-to-riches story. The history of American Financial Corporation could give Horatio Alger a run for the money. Few Cincinnati institutions have had so much written about them as American Financial. Few have been both praised and damned so enthusiastically. Few have reached its size. None has been so much the child of a single family.

AFC is a family thing. There are three brothers and a sister. The public leader of the family is Carl, yet in a sense he is not public at all. This two-sides-of-the-coin condition shows up in almost everything connected with AFC and its chief executive.

The story begins in the depression of the 1930s. The Lindner family enterprise was a dairy in Norwood. Times were hard, and the entire family—Carl, Robert and Dick—had to pitch in, working before school delivering milk and late into the evenings. To Carl it meant dropping out of high school.

Through hard work the little store grew to almost 200 stores, many of them housed in small shopping centers that the family built. Carl Lindner borrowed money to expand the dairy business and borrowed more to build shopping strips and malls. Money became a familiar tool to him. At 36 Carl became a member of the board of directors of the Central Trust Company.

United Dairy Farmers—the corporate name of the one-time dairy store—became a multi-million-dollar business, but acquaintances believe that Carl's first love became banking when he saw that there was more to be made handling money than in retailing milk.

American Financial Corporation was organized in 1959, when the Lindners acquired three small savings and loans that were combined as the Hunter Savings Association. It became a public company in 1961 and developed into a notable financial holding company, the vehicle by which the family became involved in an even greater variety of enterprises.

Carl H. Lindner, chairman of the board and president of American Financial Corporation. Photograph courtesy of *The Cincinnati Post.*

The company entered the insurance business in 1962 and in 1966 gained control of Provident Bank, which had been established around the turn of the century by grocery chain founder Barney Kroger. Provident stock was subsequently distributed to AFC shareholders in 1971.

In 1974 AFC acquired Great American Insurance Co. by purchasing its parent holding company. For a time AFC owned *The Cincinnati Enquirer.* The newspaper was sold to a communications company that later merged with the Gannett chain.

AFC's assets now take the form of substantial investments in other companies. The list of its holdings changes frequently and becomes public only when they exceed 5% of an enterprise, the point at which the federal government dictates disclosure.

AFC returned to private status in 1981. Virtually all the stock is now owned by members of the Carl Lindner family. Richard chose to go his independent way as the operator of the Thriftway supermarket chain; Robert took over direction of UDF, and Carl continued to devote himself to making AFC grow.

Since 1981 AFC has gained significant interests in other firms, including Penn Central, United Brands, Great American Communications, Circle K Corporation and American General Corporation. In some cases the Lindners exercise overall control.

When Lindner gained control of major firms through AFC, he often moved their headquarters to Cincinnati, bringing both jobs and prestige to the city. The Los Angeles-based Great American Insurance Company was relocated to the Queen City following its acquisition by AFC in the mid-1970s. In the next decade the home offices of Penn Central and United Brands, including its John Morrell meat-packing and Chiquita Brands subsidiaries, were likewise brought here.

AFC's acquisition of the troubled Home State Savings in 1985 was partially intended to prevent major losses by depositors and foster a positive image of the Cincinnati business community's problem-solving abilities.

Carl Lindner himself is often sketched as a reticent man, without emotions. This reputation stems mostly from his refusal to talk to the media about his business. The other side of the coin shows a far more human personality.

He attributes his success to his sharing with his employees through stock distributions, options and appreciation rights. He is a Baptist, and his family's gifts to Baptist institutions are in the millions. But he also is generous to institutions of other religious denominations. He is the United States' largest non-Jewish contributor to Jewish causes. Other benefactions include Lindner Hall at the University of Cincinnati and The Christ Hospital, for which he has purchased several major pieces of diagnostic equipment.

When the effort to establish a bank operated by blacks was about to founder, the Lindners provided the rescue money. When drop-outs and an apparent mismatch threatened the success of the Davis Cup Finals held in Cincinnati, Lindner bought 10,000 tickets for his employees. He once bought out a performance of the financially shaky Cincinnati Ballet Company for an employee Christmas party.

Nor has the ice cream store in Norwood been forgotten. Carl Lindner was the largest single purchaser of "I love Norwood" stickers when that city essayed an image-building program.

Amko Plastics Inc.

Greater Cincinnati's modern history has been filled with enterprise in plastics. Some local companies produce raw materials; others process plastic resins into "intermediate structures" that are incorporated into finished products; and still other firms manufacture finished plastic products. Many distributors of plastic products provide local warehousing of thousands of plastic materials and products.

Cincinnati's plastics industry is responsible for the creation of thousands of new jobs. At the root of the industry's growth has been the development of exciting new technologies, equipment and products designed to meet a continually increasing demand for new plastic products to replace paper, glass and metal.

Amko Plastics Inc. manufactures specialty printed plastic bags used in retail store packaging, industrial packaging, medical services and consumer products sales. It also markets the products and services of consumer advertisers through the automatic insertion of advertising and promotional materials into the bags that it manufactures.

The firm was founded in Cincinnati in 1966 by Irvin and Janet Makrauer. After 25 years of innovative contribution to another firm, Irvin combined economic necessity with an entrepreneurial spirit and a similarly talented spouse, establishing a small manufacturing plant in Corryville.

Irvin had been an inventor of plastic garment bags in roll form in the 1950s. This product revolutionized dry-cleaner packaging and protection of garments. Subsequent improvements in the packaging of bread, produce, meats as well as industrial and consumer products established his personal reputation for innovative leadership. This tradition still provides a solid foundation for Amko's research and development successes.

In its industry Amko has led in the development of technologies and products that serve both its customers and the community at large. Amko developed new production techniques in 1970 that revolutionized the manufacture of specialty drawstring bags. In 1979 Amko introduced to the industry a new plastic film bag whose production and use conserved energy and offered more strength at the same time.

From 1984 through 1987 Amko led the flexographic printing industry development of water-based ink printing systems to reduce air pollution by replacing alcohol with water as the solvent. And Amko was the first bag producer in the United States to develop and nationally introduce degradable plastic bags in response to international concerns about solid waste disposal and litter reduction.

The Greater Cincinnati Chamber of Commerce voted Irvin Makrauer the Small Business Person of the year in 1977. After his death in 1983, his wife Janet became Amko's president and was selected Ohio's Small Business Person in 1985. In 1986 their son, George A. Makrauer, became Amko's president and chief executive officer.

Today Amko continues to work hard to maintain its commitment to establishing long-term relationships with its customers, employees, suppliers and the Greater Cincinnati community at large.

From its inception, Amko's commitment and daily attention to quality, innovation and service stimulated productive growth. New products were developed to better serve customers' packaging needs; new production techniques were developed to allow more competitive and profitable operation, and new jobs were generated to support the growing company.

Although its original headquarters only took up 5,000 square feet of space, by 1977 Amko had outgrown a multi-story, 50,000-square-foot Corryville location and opened a new plant and office in Springdale. Amko occupied over 200,000 square feet in 1988, with plans for additional expansion.

Samples of plastic bags manufactured by Amko Plastics Inc. Photograph. Courtesy of Amko Plastics Inc.

Anderson Publishing Company

William Harvey Anderson, founder and first president of Anderson Publishing Company.

The Anderson Publishing Company, publisher of Ohio law books and national legal publications, is one of Cincinnati's oldest book publishing companies, having celebrated its 100th birthday in 1987. The company spent its first century on Main Street before moving to its new headquarters on Reading Road in 1988.

Book publishing was among Cincinnati's leading industries when William Harvey Anderson started his publishing company in 1887. Anderson had worked as a salesman for publisher and bookseller Robert Clarke for 20 years before opening the W.H. Anderson Company at 524 Main Street in a building that he designed himself. From the beginning Anderson specialized in legal publications, especially Ohio law books. He purchased Clarke's law book titles in 1908.

W.H. Anderson served as president of the firm until 1930, and during his tenure he published several books and series that still are popular today. These include *The Law Dictionary*, first published in 1888, and *Pages' Ohio Revised Code Annotated*, first issued in 1912.

The company's second and third presidents, Edwin P. Coke (1930-1936), one of the original incorporators of the company, and Clifford W. Mueller (1936-1950), whose first job at the company was as an errand boy, led Anderson Publishing through the Great Depression and were able to add numerous titles. These included *Thornton's Law of Oil and Gas*, which has become one of Anderson's best-selling national publications. Other prominent national publications include *Federal Antitrust Law* and an eight-volume, 11-book set, *Page on Wills.*

George C. Trautwein (1950-1964) was the company's fourth president, and more than 50 new or revised titles were added under his leadership. During this period the company outgrew its original building and moved to 646 Main. The fifth president, John L. Skirving, served from 1964 to 1974, adding several national publications including Anderson's first law journals, the *Journal of Law and Education* and the *Journal of Maritime Law and Commerce.*

The current president, John L. Mason, has overseen the development of Anderson's new Criminal Justice Division, which publishes books for the college market. Unlike the standard law books, which are primarily sold to lawyers, law libraries, law schools and government offices, the criminal justice books are marketed to professors of criminal justice, university book stores, police academies and correctional training facilities. The nearly 50 titles on this list include *Organized Crime in America, Fundamentals of Criminal Justice Research* and *Probation and Parole in Practice.*

The beginning of the company's second century has also been marked by a move into electronic publishing. Legal forms are now published in printed and software versions under the copyrighted name "Lawriter." In addition Anderson's *Automated Social History* software allows psychologists, probation officers and mental health workers to generate social histories from standardized questionnaires.

Anderson Publishing Company currently employs 90 people and completes all editorial and marketing aspects of the publishing business in its new Reading Road office. While most manuscripts are written by outside authors, in-house lawyers and legal scholars research and write many publications. Book design and typesetting are also in-house activities, while outside firms handle printing and binding.

The company is proud of its stability; it has never laid off an employee and has had only six presidents in 101 years. W.H. Anderson's "family-oriented" employee policies and his long-standing commitment to quality, service and "Good Law Books" still govern company standards. The Anderson Publishing Co. remains one of the last independently owned legal publishers in the United States.

Anderson Publishing Company occupied this building at 524 Main Street for nearly a century.

Illustration and photograph. Courtesy of Anderson Publishing Company.

The Atkins & Pearce Manufacturing Company

John and Henry Pearce began their careers as artists in the South, traveling from plantation to plantation painting portraits. Originally from Cornwall, England, these brothers were not only creative, but also mechanically inclined. During their travels they noticed workers using a crude form of Eli Whitney's cotton gin. Being imaginative young entrepreneurs, they decided they could go one step further.

They devised an adaptation to the cotton gin and were so pleased with the results that they decided to manufacture it. In 1817 they started their company in Cincinnati, reasoning that the city was already an established trade center with easy access to both the plantations lining the Mississippi and a supply of skilled workers. Atkins & Pearce was one of the first manufacturing concerns established west of the Alleghenies. The early days of the company were devoted to the manufacture of cotton ginning, carding and spinning machinery. Some of the original Pearce machines have been preserved and are on display at the Ford Museum in Dearborn, Michigan; the Smithsonian Institute; and the Presbyter Museum in New Orleans.

During the 1830s a nephew, Henry Pearce, came from England, bringing his expertise in spinning and enabling the company to convert raw cotton into cloth. As the Civil War halted all trade to the South, Henry's cotton processing expertise changed the direction of the company and brought it new life. By 1875 there were over 10,000 spindles in operation, processing a complete line of cotton yarns. By the end of the Civil War, the Pearce family had moved out of the machine business and into the processing of cotton.

John and Henry Pearce called their business the Pearce Bros. Co. Their nephew, Henry, succeeded them, devoting much of his spare time to civic affairs. He was a member of the first board of McMicken University, a founder of the old Marine Hospital and a director of the Mechanics Institute. For nine years he was president of the City Water Works Board, and it was during his tenure and through his influence that Eden Park was purchased and the reservoir constructed. His sons and son-in-law, Harry Thomas Atkins, took over the business in the next generation and changed its name to Henry Pearce's Sons. In 1880 the company again was renamed, becoming The Atkins & Pearce Manufacturing Company. Eventually the firm abandoned its spinning operations in favor of developing and manufacturing industrial textiles.

The firm's first location was on the corner of Seventh and Smith streets. In 1827 the plant was moved to George Street between Central and John, staying there until the 1840s when James and Henry Pearce sold the old site and moved to the corner of Fifth and Lock to take advantage of the water from the Ohio-Erie Canal. For years the canal ran through the plant, providing power to run the machinery. In 1965 the company purchased the former warehouse and general offices of White Villa Grocers, Inc. at Pearl and Pike streets. Atkins & Pearce remained there until its new facility opened in Covington in 1986.

The company has always reflected the changes in the American scene. In the early days workmen lived so close to the plant that they were called to work by a large bell placed on the factory's roof. During World War II Atkins & Pearce manufactured parachute cords and other cotton goods used in the war effort. At one time demand was so great that the company operated 24 hours a day, seven days a week, shipping the product by plane to U.S. forces in western Germany.

Today Atkins & Pearce is the world's largest producer of precision-braided textiles, using both natural and man-made fibers. At its new six-and-one-half acre plant in Covington, Kentucky, the company specializes in the field of braided narrow fabrics, operating more than 6,000 individual braiding machines with over 10,000 pieces of yarn processing and support equipment.

Most products are custom-engineered to meet exact specifications. They include electrical and thermal insulating sleeving; sleeving for mechanical reinforcement and filtration applications; lacing cords and tapes for wiring harnesses; decorative trim braids; and candlewicking, the company's original braided product. In addition, the firm converts high tech fibers into standard braided sleevings and tapes as well as complex and irregular braided preforms. Atkins & Pearce continues to develop new ways to group and orient fibers into usable fabrics and forms for composites.

The company also has developed fiber handling techniques and machinery enabling it to create fabric constructions for reinforcement in composite applications. For example, it helped Huffy and the U.S. Cycling team reduce the total weight of their bicycles by using braided preforms for some cycle components.

The aerospace industry also relies on precision-wound braider packages from Atkins & Pearce for rocket casings that employ a braided fabric of specially prepared fiberglass. Flat braided tapes are purchased by the aircraft/aerospace industry for use in wire harnesses. The electric motor industry also depends on Atkins & Pearce for twisted and braided cord.

The firm that began supplying candlewicking to candlemakers more than 130 years ago has maintained a dominant position in the domestic market and supplies over 120 different types of wicks to customers in England, Ireland, Scandinavia and South America.

Glass sleeving is sold to insulation specialists who coat and prepare the material for use in thermal and mechanical applications for the electrical and electronics industries and, increasingly, automotive markets. In addition, the firm supplies packaged yarns that are twisted and/or plied to customer specifications and then precision-wound onto braider packages for thermal, electrical and mechanical applications.

Although Atkins & Pearce thrives on the continued challenges of fulfilling the specific needs of individual companies, it also helps manufacture everyday products, including toasters, coffee makers, golf clubs, tennis rackets and personal computers. The firm remains a dominant supplier of braid and braid-related products. It continues to develop its export business and to explore new uses for braiding technology in the production of high-performance materials and components.

Cotton went into the top of this Pearce spinning gin and was spun out as yarn. One of the original machines of Atkins & Pearce, it is now on display at the Smithsonian Institution in Washington, D.C. Photograph. Courtesy of Atkins & Pearce.

The G.A. Avril Company

Lose this day loitering, 'twill be the same old story tomorrow, and the next day more dilatory. Each indecision brings its own delays, and days are lost lamenting o'er lost days. What you can do, or dream you can. Begin it. Boldness has genius, power and magic in it.

Goethe

With this inspiring advice that he kept framed on parchment on his office wall, George Anton Avril founded the G.A. Avril Smelting Works in August 1923. A World War I Army veteran and electrical engineering student, University of Cincinnati class of 1920, George had gone to work for the Brewer Company, a local processor of brass foundry waste. After several years he was earning six dollars a week. When he asked for a raise he was turned down, prompting his decision to follow Goethe's admonition to "Begin."

Shortly thereafter, with a $2,000 loan from his father, George and one employee lit up and charged a small furnace to alloy the first "heat" of brass ingot by the G.A. Avril Smelting Works. The establishment was located at 2818 Spring Grove Avenue, Camp Washington. The furnace room where melting, refining and alloying was performed was in the basement.

The firm's location was good for business. Just down the street was the J.H. Day Co., G.A. Avril's first customer for brass foundry alloys. George delivered the alloyed ingot personally in a wheelbarrow. Next door was Reliable Castings. To the south, across the street and two blocks down, was the William Powell Company, the first brass foundry west of the Alleghenies. The Schaible Foundry and Brass Works, The John Douglas Company, Lunkenheimer, D.T. Williams, Queen City Valve and Ohio Pattern Works also were nearby. Some say that more brass was cast in that two-mile stretch of the Mill Creek Valley between Colerain Avenue and Beekman Street than in any other similarly sized area in the country. This was George's market.

The company quickly replaced the wheelbarrow with a delivery truck and installed larger furnaces to increase production capacity. The business survived the Great Depression but had difficulties operating during the recurring floods of the Mill Creek Valley that inundated the basement furnace room. In 1936 George had the opportunity to buy the property occupied by his brother Arthur's company, Avril Trubatch, on the southern edge of St. Bernard in Winton Place. Sensing the advantage of high ground still in the industrial valley, he built a new one-floor smelting plant designed to facilitate and augment the unique nature of the manufacturing processes.

But "Black Sunday," January 24, 1937, put three feet of water in the new G.A. Avril Smelting Works. Flood waters reached a depth of approximately six feet on Este Avenue in front of the plant. Had it still been in Camp Washington, the company might not have survived.

World War II and the loss of many skilled employees to the military services challenged the company as never before. Its raw materials—tin, copper, nickel, zinc and lead—were in short supply and on allocation. The plant operated around the clock to keep the alloys flowing to the manufacturers of strategic war materials. In addition to maintaining production at the plant, George served as the brass and bronze ingot industry representative on an advisory committee to the War Production Board in Washington, charged with overseeing the smooth transition from peacetime free markets to wartime commitments.

In retrospect perhaps the greatest innovation that the company implemented in the 1940s was use of the fork truck. The ability to palletize, pick up and transport raw materials and finished alloy ingot with the fork truck eliminated the shovel, the wheelbarrow, cumbersome high-wheel buggies and hours of back-breaking work. Mechanized pouring of molten metal into ingot mold conveyors and installation of large rotary furnaces completed the transition from a labor-intensive operation.

In 1946 George was joined in the business by his son, Thomas B. Avril, a World War II Navy veteran. The firm incorporated and changed its name to The G.A. Avril Company, focusing on refining brass and bronze scrap.

Brass and bronze alloys consist of copper as the main element with varying amounts of other metallic elements such as tin, lead, zinc, nickel, aluminum, silicon and iron. The various alloys are blended to specifications developed to provide desired mechanical and physical properties. While in a molten state in the furnace at approximately 2,300 degrees fahrenheit, a refining process is employed to remove impurities. The metal is poured into molds to cast it into ingots which are in turn sold to foundries around the country.

Over the years the range of alloys manufactured has increased to about 40, and today the company's products are found in plumbing fittings, valves, marine hardware, gears, bearings, power transmission hardware, pumps, decorative architectural and art bronze work, paper making machinery, mining machinery, soap molds and molds for high volume glass bottle machinery – anything in which the physical properties of brass and bronze meet the requirements for quality and service.

In 1953 the company entered a related industry through the purchase of the Lead Products Division from the Eagle-Picher Company, located at the corner of Langdon Farm Road and Seymour Avenue in Bond Hill. This acquisition added tin lead alloys, solders, lead plumbing materials and fittings, babbitts, plating anodes, cable sleeving, came lead for stained glass and special shape counter weights to the company's manufacturing capacity.

In 1956 John G. Avril, after Naval service, joined with his father and brother in the business. Three years later the two sons took over the day-to-day management of the company. Plant expansion and modernization continued into the 1980s with the addition of more efficient furnaces, refining techniques and labor-saving methods.

Today the company serves a regional market extending east to New England, south to the Gulf of Mexico, west to the Rocky Mountains and north to the Great Lakes. G.A. Avril's bronze was selected for use in the casting of Cincinnatus, the statue and one of the focal points of the Bicentennial Commons. Sixty-five years of Avril employees have a share in that accomplishment. G.A. Avril remains family owned, managed and operated. It looks forward to the 1990s with great confidence in the strength of the local economy.

George Anton Avril, founder of the G.A. Avril Smelting Works.

A worker stands in front of the original factory building of the G.A. Avril Smelting Works on Spring Grove Avenue.

Photographs. Courtesy of the G.A. Avril Company.

Bartlett & Co.

Bartlett & Co. traces its heritage back to 1898, when Benjamin D. Bartlett purchased a seat on the New York Stock Exchange. Bartlett was a partner in George Eustis & Co., then the oldest investment house in Cincinnati, dating back to 1862. Bartlett continued with the Eustis firm until 1923, when the partnership was divided and Bartlett remained to carry on the business under his own name.

In 1926 Bartlett sold his investment firm to two new partners, Marcus (Mike) Fechheimer and Herbert R. Bloch. Later Joseph Marks and John R. Lewis also became members of the firm. Bartlett & Co. expanded to include Alfred J. Friedlander in 1929 and Joseph B. Reynolds in 1936. The new Bartlett partners were all prominent men, active in many aspects of Cincinnati's civic and business life.

Fechheimer, from the Krohn-Fechheimer Shoe Co. family, was first of the new partners to die; he collapsed while out for a gallop on his horse. Bloch had been a wholesale clothier and served on the board of Shillito's, among other firms. His son, Herbert Jr., became a senior executive with Federated Stores. Lewis, who had been associated with Bloch before joining Bartlett, held a long list of offices in Masonry and the Shrine.

Friedlander, the son of Dr. Alfred Friedlander, once dean of the U.C. medical school, was a partner for 37 years, all the while making his mark as a patron and fund-raiser for hospitals, charities and the arts. And Reynolds, who had organized a brokerage firm before he became a Bartlett partner, remained there until he died in 1977 at age 81. He was at one time also president of Vulcan Corp., a director of other

companies and a prominent supporter of Catholic charities.

The new Bartlett began to take form in 1957, when it absorbed J.E. Bennett & Co., with Jean Bennett and Charles Snyder joining the Bartlett partnership. Later the investment firms of W.P. Clancy & Co. and James E. Madigan & Co. were also absorbed by Bartlett & Co.

First of the present generation of Bartlett partners, Bruce R. Davies, joined the firm in 1954, and Alfred Friedlander's son, William, started in 1957 and became managing partner in 1967.

Bartlett's services and investment role has also evolved over the last 90 years. Originally a stock and bond brokerage firm, Bartlett became an investment advisory firm in 1946. By virtue of this change in direction, which really was quite innovative in its day, Bartlett is among the longest lived advisory firms in the nation. At the time of original registration, there were a total of 26 registered private investment advisors in the country; today the industry encompasses about 12,000 firms.

In 1986, after nearly 90 years in three buildings at various locations along Fourth Street, Bartlett & Co. purchased, renovated and moved into the Bartlett Building at the northwest corner of Fourth and Walnut streets, the very same place where Benjamin D. Bartlett & Co. began the firm in 1898.

Today's Bartlett & Co.'s investment advisory services have expanded to include not only management of individual investment portfolios, but also mutual funds and real estate direct investments. The firm currently manages $1.5 billion for a variety of national and regional

corporations, non-profit institutions, as well as individuals, many of whom have been Bartlett clients for decades. Bartlett & Co. is also distinguished by the long tenure of its management team.

In keeping with today's sophisticated invest-

ment environment, the Bartlett investment support team has grown to include more than 100 people with state-of-the-art technology and a sophisticated research and analytical effort, all of which compliment the firm's disciplined investment process. Today Bartlett & Co.'s investment results place it among the premier investment firms in the United States.

Benjamin D. Barlett (1859-1927)

Herbert R. Bloch (1889-1957)

Alfred J. Friedlander (1903-1966)

Joseph R. Reynolds (1896-1977)

Bethesda Hospital, Inc.

In 1896 seven German Methodist deaconesses moved into a small cottage in Mount Auburn near the foot of Auburn Avenue. They devoted their lives to caring for the sick and poor in the basin area of Cincinnati, often bringing people in need of constant nursing care directly to their home. Soon the overcrowded cottage became a makeshift miniature hospital.

Seeking better facilities the German Methodist Deaconess Home Association purchased a small, private hospital at the corner of Reading Road and Oak Street in 1898 and moved its patients to this location. This marked the beginning of Bethesda Hospital, Inc., Cincinnati's first private hospital.

Bethesda began as a 20-bed facility where the deaconesses tended the patients by nursing, cooking and doing laundry. The superintendent of the hospital from its founding through the early 1920s was Reverend Christian Golder. His sister, Louise, served as superintendent of the nurses and the deaconesses.

Under the leadership of the Golders, the hospital introduced several new programs that changed the way health care was provided in Cincinnati. It opened The Bethesda School of Nursing in 1899 with 10 students who were trained by doctors on the hospital staff. Today

the school enrolls more than 150 students in its 27-month diploma program and graduates over 50 nurses annually.

In the early 1900s Bethesda was one of the first hospitals in Cincinnati to offer maternity care. The small community hospital started doing so in 1898 and by 1902 expanded its maternity facilities by opening a large house on Reading Road that accommodated eight patients. Today approximately 5,000 babies a year are delivered at Bethesda.

In its long history Bethesda's maternity program has accomplished many "firsts," including allowing husbands to be with their wives during a Caesarean birth and offering a birthing room. Bethesda also started the first combined obstetrics and gynecology residency program for physicians in Cincinnati and offered the first classes in the Midwest for fathers. "For Fathers (and their babies) Only" is a program that encourages men to develop healthy, rewarding relationships with their babies.

The hospital introduced the community to long-term care for the elderly in 1919, when it opened the Bethesda Home for the Aged—Lafayette Hall—on the grounds of the Schoenberger mansion in Clifton. The 50-resident home was expanded in 1959, when it became known as Scarlet Oaks Manor. A new Health Center opened on the grounds in 1966, providing residents with nursing care and therapy. Today Scarlet Oaks Retirement Community offers a safe and secure living environment for about 350 older adults.

Bethesda was the first hospital in the county to open a freestanding outpatient surgery center; the first Cincinnati hospital to use a computerized electrocardiogram system; the first hospital in the Tri-State to offer a daytime outpatient diabetes management program; and the first area hospital to offer a teenage day treatment program for alcohol and drug rehabilitation.

The Bethesda Hospital complex on Reading Road and Oak Street includes numerous buildings including the Cincinnati Hospice, a facility for the terminally ill that opened in 1981 in the Golder-Gamble building, named for Louise Golder and Fanny Nast Gamble. Older buildings have been demolished over the years and a new nurses' dormitory, maternity wing, chapel, office building and out-patient surgery center constructed. A satellite hospital, Bethesda North, opened in Montgomery in 1970.

Special programs and facilities at Bethesda Hospital include family-centered maternity care (with a Level II Special Care Nursery); intensive care and coronary units; physical rehabilitation; psychiatric and mental health care; alcohol and drug rehabilitation programs; centers for cancer treatment, cardiac rehabilitation, diabetes care, fertility and sleep disorders; and outpatient surgery centers. Its corporate health services include health promotion, employee assistance and occupational nursing programs.

The Bethesda Hospital and Deaconess Association became Bethesda Inc. in 1983. Today Bethesda Hospital and its subsidiaries form one of the largest health care systems in Cincinnati, with more than 800 beds and seven occupational health centers, as well as its hospice and retirement community. Approximately 1,800 physicians are part of Bethesda Inc.'s team of 3,500 employees.

L. Thomas Wilburn Jr. is chairman, president and chief executive office of Bethesda Hospital, Inc. Larry W. Collins is senior vice president of Bethesda Oak Hospital, 619 Oak Street in Avondale. And William F. Groneman is senior vice president of Bethesda North Hospital, 10500 Montgomery Road in Montgomery.

Bethesda North Hospital opened in 1970.

Photographs. Courtesy of Bethesda Hospital, Inc.

The Bethesda Oak Hospital complex has been situated at Oak Street and Reading Road since 1898.

William Cargile Contractors, Inc.

William Cargile, founder and president of Cincinnati's first black contracting firm. Photograph courtesy of William Cargile Contractors.

The company established in 1953 by William Cargile III holds many "firsts" in Cincinnati history: Cargile was the first black contractor to perform work for the cities of Cincinnati, Norwood and St. Bernard; the first black contractor to build here for the U.S. Army Corp of Engineers; the first black construction firm in Greater Cincinnati to be awarded a contract from the U.S. Veteran's Administration and first in the Midwest to qualify for the Small Business Administration 8(a) program.

A native of Union Springs, Alabama, William Cargile III stopped in Cincinnati in 1947 en route to California to seek his fortune. He never left. Cargile took a job in construction, found the field to his liking and served in the first apprenticeship class held by the cement masons in Cincinnati area. He also took course work at the Ohio Mechanics Institute and University of Cincinnati to further his knowledge of business, construction and engineering.

In 1953 Cargile established his own company, Cargile Cement Contractor. The early years were difficult ones, but with the aid and encouragement of his family, Cargile persevered. He established a reputation for quality work and performance that enabled him to obtain the bonding required to bid on large jobs and public works. In 1961 he won a City of Cincinnati contract for the concrete work in the Findlay Street Market renovation. And although Cargile lost money, it was an important, highly visible job that provided a major breakthrough for the struggling young company.

Bill Cargile was determined to broaden his expertise beyond cement and concrete work, a trade that historically had been assigned and open to blacks. He made a concerted effort to be allowed to bid on all types of building and highway construction, gaining valuable experience in those areas along with historic restoration and remodeling. In 1968 the name of the company was changed to Cargile Contractors, Inc., in recognition of the broadened scope of the firm's activities. The company grew as its reputation became known and as the opportunities for minority contractors expanded.

Cargile has completed many major jobs in the last three decades, including the Elm Street Health Clinic, the U.S. Veteran's Administration Medical Center in Dayton, the St. Bernard Police Station, Millcreek Flood Wall for the U.S. Army Corps of Engineers and the State of Ohio Workman's Compensation Building in Columbus. Cargile Contractors, Inc. took its first construction manager project as a joint venture with Turner Construction for the expansion of the Cincinnati Convention Center, completed in 1986, and it is a partner with Frank Messer & Sons Construction Company for the renovation of Cincinnati Union Terminal, which will become a museum complex housing The Cincinnati Historical Society and the Cincinnati Museum of Natural History. Cargile Contractors has expanded the geographic area of its operations considerably, being one of the prime subcontractors for what is currently the largest job in the country, the U.S. Army Corps of Engineers base at Ft. Drum, New York.

Over the years Cargile has developed several construction-related companies that operate under the name of Cargile Enterprises; they include Wm. Cargile Contractors, Inc. and Cargile Supply Company in Cincinnati, and Cargile Builders, Inc. in West Palm Beach. The entire Cargile family—Bill's wife, Novella, and five children—is actively involved in the success of Cargile companies. Mrs. Cargile is vice president and a member of the board of directors of Wm. Cargile Contractors, Inc.; Kimberly is president of Cargile Builders, Inc.; William IV is president of Contractors Four, Inc.; and Carol, Jimmie and Jeffrey work in Wm. Cargile Contractors, Inc. Carol is also a psychologist on the faculty at the University of Cincinnati.

Bill Cargile is active in a number of local, state and national organizations, particularly those that seek to foster economic opportunities for minorities. He was the founder and first president of the United Minority Contractors Association of Cincinnati (est. 1968) and is currently a consultant for the national organization's Big-Brother program, which sends mentors all over the country to assist aspiring minority contractors in such areas as preparing bids and securing bonds. In addition he is a member of St. John's Lodge, the Association of Ohio Commodores, the advisory board of the 1988 Ohio Black Expo and the Black Male Coalition.

Cargile also regularly sponsors athletic, educational and human service projects for youths, especially in the black community. He sponsored the Miss Black Teen Cincinnati pageant, the Curry Cargile Lions baseball team—which won the Continental Amateur Baseball Association World Series in 1984-1985, and has been a scoutmaster for Pack 292. And once he purchased groceries for an entire neighborhood of 200 families whose refrigerated food supply had spoiled during a power outage.

A member and past board member of the Greater Cincinnati Chamber of Commerce, Cargile won the Greater Cincinnati YMCA Black Achiever of the Year award in 1981. He has been recognized as one of the top 100 black businessmen in the nation by ***Black Enterprise Magazine*** for the past six years.

Carlisle Companies, Inc.

What began as a two-man inner tube plant during World War I is now listed among the 500 largest U.S. industrial corporations as ranked by *Fortune* magazine.

Carlisle Companies Incorporated manufactures and distributes products of rubber, plastic and metal content for industry, both components used by other companies in the manufacture of capital and consumer goods and those for the aftermarket. The leading producer or among the leading producers of many of its lines, Carlisle currently employs 4,200 people, and its corporate headquarters has been in Cincinnati since 1971.

The firm was incorporated as Carlisle Tire & Rubber Company in September 1917 by Charles S. Moomy and James T. Johnstone in Carlisle, Pennsylvania. Moomy was experienced in the manufacture of inner tubes, and Johnstone was a New York rubber broker and merchant. Together with a small amount of cash and machinery, the founders began to produce inner tubes in a leased brick mill building under an agreement with Montgomery Ward.

The business grew and prospered until the depression of 1921, when it as well as many other rubber companies in the United States had financial difficulties. It lived through this, however, and a few years later acquired land for expansion adjacent to the original site. In the late 1920s the company developed the first commercial, full-molded inner tube process in the world, which became the basis for later growth. During the 1930s Carlisle Tire & Rubber Company again suffered reverses and did not completely recover until the next decade.

In 1944 Carlisle Tire & Rubber Company was acquired by Pharis Tire & Rubber Company, a tire manufacturer in Newark, Ohio that was in need of additional inner tube production facilities. With construction of plant and equipment limited because of World War II, acquisition of Carlisle was the easiest way for Pharis to secure the additional capacity it needed.

Carlisle was run as a subsidiary of Pharis until 1949, when Pharis ceased operations because of a difficult labor strike that lasted for three months. In that year Pharis transferred its bicycle tire production equipment to Carlisle Tire & Rubber Company along with the assets and business of Molded Materials Company, a brake lining manufacturer located in Ridgway, Pennsylvania. The name Carlisle Tire & Rubber Company was changed to Carlisle Corporation, and two operating divisions were designated as Carlisle Tire & Rubber Division and Molded Materials Division.

In 1949 Pharis distributed the Carlisle Corporation stock to its own stockholders and liquidated its business in Newark, Ohio. Carlisle became a public company with its stock trading on the Curb Exchange. The stock was listed on the New York Stock Exchange in April 1960.

Since its formation Carlisle has sustained an impressive growth record by finding new product niches for its relatively unglamorous product lines and by gradually acquiring new businesses that complement the old. Along the way the company has dropped many of its original lines because of changing technologies and increased competition, principally foreign, that rendered the margins too low to justify continuing production.

In 1986 the firm was reorganized as a holding company with the name Carlisle Companies Incorporated. Today Carlisle is made up of 12 separate operating units with over 20 plant sites in 14 states. Its operations and product lines include: Carlisle SynTec Systems and Geauga Company, both of which produce construction materials; Braemar Corporation, Data Electronics Incorporated, Digital Controls Corporation, DSI Incorporated, Graham Magnetics Incorporated, Tensolite Company and Zetaco, Inc., dealing in data communications and electronics; and Carlisle Tire & Rubber Company, Continental Carlisle Incorporated, Geauga Company, and Motion Control Industries, Inc., which are part of the automotive/industrial industries.

One of the most significant internal developments in recent years has been the pioneering effort of Carlisle SynTec Systems in the development of single-ply, synthetic-rubber roofing systems for commercial/industrial use. The company's single-ply roofing systems last longer, require less maintenance and are price-competitive when compared with conventional asphalt built-up roofing. Carlisle SynTec not only got a head start on the big rubber companies in the mid-1970s and stayed there, but also pushed aside the old built-up roofing giants and ended up with a dominant position in the commercial/industrial roofing industry.

Carlisle's involvement in data communications/electronics markets extends back to the late 1950s, when a manufacturer of specialty wire and cable was acquired. Acquisitions completed since then, most in the mid-1980s, have contributed to a base of business currently amounting to about $200 million. Most products are specialty in nature and serve small niches in their respective markets.

Carlisle's automotive/industrial lines include products that it has manufactured for over 40 years. Carlisle was the first to introduce non-asbestos brake lining to the heavy duty truck market in the late 1970s and currently has a leading market share position.

In 1988 Stephen P. Munn became president and chief executive officer of the company, succeeding Malcolm C. Myers, who had been chief executive officer since 1970. George F. Dixon Jr. retired from his position as chairman of the board and was succeeded by Myers.

Headquartered in Cincinnati since 1971, Carlisle Companies, Inc. is made up of more than 20 plants in 14 states.

The Central Trust Company

The name Central Trust appeared here on the company's first offices at 111-115 East Fourth Street in 1917.

The Central Trust Company, N.A. (National Association) traces its roots to 1862, when the Franklin Bank was incorporated with a state charter, and 1883, when the Fidelity Safe Deposit and Trust Company was chartered as the first trust company in Ohio. Fidelity's president, Julius Dexter, was an Ohio senator and chief architect of the original statute providing for the creation and regulation of trust companies in the state.

Trust services have remained an area of specialization over the years. Today Central Trust has one of the largest trust divisions in Ohio, with total assets exceeding $8.4 billion in June 1988. Proof of its continuing influence in trust services lies in its role as investment advisor to the Tecumseh family of mutual funds—money market, equity and bond portfolios with $600 million in assets at June 30, 1988.

Throughout its 125-year history, The Central Trust Company has continually broadened its financial services. As early as 1888 new bank services were emerging. Not only did the bank offer safe deposit and trust services; the company also was accepting savings deposits. Its official savings department opened in 1892. Other areas in which Central Trust has pioneered include common trust funds, consumer installment and small business loans, electronic and drive-in banking, direct leasing, securities trading, lines of credit, and international banking.

The now-familiar Central Trust Company name appeared in 1917. Two years later the firm moved from its original site at 111-115 East Fourth Street to the Central Trust Tower at Fourth and Vine, its headquarters for the next 60 years.

In 1898 Central Trust acquired the Cincinnati Safe Deposit and Trust Company; however, this type of expansion was not prevalent until the 1920s, when Central Trust acquired or merged with six other financial institutions. Total assets grew from $9.3 million in 1922 to $73.1 million by the end of 1930, when banking offices numbered 11. When Central Trust merged with Citizens National Bank in 1927, Central Trust President A. Clifford Shinkle became chairman of the board. Citizens' President Charles W. Dupuis served as the new firm's president through 1949 and then served another 10 years as chairman of the board.

Central Trust initiated branch banking in 1922 with the establishment of the East Hill office on Victory Parkway. By 1925 there were additional branches in Avondale, Mariemont and Price Hill. Expansion into the northern suburbs began in 1957 with the opening of the Brentwood Office. In 1960 there were 18 Central Trust locations; by 1970 there were 25.

The company's first automated teller machine was installed at its Northgate Office in 1973. Thereafter, electronic banking services grew rapidly in presence and popularity. The Owl automated teller network was formed in 1975 and by 1988 had become the sixth largest in the nation, with nearly 300 financial institutional members. Through its regional and national affiliations, The Owl makes available some 20,000 machines nationwide.

In 1968, under Fletcher E. Nyce, The Central Trust Company and Citizens National Bank of Marietta formed the Central Bancorporation, Inc. holding company, which became the parent organization of Central Trust. A year later, Oliver W. Birckhead was elected president and chief executive officer of Central Trust. He also became chief executive officer of Central Bancorporation in 1971.

During his tenure the bank converted from a state-chartered to a national bank in 1974, effecting its final name change to The Central Trust Company, N.A. In 1979 it moved into its new headquarters, the Central Trust Center at Fifth and Main streets. The bank grew from 26 to 51 banking offices, and total assets increased from $631 million to $2.6 billion. Adding to its growth was the 1979 merger of Central Bancorporation's Dayton bank, The Central Trust Company of Montgomery County, N.A., with the Cincinnati affiliate, forming one of five regional Central Bancorporation financial institutions serving the state of Ohio.

Then in 1985 the Southern Ohio Bank merged with Central Trust, creating the city's largest bank and adding 13 new branches. That same year Central Trust acquired Molitor Loan and Building Company followed by the Madison Savings Bank in 1986. Central Bancorporation next merged with PNC Financial Corp., a super-regional bank holding company headquartered in Pittsburgh. To Birckhead the 1988 merger was the high point of his 50 years in the banking business.

Gary N. Kocher, president and chief operating officer of Central Trust since January 1987, became chief executive officer in June of that year. Upon the PNC merger he also became president and chief executive officer of Central Bancorporation.

As of July 1988 Central Trust had $3.2 billion in total assets and 55 branch offices in Greater Cincinnati and Dayton. Central Bancorporation, with assets of $5.3 billion, operated some 130 banking offices through its seven regional banks serving Ohio and Northern Kentucky. And PNC Financial Corp., the nation's 12th largest bank holding company with assets of $37 billion, operated roughly 475 banking offices in Pennsylvania, Ohio, Kentucky, Indiana and New Jersey. PNC also conducts business in 19 states and nine foreign countries.

Central Trust moved to its new headquarters at Fifth and Main streets in 1979.

Photographs. Courtesy of Central Trust.

Chemed Corporation

Chemed Corporation, with two successful lives behind it, is thriving in its third—stronger and fresher than ever.

Chemed's origin lies primarily in the DuBois Soap Company; its middle years were spent as an arm of W.R. Grace & Co., and it now operates as a totally independent public company.

The DuBois Soap Company was started by Tunis Vanderveer DuBois, whose entire career was given to selling. The new Chemed Corporation is the work of Edward L. Hutton, its president and chief executive officer, who carefully reshaped DuBois' small but prosperous company into a dynamic and flourishing one.

T.V. DuBois came to Cincinnati in 1910 in search of a career. He found a job first at Philip Carey and then at the Hunnewell Soap Co., where he picked up management skills and began to yearn for his own company. In 1920, with a loan of $2,000, he started the DuBois Soap Company, later known as DuBois Chemicals.

DuBois' first plant, a four-story red brick building at the western end of what is now Mehring Way, made soap chips and powders for Cincinnati restaurants. A metal cleaner was among the first products that broadened the company's customer base during World War II.

Demand for DuBois' products continued to increase after the war. To accommodate this growth the company made its first acquisition—a West Coast firm—and moved its general offices to 634 Broadway. DuBois maintained its growth rate through international expansion into Canada and the British Isles and through its reputation for quality products and services, reflected in the DuBois motto, "Sell, Service, Satisfy."

DuBois' success made it a prime acquisition candidate, and on May 7, 1964, DuBois Chemicals Inc. became the DuBois Chemicals Division of W.R. Grace & Co., a New York-based conglomerate. Edward L. Hutton, then a vice president of W.R. Grace, became general manager of the DuBois Division and group executive of Grace's Specialty Products Group, of which DuBois was a part. New products were added to the DuBois product line; new plants and agencies were established to sell these products all over the world, and a new plant was built in Sharonville to handle increased demand.

In 1970 the company moved its general offices into the new 31-story DuBois Tower on Fountain Square. A year later Grace spun off its Specialty Products Group into the company known today as Chemed Corporation. Although Grace maintained 84% ownership, Chemed functioned fairly autonomously as a public entity. Hutton and staff embarked on an 11-year forging process, growing without straying from Chemed's basic philosophy of acquiring only those businesses that are people oriented, non-capital intensive and recession resistant.

In 1981 Chemed combined several of its health-care operations with a California based pharmacy services company to form Omnicare, Inc., a health-care services corporation that it took public in July 1981. Chemed maintains 26% ownership in Omnicare, and Hutton serves as Omnicare's chairman. Reflecting Hutton's pride in Cincinnati, he opted to keep Omnicare's headquarters in Cincinnati rather than moving it to Los Angeles, home of Omnicare's largest subsidiary. Similarly, when Chemed acquired the Iowa based Roto-Rooter Corporation in 1980, Hutton moved Roto-Rooter's headquarters to Cincinnati, bringing another highly profitable company to the Queen City.

Chemed reached a milestone in its history in 1982, when it traded a $250 million operating division plus another $185 million in cash to W.R. Grace for Grace's entire holding of Chemed's stock. Having become a totally independent company, Chemed listed its shares for trading on the New York Stock Exchange under the ticker symbol CHE.

After it gained its independence, Chemed's expansion accelerated. The firm purchased two commercial laundry products businesses which were combined to form a Cincinnati-based subsidiary called Fabrilife Chemicals. Chemed also purchased National Sanitary Supply Company, the largest janitorial supply distributor in the country, thus entering a lucrative new market with excellent growth potential.

Throughout the years Hutton has worked to develop Chemed's businesses into companies that can stand on their own, with separate management teams and corporate identities. His unique and extremely successful philosophy has resulted in a highly motivated cadre of managers, each striving for consistent earnings growth. This philosophy has resulted in the public offerings of Roto-Rooter in 1985 and National Sanitary Supply in 1986, with Chemed maintaining a majority ownership in each company. As chairman of these two companies, Hutton can today be credited with keeping Chemed and its sister companies—National Sanitary Supply, Roto-Rooter and Omnicare, with a combined market value approaching $600 million—prospering in Cincinnati.

Because of Chemed's origin as the DuBois Soap Company, it tends to be viewed by Cincinnatians as strictly a soap company. Yet Chemed now manages from within the Cincinnati community several diversified, highly successful businesses. DuBois Chemicals is #1 in the United States in the sale of industrial cleaning compounds and #2 in institutional cleaning compounds. Chemed's other subsidiaries also share the limelight—its Roto-Rooter subsidiary is the largest sewer and drain cleaning company in the United States, and its National Sanitary Supply subsidiary is the country's largest distributor of sanitary maintenance supplies. With sales of roughly $400 million and after-tax profits of approximately $24 million, Chemed is now one of the nation's 500 largest companies.

In short Chemed Corporation, with E.L. Hutton at the company helm, is a strong, independent corporation with operations from Canada to Latin America, from England to Japan, from Fountain Square to all of the Americas.

Tunis Vanderveer DuBois (1890-1957) Founder of DuBois Chemical Company.

Edward L. Hutton (1919-) The current president and chief executive officer of Chemed Corporation.

The original DuBois soap plant at 1120 West Front Street. Edward Breckel, a founder of the company, is pictured at the front left. (c.1935).

Photographs courtesy of the Chemed Corporation.

Children's Hospital Medical Center

Children's Hospital Medical Center (CHMC) has a history of excellence dating back to November 1883, when a group of Episcopal church women determined that Cincinnati needed a hospital exclusively for children. They rented a home in Walnut Hills and converted it into the Episcopal Hospital, later to be named Children's Hospital. The hospital's first home was equipped with 12 beds, one bathroom but no operating room.

Within a few years John and Thomas Emery, sons of the founder of one of Cincinnati's most prominent industries, donated land and building costs for a new hospital in Mt. Auburn. The new quarters, opened in 1887, were well-equipped for the time, containing about 50 beds, an operating room and an improvised chapel. Later enlargement of this building increased capacity to 80 beds.

Plans for a new Children's Hospital were drawn in 1921, and in 1923 six acres of land at Elland and Bethesda avenues were transferred from the city of Cincinnati. Construction began in 1925, and patients moved into the new hospital in December 1926.

With a significant gift from William Cooper Procter, grandson of the co-founder of the Procter & Gamble Company and president of the hospital's board of trustees, Children's Hospital Research Foundation was dedicated in 1931. The hospital's first outpatient clinic was housed in the research building. In 1950 the Procter Memorial Wing was added to provide laboratories and quarters for resident physicians. The first comprehensive laboratory for laser medicine in the world was established at Children's Hospital in 1963.

In 1968 a second research building, the Institute for Developmental Research, was completed. Extensive renovations and expansion of the Children's Hospital building took place from 1968 to 1972. The Convalescent and Services Pavilion opened in 1973, with spacious new quarters for Convalescent Hospital for Children (founded in 1832 as the Cincinnati Orphan Asylum), formerly located in Mt. Auburn. The Pavilion also brought together the four other affiliates of what had now become Children's Hospital Medical Center—Cerebral Palsy Services Center, Children's Dental Care Foundation, Cincinnati Center for Developmental Disorders and the Division of Adolescent Medicine.

In 1987 the medical center opened its first off-campus facility. Children's Outpatient North in Mason is a modern, one-story structure especially tailored for pediatric outpatient surgery and specialty examinations.

The Ambulatory Services Building opened in 1983 and expanded in 1988. The building consolidates all ambulatory care services and administrative offices. Major expansions of the emergency department and the Clinical Research Center also took place in 1988.

New research and patient-care buildings are in the planning stage for completion in the early 1990s. These high-technology facilities will keep Children's at the leading edge of pediatric research and patient care.

Paralleling its physical growth over the past century, CHMC's growth in services has been notable in virtually every area of patient care, teaching and research. Children's is especially noted for its accomplishments in treating childhood cancer, severe illness in newborns, endocrine, diabetes, heart, kidney and liver problems, congenital malformations, and mental retardation and other developmental disorders.

Over the past 55 years, Children's research programs have resulted in more than 2,500 contributions to pediatric knowledge. Most widely recognized have been the development of the first practical heart-lung machine for open-heart surgery in 1952; the Sabin oral polio vaccine in 1960; and the identification of many inborn errors of metabolism, among them PKU, a disease that can be corrected through special dietary restrictions but which causes severe mental retardation if undetected at birth. The first artificial blood compounds that have been successfully tested as substitutes for whole blood were developed at CHMC in the late 1960s.

In 1970 CHMC pioneered the use of ultrasound as a diagnostic tool in cardiac disease. Children's also has been instrumental in developing pediatric pacemakers as well as the standard pediatric balloon catheter now used worldwide. As a pioneer in open-heart surgery, CHMC also stands as a leader in this field, treating cardiac patients not only from the Cincinnati area but from other cities and countries as well.

Children's today is renowned for its surgical expertise, performing more surgical procedures annually than any other pediatric hospital in the country. Several procedures first done at Children's are now being performed around the world.

The first pediatric kidney transplant in Ohio was performed at CHMC in 1965. Children's today is one of the leaders in the United States in the total number of pediatric kidney transplants performed, with 218 procedures. In 1986 Children's Hospital Medical Center joined the Ohio Solid Organ Transplant Consortium and began performing pediatric liver and heart transplants. Currently CHMC transplant surgeons have performed one heart transplant and nearly 30 liver transplants, including three segmental transplants in which larger livers are pared down to accommodate tiny infants and children.

One of the largest and most sophisticated newborn intensive care units in the world is at CHMC, treating nearly 800 babies a year. In August 1986 the Perinatal Research Institute was established as the first interdisciplinary institute in the country dedicated to research related to the period before, during and after birth.

Currently Children's Hospital Medical Center, a private, not-for-profit facility, has 350 beds, making it the largest pediatric facility in the country. Children's furnishes most of the pediatric inpatient care within a 50-mile radius of Cincinnati and virtually all tertiary care within a 100-mile radius. CHMC records approximately 15,000 inpatient visits, 115,000 ambulatory care visits to its 56 specialty clinics and 71,000 emergency visits annually.

Through its affiliation with the University of Cincinnati, CHMC's full-time medical staff of about 175 constitutes the faculty of the department of pediatrics of the U.C. College of Medicine.

Because teaching and research are totally interrelated with patient services at Children's Hospital Medical Center, the most highly qualified medical staff, researchers and students are attracted to CHMC. Children's has the largest pediatric training program within a single institution in the United States, with about 180 postgraduate fellows, residents and interns rotating through the center each year.

Today over 3,000 talented and dedicated employees make CHMC a valued asset to the city, the region and the nation.

On "Sabin Sunday," April 24, 1960, Cincinnatians lined up to receive doses of the new oral polio vaccine at Children's Hospital.

Photograph. Courtesy of Children's Hospital Medical Center.

The Christ Hospital

The Courtyard Atrium at The Christ Hospital's Cancer Center offers visitors and outpatients some of the comforts of home. Photograph courtesy of The Christ Hospital.

The Christ Hospital's tradition of excellence in medical care can be traced to 1888, when conditions in Cincinnati's crowded West End were bleak for the poor and sick who lived there. James Gamble, whose soap business was flourishing, read of the work in Chicago of a missionary on leave from India, Isabella Thoburn. Impressed by an account that she wrote for Cincinnati's Methodist newspaper, he persuaded Thoburn to start a program here in the basin of the city.

Gamble and other concerned citizens founded an association on December 23, 1888, naming it for James Gamble's wife Elizabeth, a strong supporter of charitable work who had died that September. The goal of the new Elizabeth Gamble Deaconess Home Association was "to train deaconesses and missionaries, and to carry on religious, educational and philanthropic work."

Not long thereafter the most far-reaching legacy of Isabella Thoburn and her deaconess work began. Early in 1889 Thoburn encountered a woman who was desperately ill and crying on the street. Being from out of state, the woman could not be admitted to the city hospital. Thoburn took her to the Deaconess Home at 50 York Street and cared for her in her own room.

In March Thoburn shared this story with the board of The Elizabeth Gamble Deaconess Home Association, which endorsed her action and acknowledged the need for a hospital that would accept non-city residents. On September 23, 1889, Christ's Hospital opened at 46 York Street in a house that James Gamble donated. The name was officially changed to The Christ Hospital in 1904.

By 1893 the tiny, four-building complex on York Street was taxed to its limits. The Gamble family again came to the rescue and purchased a building and four acres of land from the Thane Miller Boarding School for Girls on Auburn Avenue. After some renovations the new hospital opened June 2, 1893, on the site that has become its permanent home. The seemingly spacious, 60-bed capacity doubled within 10 years.

From the beginning of their work, the deaconesses valued education. They trained the women who joined them both in religious studies and in nursing. By 1901 young women were accepted for training as nurses regardless of whether they intended to become deaconesses, paving the way for formation of The Christ Hospital School of Nursing in 1902.

According to a hospital annual report, almost as many patients had to be turned away as were received in 1913 due to overcrowding. The solution was a new building that opened in 1915, offering three times as many private rooms as well as moderately-priced rooms and wards in the old building. Modern conveniences abounded—from hot and cold water to electric reading lamps and telephones.

The hospital confronted new problems during World War I, when a worldwide influenza epidemic nearly depleted the supply of available nurses in 1918 and 1919. Christ Hospital nurses went to General Hospital and area communities to answer appeals for help, and 75 enlisted in Red Cross work. One nurse and two doctors died while caring for influenza victims, and nearly 80 students contracted the disease, but none died.

In 1927 James Norris Gamble, chemist and long-time benefactor of The Christ Hospital, donated $100,000 to start a research institute that now bears his name. Originally located on the ninth and 10th floors of the hospital, it moved to separate quarters adjacent to the hospital in the mid-1950s.

The next hospital expansion, in 1930, added the north wing and the most visible part of The Christ Hospital—the tower that lights up the skyline at night. The beacon attracted many public dependents seeking free or partially free medical services during the Great Depression.

World War II also brought new challenges. School of nursing enrollment increased to fill a nearly insatiable demand for nurses. Nurse aides and assistants left for better paying jobs in defense plants, and 147 nurses, 30 medical and surgical staff members, and 62 doctors served in the Armed Forces. The 1944 annual report called Christ Hospital "overcrowded and understaffed."

Overcrowding remained a theme in the years following the war. Ground was broken in 1958 for a new west wing, and construction on the first nine floors was completed in 1960. Remaining floors of the 13-story wing were completed in 1968, bringing the hospital's capacity close to 700 beds. The south wing built in 1915 was replaced in 1978 by new south and southwest wings.

Throughout The Christ Hospital's history, there have been a number of firsts. Elizabeth Campbell, M.D., who was hired in 1902, was the first woman physician in Cincinnati to be admitted to a hospital medical staff. In 1931 the first drinker respirator arrived for treatment of people whose chest and diaphragm muscles had been temporarily paralyzed. The first mechanical kidney in Cincinnati, forerunner of today's hemodialysis units, was installed at The Christ Hospital in 1951.

Other innovations include the first hyperbaric chamber in the Ohio Valley, installed in 1971 for the treatment of advanced cancer, gas gangrene, carbon monoxide poisoning, tetanus and decompression sickness; the city's first coronary balloon angioplasty, which opens clogged arteries without surgery, 1980; the first ceramic hip joint replacement in the United States, 1982; and one of the first U.S. hospitals to test Tissue Plasminogen Activator (TPA), a drug that dissolves blood clots that cause heart attacks, 1986.

Today The Christ Hospital is a 660-bed, non-profit, acute care facility with extensive programs in such areas as heart disease, women's health, internal medicine, cancer care, advanced orthopedics, surgical specialties and behavioral medicine. As a referral center, it serves more patients from outside Hamilton County than any other area hospital.

The Christ Hospital also is a teaching hospital, with a highly regarded, independent, internal medicine residency program affiliated with the University of Cincinnati College of Medicine.

"Changing technology, unchanging values" is the slogan adopted for The Christ Hospital's centennial and second century. One tangible example of this is its new Courtyard Atrium, completed in 1988 and geared toward the growing needs of outpatients.

Cincinnati Bell Inc.

The accepted image of a Cincinnati enterprise is that of thoughtful, stable progress, a matter of taking one well-considered step after another. None fits it better than Cincinnati Bell Inc.

Communication by wire came early to the city in the form of the telegraph. It was an important tool, but it had to be supplemented by an army of messengers.

Charles H. Kilgour, a banker and transit company investor, had a telegraph in his home —a rare, if not the only such installation in town. Kilgour had fallen from a horse frightened by one of his own steam traction cars and had taken to working from his home while he healed. A clerk named Thomas Bell carried messages between the Kilgour home and office. His name sounds portentous, but he was related to the famous inventor only by ingenuity. Young Bell, tired of running uphill every day, suggested a telegraph would save time and money. Kilgour had one installed and, accustomed to financial adventure, also formed a company to offer such service to any who wanted and could afford it.

The City and Suburban Telegraph Association was incorporated in July 1873. Kilgour had to take almost two-thirds of the stock himself, and even some of the daring few who joined in the beginning dropped out when the company showed no sign of becoming profitable. It eventually installed about 50 private telegraph lines, in most cases connecting a company with a branch or factory. It was not a promising business because of the difficulty in communicating by code.

In 1877 James Shiras arrived to show Cincinnati a year-old device which would carry voices over a wire. City and Suburban was a natural prospect because it was the one company which already had a lot of wire stretched around the area. Shiras demonstrated his telephone on a telegraph line which ran from Kilgour's downtown office to a traction company office in Mt. Lookout. City and Suburban not only bought the idea, but it also signed up Shiras to sell telephones to the rest of Cincinnati. His first sale was to Cincinnati Gas Light & Coke Co., the forerunner of C.G. & E.

Thomas Watson, who had answered Bell's historic initial call, came to Cincinnati to help lay out the system, the first in Ohio and the 10th in the U.S. The company name changed to The City and Suburban Telegraph Association and Telephonic Exchange. Bell's and Western Electric Manufacturing equipment were used from the beginning, but there were competing systems, notably one based on Edison patents. In 1878 the City and Suburban signed a contract with Bell Telephone of Boston to be the exclusive agent for Bell in Cincinnati and the 25-mile area surrounding it.

The progress of the telephone company is most visible in the directories. The first directory was published in 1879. It was a single page and new pages had to be printed every week. Subscribers did not have numbers. Operators had to memorize every name and know on which switchboard a given subscriber's line was to be found.

Stockholders remember 1879 for another reason—the company issued its first dividend. It has not missed a year since.

Other milestones in Cincinnati Bell's history:

1882—City and Suburban contracted with American Telephone & Telegraph for long-distance service. "Long distance" was about 100 miles at the time.

1891—The first underground cable was installed.

1903—The company name was changed to Cincinnati and Suburban Bell Telephone.

1904—Coin-operated telephones arrived. The first street phone was between Walnut and Main on Fifth Street.

1909—The company bought its first automobile. Cincinnati Bell has a picture of workmen hauling a telephone pole on a motorcycle and sidecar; trucks were a major technological advance.

1913—A new headquarters building was completed on Fourth Street between Main and Sycamore.

1914—Hazelhurst, a vacation resort for female employees of the company, was opened on what was then a rural stretch of Hamilton Pike. Hazelhurst was closed in 1929.

1915—Transcontinental calls became possible.

1928—A cable to Covington was laid on the bottom of the Ohio River.

1930—Conversion to dial service started; it was completed after World War II.

1931—The company's building at Seventh and Elm streets opened. In the public mind, this was the Telephone Building, although the company's headquarters were in the more ornate building on Fourth Street at Hammond Alley. In 1981 headquarters moved next door into the new Atrium One where Cincinnati Bell is the principal tenant. In 1982 the old headquarters building was razed to make room for Atrium Two.

1946—Mobile telephones made calling the office a moving experience.

1952—The switchover to dial service was completed. Cincinnati was the first of the Bell companies to become 100% dial and parents had to begin explaining to teenagers how "Hello, Central, Give Me Heaven" could have become a hit song.

1968—Electronic switching and musical beeps took over. Prosaic numbers already had replaced the traditional names of the various exchanges. Dropping Canal, Avon, East, Central, Walnut, Beechmont, Redwood, Main, Grandview and the rest was one of the telephone company's major public relations headaches, but expanding usage and services dictated beeps and numerals.

1971—Another name change, this time to a simple Cincinnati Bell.

1973—Mr. Kilgour's company became 100 years old!

1976—A larger new building at Seventh and Plum was joined to the older "telephone building" at Seventh and Elm.

1983—Cincinnati Bell was reorganized as a holding company to permit entry into diversified ventures beyond the core local telephone services.

Today Cincinnati Bell Inc. is an information services company that competes in markets nationally and internationally.

Besides basic telecommunications services, the Cincinnati Bell family of companies markets communications equipment testing, circuit board repair, discount long distance, telemarketing and computer software with a full range of consulting and software design services.

The Cincinnati Bell Telephone Company's first means of making emergency repairs. Photograph courtesy of Cincinnati Bell.

Cincinnati Butchers' Supply Co.

Our Meat Market on Wheels

Customers waited upon without leaving Wagon.

This represents our No. 101 Wagon with refrigerator placed in rear of wagon. Ice door is in rear, meat doors in front. Wagon is equipped with stool and chopping block. Axles 1¼ inch, body 7 feet 6 inches long, 42 inches wide, weight 860 lbs., capacity 1200 lbs. Price on application.

Every Cincinnatian has heard of Porkopolis, that industrial Camelot where roamed entire herds of Poland-China hogs. Much of it was true; there really was a Comstock Lode of ham, and it created more wealth than did the silver.

It also is true that Cincinnati's meat-packing kingdom faded as did the mines. Among its most prosperous and important survivors is a firm which attracts little public notice in today's Cincinnati, but which has outlived nearly all its contemporaries in that long-ago time. The company is The Cincinnati Butchers' Supply Co. Its product is machinery.

The boom in hog processing had peaked in Cincinnati by 1870, the year the C. Schmidt Co. went into business. C. Schmidt was Carl Schmidt, who was joined by his nephew, also named Carl. Carl's sister had married Christoph Bruckmann, a brewer, and his original intention was to apprentice himself in that industry. He joined his uncle, instead, and learned about meat packing. Carl insisted that the nephew call himself "Charles" to avoid confusion. Charles he became, but his male descendants all used Carl Oscar Schmidt as their formal names.

The new Charles Schmidt remained with his uncle until 1886, when he went into business on his own as Cincinnati Butchers' and Packers' Supply Co. The "packer" part was dropped because the whole name was burdensomely long. The home office was on Central Avenue until 1940 and is now on Helen Street in the industrial area of Elmwood Place, just north of the Ivorydale Procter & Gamble plant.

By this time Carl (Charles) had become a kind of engineering trouble shooter for his business. It is obvious the family had a bent for engineering. His son, Oscar, was to receive about 100 patents and his grandson, C. Oscar Schmidt Jr.—the current company head—has about 35.

Grandfather's first designs were for a machine which cleaned sausage casings and a cooler which protected the meat from the drip of melting ice. In time the company produced an entire line of packing machinery which helped revolutionize the industry. The basic principles developed here continue to be used today. Only sausage machinery was made at first, but the line now includes equipment for slaughtering.

Slaughtering machinery, which is made for both hog and cattle packers, is the company's major accomplishment. Not all of the firm's innovations have resulted from the profit motive. It developed an electric stunning device with a restrainer that enabled packers to meet the requirements of the humane slaughtering act. Schmidt sees the cost of developing it as a gift to the industry because it was far cheaper than the devices it replaced.

In the long haul Butchers' Supply Co. made mechanization of the industry its real contribution. Some companies routinely process 1,200 hogs an hour on its equipment.

The success of Cincinnati Butchers' Supply Co. has at times made its own survival difficult. It has received orders for replacement parts for machinery made 90 years ago. And the faster the machines work, the fewer packers need. As a result the size of the industry shrinks, even as its product increases.

Cincinnati Butchers' Supply succeeds because of innovation, vigorous pursuit of new products and fields, and because it has had the stamina to hang in there. It has absorbed competing or allied companies when they faltered.

Schmidt, looking back on the 1960s (the hard times of the packing business), says now that his company has managed to become a specialist in the slaughtering field. "We just sort of forgot about the sausage industry," he says.

In 1980, the company bought Omeco-St. John Co., of Omaha, a producer of material-handling and food-processing equipment. Another Cincinnati Butchers' Supply offshoot is EscoBoss of Mexico City. EscoBoss' owner is now over 90 but is an active executive. Oscar Schmidt is affiliated with EscoBoss, but the president and managing stockholders must be Mexican nationals.

The corporate structure also has been re-designed. William Schmidt, a brother of Oscar, took over the LeFiell Co. of San Francisco in 1982, leaving Oscar the sole owner of the Cincinnati firm. LeFiell had been purchased by Butchers' Supply in 1960.

A holding company, Schmidt Boss, has been formed for the companies remaining with the Cincinnati firm. (The "Boss" in the company names and brands dates back to the founder's time, when "boss" was a favorite label among manufacturers.) The subsidiaries are Omeco-Boss, of Omaha; Winbco Tank Co., of Ottumwa, Iowa; Mobile Crane Service, of Ottumwa; and BEC, Inc., of Trussville, Alabama. Schmidt owns an interest in EscoBoss. All the companies deal in equipment parts, or services for meat packers.

And there is a fifth generation of Schmidts, both sons of Oscar Jr. They are Milton, vice president and general manager of Butchers' Supply, and Christoph, vice president of administration.

Our Meat Market on Wheels. "This represents our No. 101 Wagon with refrigerator placed in rear of wagon. Ice door is in rear, meat doors in front. Wagon is equipped with stool and chopping block. Axles 1¼ inch, body 7 feet 6 inches long, 42 inches wide, weight 860 lbs., capacity 1200 lbs. Price on application." *The Cincinnati Butchers Supply Co. Catalog No. W-17* (also numbered 31) n.d. Courtesy of Cincinnati Butchers Supply.

The Cincinnati Cordage and Paper Company

John A. Church, who joined Cordage in 1897, was elected president of the National Paper Trade Association in 1903. He also was active in civic affairs and was president of the Business Men's Club of Cincinnati when it sponsored the successful 1901 Cincinnati Fall Festival.

Cincinnati was still something of a riverboat town in 1892 when The Cincinnati Cordage and Paper Company was formed by two young brothers, Edward F. and Llewellyn Evans. Cordage began as a "coarse paper" house, a jobber that sold cordage (heavy rope such as that used to rig ships and lighter lines such as twine) along with heavy papers used to wrap packages.

Rope became less important with the city's declining river trade, but the twine industry remained strong. At the turn of the century, Cincinnati was the largest soft-fiber twine and cordage center in the United States, both in manufacturing and jobbing. Soft twine was made from Kentucky hemp and jute. The Cordage house on Main and Sixth streets sold to river and rail shippers and retail merchants.

The Evans brothers lived in Norwood. Edward, the elder of the two, became president of the company. Llewellyn, who had studied at a printing school in St. Louis, was vice president.

In 1897 Abner L. Whitaker and John A. Church, who were both natives of Windham, Connecticut, and graduates of the National Normal University at Lebanon, Ohio, joined Cincinnati Cordage. Whitaker had been an agent with the Graham Paper Co. of St. Louis that had a business office in Cincinnati on Third Street. Church had attended the Miami Medical School but did not practice. He taught in Cincinnati at Springdale School before joining the Graham Paper Co., managing its Nashville office. Graham specialized in fine (printing) paper, and Church and Whitaker were instrumental in steering Cordage from coarse paper to fine paper products.

Cincinnati had no paper manufacturers within the city, but there were approximately 50 mills in the Miami Valley at Lockland, Hamilton, Franklin and Middletown. The two Hamilton mills, The Champion Paper and Fibre Company (U.S. Champion/Plywood) and Beckett Paper Company were Cordage's earliest suppliers.

It was a good time and a good place to be manufacturing paper. Increased mechanization in industrial production and the substitution of wood pulp over rag as a raw material had lowered costs and Cincinnati's numerous printing, lithographic and publishing concerns created a strong demand for fine paper.
Five years after its founding, Cordage opened a branch in Pittsburgh. It was sold in 1903, the year A.L. Whitaker resigned to form the Whitaker Paper Company on Eggleston Avenue. John A. Church bought Whitaker's stock and gained control at that time.

Cordage joined other paper distributors across the country to form The National Paper Trade Association in 1903. John A. Church was its first president. Cordage's current president, John F. Church Jr. (a grandson of John A.) was president of the association in 1982.

Llewellyn Evans, founder of the Cincinnati Cordage and Paper Company.

Photographs courtesy of Cincinnati Cordage and Paper Company.

The Cincinnati Cordage and Paper Company from George W. Engelhardt's *Cincinnati: the Queen City* (Cincinnati, 1901) p. 215.

Over the years Cordage has expanded into five neighboring states with divisional or sales offices in Akron, Cleveland, Columbus, Dayton and Youngstown, Ohio; Pittsburgh, Pennsylvania; Huntington, West Virginia; Indianapolis and Ft. Wayne, Indiana; and Nashville and Knoxville, Tennessee; and four retail stores in Ohio and Pennsylvania.

A subsidiary, Cordage Packaging in Springboro, fabricates and prints paper and polyethylene bags which are used in packaging fruits and vegetables for the retail market. The idea for this operation came from a salesman's call upon an apple grower who described the need for attractive and practical packaging. They have moved into the industrial, distribution and retail markets and expanded their traditional position in the horticultural market.

The type of paper Cordage distributes today varies with the particular sales area. Cincinnati, for example, is still a major publishing center which uses large quantities of printing paper. Cordage stresses helping artists, advertising directors and design agencies select the right paper for a particular job to produce high-quality printed materials.

Cordage has a tradition of family management with the presidency alternating between members of the Evans and Church families except for 1936-1949 when A.T. Nesbitt was president. E.F. Evans died in 1913 and Llewellyn died in 1936; they were succeeded by Llewellyn's son, R. Gale, who joined the firm in 1926 and became president and treasurer in 1949. John A. Church died in 1929. His son, John F. Church, joined the company in 1949, becoming chairman of the board in 1974. On December 31, 1975, John F. Church and R. Gale Evans retired and their sons, John F. Church Jr. and Richard G. Evans Jr., became president and executive vice president, positions that they hold today.

Since 1955 Cordage has been located in a modern office and warehouse facility off East Ross Avenue in St. Bernard. It was the first one-story paper warehouse in Cincinnati. Today Cordage has sales of close to $150 million and 325 employees. It is well-positioned as an independent to grow in the future despite a very competitive environment.

The Cincinnati Enquirer

The Cincinnati Enquirer has reported the national and local news since 1841. Photograph courtesy of the Cincinnati Enquirer.

Thanks to the volatile state of publishing in the 19th century, *The Enquirer* can claim more than one founding date, but either would make it the oldest daily newspaper in the city with the oldest Sunday edition in the nation.

Its official history uses 1841 as the year of its birth, but it actually springs from a paper which began publishing in 1818—*The Advertiser. The Advertiser* (which also incorporated "Inquisitor" and "Journal" into its flag at various times)—spent most of its 23 years as the property of Moses Dawson, a political activitist, who in 1841 was driven by advancing age to sell it. John and Charles Brough, experienced printers and publishers, bought the paper for $3,250. On April 10, 1841, the brothers published it as *The Enquirer* for the first time.

In 1843 the Brough brothers sold the paper, by then a morning daily, to Hiram Robinson. In 1846 James J. Faran bought it and the Brough brothers returned to run it, until Charles left again to fight in the Mexican War. John Brough was to become an Ohio governor and Charles a common pleas judge. Under Faran's ownership, the paper launched its Sunday edition in 1848, dropping the Monday morning paper to do it.

In general the owners to this point were interested in profit but were mostly politically motivated, and all had been active in state and national politics. The first of the new type of owners was Washington McLean. He was a builder of steam engines for marine use and bought into the paper in 1857. He and Faran added job printing to *The Enquirer's* income and built that subsidiary function into a company which eventually became U.S. Playing Card.

The 1866 Pike's Opera House fire also destroyed *The Enquirer's* plant at Vine and Baker streets, causing a one-day interruption in its publication. McLean then purchased the site at 617 Vine Street, where the paper's business and editorial offices remain today. The present building, however, was built in 1924.

Washington McLean gave his interest in the paper to his son, John R., in 1880 and three years later the younger McLean bought out Faran. McLean strove to make *The Enquirer* a national paper and broadened its coverage to that end. He later added *The Washington Post* to his holdings and moved to the national capital. Before that, however, he brought in William F. Wiley as an aide in a variety of positions and who took full charge of *The Enquirer* when McLean died in 1916. During Wiley's regime the paper purchased the rival *Cincinnati Commercial Tribune* and absorbed it entirely during the depression.

As his own successor, Wiley hired Roger Ferger, a former advertising manager of *The Enquirer,* who had become business manager of a Pittsburgh paper. Ferger became publisher at Wiley's death in 1944. Although the paper's economic progress was never jeopardized, Ferger's tenure was one of tumult, none of it his own making.

In 1952 the McLeans announced their intent to sell the paper to the afternoon *Times-Star.* The announcement touched off an employee movement unmatched in U.S. journalism. Within weeks they organized a counter offer by rounding up a combination of wealthy sponsors and friendly brokers to raise the money. In the end the employee group had $7.5 million cash to buy the paper, including $1.5 million raised among the employees and bonds sold by the brokers.

After four years, management of the paper began to develop problems and the employee organization deteriorated as the struggle for control increased. In 1956 Scripps-Howard purchased a majority interest in *The Enquirer's* stock but never exercised control.

The various changes did not jeopardize the paper's prosperity. Francis L. Dale, an attorney who had participated in the employees' coup, eventually became president and publisher.

In 1971 a consent decree in federal court caused Scripps Howard to divest itself of *The Enquirer*, and American Financial Corporation bought it. Dale continued as publisher until 1973, when he was succeeded by Carl H. Lindner, chairman of American Financial. William J. Keating, a former Cincinnati City Council member and judge, resigned from the U.S. House of Representatives in 1973 to become president and chief executive officer of *The Enquirer.*

American Financial sold *The Enquirer* in 1975 to Combined Communications Corporation, a company with operations in publishing, broadcasting and outdoor advertising. Combined Communications merged with Gannett Co., Inc. in 1979, and Keating succeeded Lindner as publisher.

In 1979 *The Enquirer* moved its production facilities to a new printing plant on Western Avenue. Advertising, circulation, personnel and news operations remained at 617 Vine Street. The news division was linked to the printing plant with computers. The *Cincinnati Post* and the *Kentucky Post* also were linked to the plant and are produced there.

When Keating moved to Gannett's corporate headquarters as president of the company's newspaper division in 1984, he was succeeded as president and publisher of *The Enquirer* by Gary Watson. In late 1985 Watson moved to Gannett headquarters, and John P. Zanotti became president and publisher.

Cincinnati Financial Corporation

In the book of Cincinnati legends, one of the newest stories is that of Cincinnati Financial Corporation. The plot is an old theme with a new twist—local boys make good...right here at home.

Four partners launched what was to become CFC, but John Schiff, chief executive officer, is the public figure seen by the town as the driving force and the man around whom the company image is built. That image is one of old-fashioned virtues, devotion to country, respect for the work ethic and admiration for the results of thrift.

For many years Schiff interviewed teenagers when they became eligible for coverage under the family auto policy. He told the Newcomen Society that this was merely good business practice inaugurated when the son of a client with a record of repeated accidents applied for insurance. The father averaged a damage claim every 18 months. Fear that the sins of the father had infected the son made Schiff blanch. He asked the father for a chance to talk to the boy.

The idea was to impress the youth that coming of driving age was a serious business, important enough to engage the attention of the highest officer in the company. The idea worked. The youngster grew up to become the president—the safe-driving president—of a manufacturing concern. Even the father was impressed, although the record does not show if he turned over a new driving leaf.

Shortly after World War II, Schiff, his brother Robert, Harry M. Turner and the late Chester R. Field set about forming their own insurance company. As independent insurance agents living and working in Ohio, they wanted to avoid the inconvenience of dealing with large insurance companies in distant cities. The four men pooled their expertise and energy to form The Cincinnati Insurance Co., an Ohio stock company committed to helping local agents sell insurance in their own towns. In 1950, at a cost of only $249.07, the 12 original directors raised $200,000 capital.

In the early days, as now, everybody pitched in. Company officers cleaned up the grounds of the first home office—on Saturdays, of course—and once started a brush fire doing it. Other domestic efforts turned out better. Faced with a claim involving a truckload of bakery goods, the company peddled cookies to employees and friends and recovered the $2,000 loss.

This first company, the Cincinnati Insurance Co., started small but grew quickly. In its first year gross premiums came to $92,052. The company that it grew into had gross revenues of $883,077,000 in 1987. The Cincinnati Insurance Co. was chartered to deal in property and casualty insurance. Though successful it was restricted to the stated field, and new companies had to be formed to permit wider growth. The first was Cincinnati Financial Corp., the holding company that is the parent for all other operations. It was founded in 1968 and a year later absorbed CIC through a stock exchange. A real estate operation called CFC Investment Co. was formed in 1970, and it, in turn, established a computer and office equipment leasing division.

In 1973 CFC arranged a merger with Inter-Ocean Corporation, a life, health and accident insurance company founded in St. Louis and based in Cincinnati since 1917. That same year CFC incorporated two new enterprises: The Life Insurance Co. of Cincinnati and Queen City Indemnity Co., a fire and casualty insurer renamed The Cincinnati Casualty Co. in 1987.

The two life insurance companies merged into the new Cincinnati Life Insurance Co. in 1987, rededicated to making life insurance products available through independent agents representing The Cincinnati Insurance Co. Because The Cincinnati Insurance Co. and The Cincinnati Casualty Co. serve preferred markets, an additional property and casualty company was founded in 1988 to serve agents who needed to place nonpreferred business. The Cincinnati Indemnity Co. rounds out the family of Cincinnati companies.

All CFC insurance is sold through independent agents, which now number more than 750. Although it is a thoroughly Cincinnati establishment, CFC does business over all the United States. The company has more than 1,500 employees and has outgrown its original offices.

Cincinnati Financial Corporation headquarters opened in 1986 in Fairfield, Ohio. Illustration. Courtesy of Cincinnati Financial Corporation; Warren Stichtenoth, artist.

It began in modest quarters on Central Parkway—scene of the Saturday morning brush fire—then moved to larger offices nearby, and in 1973 to a handsome Georgian building on Princeton Pike that once had been the home of the Glenmary Missionaries. The building is a stylish landmark, but it also failed to contain CFC growth. The Cincinnati companies moved to Fairfield in 1985. The state-of-the-art headquarters building designed specifically for operation of their insurance business measures 300,000 square feet—grown from the 1,200 square feet of the original Central Parkway home.

Insurance companies all depend on investments as well as the profitable balancing of premiums against risks. Careful management of investments coupled with conservative insurance operations resulted in assets that topped $2 billion in 1988, a 10,000-fold return on the original capital raised in 1950.

The three surviving founders still are active in the company. They and other executives routinely work on Saturday mornings. Running one of the most profitable, diversified insurance companies in the nation, the current executive team of Schiff, Robert B. Morgan, John J. Schiff Jr., and William H. Zimmer still practices hands-on management. They greet most of their 1,500 associates by name and leave their comfortable offices to travel to meetings in 23 territories each year, giving the agents they serve unparalleled personal access to top management. While success broadened the scope of operations, it has not changed the goals. The Cincinnati companies remain agent-sponsored, with fully half of the CFC board members being independent agents. And John Schiff still promulgates his credo: "It is our responsibility—as recipients of the good fortune of living in a free country, under God, and with His guidance and with His inspiration—to motivate others who are establishing their own goals and objectives."

The Cincinnati Gas & Electric Company

The Ohio River, which put Cincinnati where it is, is largely responsible for making The Cincinnati Gas & Electric Company what it is.

Waterways gave access to plentiful coal in the Appalachian mines of Ohio, Kentucky and West Virginia. Barges on the Ohio River remain the least expensive method of transporting coal to CG&E's electric generating plants, helping make low-cost electric power among the city's most important assets.

The Cincinnati Gas & Electric Company grew from a tiny seed planted near Fourth and Main streets, the site of its main headquarters building since 1930. Thomas Lawson, an immigrant English tin and coppersmith, lighted his shop with homemade gas on Main near Fifth Street in 1825, when heat, light and power had not gone far beyond that produced by the axeman, the candlemaker and human muscle. Lawson supplied a few neighbors with his "city gas" but never really organized it into a business.

In 1837, six years after Lawson had been ordered by Cincinnati City Council to "put out his light" following a fire in the immediate vicinity of his gas plant, a group of local citizens secured a charter from the Ohio Legislature founding The Cincinnati Gas Light & Coke Company.

It was not until 1843, however, that operations actually began. On January 14 of that year, the system's first gas light was lit at the W.H. Harrison drug store, corner of Fourth and Main streets.

The company's name accurately reflected its interests – lighting was the principal use of gas which was made from distilling coal. The residual coke was sold for heating. Streets and business places were the first to enter the gas-light era, but in time thousands of homes were lighted by this artificial gas. Gas was coming into use for cooking by 1874, and shortly after that natural gas fields began to be tapped.

Then Thomas Edison turned on a new kind of light. Electric lighting was at first a kind of sophisticated do-it-yourself project. Manufactures of generating equipment sold it to institutions and factories. It was expensive, and in 1883 The Cincinnati Electric Co. and the Brush Electric Co. went into business as central generators of electricity. Although this reduced the cost, these "central" plants were small, and private plants abounded.

Despite the skepticism of its president at the time, General Andrew Hickenlooper, The Cincinnati Gas Light & Coke Co. bought a few of the plants and got into the electric business. Eventually the business was divided between Gas Light & Coke and its largest competitor, The Cincinnati Edison Electric Co. In 1901 the two companies consolidated.

By that time Cincinnati had 325,000 inhabitants, and the suburbs were growing. The problems of staying ahead of the city's expansion were staggering. However, CG&E's foresight has prevented the area from experiencing a blackout caused by a lack of capacity. And the efficiently managed company has never missed paying a dividend annually to its investors since it began doing so in 1853.

An exceptionally cold winter in 1917 brought gas shortages that compelled the company to build new stand-by gas storage caverns. There are several man-made caverns in CG&E's service area today where propane is stored against winter demands. Those facilities proved useful when record cold weather hit Cincinnati in 1977-1978, straining the gas supply. Service to residential customers was never curtailed.

The demand for electricity has continued to grow over the years, and CG&E has kept up by building new generating units, most of them coal-fired. In recent years CG&E joined the utilities in Columbus and Dayton to finance new generating plants. In the 1970s the three utilities began building the Wm. H. Zimmer Generating Station, which originally was intended to be a nuclear power plant. The project was delayed by a number of problems, including numerous additional federal regulations. Ultimately the utility partners decided in 1984 to convert Zimmer Station to a coal-fired plant, the first such conversion ever attempted, which is expected to go into service in 1991.

CG&E also has been a national leader in the renovation of existing power plants. Refurbishment of three units at its W.C. Beckjord Station has been completed and is expected to add 25 years to the lives of those units, saving CG&E customers millions of dollars compared to the cost of building new units.

CG&E celebrated its 150th anniversary in 1987 by making two major gifts to the community: exterior lighting to the facades of Cincinnati's City Hall and Music Hall. The company has continued to increase its involvement in the community, reflecting its new motto of "The Energy Service Company," and is rededicating itself to serve the customer better.

CG&E's mission is to become "the best energy service company in the United States." It has pledged to its customers, shareholders, regulators and employees that it will provide the energy service activities that best meet customer needs and expectations, in keeping with its long tradition of serving Cincinnati.

The Gas, Light and Coke Company building at Fourth and Plum streets became the Cincinnati Gas and Electric Company offices after the companies merged in 1901. In 1981 the newly renovated building was converted to apartments. Engraving. From *The Cincinnati Southern Railway, a History* (Cincinnati, 1902), p. 194.

The Cincinnati Gear Company

The founders of The Cincinnati Gear Company had sharp eyes and logical minds. They were John Christensen and Soren J. Sorensen. Both were born in Denmark and both showed early-on that they were ambitious for a larger world.

Christensen went to sea while still in his middle teens—about 1885, when sailors still worked with sails. After a few years he settled in Philadelphia, where he found a job with Bilgram Machine Works. At this time he and his wife used their combined thrift to buy a hardware store. Christensen kept his job at the machine works, and Mrs. Christensen ran the store.

Sorensen's early history was much the same. He was four years older than his future partner, but shared his outlook. Sorensen left Denmark as a youth to work as a farm hand around Philadelphia and in time he, too, wound up at the Bilgram factory.

Bilgram made gears. The two Danes noted that much of the product was shipped to Cincinnati, which at the turn of the century was just beginning to establish its place as the world's machine tool capital. Obviously, if Cincinnati was a place where a lot of people were buying gears, it would be a dandy place for a gear factory.

Christensen and Sorensen pooled their funds and bought a carload of machinery. They never had been to Cincinnati, so they shipped the machinery to Brighton Station, Cincinnati, Ohio, an address they took from a railroad timetable. A passenger train got them here just ahead of their "factory," which they installed in rented space on Opera Place. (The Skywalk and Convention Center effectively hide Opera Place now.)

It was 1907 and the country was living through one of the financial panics given to every generation. Cincinnati industries were making do with what little money was available and emergency scrip issued by the banks. Christensen and Sorensen were the sales and production staff, their company's only employees and, at the $10 a week they allowed themselves, the highest paid.

They called their tiny company The Ohio Bevel Gear Company. It had equally tiny competition, The Cincinnati Gear Works, just across the street. A year after Ohio Bevel went into business, it consolidated with Cincinnati Gear and continued as The Cincinnati Gear Company. Christensen and Sorensen were the active management of the young company and remained close friends until death.

Business was good and the factory was moved to Ninth and Broadway, the site of a fire station now, where it occupied the second floor until a new plant was built at 1825 Reading Road in 1911 and expanded in 1918.

Despite this growth Cincinnati Gear remained relatively small. Much of the product turned out was repairs for existing machinery. The company was not equipped with either the tools or processes to handle gears called for by modern machinery until 1936.

In 1937 Christensen, by then a Danish knight, died at sea while enroute with his family to the coronation of George VI in London. He was president of the company at his death and Sorensen the treasurer. Sorensen succeeded to the presidency, but in 1941 he, too, died. Neither of the founders was to see the flowering of the company. Each had sons, however, who had been active in management. Paul Christensen became president, but Frank Sorensen eventually left the firm to become president of an aircraft products company in Dayton, Ohio. (He already had gained fame as the All-American captain of an Ohio State football team.)

A grandson of the founder, Paul Christensen Jr., served as president from 1958 to 1978 and as chairman of the board from 1978 to December 1987. In 1978 Walter Rye became the first president outside of the founding families. In December 1987, after 80 years of continuous ownership, the Christensen family sold The Cincinnati Gear Company to Rye.

World War II production efforts by 1942 required the doubling of manufacturing space and forced another move, this time to Mariemont, where the company remains headquartered today. Through the addition of a neighboring facility in 1974, Cincinnati Gear again doubled in size to accommodate a greatly expanded Engineering Department and growing assembly and testing facilities requirement.

From its beginning Cincinnati Gear specialized in custom work. All its work is customized, although the scope of what it makes has expanded steadily since the milestone 1936 year. The one-time small orders evolved into large production efforts and, in 1963, the manufacture of enclosed drives, the special assemblage of gear systems into a housing commonly referred to as a gearbox or transmission. The year 1963 also marked CGCO's introduction of automated machinery.

Nearly doubling in size again in 1982, Cincinnati Gear purchased and improved a manufacturing and assembly facility in Lebanon, New Jersey capable of producing ultra precision gears up to 200 inches in diameter. Included was a large metal fabricating shop, which enables the company to build the housings required for enclosed drives.

Cincinnati Gear products are to be found in machine tools, earth moving equipment, food processing machines, jetfoil boats, dredges, rapid transit cars, hydraulic pumps, medical equipment, compressors, blowers and dozens of other applications all over the world.

Market changes in the late 1970s and early 1980s led Cincinnati Gear to enter into the design and manufacture of large, high-performance marine gearboxes installed in U.S. Navy ships. The company quickly took a leadership role in this field with its ability to build "quiet gears." Looking toward the year 2000 and beyond, CGCO is strongly advocating the use of epicyclic gears for quiet, high-powered applications.

Internationally Cincinnati Gear developed a close relationship with BHS-Werk in Sonthofen, West Germany. Cinti-BHS products are used in marine and industrial products throughout the world and enjoy a reputation of superiority for design and service. A warm personal and technical interaction between the companies keep them at the cutting edge of gear technology.

A manual issued to employees assures them that the opportunity to learn and advance is available to all. It cautions that a customer is somone whose needs are to be filled and not someone with whom the company matches wits.

John Christensen and Soren Sorensen would applaud.

"Full load, back-to-back" testing of the T-AO 187 class gearboxes being conducted in the Lebanon, New Jersey facility. Designed for 16,000 horsepower, the gearboxes were tested to power loads above 18,000 horsepower. Photograph. Courtesy of Cincinnati Gear Company.

The Cincinnati Herald

The Cincinnati Herald, Cincinnati's only local black weekly newspaper, was founded in 1955 by the late Gerald L. Porter.

A few years earlier Porter, a social worker by profession, had come to Cincinnati from his native Illinois to work for the *Independent,* a black paper published by Mary M. Andrews, a funeral director.

Porter had first tried his hand at publishing in Norwalk, Connecticut while working as the director of a community center there. After leaving employment at the *Independent,* his first publishing effort in Cincinnati was a pocket-sized magazine known as *Talk.*

Talk was only in publication for a short time, and public interest in the *Independent* was waning. Realizing that Cincinnati had not had a viable, widely read black publication since W.P. Dabney's *Union* ceased publication in the late 1920s or early 1930s, Porter set out to publish the *Cincinnati Herald* in 1955.

An office was established in the building that housed the Better Business Bureau at 406 Elm Street near Fourth Street in downtown Cincinnati. The first issue was printed by N.A. Sweets, a black publisher friend of Porter's and publisher of the *St. Louis American,* a weekly still being published in St. Louis, Missouri.

A nearby printer was engaged, and the *Herald* proceeded with weekly publication at first the Fourth and Elm location and then at 432 Elm until about 1960 or 1961, when the office was moved to another downtown location at 131 Opera Place.

Production of the newspaper was almost a one-person operation with the publisher selling the advertising and doing most of the mechanical work. There was a small supporting staff consisting of a clerk, typist, receptionist, part-time person for distribution and the late Al Roman for news and editorials. During 1961 two advertising salesmen joined the staff, and two young men, journalism graduates from Atlanta, were with the *Herald* for a brief period.

The *Herald* struggled on through 1961 and 1962 battling against the odds facing small business in general and black business in particular. In January 1963 a young man, Samuel Logan, came from Detroit, Michigan to join the *Herald* staff. Sam, who now manages the *Michigan Chronicle* in Detroit, is an extraordinary advertising salesman.

Before the impact of the sales expertise of Sam Logan could be felt a tragedy struck, changing the entire direction of the *Herald.* In the early morning hours of February 23, 1963, founder, owner and publisher Gerald Porter driving home fell asleep at the wheel and hit a guard rail. He was taken to the nearest hospital, which x-rayed him but denied him bed care because he was black. Upon arrival of his wife, Marjorie Brower Spillers, a nurse actually told her that they would not administer bed care to a Negro patient. He was moved to another hospital where he died 14 hours later from shock.

On Monday morning, February 25, 1963, Porter's widow walked into a business, the workings of which she knew nothing. She was soon to learn that the greatest feat that the *Herald* had accomplished was uninterrupted publication. It had come off the press every week but in doing so had compiled monumental debts and because of delinquent obligations, among other things, had acquired a negative public image.

In the past 20 years women have made significant inroads in the newspaper business, but in 1963 publishing was (and to a great extent still is) a man's world.

A newspaper publisher who was female, black and in debt, with an insufficient cash flow to pay those debts, was not someone that the business community was prepared to take seriously and do business with. All indicators pointed to failure, but Marjorie saw potential in the business and was determined to make it work.

The first order of business was to get someone to help who would not think in terms of salary that did not exist. Her son William (Bill) Spillers had worked at the paper during vacations since its beginning and had an affinity for it. However, his step-fathers' death found him serving his mandatory time in the United States Army with more than a year to go.

Good friends in high places in Washington came to the rescue, and he was at home and on the job by early April, under the tutelage of Sam Logan. Bill was ready to carry on when Sam left to return to Detroit.

Early in the Spring of 1963, publisher Majorie Porter decided to take steps toward a business and image change by going out of business with the original structure of the *Cincinnati Herald* and forming a corporation known as the Porter Publishing Company dba the *Cincinnati Herald.* She also decided to move the business out of the downtown area into the heart of the black neighborhood. On November 1, 1963, the *Herald* moved to 3488 Reading Road, where it remained until the present location, 863 Lincoln Avenue, was purchased in February 1966.

Following the death of newsman Al Roman, the *Herald* hired veteran news editor Ray Paul, who is still with the *Herald* after 24 years.

In 33 years of publishing the *Herald* has missed one issue when copy en route to the printer was misplaced by the carrier and was not located until it was too late for the publication date.

The *Herald* has a policy of honest reporting as void of sensationalism as possible and a policy of political independence.

The principals of the *Herald's* staff are: Marjorie Parham, president and publisher; William Spillers, vice president and advertising manager; and Ray Paul, news editor. Several young people have recently been added to our clerical, advertising, reporting and circulation staff. We look forward to carrying on in the tradition of a voice and champion of the Black Community.

The *Cincinnati Herald* has been the voice of the Black community since 1955. Photograph. Courtesy of *Cincinnati Herald.*

Cincinnati Microwave, Inc.

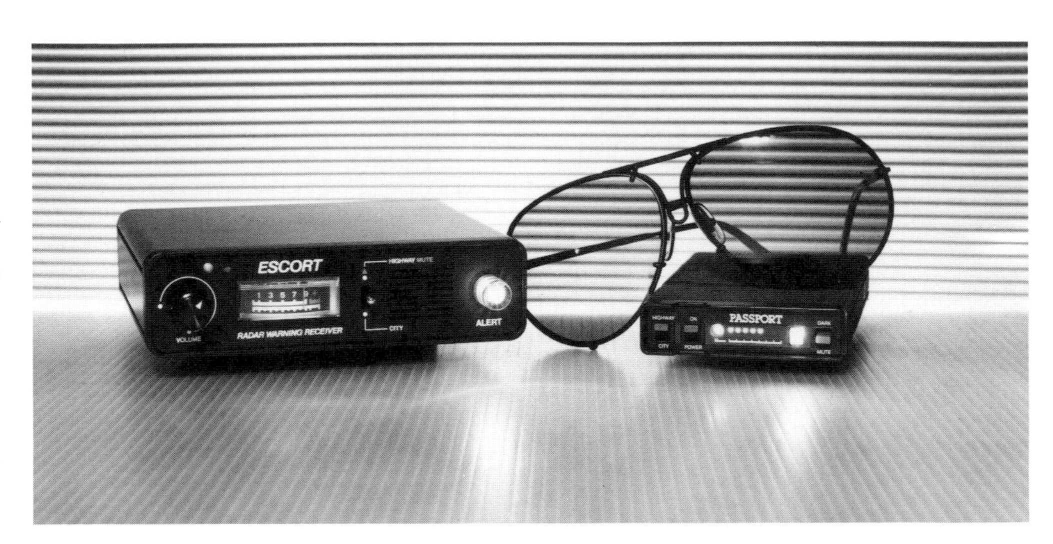

The popular *Escort* and *Passport* models have been consistently rated tops among radar warning devices.

Photograph. Courtesy of Cincinnati Microwave.

Although the company name is Cincinnati Microwave, Inc., most people know the firm for ESCORT or PASSPORT radar warning receivers. Many products are invented by men who find better ways of doing something. James L. Jaeger and Michael D. Valentine began thinking in 1975 that radar detectors already on the market could be greatly improved with different, more advanced technology. In 1976 they founded Cincinnati Microwave with the financial support of Valentine's father, James.

Jaeger and Valentine were serious driving enthusiasts. They were, and continue to be, men who love cars. Thus they saw an opportunity to use such a device themselves and also market it to other enthusiasts. They built a prototype in Jaeger's basement and found that it worked remarkably well. They were the pioneers in utilizing dual band, superheterodyne microwave reception technology for radar detectors, which has become the industry standard.

The ESCORT, Cincinnati Microwave's first detector, sold for $245. This was considerably more than the best-selling detectors at that time, but because of its vast superiority, it quickly became the market leader.

One of the first questions addressed was how to market the ESCORT. The owners decided not to sell through retailers. By cutting out the middleman and selling directly to consumers, Cincinnati Microwave could put more money into quality components and advertising and at the same time better serve customers by dealing with them personally.

Advertising and word of mouth soon built up clientele for the ESCORT. Then in 1979 a national car magazine, *Car and Driver*, rated the ESCORT as the best radar detector on the market. Cincinnati Microwave's manufacturing couldn't keep up with the demand created by this acclaim, and soon there was a six to eight month backlog for customers to receive their unit. Nevertheless, Cincinnati Microwave has remained a strictly direct mail company. And ESCORT and, subsequently, PASSPORT have been consistently rated the best detectors in magazine comparison tests.

In addition to magazine advertising, Cincinnati Microwave provides a significant amount of support to motorsports. Many buyers are automotive enthusiasts, so racing programs serve a dual purpose—they provide a goodwill gesture to those who have helped the company get where it is and serve as a way of generating new and continued interest. The ESCORT Endurance Championship, ESCORT Radar Warning 200 Indy car race at Mid-Ohio, and the ESCORT Trans-Am are just a few of the events sponsored by Cincinnati Microwave.

In 1982 the company outgrew its modest manufacturing and sales quarters near the Tri-County Mall in Springdale and moved to a high-tech, 75,000-square-foot facility in Warren County. Even this amount of space failed to contain Cincinnati Microwave's growth, and an additional 100,000 square feet was added in 1987.

The partnership between Jaeger and Valentine ended in 1983, when Jaeger bought out the Valentines. Jaeger took the company public in December 1983 to help pay off the debt incurred in the buy-out, but he still retains controlling interest.

One of Jaeger's first major decisions as president was hiring a professional to run the organization. John O'Steen, a racing acquaintance of Jaeger's, was the person selected. While gaining experience on the amateur racing circuit, O'Steen was also climbing the corporate ladder at Procter & Gamble.

O'Steen had made up his mind to accept an enticing offer from a professional racing team when he had a chance meeting with Jaeger. After a month of negotiating, O'Steen turned down the racing offer and accepted the offer at Cincinnati Microwave. O'Steen now competes only occasionally in selected races.

Although the Cincinnati Microwave empire had been built on radar detectors, Jaeger, O'Steen and the company officers were aware that someday the market would slow and they would need to diversify. In 1986 a subsidiary of Cincinnati Microwave acquired Guardian Interlock Corporation, which shared Cincinnati Microwave's tradition of technological innovations.

The Guardian product is a motor vehicle ignition interlock that deters a driver from drinking and driving. The device requires that the user pass a sobriety test before the vehicle can be started. The system was designed to help the courts keep convicted drunk drivers off the road. Legislation endorsing the use of the interlock device as an additional sentencing measure has passed in 10 states and continues to gain support in many others.

Guardian also entered the home incarceration business in 1987. Designed in response to the problem of prison overcrowding, the Guardian system monitors an offender's whereabouts as well as measures the offender's blood alcohol count over the telephone line. Guardian has signed contracts with several jurisdictions to provide "home arrest" systems and monitoring services and was awarded the first federal contracts for such systems.

As Cincinnati Microwave looks to the future, it will continue to concentrate on developing its current business, as well as pursuing other opportunities that fit its strategy. In the radar warning receiver business, emphasis will be on developing technical advances and offering them to customers who want premium performance and premium service. Guardian Technologies will continue to develop products and services to maximize opportunities in the alternative sentencing area of the judicial sector.

Cincinnati Milacron

It has been known as Cincinnati Milacron since 1970, but most people still call it "The Mill."

Milacron's story begins in 1884 with the incorporation of The Cincinnati Screw and Tap Co. Fred A. Geier was working as a bank clerk in Kansas and came home to help settle his father's estate in 1887. He met Fred Holz, one of the partners and probably the genius behind Screw and Tap. The company had a small shop in rented space on the second floor of a building at Pearl and Plum streets. Geier's visits aroused his interest in the company, and he joined it.

Holz had designed a small milling machine used in the company's own manufacturing operations and had sold one to another local firm. A milling machine is a versatile machine tool which changes the shape of metal by cutting—as contrasted with pressing, forging or casting it.

Geier, primarily a salesman and administrator, saw the future in terms of the little milling machine and not screws and taps. In 1889 the company changed its name to The Cincinnati Milling Machine Company. Holz took charge of engineering, design and production at The Mill, and Geier did everything else.

In 1890 the company made its first international sale and by 1910 its exports accounted for 30% to 40% of its business. Today Milacron has manufacturing operations in four overseas countries and sales in a hundred more.

By the end of the century, the company had its own plant on Spring Grove Avenue and several hundred employees. During hard times The Mill resorted to unusual methods to keep people working. In 1893 it took orders on credit and paid its employees half in cash and half in scrip—all of which was later redeemed in full. Forty years later it kept much of its payroll intact during the Great Depression by finding new things to make and sell.

Milacron displayed its concern for its employees in other ways as well. In 1914 Fred Geier's brother, Otto, a Cincinnati physician, set up a fitness and health department at The Mill. It was one of the earliest and most complete in the United States at that time.

While the flow of improved products was unending, for 30 years The Mill's mainstays were milling machines and cutter grinders, which had been introduced in 1890. In 1900 one of its milling machines won a gold medal in the Paris Exhibition. (It was one of two Cincinnati companies thus honored; Baldwin's grand piano also won.)

In 1911 the company moved to Oakley when it was almost rural. Oakley is still the world headquarters of Milacron.

After World War I the machine tool business went into a slump, but by 1926 it had rebounded and The Mill had become the nation's leading machine-tool producer. It added other basic machine tools to its line, including the centerless grinding machine. This unique machine, still widely used throughout the metalworking industry, allowed manufacture of precision cylindrical parts for expanding industries such as automotive and aircraft. Some unique applications included the first perfectly round bowling balls and the first perfectly smooth surgical sutures.

The Mill played an important role during World War II. In the years just prior to Pearl Harbor, its floor space had been doubled. This allowed production and shipments to increase in 1942 to seven times the 1939 level: 17,511 machine tools were produced during 1942, 7.8% of the nation's machine-tool production.

In the postwar years The Mill introduced a variety of new products. At the national machine tool trade show in 1947, The Mill exhibited 54 machines, 31 of which were being shown for the first time. By this time the company had a complete line of basic machine tools and was in search of new fields.

It developed the first water-based cutting fluids in 1944. In contrast to commonly used oils, the new synthetic fluids did not smoke or burn. In the 1960s widespread use of plastics dictated new machines. The Mill has become the world leader in production of machines to process plastics into products as diverse as automobile bumpers and soft drink bottles.

In the area of automation, it was not until the 1950s that the first numerical controls were introduced. From its pioneering role in this new technology, Milacron has grown to be a U.S. leader in the production of highly sophisticated computer numerical controls for machine tools. These controls make it possible for less-skilled workers to perform complex machining operations easily.

The step to other areas of electronics was a short one, and Milacron-built computers and software now control the company's robots and plastics processing machines as well. Through acquisitions in the 1980s, the company expanded its products for factory automation to include metrology and inspection systems and industrial laser machines.

Not all presidents of The Mill have been Geiers, but the Geier family has been the driving force. Fred A. was followed by his son, Frederick V. Geier. For a time Frederick's cousin, Philip O. Geier Jr., ran the company. Today's chief executive officer is James A.D. Geier, and its president and chief operating officer is Daniel J. Meyer.

Milacron is a publicly held company and has been listed on the New York Stock Exchange since 1946.

In 1921, 10 years after the firm moved to Oakley, the Cincinnati Milling Machine Company's plant was the largest in the world devoted exclusively to the manufacture of milling machines and milling cutter grinders. Today these buildings are part of the complex which still is Cincinnati Milacron's world headquarters. Gift of J. P. Northcutt.

Cincinnati Milacron's history developing and building machines to boost productivity and quality levels in customers' manufacturing plants continued with the introduction in the early 1970s of the computer-controlled industrial robot. Today, Cincinnati Milacron is the largest U.S. manufacturer of robots used by industry for such diverse operations as arc welding, materials handling, machine loading, spot welding, drilling, riveting and grinding. Photograph. Courtesy of Cincinnati Milacron.

Cincom Systems Inc.

Although it is one of Cincinnati's youngest companies, Cincom already has made headlines as a leader in the development of computer software.

At the age of 20, CINCOM is not an old Cincinnati company. But within its field, the development of computer software, Cincom is one of the oldest in the business, and, because of the vision of its owner, Thomas Nies, one of the most successful. In two decades Cincom has grown out of its Hyde Park basement office and into one of the top dozen software firms worldwide.

In the 1960s Nies, a native of Cincinnati and an account executive for IBM, became convinced that the future of the computer industry lay not in computer equipment, or hardware, but in the programs, or software, that enable people to use computers. This was a revolutionary idea for its time, for it turned the existing computer world upside down.

Computers of this era were enormous machines, room-sized behemoths that were used almost exclusively for data processing. Data was entered on computer punch cards, and computer specialists ran the machines. The industry focused on the machines themselves and put much less emphasis on improving the software programs that ran the machines.

Cincom's world headquarters on Montana Avenue supports sales and service operations from Europe to Australia. Photograph courtesy of Cincom.

Nies pushed his ideas for software development at IBM, trying to interest the company in software that could be sold independently of the computer itself. The company showed little interest, so in 1968, Nies left IBM and with two other associates started a new business in the basement of the Nies' home in Hyde Park.

At first Cincom (the name is a meld of "Cincinnati" and "computers") was a distributor of a few small software products and services. But the focus of the founders' energy was in developing a new data base management program that would be more functional and flexible than the existing programs. A data base program allows users to store, update and retrieve information. Cincom introduced its new program, TOTAL, in 1969.

The market for Cincom's software was among large "mainframe" computer operations run by the world's largest companies and organizations. TOTAL's clients included everything from hotel chains to banks to government agencies. The product was enormously successful, and Cincom had carved out a dominant role in the emerging software development field.

The success of the company generated a need for more and more office space. Cincom moved out of Nies' basement into a modest two-room office on Victory Parkway that lacked not only a computer, but also a copying machine. Employees had to borrow computer time from their customers. Eventually Cincom took over the entire building and finally in 1974 moved to its world headquarters at 2300 Montana Avenue. Today Cincom employs about 1,600 people worldwide, including 600 in Greater Cincinnati.

Cincom introduced additional software programs in the 1970s, including MANTIS, a new computer language which is part of a complete set of application development products. These originally were intended to increase the productivity of application development programmers handling increasing volumes of work. Now some of these products even allow non-technical users to manipulate the power of a computer to meet the unique requirements that individual businesses have.

Cincom grew at phenomenal rates in the 1970s, but Nies was convinced that the market for mainframe software would flatten out in the 1980s, with the increased availability of mini computers, less powerful but less expensive cousins of the mainframe. In 1980 Cincom began a major research and development effort to produce new software for the expanding mini computer market, as well as for mainframes. A second key decision was to produce software that was compatible with IBM's main competitor, Digital Equipment Corporation (DEC), as well as NCR Corporation, WANG and Honeywell Bull.

Cincom began introducing its new product lines in 1983 and 1984. The new software included SUPRA, with even more data base management capabilities, and NET/MASTER, a program that automates the manual operations of a computer network. NET/MASTER allows a network to build in automatic responses, solve problems and monitor multiple operations from a single console.

One of the most successful of the new products, especially in the digital marketplace, is CONTROL:Manufacturing. This program manages the information systems of large manufacturing companies. Customers include giants such as Michelin and American Standard.

By 1989 the new products are expected to account for 83% of Cincom's nearly $200 million in revenue, making this development effort a well-timed, high-stakes gamble. The new products have helped Cincom make the transition from a mid-size firm with a few product offerings to a large software organization with perhaps the most extensive product line in the industry.

In addition to the development of innovative products, much of Cincom's success can be attributed to its aggressive pursuit of international markets. It is one of Cincinnati's most successful exporters, having won national awards for Export Excellence. The company first entered the international market in 1971 with sales to Canada. A year later Cincom became operational in Europe with sales to 3M and the Procter & Gamble Co.'s European division. Today Cincom is active on six continents, with installations in over 70 countries. International sales account for 60% of gross dollars.

Each year Cincom hosts CinterAct, an international conference for its clients and potential clients. In June 1988, in honor of the city's bicentennial, Cincom held the conference in Cincinnati and flew in 70 European clients on a Concorde, marking the first appearance of the jet in Cincinnati.

COMAIR, Inc.

What began as a father and son's dream of starting a commuter airline service has become the nation's fastest-growing regional carrier.

Comair has had one of the most exciting growth records of any business in America. The airline was founded by Raymond Mueller and his son, David, with their personal assets. Raymond served as president, and David not only performed as executive vice president but, being a certified pilot, flew many of the routes. The original Comair fleet consisted of a seven-passenger Piper Navajo aircraft.

Comair began scheduled flights between the cities of Cincinnati, Cleveland and Akron-Canton in April 1977. The company's original purpose was to provide frequent flights to medium-sized cities that lacked good, efficient air service. Although deregulation of the airline industry became effective in 1978, major jet carriers already were cutting back service in short-haul markets in 1977, creating a market niche for regional commuters like Comair.

In 1983 Comair became the first U.S. carrier to receive the new Saab-Fairchild SF-340 airliner, which has the latest state-of-the-art technology equipment for regional airline service. Manufactured by Saab-Scania of Sweden, the 33-seat pressurized aircraft offers full in-flight service and comfortable flights to Comair's most distant cities.

In October 1983 Comair purchased Servair, Inc., a fixed-base operation at the Greater Cincinnati International Airport, and changed its name to CVG Aviation. Comair's wholly-owned subsidiary now provides outside aircraft owners and transient aircraft with the best fleet base of operations service available anywhere. The following year Comair purchased a Learjet 25, which it offers for private charter through CVG Corpflite, a subsidiary of CVG Aviation.

As of March 1988 Comair operated a total of 50 aircraft—12 Embraer Bandeirantes, 23 Fairchild IIIs and 15 Saab SF-340s—and served 42 cities in 11 states as well as Toronto, Canada and Freeport, Grand Bahama.

A solid marketing agreement with Delta Air Lines has contributed significantly to Comair's growth. Comair has been a "Delta Connection" carrier since September 1984. This marketing agreement allows Comair to offer passengers lower joint fares, coordinated schedules and Delta Frequent Flyer mileage. In November 1987 Comair became the Delta Connection in Florida, feeding Delta flights in Orlando and Ft. Lauderdale.

Comair issued a public stock offerings in July 1981, when Raymond Mueller was elected chairman of the board and David, president. Additional stock offerings were issued in June 1983 and May 1985. Delta purchased 20% of Comair's common stock in July 1986, cementing the partnership between the two in the Delta Connection program. In October 1987 Comair's board of directors approved an initial quarterly cash dividend.

Comair's total passenger boardings have soared, rising to more than 625,000 through September 1988, from 430,000 the previous year. And 30-day advance bookings averaged 51,000 versus 37,000 during the same period.

Comair has 1,500 employees, whom its president credits for the growth that the airline is experiencing. In October 1988 Comair announced plans to add 25 more planes to its fleet: five Swedish Saab SF-340s and 20 Brazilian Embraer Brasilias worth $165 million.

A Comair flight prepares to land at Greater Cincinnati International Airport. Photograph. Courtesy of Comair Inc.

The Delta Queen Steamboat Company

The *Delta Queen* looks like a riverboat, but she is really a time machine for people who want to visit golden days accompanied by good food and a comfortable bed. As a landmark, she may be Cincinnati's best known symbol. The *Queen* has shown up in movies, in magazines, in television commercials. She was the star in a campaign that made her a historical asset. She is a beautiful boat and can go anywhere there is enough water to float her.

Her present owner is the Delta Queen Steamboat Company.

Her first Cincinnati owner was the Greene Line, a family-owned company which came into being in 1890 as an operator of packet boats. The Greene family boats also carried passengers, and after World War II they took precedence over freight. Capt. Tom Greene purchased the *Queen* from the Maritime Commission in 1947.

For a vessel which has come to symbolize American inland river life, the *Delta Queen* has an unusual history. The boat was designed by an American, James Burns, of Oakland, California, but her hull was built on the River Clyde in Scotland in 1926. She was one of two identical vessels designed for use in the United States and the most expensive crafts of their type ever built.

The *Delta Queen*, a favorite excursion boat on the Ohio and Mississippi rivers for more than 40 years. Photograph. Courtesy of the Delta Queen Steamboat Company.

The *Delta Queen* twice has crossed open sea, once to come to the United States and once to reach Cincinnati. For her first trip, she and her sister vessel were disassembled and loaded on a freighter in Scotland. They were taken to San Francisco, where the *Queen* did packet duty on the Sacramento River. During World War II she was used to ferry U.S. troops in San Francisco harbor and thus came into the hands of the Maritime Commission.

Capt. Frederick Geller, a sea captain, with the help of a tug took the *Delta Queen* to the ocean again. She went down the Pacific Ocean to the Panama Canal, then north through the Caribbean Sea, across the Gulf of Mexico and up the Mississippi to New Orleans. From there she traveled under her own steam power up the Mississippi and Ohio rivers to Cincinnati, with veteran river pilot Capt. Fred Way, Jr., in charge. The total trip was more than 7,000 miles.

What the Greene Line acquired was picture book material—a boat 285 feet long and 58 feet across the beam. She can carry 192 passengers at an average of seven miles an hour. Her 2,000 horsepower steam engine turns a paddlewheel 29 feet in diameter and 18 feet across. The hull is galvanized iron and her interior is of oak, teak, and mahogany. There are stained glass windows, but for the modern traveler there is air conditioning, too. Since she arrived in Cincinnati in 1947, about $7 million have been spent on her, eight times what she cost to build.

In 1970 she was registered as a National Historical Place. She also came up against congressionally created safety codes that had been written for sea-going vessels but which applied, albeit unrealistically, with equal effect to a river steamer that would never get 200 yards away from shore. A remarkable Cincinnati woman, Betty Blake, led the campaign that achieved congressional exemptions from certain aspects of the new law. The boat's current exemption is the seventh, and it runs until 1992. The *Queen* looks as if she were built for Scarlett O'Hara, but she also has a modern sprinkler system, smoke and heat sensors and other safety devices in her wood superstructure.

The *Delta Queen.* Photograph. The Paul Briol Collection.

The legendary *Queen* is a familiar sight to Cincinnatians and is the city's special pride, but she has a bigger, newer and more costly sister, the luxurious *Mississippi Queen.* Christened in August 1976 the *Mississippi Queen* is the first river craft of her type to be built in more than 50 years.

The *Mississippi Queen* was designed by the English craftsmen and decorators who turned out the *Queen Elizabeth II.* She was built at Jeffersonville, Indiana, at a cost of $27 million. She is the largest paddlewheeler ever built—382 feet long and 68 feet wide. Her paddlewheel is 36 feet across and 22 feet in diameter. Her engines supply 2,000 horsepower, allowing an average speed of eight miles per hour.

She carries 406 passengers and averages a crew member for every two-and-a-half passengers. She is undeniably a river boat, but the ambiance is more nearly that of an ocean liner, thanks to her size. She has a Jacuzzi pool, elevators between her seven decks, a movie theater, sauna, gym and library.

The Delta Queen Steamboat Company is privately owned. Patrick T. Fahey is president and chief executive officer.

Didier Taylor Refractories Corporation

Didier Taylor Refractories Corporation serves industries around the world with a combination of high-quality refractory product selection, dedicated technical development and engineering services. The company's beginnings can be traced to a small firebrick business founded in Cincinnati by Charles Taylor in 1864.

Shortly after the American Revolution ended, the industrial revolution began to reach the Ohio Valley. Firebrick became one of the basic and essential tools. The producers of iron, glass and many other industries, such as steamboats, required high-temperature furnaces which, in turn, depended upon firebrick lining to operate properly.

As the country moved westward, brickmakers located near the sources of fireclays. The first brickyard (later known as a refractory plant) in Ohio was started in 1841 at East Liverpool. Over the next fifty years, another forty would join this pioneer in the Ohio Valley.

Charles Taylor was an English immigrant who found his way to Covington, Kentucky, where he was employed as a potter. The pottery's owner had a daughter who in time became Mrs. Charles Taylor. The young couple was ambitious. In 1861 the Taylors crossed the Ohio River to start their own pottery business on Burns Street in Cincinnati. This area was one of the first industrial sections of Cincinnati.

Foreseeing the continuing growth of the firebrick industry, the young potter founded Charles Taylor and Company in 1864. Clay was shipped from Eastern Ohio by barge to his refractories plant at Cincinnati. Raw clay was converted into linings for heating stoves and retort vessels, used in producing fuel gas from coal. In 1865 he merged with three partners who owned a new operation called the Scioto Fire Brick Company. The name Charles Taylor and Company was maintained.

By the time of his death in 1891, Charles and his three sons, Charles F., William and Arthur, had established plants in West Virginia and Alabama, and the company had become a leader in both the technology and the economics of the industry. William Taylor died soon after joining the company, but Charles and Arthur spent their entire business careers developing it. During this period the name was changed to Charles Taylor and Sons Company.

The sons continued producing firebrick in Cincinnati and opened another plant on the Ohio River across from Portsmouth. A sophisticated laboratory and dedicated technicians became an important factor in Taylor's growth as the expanding industry turned to more complex products. New Taylor products were developed which could withstand extraordinary high temperatures employing such exotic ingredients as zircon, corundum and even kyanite brought all the way from India. The new refractories completely protected expensive equipment from the astonishing heat developed by the many modern manufacturing processes. These refractories were and still are expendable in the process and must be replaced—some in a few days, others after many years, depending on the application and refractory itself.

Clifford Taylor, a grandson of the founder, became president in 1942 and continued developing the business until 1951 when he sold it to National Lead Company, later to become NL Industries, Inc. The subsidiary maintained its identity as Charles Taylor and Sons and became a world leader in its fields. It expanded into Europe by establishing a new enterprise, Charles Taylor Sons S.A., and opened its first overseas plant at Ghent, Belgium in 1962. The company has customers in the glass, metallurgical and steel industries in countries around the world.

A new plant, general office and laboratory were built on Broadwell Road in Anderson Township in 1969, and the company moved from its original location on Burns Street after 100 years.

At about the time Charles Taylor was born in England (around 1833), Friedrich Didier opened a refractory shop in Rostock, Germany. He expanded the business and added other facilities to his original plant, one of which was a lime plant started in 1310. The mines supplying the lime kiln also contained gravel and sand needed for a type of heat-resistant refractory brick.

Didier's partner, Wilhelm Kornhardt, continued the small and developing business until his death in 1871. The firm then evolved into a public stock company. Eventually it had an American subsidiary, which was dissolved during World War I. A second start in North America was made in 1975 when Didier built a plant in Becancour, Quebec. Further expansion into North America materialized with Didier's 1978 purchase of the Taylor Refractories Division of NL Industries.

Thus, the one-time brickyard on Burns Street became Didier Taylor Refractories Corporation. The special high-temperature products developed by Didier Taylor and Didier-Werk A.G. are manufactured in the plants of both companies now, and Taylor remains in its Cincinnati headquarters at 8361 Broadwell Road.

Charles Taylor (1832-1891), founder of Charles Taylor and Company.

In this quality control laboratory at Didier Taylor Refractories, technicians are inspecting a feeder tube through which molten glass will pass. The seven-hole cylinder in the lower center of the photograph is a blast furnace checker. Each is 12 inches in length, and they are stacked to a height of 80 feet forming tubes, or flues, to preheat combustion air for blast furnaces. The brick-like tiles in the foreground are used to line a wide variety of industrial furnaces.

Photographs courtesy of Didier Taylor Refractories.

Drackett Company

Give Cincinnatians a word-association test and one of the pairings is a certainty. You say "Drackett", and the answer will be "Drano." Like saying "please" when you have not quite heard a companion's comment, it's a classic Cincinnati reaction: identifying a company with the first-born of its brand names to become a part of the language. Drackett is a company which produces household words.

Check your own cupboards. Chances are you will find a Drackett Household word: Drano, Windex, Vanish, Behold, Endust, Mr. Muscle, Renuzit, Twinkle, O-Cedar and—surprise—a food supplement called Nutrament.

The founder, Phillip Drackett, turned his back on the family craft—shipbuilding—to become a pharmacist. He seems to have been born a chemist, and, though he operated a drugstore near Cleveland for a while, it was not enough. He spent most of his life experimenting with chemicals as he worked selling pharmaceuticals, a career which brought him to Cincinnati.

It took him a long time, but finally he gave in completely to his chemical itch at age 56. He and his wife, Sallie, started brokering bulk chemicals in 1910. Phillip was the salesman, Sallie was the home office. They sold soda ash, caustic soda, chlorinated lime and denatured alcohol.

The expanded use of indoor plumbing brought new conveniences—and new headaches. The power of Drāno to unclog stubborn, stopped-up drains became the basis for the development of a full line of household products by the Drackett Company.

In 1915 their sons, Phillip Jr. and Harry, joined the business and the company became P.W. Drackett & Sons. By this time, the Dracketts were packaging the chemicals they sold under the family name. During and immediately after World War I, Drackett was the major producer of pharmaceutical-grade Epsom salts.

The young company's trademark was a capital "D" with a horizontal diamond. The "diamond D" symbol still can be seen on the Drackett plant built in 1919 at 5020 Spring Grove Avenue, a facility still there, though much changed.

The Drackett Company has changed the formula of Windex glass cleaner about 60 times in the past 30 years to keep the product effective and ahead of its competition. Illustrations from *The History of Drackett,* courtesy of The Drackett Company.

Phillip Drackett's chemical curiosity led to the company's first major consumer-product breakthrough. As indoor plumbing and its inevitable companion, stopped drains, became commonplace after World War I, Phillip tinkered up a mixture of caustic soda and tiny aluminum chips whose churning reaction in water cleared the most stubborn goose-necks. Sallie, a language purist, created the name, "Drano," and insisted on the macron—the little dash—above the "a" to insure their household word was pronounced in a way that left no doubt about its intended use.

The Dracketts were phenomenal salesmen and promoters. In seven years their Drano swept the United States and Canada. Their early Drano symbol, a dotted line showing flow through a goose-neck, has remained unchanged except for graphic refinement.

The Drackett name stayed with the company as Phillip was succeeded by his son, Harry, and a grandson, Roger, the last of the family name to head up the company.

Their tenures were periods of vigorous expansion and experimentation. In 1934 the company introduced Windex, the first glass cleaner and still the leading brand; in 1937 it built a plant for product processing and research with soybeans, which led eventually to interest in food products and plastics. A Sharonville facility turned out soybean oil and cattle meal as World War II began. After the war Drackett added to its soybean processing business an experimental textile fiber called Azlon, a "dessert" for pets called Charge Dog Candy and raw materials for the plastics industry. The entire soybean operation was sold in 1957 when Drackett decided to focus all of its attention on household products.

Expansion continued in other ways at the same time. In 1955 Drackett purchased two companies—Calmar and Maclin—which produced packaging supplies the company could use for its own wares. In 1958 it acquired Vanish bowl cleaner by purchase of the Judson Dunaway Corp. and made it the industry leader. In the 1960s it introduced Twinkle Silver Polish and acquired a list of nationally known products and brand names by purchasing the O-Cedar line from the Martin-Marietta Co.

Renamed simply, "The Drackett Company," it went public in 1944. Its stock was listed on the New York Stock Exchange in 1964, and the growing company was acquired by Bristol-Myers in 1965. Nicholas Evans became president in 1969 and Roger Drackett retired as chairman in 1972, ending 60 years of family management. Douglas G. Cowan is now president of Drackett.

Bristol-Myers expanded Drackett's role in food marketing, adding Metrecal, Nutrament, an energy food supplement, and a line of "Weight-Watchers" foods to its marketing mix in the mid-1960s. Changing dieting trends and a desire to concentrate on household product marketing produced a series of planned divestitures. Calmar and Maclin were sold in 1967 and the Weight-Watcher division was sold in 1979, leaving Drackett once more a premier dealer in products for the home. In 1982 Drackett could boast it had eight household words which were the biggest sellers in their fields, including, of course, Drano. Drackett products are sold in Europe, Australia, Canada and the United States through its parent, the Bristol-Myers Co.

Through almost 80 years Drackett has adapted to a changing pattern of consumer needs. For example Windex glass cleaner has undergone about 60 formula changes in the past 30 years to keep it effective and ahead of its competition. Drackett's growing research operations are occupying an ever-larger part of the firm's Spring Grove plant, and new offices downtown have become necessary in order to make room for the company's continued curiosity with chemical products for the home.

Eagle-Picher Industries, Inc.

From modest beginnings in 1843 in Cincinnati, Eagle-Picher has become a highly diversified manufacturer of industrial products that touch virtually every segment of the American economy. Courtesy of Eagle-Picher.

Eagle-Picher Industries, Inc. is a diversified manufacturer of industrial products operating over 90 plants in 34 states, Canada, Spain and West Germany. William D. Atteberry, who rose through the ranks from production manager to president and chief executive officer in 1967, was elected chairman of the board in 1982, and a Cincinnatian, Thomas E. Petry, was elected president and chief executive officer the same year. Sales of $677 million in 1987 were the highest in the company's long history, which began in 1843 with the founding of Conkling, Wood & Co. on the east side of Spring Street, north of Court Street, by Edgar Conkling and William Wood.

The firm manufactured white and red lead, litharge and chromes, ingredients in paint pigments and sold under the "Eagle" trade name. In 1867 Wood and other local investors incorporated the business as The Eagle White Lead Company with Wood as president. While Eagle White Lead was growing in Cincinnati, Oliver H. and William H. Picher organized The Picher Lead & Zinc Co. in Joplin, Missouri in 1876. It later became an important lead supplier to Eagle White Lead.

A significant financial reorganization took place in 1891, when John B. Swift of Cincinnati and his associates bought The Eagle White Lead Co. and Swift became president.

In 1904 the Cincinnati firm bought control of Picher Lead to insure the availability of lead and, after Picher's 1914 rich strike of lead and zinc in northeastern Oklahoma, the Eagle-Picher Lead Co. was formed by a merger of the two. John B. Swift became chairman and Oliver S. Picher, president. Following Picher's untimely death in 1920, Swift stepped back into active management until 1928, when he was succeeded by Arthur E. Bendelari, the head of the mining operations.

During the depression of the 1930s, the company's sales fell from a 1929 high of $26 million to $7 million in 1932. The depression was as difficult for Eagle-Picher as it was for the nation, and many insiders gave credit to Joseph Hummell, Jr., an employee since 1892 and president from 1937 to 1941, for his efforts in achieving the company's survival. In the 1940s while Joel M. Bowlby was president, commercial germanium dioxide was produced in the company's research facilities in Joplin, aiding in the development of revolutionary transistors during World War II and led to Eagle-Picher being the sole source of isotopically pure boron for government nuclear and defense applications in the 1980s. Also, through the acquisition of diatomaceous earth deposits in Nevada, production of Celatom products began and has grown significantly in importance. In its 100th anniversary year, 1943, the company's stock was listed on the New York Stock Exchange.

T. Spencer Shore, a director since 1943, succeeded Bowlby as president on January 1, 1949, and under his leadership a strategic change of corporate direction began, designed to eliminate Eagle-Picher's dependence on the non-ferrous metal market. The company strengthened its cash position and made a basic decision to move away from lead and zinc related businesses into manufacturing products for industrial markets. This was accomplished by making acquisitions and developing new products internally. Three acquisitions made in the 1950s positioned the company as a manufacturer of industrial rubber products primarily for the automotive industry; interior trim and insulations for the automotive market; and porcelain enamel frit for the major appliance industry.

Through the 1960s and 1970s, the company continued its diversification strategy but with an ever-increasing emphasis on the development of high technology products. Today products manufactured by Eagle-Picher touch virtually every segment of the American economy. From earth-moving machinery to vibration-dampening products which provide the quiet ride in an automobile; from the filter medium of diatomaceous earth that gives wine and beer sparkle and clarity to high-purity boron to make nuclear energy safe; from giant can-washing machines for beverage cans to cast-aluminum impellers in a turbocharger; from satellite batteries to wrappers for confectionery and dairy products, Eagle-Picher products provide a quiet quality and a subtle improvement to thousands of products which are essential in our everyday lives.

A most notable area of the company's involvement in industrial America is a direct outgrowth of Eagle-Picher's origins—lead and zinc mining and the establishment in 1912 of a research laboratory for battery research. Eagle-Picher Industries is the leading manufacturer of sophisticated special-purpose battery systems primarily for aerospace and defense applications. In every manned space flight from Project Mercury to the flight of the space shuttle *Discovery*, electrical energy was supplied by batteries developed by Eagle-Picher Industries.

From the modest beginnings in Cincinnati in 1843 on Spring Street to its present headquarters in the 580 Building, Eagle-Picher Industries has grown into one of the truly unique corporations in America today.

From Project Mercury to Sky-Lab to the flight of the space shuttle *Columbia*, Eagle-Picher special purpose battery systems provided virtually all of the electrical energy on these missions. Photograph courtesy of Eagle-Picher.

Fifth Third Bank

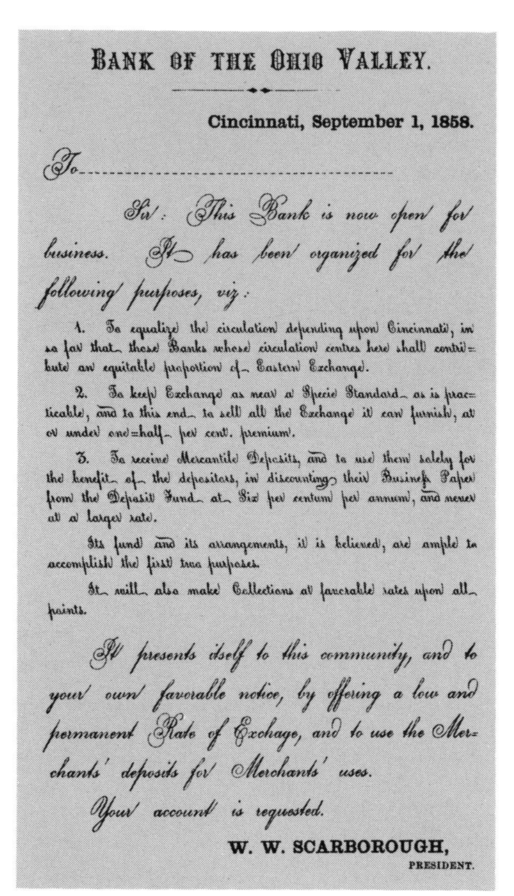

BANK OF THE OHIO VALLEY.

Cincinnati, September 1, 1858.

To..

Sir: This Bank is now open for business. It has been organized for the following purposes, viz:

1. To equalize the circulation depending upon Cincinnati, in so far that those Banks whose circulation centres here shall contribute an equitable proportion of Eastern Exchange.

2. To keep Exchange as near a Specie Standard as is practicable, and to this end to sell all the Exchange it can furnish, at or under one-half per cent. premium.

3. To receive Mercantile Deposits, and to use them solely for the benefit of the depositors, in discounting their Business Paper from the Deposit Fund at Six per centum per annum, and never at a larger rate.

Its fund and its arrangements, it is believed, are ample to accomplish the first two purposes.

It will also make Collections at favorable rates upon all points.

It presents itself to this community, and to your own favorable notice, by offering a low and permanent Rate of Exchage, and to use the Merchants' deposits for Merchants' uses.

Your account is requested.

W. W. SCARBOROUGH,
PRESIDENT.

Established by capital from outside Cincinnati, the Bank of the Ohio Valley opened in June 1858. Its first President was distinguished businessman William W. Scarborough; in 1860 Miles Greenwood and Reuben R. Springer served on its board. The bank was purchased by the Third National Bank in 1871. From the John J. Rowe Collection.

The way banks grow—by consolidation and merger—has made some fine contributions to orotund nomenclature, none more ear-filling than The Fifth Third Union Trust Company.

On June 17, 1858, The Bank of the Ohio Valley opened its doors, becoming the first element of what was to become Fifth Third Bank.

In 1863 Congress passed the National Bank Act, stating that banks had to deposit bonds equal to one-third of their capital stock to back up the new federal currency. Within weeks a federal charter was issued for a new bank called the Third National, with offices at Third and Walnut. Third National bought the Bank of the Ohio Valley in 1871 and on the basis of its capital became Ohio's largest bank.

Coincidentally, on September 28, 1882, The Queen City National Bank of Cincinnati opened at 53 West Third Street. Presumably for security purposes each customer had to register his or her signature at the bank in a permanent journal, which still exists.

On April 2, 1888, The Queen City National Bank of Cincinnati changed its name to The Fifth National Bank. Under that name it moved to the Chamber of Commerce building at Fourth and Vine.

The Third National and The Fifth National merged on June 1, 1908, and did business at 14-16 West Fourth Street. The combined banks adopted a new name, The Fifth Third National Bank. In 1908, 1910 and 1919, it purchased the American National, S. Kuhn & Sons and the Market National banks, but it could not open branches as only state-chartered banks could do that.

New Union Trust Building. The Gibson House, Walnut and Fourth streets. Jacob G. Schmidlapp, founder and president of the Union Savings Bank and Trust Co., commissioned famed Chicago architect Daniel H. Burnham to design Cincinnati's first "skyscraper," or steel-skeleton office building. The Union Trust Building was completed in 1901, with additions added in 1914 and 1927. The building served as the main office of the Fifth Third Union Trust Co. from 1931 to 1971, when Fifth Third moved to a new building on Fountain Square. It is now known as the Fourth and Walnut Building. From promotional brochure for George W. Englehardt's *Cincinnati, the Queen City* (Cincinnati, 1901), p. 18.

Enter the Union Savings Bank and Trust Co., which was organized in 1890. By 1901 it had built its own 18-story office building at Fourth and Walnut streets and was permitted to have branches. In 1903 Union Trust bought The Cincinnati Savings Society and opened the city's first branch bank in 1904 at 1127 Vine Street.

Stockholders of Fifth Third and of Union Trust became stockholders in both banks in 1919. After the affiliation Union Trust expanded rapidly. It bought the Security Savings Bank and Safe Deposit Co., The Mohawk State Bank and the Walnut Hills Savings Bank. Then came the Court House Savings Bank (1922), Home Savings Bank (1923), Winton Savings Bank (1924) and the First National of Madisonville (1927).

And at long last on February 23, 1927, The Fifth Third National Bank and The Union Trust Co. were consolidated into a single bank and under the latter's state charter began operating as The Fifth Third Union Trust Co. in the Union Trust Building.

Cincinnati's financial institutions survived the depression relatively well, but the city was not unscathed. In 1930 the Ohio superintendent of banking had to take over The Cosmopolitan Bank and Trust Co. and eventually sold its assets to The Fifth Third Union Trust, adding five branches to Fifth Third's operation. It also bought the Oakley Bank in 1930. Three years later the Ohio bank superintendent liquidated The Washington Bank and Trust Co., one of whose branches became Fifth Third's Pleasant Ridge branch. In 1969, when Fountain Square was redesigned, the bank's headquarters were moved into a new Fifth Third Center on the north side of the square. The bank's decision to build there allowed the renewal of the square to begin.

For many years the Rowe family presided over Fifth Third management. John J. Rowe was president of a rival bank—First National—but resigned to become president of Fifth Third. His son, William S. Rowe, followed him as president and chairman of the board. The main office of Fifth Third was named in his honor upon his retirement from the board in 1987. The current president and chief executive officer is Clement L. Buenger.

Fifth Third Bancorp was established in 1975 as a holding company to purchase other banks. Its lead bank, Fifth Third Bank, has several affiliates, including Fifth Third Securities, Fifth Third Travel and Midwest Payment Systems. By 1988 Fifth Third had 72 branches serving the Tri-State, including: The Fifth Third Bank of Northwestern Ohio, N.A., based in Findlay; The Fifth Third Bank of Western Ohio, N.A., headquartered in Wapakoneta; The Citizens Heritage Bank N.A., with main offices in Piqua, Ohio; The Fifth Third Bank of Southern Ohio, based in West Union; The Fifth Third Bank of Columbus; The Fifth Third Bank of Boone County in Florence, Kentucky; The Fifth Third Bank of Kenton County in Covington, Kentucky; The Fifth Third Bank of Campbell County, N.A., Ft. Thomas, Kentucky; and The Fifth Third Bank of Southeastern Indiana, located in Batesville, Indiana.

Fifth Third is proud to be involved with the Cincinnati community as a sponsor of the Cincinnati Bicentennial Commission, the Cincinnati Symphony Orchestra's summer concerts, and the Cincinnati Regatta.

Franciscan Health System of Cincinnati, Inc.

The Franciscan Health System of Cincinnati, Inc., incorporated in 1987, is composed of three hospitals—St. Francis-St. George, Providence and Emerson A. North; two social service agencies—St. John and St. Raphael; two long-term care and retirement communities—Franciscan Terrace and West Park; and dozens of outpatient and acute care services. The system traces its healing mission in this community to 1858. In that year six Sisters of the Franciscan Sisters of the Poor came here from Germany at the invitation of Archbishop John B. Purcell.

They established St. Mary Hospital on West Fourth Street in a building that had previously housed the St. Aloysius Orphan Asylum. St. Mary's quickly acquired a reputation as a place of healing and comfort, where the clinical expertise and medical knowledge of the time was available to travelers as well as residents and to the sick and poor of all faiths.

In 1859 the Sisters built a modern hospital that could accommodate 75 patients at Betts and Linn streets in the West End.

Thirty years after St. Mary's opened its doors, the Sisters opened St. Francis Hospital in South Fairmount to meet the health care needs of a new generation of west and northwest residents. From its inception in 1888, St. Francis was gratefully acknowledged for its exceptional efforts in caring for the chronically ill and aged poor.

What began with St. Mary's has grown through more than six generations of challenge and change into a state-of-the-art network of health care services and facilities—the Franciscan Health System of Cincinnati. Sponsorship of the system is shared by the Franciscan Sisters of the Poor, Brooklyn, New York—the fifth largest Catholic health services system in the country—and the Dominican Sisters of Saint Mary of the Springs.

The Dominican Sisters founded St. George Hospital in the Cincinnati suburb of Westwood in 1944, and the two orders were brought together with the merger of St. Francis and St. George hospitals. The new St. Francis-St. George Hospital, which opened atop Western Hills at the corner of Queen City and Boudinot avenues in 1982, replaced the two older hospitals. The 290-bed hospital offers a wide range of health care services and programs. The St. Francis-St. George Surgical Center is also located on the grounds. Adjacent to the hospital is the Breast Imaging Center.

After more than a century of service, St. Mary Hospital closed in 1971, the same year that Providence Hospital opened. Located on Kipling Avenue in Mt. Airy on the grounds of the Powel Crosley Jr. estate, Providence is a 372-bed community hospital with a full range of major medical/surgical services. Its Emergency Care Center, opened in 1984 off of Interstate 74 in Harrison, serves western Hamilton County and southeastern Indiana.

Emerson A. North Hospital, a 115-bed psychiatric and chemical dependency facility, is the newest member of the health system but one with a venerable history. Located on 25 wooded acres on Hamilton Avenue in College Hill, the original building was first used as the Ohio Female College and converted in 1873 to a private psychiatric hospital, the Cincinnati Sanitarium. In 1956 the hospital changed its name to memorialize Dr. Emerson A. North, a leader in the field of psychiatry in Cincinnati. And in 1988 the staff completed a long-awaited move from the original building to a striking new facility on the same grounds.

St. John Social Service Center in Over-the-Rhine was established in 1936 by the Franciscan Sisters of the Poor at the request of Archbishop John T. McNicholas. The center targets the needs of the poor, focusing on single, female heads of households, low-income teen fathers, the elderly, homeless families, and families on public assistance.

The Franciscan Sisters of the Poor established the St. Raphael Social Service Center in Hamilton, Ohio in 1942. The center provides a variety of programs including: emergency money and supplemental food; individualized case work; telephone calls to the elderly and handicapped; clothing, furniture and appliances; and a layette service.

One of the system's long-term care facilities, Franciscan Terrace at St. Clare Center, opened in 1971 north of Cincinnati in Wyoming. Included are 110 nursing home beds, 50 rest beds, 11 independent living apartments, and a variety of services, including outreach, for senior citizens.

West Park, composed of 118 independent living apartments, 56 assisted living units, and 100 health care or skilled nursing beds, opened in 1983. In addition, 72 new "assisted living plus" units have been added, and furnished one-bedroom apartments are available for respite care.

The system's most recent development, Senior Network, combines all of its various programs and services into one comprehensive health care network for people over 55. The Senior Network Resource Center at West Park provides information on aging health and lifestyles to health care professionals and people in the community.

The foundress, Blessed Frances Schervier, never could have imagined such far-reaching advancements. Today a staff of more than 3,000 experienced professionals in dozens of specialized areas use the most advanced life-saving technologies available. With 777 combined hospital beds and 471 additional units in the retirement communities, the Franciscan Health System of Cincinnati is the largest network of health care services in the Tri-State area. Together the emergency departments at Providence and St. Francis-St. George hospitals treat more patients than any other facility in the Cincinnati area, making it the busiest emergency system in the region.

Much more than a collection of services and institutions, the Franciscan Health System of Cincinnati is a system of beliefs, principally the same reverence for life and the healing mission that guided the original six Sisters on their journey from Germany. Through six generations of challenge and change, the Franciscan Sisters of the Poor have remained a vital part of the lives and the dreams of this community, this city, this region. Because they've never stopped finding better ways to serve.

St. Mary Hospital was established in 1858.

Photograph. Courtesy of Franciscan Health System of Cincinnati, Inc.

Frisch's Restaurants, Inc.

Frisch's had its beginnings in 1905, when Samuel Frisch opened his lunch stand on Freeman Avenue. Ten years later, he opened Frisch's Stag Lunch in Norwood, and in 1921, his three sons—David, Irving and Reuben—joined him in the restaurant business. Dave was only 21 when he took over management of the Stag Lunch upon his father's death in 1923.

Dave opened Frisch's Cafe at the turnaround of the Oakley car line on Madison Road after selling his interest in the Stag Lunch to his brothers in 1932. This store closed in 1939 when Dave opened the first year-round drive-in of the Cincinnati area in Fairfax. Hailed as a Frisch's Restaurant, Dave named it the Mainliner after a tri-motor commercial passenger plane that flew into Lunken Airfield. A replica of this plane appears on the restaurant's exterior sign to this day. Dave added a second restaurant in 1944 on Reading Road. Because the building resembled George Washington's Virginia residence, he named it Mt. Vernon.

Two years later Dave visited Glendale, California, where a man named Bob Wian was selling a double-decked hamburger called "Big Boy." Realizing that the cooking process of two smaller hamburger patties was faster than that of a single patty of equal weight, Dave brought the idea back to Cincinnati and began selling the sandwich in his two restaurants. There was one ingredient change. While Wian served his sandwich with a Thousand Island dressing, Dave created a specially formulated tartar sauce. The recipe was unique to Frisch's and still is served with many of its sandwiches and dinner entrees today.

The Big Boy chain expanded when a franchise agreement was signed with Bob Wian in 1946 and Frisch's Restaurants, Inc. was incorporated in 1947. The agreement provided for exclusive rights to open and sub-franchise Big Boy restaurants in Ohio, Kentucky, Indiana and Florida. That same year, the first Big Boy restaurant opened on Central Parkway in Cincinnati, and Jack C. Maier joined the company as a part-time car attendant and fountain boy at the Mainliner.

Selling hamburgers through a drive-in restaurant and offering sandwiches quickly cooked to order were novel concepts. So were electronic speaker phones from the curb to the building to assist car hops who delivered the orders. During the next three decades, Frisch's Big Boy restaurants were the gathering place for teens, cruising past the canopied curb service in their cars. Whether neighborhood or small town location, it was the place to see and be seen. Generations grew up recognizing the statue of the chubby boy in striped overalls with a slingshot in his hip pocket permanently stationed outside the restaurant. Pranksters sometimes removed the statues, giving Big Boy a temporary home on high school property.

By 1961, the year after Frisch's first sold its common stock to the public on the over-the-counter market, there were 140 Frisch's locations, including franchises. Several proprietary products—the Big Boy sandwich, the Brawny Lad steak sandwich and the Buddie Boy ham and cheese sandwich — were developed and trademarked.

Expansion in the late 1960's included the opening of Annette's, a white tablecloth restaurant named after Dave's wife; the Quality Hotel Central in Norwood, across from the original Stag Lunch; and the round Quality Hotel Riverview in Covington, Kentucky, featuring a revolving restaurant on its 18th floor and a panoramic view of the Cincinnati skyline and Northern Kentucky hillsides.

When David Frisch died in 1970, the company had $30 million in retail sales. Jack C. Maier, who guided the company as executive vice president during Dave's lengthy illness, was elected to his current position as president and chairman of the board.

Jack has directed company growth that has included the purchase of the Kip's Big Boy franchise of Texas, Oklahoma and Kansas, and entry into the fast foods arena with the addition of a Roy Rogers Roast Beef Restaurant franchise. The hotel and specialty restaurant division has also grown following the successful conversion of Annette's to Prime 'n Wine. The concept of fine dining in a casual atmosphere has become popular at the three Prime 'n Wine locations, noted for their twin salad bars and prime rib entrees. Seafood is the specialty of Dockside VI, the restaurant in Quality Hotel Central in Norwood.

Big Boy restaurants also have changed over the years. The evolution from fast food to coffee shop to family restaurant is apparent in today's latest Big Boy building layout. Atriums provide dining in a homey atmosphere of soft colors, bentwood chairs, plants and stained glass. Sandwiches—the Big Boy in particular—are still a large portion of daily sales. All meal periods are served, beginning with breakfast a la carte or buffet style. Sandwiches are complemented by the soup, salad and fruit bar or served to go at drive-through windows. Dinner entrees include grilled or stir-fried chicken and seafood, as well as spaghetti and choice strip steak.

Frisch's Commissary manufactures much of the food for the restaurants, including hamburger patties, soups, salad ingredients and homemade bakery products, notably the pumpkin pie offered only in the fall. The popularity of preservative-free soups, chili and salad dressings made in the soup kitchen are due to timeless recipes that represent Frisch's philosophy: serve quality food in clean, pleasant surroundings at a price value to the customer.

The company now achieves $136 million in retail sales annually, and its stock is traded on the American Stock Exchange. In addition to 73 franchised restaurants, there are 129 company-operated units that employ almost 6,000 people. Serving on the Board of Directors with Mr. Maier are Marvin G. Fields, chief operations officer and senior vice president-operations; Louis J. Ullman, senior vice president-finance; Alfred M. Cohen, partner in an outside law firm; Blanche F. Maier, daughter of the founder; and Craig F. Maier, executive vice president and one of five members of the fourth generation currently working for Frisch's. He joined the company in 1973 as a manager trainee.

Frisch's Mainliner was a popular Cincinnati hangout in the early 1940s. Photographs courtesy of Frisch's Restaurants, Inc.

Frisch's cafe on Madison Road in Oakley, 1927. Irving Frisch is at far left, behind counter; David Frisch is at far back on right in bow tie. Photograph. Courtesy of Frisch's.

Gateway Federal

Now the largest publicly owned savings and loan headquartered in Cincinnati, Gateway Federal owes much of its growth to a supermerger of two equally large lenders.

Gateway, a unique nationally-registered name, sprang forward full grown on April 1, 1981 with assets of about $450 million. Before that date, there was no Gateway, only Standard Federal and Home Federal.

Standard Federal, the older of the two, was incorporated as Standard Building & Loan Co. in November 1908 with H.W. Taylor as president. Initially it operated out of a storeroom in Pleasant Ridge. The rent, including utilities, and the first teller's salary were the same—$7.50 a month. At the end of the first year, assets stood at $11,153.14. By year-end 1918, that had grown to $56,669.35.

The company opened offices in Kennedy Heights in 1923 and in Pleasant Ridge, at 6070 Montgomery Road, in 1958. The Montgomery Road office served as Standard's home office until Jan. 1, 1973, when that designation was shifted to the two-year-old branch at 525 Vine Street. This office also was home to the Statesman's Club, offering a lounge and free services to major depositors. Gateway now operates five Statesman's Club clubrooms.

Standard Federal, which became federally chartered in 1966, grew by acquisition and by opening new offices throughout the 1970s. In 1971 it acquired Hillsdale Loan and Building Co. and O'Bryonville Building and Loan Co., both founded in 1890. It added offices in Northgate in 1979 and Cherry Grove in 1980; assets had grown to nearly $206 million.

Home Federal started out in 1910 as West Price Hill Building and Loan Co., with a capitalization of $20,000. Its seven organizers held their first meeting at the Crow's Nest, a landmark family restaurant at the end of the Elberon Avenue car line.

When the assets of the company grew to $100,000, the cautious directors finally decided to acquire an office building. In February 1919 they built a one-story frame office on West Eighth Street at a cost of $2,883. Within nine years the assets of the association doubled and additional space was needed. The directors built a two-story building at 4520 West Eighth Street, moved the existing structure to the rear of their lot and rented it to a dry cleaner.

West Price Hill weathered the Depression and became the second thrift institution in Hamilton County to join the newly organized Home Loan Bank System in 1934. At the same time, it became a federally chartered association under the Home Federal name.

The renamed association moved downtown, to 130 East Fourth Street, in search of a larger home in 1936 and down the street to 120 East Fourth for still bigger quarters in 1938.

In 1949 Home Federal expanded in a different way—by opening a branch office in Lebanon. A second branch, added four years later in Wilmington, was so successful Home Federal built a new and larger office to hold it.

Meanwhile the growing institution—now with assets of $31.5 million—kept its faith in downtown. The association bought and thoroughly remodeled the Kreimer Building at 128 East Fourth Street as its new home office. When urban renewal demolished the north side of Fourth between Main and Walnut in 1969, Home Federal temporarily moved its headquarters. But it came back to 128 East Fourth, in the new Mercantile Center, formerly the Formica Building, in 1970.

Home Federal merged Northside Federal in 1966, Champion-Lion and Mutual in 1968 and opened a branch in Blue Ash in 1981. The company became heavily involved in housing rehabilitation lending in the 1970s.

Faced with the tremendous pressures of disintermediation, spiraling interest rates and regulatory constraints, Gateway Federal sold its Lebanon, Wilmington and Vine street locations in 1982 and 1983. But armed with a new management team, new banking services such as commercial lending, business equipment leasing, consumer lending and adjustable rate mortgages, Gateway has reestablished itself as a leader in providing financial services.

In June 1987 Gateway Federal received approval from federal regulators for permission to change from a mutual form of ownership to a publicly owned stock corporation and issued 1,955,000 shares of stock. The association became the largest publicly owned savings and loan headquartered in Cincinnati.

Within less than a year, Gateway opened two new offices, one at the Home Center Mall on Mosteller Road in March 1988 and the other at Kings Mall on Fields Ertel Road in April 1988.

Its current theme line, "Bank With the People You Know," reflects the commitment that the association has to providing personal banking services to the Cincinnati market.

Gateway Federal's headquarters office building at 128 East Fourth Street. Photograph. Courtesy of Gateway Federal.

General Electric Company

The shape of the propulsion future is this ultra high bypass engine called the Unducted Fan by GE Aircraft Engines. The UDF has been undergoing extensive ground and flight testing since 1985 and will be ready for commercial and military service in the 1990s. Ground testing, shown here, is conducted at GE's outdoor test site at Peebles, Ohio, 60 miles east of Cincinnati. Photograph. Courtesy of GE.

The presence of the General Electric Company can be found in Cincinnati in 27 different plants and offices, but the one which most Cincinnatians see is the huge jet engine plant along I-75 in Evendale. About 13,000 persons are employed there. About 1,600 are employed in the other 26 installations.

The Evendale plant is not only the largest of the local group, it also is the headquarters and largest unit of General Electric's Aircraft Engine Business Group, a 15-site operation which designs, develops, builds, tests and services gas turbine engines. Most of these engines go into military or commercial planes, but they also are to be found on private jets, helicopters and in naval vessels. Some, such as those which power a standby generator operated by Cincinnati Gas & Electric in Butler County, are in industrial service.

A GE scientist, Dr. Sanford Moss, spun the first gas-driven turbine in the United States in 1903. Its first extensive aviation use was to drive superchargers for the famous B-17s of World War II. In October 1941—even before World War II touched the United States—GE had begun work on a jet engine. America's first jet-powered aircraft, the Bell XP-59, flew exactly one year later. GE had assembled and tested this pioneering engine in just six months.

The company's early engine work was done in plants at Lynn, Massachusetts, and Schenectady, New York, and the first of its J47 engines were made there. The J47 was both a breakthrough and mainstay for GE because it was to become the most widely used jet engine ever made in the United States. In the 1940s and 1950s it powered the F-86, the Boeing B-47, the Convair B-36 and the North American B-45, all of them honored, pace-setting Air Force aircraft. It was in production until 1956, and GE made 29,678 of them, mostly at Evendale.

Production requirements exceeded the capacity of GE's eastern plants, so it took over part of what had been the Curtiss Wright piston engine plant on what was then called the "Lockland Highway" north of Cincinnati. This highway had been built to service the monster plant in World War II. It later became part of southbound I-75, and the area around the plant was eventually incorporated as Evendale. Curtiss Wright had stopped operations with the end of the war and parts of its former plant were occupied by other industries before GE arrived. GE's initial operation covered 700,000 square feet and proved too small in two years.

The first J47 from this plant was delivered to the Air Force on February 28, 1949. At that time the plant employed 500 persons and there were predictions the payroll "might some day reach 1,000."

GE began a series of expansions and developments on its plant until today it represents an investment of $1 billion. In 1951 it bought or built facilities which brought the plant to 3,000,000 square feet. In 1952 it started a $30 million laboratory complex. In 1957 it purchased more space and now covered 6,000,000 square feet (including space leased from the government). Building and rebuilding have continued over the past 25 years as well.

GE has made a succession of engines in its Evendale plant. The J47 was succeeded by the J79. The first were made in 1956, and GE made 13,683 of them. J79s powered the B-58 "Hustler," the world's first supersonic bomber, the Lockheed F-104 "Starfighter," and the F-4 fighter. The latter two are still being used. The newest model of the J79 is being considered for a low-cost international fighter. Commercial versions of the J79 also powered Convair 880 and 990 airliners.

For a time, some of the Evendale staff was engaged in research in fields exotic even to the jet age. Its scientists studied such ideas as plasma engines for space travel. Some of this research was turned to practical use in 1958 when a GE-made rocket engine, the X-405, powered the Vanguard rocket.

Jets continue to be the core of the Evendale business. A new engine, the J93, took the XB-70 to three times the speed of sound. The TF39 powers the world's largest aircraft, the Lockheed C-5A, and led to the GE line of commercial airliner engines which are designated CF6.

Asked to build an engine for the proposed U.S. supersonic airliner, in 1968 GE demonstrated what is still the most powerful jet engine built. It produced 63,900 pounds of thrust, but the plane itself was never built.

Until the late 1960s GE engines with their reputation for reliability and power were dominant in the military field. The CF6 engines enabled GE to compete for commercial airliner business because they were fuel efficient, quiet and low in emissions. In 1981 over half of the Evendale output involved commercial engines. CF6 engines are on McDonnell-Douglas DC-10, Boeing 747 and Airbus Industrie A300 wide-body transports; a new version is being made for the new Boeing 767 and the Airbus Industrie A310. Another engine, called the CFM56 and developed jointly with the French engine maker, SNECMA, powers re-engined DC-8s, and an advanced version will power Boeing's 737-300 airliners. Marine and industrial versions of the CF6 are powering ships in the United States Navy, gas-line pumping, providing power for offshore drilling rigs and generating industrial power.

GE's engine production depends on government needs and airline prosperity, and GE's prosperity makes it one of the half-dozen industries on which Cincinnati's own economic health depends. GE is Cincinnati's largest industrial employer. Its payroll since 1948 totals $6 billion and is running at a $400 million-a-year clip now. Other Cincinnati businesses sell it $100 million worth of goods and services a year.

The company's second-largest installation in Cincinnati is the Cincinnati Aviation Service Operation which employs about 700. Other major GE units in residence include major appliance sales and service, industrial equipment sales and service, GE Credit Corp., mobile radio sales, medical systems division, computer time-sharing service and lamp sales and distribution and sales. They are scattered over all the Greater Cincinnati area.

Brian H. Rowe heads the Aircraft Engine Business Group headquartered at Evendale and is the Cincinnati area executive for GE. W. George Krall is vice president and general manager of the Group's Evendale Production Division.

Gibson Greetings, Inc.

The history of Gibson Greetings, Inc. began with a family's faith in American opportunity.

Early in 1850 George Gibson, his wife, five sons and two daughters left their native lands of Scotland and England in search of opportunity in America. The elder Gibson had run a small lithographic and copperplate engraving business from his home. His entire family assisted in the work, and the five sons became adept at the then-new process of lithography, as well as the older craft of copperplate engraving.

Upon arrival in America with very meager funds and a French-made lithographic press, the Gibson family journeyed westward by way of canal routes. The third oldest son, John, found work with the Erie and Miami canals to Cincinnati, the river port that was gaining fame as the "Queen City of the West." The future looked promising, so the press was given to the four sons—Stephen, 34; Robert, 18; George, 14; and Samuel, 12—who decided that Cincinnati was a good place to go into business. Their parents and sisters moved onward to St. Louis. With the small printing press, the four brothers founded Gibson & Co. in 1850 on Gano Alley.

Their adventurous spirits, Scottish thrift and a variety of aptitudes formulated an ideal business team. Stephen, the eldest, was particularly artistic and gave exceptional quality and character to the earliest products of the Gibson press. Robert possessed a talent for business management and soon became the office and financial man. George, who had a mechanical bent, took over the practical operation of the press and general production. And Samuel, the youngest, made himself useful running errands and helping with all the work.

They printed bonds, stock certificates, checks, business cards and labels. Their business thrived, and in 1853 they moved to Third and Main streets. In 1856 the brothers expanded their facility to 121 Main and in 1858 again moved to larger quarters at the northwest corner of Third and Main, where they remained for the next 10 years.

By 1900 the company's facilities included every existing graphic arts process—lithography, letterpress, gravure, and steel and copper engraving. In 1925 they erected a new seven-floor building at Fourth and Plum streets. Then in 1956 Gibson moved to its present corporate headquarters and primary manufacturing facility at 2100 Section Road in Amberly Village.

Even in their earliest business years, the Gibson brothers preferred to sell printed products at retail rather than for commercial printing. Long before the introduction of imported Christmas cards in the American market in 1880, Gibson & Co. both produced and "jobbed" many artistically printed articles that were retailed through stationery, novelty and art stores.

Among these early products were patriotically decorated stationery and prints of Civil War scenes and heroes. Later Gibson & Co. became important producers of honor and reward cards for schools and Sunday schools. Beribboned novelties for Valentine's Day and Easter entered the lines in the 1870s. Chromo-lithos for framing, such as Currier & Ives prints, also were a big item. In fact Gibson & Co. jobbed early Currier & Ives prints that were exported to Europe.

The early 1880s marked the real beginning of the greeting card business. Gibson & Co. acted as Midwest jobbers of imported German-lithographed Christmas cards and also wholesaled many of the Louis Prang productions, the first Christmas cards and Valentines made in America. As manufacturing lithographers Gibson soon produced its own lines of Christmas cards, Valentines and Easter novelties.

In 1883 Robert Gibson purchased the interests of his brothers and continued as sole proprietor of Gibson & Co. until his death in 1895. His will stated that his business was to be incorporated as The Gibson Art Company, with equal shares given to his four children: Charles R., 29; Arabella, 26; William H., 23; and Edwin Percy, 17. The company's name was changed in 1960 to Gibson Greeting Cards, Inc.

The popularity of greeting cards grew during World War I as Americans communicated with their loved ones away from home. After the war the industry continued to thrive. As a pioneer and leader Gibson contributed greatly to the foundation of today's greeting card industry. It has been recognized as an industry leader in innovations since its inception. Gibson popularized the "French Fold" card, which is by far the best-selling modern form.

In the 1930s Gibson started another trend that would characterize its success in later years—putting the retail customer first. The company also developed revolutionary merchandising methods and designed display fixtures to better control inventory and increase sales for the retailer. And Gibson's electronic reorder system, the first in the industry, provided individual stores with a profitable product mix, the most efficient in-store layouts and constant monitoring of product sales.

Gibson common stock was listed on the New York Stock Exchange from 1962-1964. C.I.T. Financial Corporation acquired all of Gibson's assets in 1964, and in 1980 RCA Corporation acquired C.I.T. Gibson thereby became a subsidiary of RCA. The Wesray Corporation and Gibson management purchased the company from RCA in January 1982. Subsequently, in May 1983, Gibson again became a publicly owned company, changed its name to Gibson Greetings, Inc. and is now traded on the National Association of Securities Dealers exchange.

Today Gibson designs, manufactures and markets everyday and seasonal greeting cards, gift wrap, paper party goods, candles, calendars and related specialty products. These products are marketed under the brand names of Gibson, Buzza and Cleo, and Pleasant Thoughts and Success.

It took 67 years for the company to reach its first $1 million in annual sales. In 1979 sales reached almost $139 million. And over the last eight years Gibson's sales have increased over two and a half times, resulting in revenues of over $359 million for 1987.

As Gibson approaches 150 years of production, it is still a company committed to quality, creativity and excellence in all phases of its business.

Robert Gibson founded Gibson & Co. with his three brothers and later became sole owner in 1883.

The corporate headquarters of Gibson Greetings, Inc. is 2100 Section Road, Amberly Village.

Photographs. Courtesy of Gibson Greetings, Inc.

Graydon, Head & Ritchey

In 1871, shortly after the Cincinnati Suspension Bridge was opened, Stanley Matthews and William Ramsey established the law firm now known as Graydon, Head & Ritchey.

In addition to U.S. Supreme Court Justice and founder of the firm Stanley Matthews, the firm's roster over the years has included many distinguished lawyers, some of whom became notable judges, such as Louis J. Schneider and Robert L. Black Jr. For a brief period, Robert A. Taft, later to become a U.S. Senator and presidential contender, practiced with the firm.

Perhaps the most celebrated has been Lawrence Maxwell, who, in 1884 at the age of 31, seized an opportunity occasioned by the illness of the senior member of the firm and made a memorable argument before the U.S. Supreme Court in *McArthur v. Scott* (113 U.S. 340), attracting the attention of important members of the bench and bar. Maxwell thereafter distinguished himself as a lawyer of uncommon intelligence, tenacity and devotion to the law.

In 1893 Maxwell was appointed Solicitor General of the United States by President Cleveland, serving until 1895. Preeminent in the Midwest during most of his career, Maxwell's prowess won him many accolades. Among the highest was the statement by Justice Oliver Wendell Holmes Jr., who, when asked to name the ablest advocate who had appeared before the Supreme Court in his time, named two men: John C. Johnson of Philadelphia and Lawrence Maxwell of Cincinnati.

In many ways the careers of the lawyers for whom the firm is now named—Joseph S. Graydon, Joseph H. Head and Hugh McDiarmid Ritchey—exemplify the current nature of the firm. The 60 lawyers who have succeeded them conduct very active practices and are engaged in a host of activities spanning the cultural, civic and political life of the Cincinnati community.

1860	King & Thompson
1865	Civil War Ends
1866	Roebling Suspension Bridge opens
1869	U.S. Grant President of U.S.
1873	King, Thompson & Longworth
1875	Lawrence Maxwell joins firm
1877	King, Thompson & Maxwell
1884	Lawrence Maxwell joins Ramsey & Matthews

1871	**Matthews & Ramsey** Tyler Davidson Fountain Dedicated
1872	**Matthews, Ramsey & Matthews**
1877	First telephones in Cincinnati
1878	Cincinnati Music Hall opens
1879	Edison's incandescent bulb
1881	Stanley Matthews appointed to U.S. Supreme Court
1882	**Ramsey & Matthews**
1884	Lawrence Maxwell joins firm **Ramsey, Maxwell & Matthews**
1888	**Ramsey, Maxwell & Ramsey**
1893	Lawrence Maxwell appointed Solicitor General of U.S.
1898	Spanish American War **Maxwell & Ramsey**
1902	Joseph S. Graydon joins firm
1903	Wright Brothers flight at Kitty Hawk
1914	Firm moves to Union Central Building (from Neave Building)
1918	World War I ends
1920	First radio station in U.S.
1929	Stock Market Crash Joseph H. Head joins firm
1932	Hugh McD. Ritchey joins firm
1936	Firm moves to Union Trust Building
1941	**Graydon, Lackner, Head & Ritchey**
1944	**Graydon, Head & Ritchey**
1945	World War II ends
1953	Korean War ends
1969	Firm moves to Fifth Third Center
1975	Vietnam War ends
1988	**Cincinnati's Bicentennial Graydon, Head & Ritchey's 117th Anniversary**

Graydon, Head & Ritchey's growth, highlighted in this timeline, has paralleled more than half of Cincinnati's 200 years.

Illustrations courtesy of Graydon, Head & Ritchey.

Stanley Matthews (1824-1889), the firm's founder, was a U.S. Supreme Court Justice.

William M. Ramsey (1837-1896) helped establish the law firm in 1871.

Lawrence Maxwell (1863-1927), the firm's celebrated trial lawyer, served as U.S. Solicitor General under President Cleveland.

Great American Broadcasting Company

The Great American Broadcasting Company headquarters atop historic Mt. Auburn.

Great American Broadcasting Company, formerly Taft Broadcasting Company, had its origins in a newspaper called *The Spirit of the Times*. It has reflected that spirit ever since through timely moves into radio, television, amusement parks, cable television, the entertainment industry, satellite services and teletext broadcasting.

The Tafts and the *Times* came together in 1873, when Charles Phelps Taft purchased the 33-year-old newspaper. He was the son of Alfonso Taft and half-brother of William Howard Taft, the 27th president of the United States.

Taft merged the paper with *The Chronicle* and *The Evening Star* to create *The Cincinnati Times-Star* in 1880. Upon his death in 1929 he was succeeded as publisher by nephew Hulbert Taft Sr. It was Hulbert "Hub" Taft Jr. who persuaded the *Times-Star* board to enter broadcasting. The company bought WKRC in Cincinnati from Columbia Broadcasting Co. for $175,000 in December 1939.

For two years the radio station run by Hub Taft and his younger brother, David, drained *Times-Star* revenues. But development of popular local talent—including Waite Hoyt, Ruth Lyons and Tom McCarthy—turned things around by World War II.

After the war the brothers tried to diversify. "Transit Radio" provided music and shopping advice to streetcar and bus riders over the WKRC-FM signal. It bombed. WKRC-FM went back to broadcasting and became the nation's first commercially profitable, independently programmed FM station.

Then came television. WKRC-TV began broadcasting in the spring of 1949, joining Cincinnati's pioneer stations WLW and WCPO. In the days before the networks and with only about 20,000 local television sets, the station was a big money loser. But by the early 1950s, sales of sets and advertising revenues soared. In a classic turnaround the once thriving *Times-Star* was now being subsidized by the company's broadcast operations.

The first of the company's many broadcast acquisitions outside Cincinnati came with the purchase of WTVN-TV of Columbus in 1953 and a companion radio station in 1954. In July 1958, after buying radio and television stations in Birmingham, Alabama and a television station in Lexington, Kentucky, Taft sold the *Times-Star* to Scripps Howard Newspapers, which merged it with *The Cincinnati Post*. The separate Taft radio and television operations were consolidated into Taft Broadcasting Co. in 1959. It was listed on the New York Stock Exchange in 1962.

Two years later Taft was the buyer in the biggest broadcasting transaction in history—a $33 million deal to buy radio and television stations in Buffalo, New York, Kansas City, Missouri, and Scranton/Wilkes Barre, Pennsylvania. The company became the first broadcaster to own the legal limit of seven television stations.

That milestone reached, Taft looked outside broadcasting for growth. Television program production looked promising, so in 1966 Taft bought Hanna-Barbera Productions Inc., the world's largest producer of animated programming.

In 1969 Taft entered another entertainment area when it acquired Cincinnati's Coney Island amusement park—and with it the management team to build giant theme parks in major metropolitan centers. The first such park was Kings Island just north of Cincinnati. Except for Coney Island these parks were spun off in 1982 when the company's park team started its own organization.

The company expanded its involvement in the television entertainment business in 1979 by acquiring Worldvision Enterprises, an international distributor of television programs made in the United States. As a supplier to broadcasters in more than 100 countries, Worldvision put its Cincinnati parent in the middle of the global business community.

Hub Taft, the company's founder and chief executive officer, was killed in an explosion at his home in 1967. He was succeeded as chairman by Charles S. Mechem Jr., the company's general counsel. Mechem remains the chairman and chief executive officer of Great American Broadcasting, with George E. Castrucci serving as president.

It was October 1987 when the company became Great American Broadcasting Company. The new owner is Great American Communications Company, a public holding company whose largest shareholder is Cincinnati's American Financial Corporation.

Today Great American Broadcasting remains a leader in the Cincinnati community as well as in the broadcasting and entertainment industries. Its current operations include five network-affiliated television stations; 15 radio stations; part ownership in cable television's Black Entertainment Television; Hanna-Barbera Productions; Ruby-Spears Enterprises, both animation-production studios; and Worldvision Enterprises, a program distribution subsidiary.

Great American also owns and operates Hamilton Projects, a leader in licensed merchandising, as well as a satellite services operation in Boston. In the leisure-facilities arena, the company is the owner of Cincinnati's Coney Island and the Jack Nicklaus Sports Center, home of the world-renowned ATP Tennis Tournament. Great American is currently expanding into the home video market and testing Teletext, a text-on-screen television information service.

Greater Cincinnati Chamber of Commerce

The year was 1839. Cincinnati had grown to a population of 45,000 and was among the country's fastest growing cities.

River commerce had fueled the city's early growth, and business was playing an increasingly important role in life in this Queen City on the Ohio River. The F.H. Lawson Company, William S. Merrell Co., Procter & Gamble Co., and Cincinnati Gas, Light and Coke Co. were already on the Cincinnati scene, and new companies seemed to spring up daily. Managing and encouraging growth was as big a business concern in the early 19th century as it is a century and a half later.

And so it was that on October 15, 1839, 76 firms and individuals placed an advertisement in the *Cincinnati Daily Gazette* urging local businessmen to attend a meeting at the young Men's Mercantile Library Association headquarters in the old Cincinnati College Building at Fourth and Walnut streets. That meeting led to the founding of "a Chamber of Commerce and Board of Trade for the purpose of uniform regulations and unison of action in the promotion of its mercantile interests."

"Prodigious wonders have been worked since that first gathering," Charles Ludwig wrote in *The Cincinnatian* 88 years later, describing the Chamber's history in words that still apply today. "They launched trade fairs, festivals, expositions, and exhibitions to attract people to Cincinnati...conducted good will excursions to extend Cincinnati's market area...(and) made Cincinnati a famous convention city.

"They built at Fourth and Vine street the world's most beautiful, remarkable, massive and monumental temple of trade— and when that was destroyed by fire, they calmly proceeded to build anew, and better than ever.

"They helped every forward cause in the history of the city," Ludwig wrote. "They led in the movement for the City Beautiful, for city planning and zoning...and all the other good things that make for a finer, richer, happier, more abundant life."

Arbitrating disputes within the business community was one of the first major activities of the young Chamber of Commerce. With no generally accepted legal or ethical standards of business practice in place, conflicts between businessmen were frequent. The Chamber's role as arbiter grew, often eliminating costly and time-consuming litigation. Its role also enhanced and strengthened its image, adding to its stature in the business community, for threat of expulsion from the Chamber often was stronger than existing legal sanctions.

Promoting Cincinnati's "mercantile interests" became increasingly complex. In 1854 a Chamber committee lobbied Congress to improve traffic on the Ohio River, and in 1861 another petitioned legislators to continue railroad access to Cincinnati during the Civil War. The Chamber protested when the bulk of Civil War munitions contracts was awarded to eastern companies, insisting that western producers be given their fair share. And in 1865 the Chamber aggressively championed a post-war reconstruction program that included a railroad system to tie Cincinnati to its markets in the South.

The Cincinnati Chamber also exerted its influence nationally by launching the movement for the formation of a national Chamber of Commerce. A forerunner of today's U.S. Chamber of Commerce, that organization held its first meeting in Cincinnati in 1869.

In that same year the Cincinnati Chamber began compiling and publishing its now-famous Daily Weather Bulletin, which eventually led to the creation of the U.S. Weather Bureau.

The Chamber was actively involved in Cincinnati's Centennial of 1888 and the industry and trade expositions held in conjunction with that celebration.

One of the Chamber's major accomplishments was its role in the development of a city plan for Cincinnati. In 1912 it urged the appointment of a planning commission. The eventual result was the City Plan of 1925, which was hailed as the most comprehensive such plan of any city in the United States. It became the forerunner of the 1948 Master Plan, subsequent updates in the early 1960s, and eventually the Year 2000 Plan, under which the city currently operates. Good planning and good follow-through have long been identified as Cincinnati strengths, and the Chamber takes pride in its early role.

From 1889 to 1911 the Chamber of Commerce occupied this Romanesque building designed by Henry Hobson Richardson, one of 19th century America's foremost architects. The building, on the southwest corner of Fourth and Vine streets, burned in 1911. Photograph. Courtesy of The Cincinnati Historical Society.

In 1915 the Chamber protested vehemently against making Louisville the terminus of the "Dixie Highway" and successfully urged Cincinnati as the logical end point. In the late 1940s the Chamber led the successful effort to enact the Ohio Valley Water Sanitation Compact, a pioneering environmental proposal. A year later a long campaign by the Chamber ended successfully with the passage of an urban redevelopment bill by the Ohio Legislature.

As Cincinnati grew more suburban and became an eight-county metropolitan area in the mid-1960s, the Chamber changed its name to the Greater Cincinnati Chamber of Commerce to reflect its role as an organization representing businesses throughout Southwestern Ohio, Northern Kentucky and Southeastern Indiana.

Beginning in 1965 the Chamber led the campaign to build Riverfront Stadium to attract a National Football League franchise and head off the threat of the Cincinnati Reds moving from the city.

Image studies in the 1960s and 1970s identified that while Cincinnati did not have a negative national image, it also did not have a positive one. In effect Cincinnati lacked an image. An "Action Cincinnati!" campaign began in 1971 to promote Cincinnati's economic development advantages regionally and nationally. This program gave way to the "Blue Chip Campaign for Economic Development" in the 1980s, and the Chamber undertook the role of coordinating economic development.

To write a history of the Chamber would be tantamount to writing a history of the city itself, for, as Charles Ludwig noted, the Chamber has been involved in virtually every significant city development since its inception.

In 1839 they called it the promotion of "mercantile interests;" 150 years later the term had changed to "economic development." Throughout the years, however, the basic purpose, mission and objectives of the Chamber have remained remarkably unchanged: to serve its members by improving the city's economic vitality and quality of life, luring business investment and helping businesses be better businesses, creating jobs and a better community for all.

Greater Cincinnati Convention & Visitors Bureau

The Greater Cincinnati Convention & Visitors Bureau formally incorporated in 1945, but the city had appreciated the significance of conventions and tourists long before that. Since the 1850s Cincinnati civic and business leaders have promoted the city through major conventions and industrial expositions, attracting national events including Democratic and Republican Presidential conventions. And in the late 1800s, the city began a series of Fall Festivals designed to showcase its manufacturing and cultural achievements and to attract visitors.

Prior to the 1930s, these events typically were sponsored by *ad hoc* groups and volunteer committees with no overall plan for bringing conventions to the Queen City. In 1932 Cincinnati's Chamber of Commerce, Hotel Association and Restaurant Association, along with other downtown merchants, created the Cincinnati Convention Committee. Headed by Col. C.O. Sherrill, the city's former city manager, and Warner Sayers, president of the last Fall Festival in 1923, the committee competed nationally for convention business and arranged local hospitality for visitors.

Major convention facilities in the 1930s and 1940s included the Hotel Netherland Plaza, Music Hall, Taft Auditorium, Emery Auditorium and Masonic Temple. The Convention Committee attracted the support of the local business community by reporting that, in addition to hotel, restaurant and taxicab expenses, conventioneers contributed to the local economy by purchasing cigars, candy, flowers, straw hats, theater tickets, photographs, baseball tickets and street car fares. By the late 1940s, the typical Cincinnati convention-goer stayed three days and spent an average of $27 a day.

The Chamber of Commerce had taken over the work of the Convention Committee by 1945. That year the Cincinnati Convention and Visitor's Bureau spun off from the Chamber, becoming the private, non-profit entity that it remains today. Joseph S. Turner, who had been the chamber's convention manager since 1935, became the bureau's first director and served until 1962.

One of Turner's top priorities was to develop a new convention hall for Cincinnati because he and other city leaders recognized that they were losing conventions to other cities with better facilities. In the mid-1940s, land was acquired at Second and Main for a 9,500-seat convention hall that could host conventions and indoor sporting events. But the project was abandoned.

Throughout the 1950s, the bureau issued a series of annual reports showing that Cincinnati's convention business was doing well but still remained far less than what it could be with a new facility.

At last City Council selected the block bounded by Fifth, Sixth, Elm and Plum as the site for a new convention hall, and construction began in 1965. The Cincinnati Convention Center hosted its first national meeting, held by the American Bowling Congress, in 1968. The new convention center allowed Cincinnati to compete nationally for conventions with up to several thousand delegates. The center was also a catalyst for the revitalization of downtown, helping lure new hotels and additional support for the city's new skywalk system.

By the early 1970s, conventions pumped over $20 million annually into the city, up from $8 million-$10 million in the early 1960s. The bureau was renamed the Greater Cincinnati Convention & Visitors Bureau in 1975, reflecting its expanding role as a community-wide organization. At the same time the convention and trade show market was evolving into a much more sophisticated industry that represented an increasingly important part of Greater Cincinnati's overall economy. With the explosion in new technology and consumer products, hundreds of new opportunities for meeting and trade show business became the bureau's focus.

Conventions brought $87 million into Cincinnati annually by 1983. The average conventioneer spent $237 over three days. But by that time Cincinnati was losing millions more to cities with larger, more attractive facilities with "high-tech" capabilities. The original convention center was slowly becoming antiquated and obsolete in comparison to other such facilities across the country. Less than 10 years after its opening, it was apparent that the city needed a new center if it was to remain competitive.

The expanded and remodeled Dr. Albert B. Sabin Cincinnati Convention Center opened in 1986, renamed for the developer of the oral polio vaccine. The center features a marble facade from the old Albee Theater above its Elm Street entrance. The impact of increasing the center's exhibit space from 95,000 to 162,000 square feet was immediately apparent. As of 1988 the bureau had reported over $160 million of new convention business that had been confirmed for Greater Cincinnati exclusively because of the expanded convention center's increased capabilities.

The main emphasis of the Greater Cincinnati Convention & Visitors Bureau remains attracting major conventions and trade shows to the Cincinnati area. The economic benefits of the convention industry continue to grow: in 1988 each convention delegate spent over $550 during the typical three-day visit.

The bureau competes nationally and internationally for convention business and for special opportunities that favorably reflect upon the Greater Cincinnati area. As a membership organization, it currently represents the interests of over 750 local member companies.

In the past decade, the bureau has also given significantly more attention to the promotion of Cincinnati as a destination market for tourists. Its work is paying off: Cincinnati was ranked in one U.S. survey as the nation's 11th most visited city in 1987.

The main entrance to the Dr. Albert B. Sabin Convention Center. Photograph. Courtesy of the Greater Cincinnati Convention and Visitors Bureau.

The Hennegan Company

The bright, clean buildings at Plum Street and Central Parkway and the scarlet trucks in downtown traffic make Hennegan a Cincinnati landmark. Throughout the country The Hennegan Company is known for its color posters for the entertainment industry and its reputation for high-quality color lithography. Printing Industries of America has named Hennegan as the number one printer in the United States for the past two years.

The theater displays and posters from the Hennegan archives are like a history of Hollywood. They include examples from *Top Gun* to *Popeye, Snow White and the Seven Dwarfs* and *Oliver Twist*. John Hennegan, son of founder James Hennegan, always felt that Walt Disney's selecting Hennegan to reproduce art work for many Disney movies was the crowning feather in the company cap.

James Hennegan led his brothers, John and Joseph, into printing in 1885. Originally the company printed receipts, letterheads, laundry slips and campaign posters. Because the company could not afford steam-powered presses or electric lights, printers worked hand- or foot-driven presses by daylight only, six days a week. Hennegan and Company's first substantial job came in 1888: an order for 150,000 centennial labels and 192,000 sets for the Christian Moerlein Brewery.

Hennegan began its show business printing in the 1890s, a period of explosive growth in leisure-time activities. The fledgling movie industry of the early 20th century signalled new opportunities. Show posters were among the first advertisements to take advantage of color, and Hennegan quickly was recognized as specialists in the color poster at a time when all other advertising was black, white or gray.

The entertainment advertising field was growing so fast that James Hennegan persuaded a friend, William A. Donaldson, to join him in a new publication to serve the industry. They agreed, reportedly over two schooners of beer at Weilert's Cafe, to launch a magazine called *Billboard Advertising*. The first issue appeared November 1, 1894. Hennegan printed it, while Donaldson edited it and kept the books.

Now known simply as *Billboard*, the magazine is a show business staple. Although Hennegan dropped its interests in it in 1900, the magazine established the Hennegan name in show business. For a time the Hennegan brothers even were showmen of their own. They opened a nickelodeon, the Lubin Amusement Company, in 1908 but pulled out after a short time to concentrate on printing.

By 1910 Hennegan was shipping theater posters and other entertainment displays all over the United States and Canada. In 1913 the company purchased its first offset lithography press and added capabilities for photographic plate-making. Lithography, a process of transferring special inks from engraved plates, is an ancient form of printing, one prized for its high quality. Hennegan received a medal for "American Lithography" at a 1914 international printing show in London, thus establishing the company's international reputation.

From the start Hennegan more than mechanically translated someone's ideas and drawings into print. It created much of what it sold under the name "Hennegan Money Getters," items including handbills and giant posters and banners.

In 1937 the company began a long association with Walt Disney by printing promotions for *Snow White and the Seven Dwarfs*. The insert that Hennegan published for *Snow White* became one of the most popular of all time. Hennegan also provided printing services for MGM Studios, including the contract for *Gone With the Wind*. Such contracts ensured Hennegan's high visibility.

Hennegan & Company, now officially The Hennegan Company, has always been run by a member of the family. The founders died in the 1920s and 1930s, passing control to John Hennegan, who headed the company for 30 years. His nephew, Robert B. Ott, a remarkable look-alike, became president in 1968 and manages the firm today. Together with his sons, Robert Jr. and Kevin, he presides over an operation that would have made his grandfather proud.

State-of-the-art equipment in Hennegan's plants in downtown Cincinnati and in Northern Kentucky helps produce a colorful array of annual reports, catalogs, corporate brochures, posters and point-of-purchase materials. Taking a cue from its show business heritage, Hennegan's motto is "Showmanship in Printing." The continuing success of its performance is evidenced by the major corporations, designers and agencies that are its customers and by the international awards it continues to receive for the outstanding quality of its work.

There have been many changes during the century since The Hennegan Company was founded, but one thing has remained constant—the dedication of its owners and employees to the tradition of the highest quality product and the ultimate in customer service and satisfaction.

A logo (c. 1916) courtesy of The Hennegan Company.

Among the numerous movies for which The Hennegan Company has printed display materials was David O. Selznick's production of *Gone With the Wind* in 1939. Courtesy of The Hennegan Company.

The Hill Top Companies

Since its reorganization in January 1987, The Hill Top Companies have consisted of three independent, privately owned companies providing life science research, consulting and testing services: Hill Top Research, Inc., Hill Top Pharmatest, Inc. and Hill Top Biolabs, Inc.

The companies focus on skin effects testing and clinical research to ensure the safety and effectiveness of consumer and medical products. Since 1985 the group also has sought to create a secondary niche in the market for pharmaceutical clinical research, not just in skin products, but in all therapeutic areas. Hill Top Companies aim to win recognition as the world's leading life science testing laboratories in these market areas.

Founder Robert A. Quisno is chairman of the board, and James Pearce Jr., chief executive officer of all three companies, which share many other officers and board members as well. In 1987 total full-time equivalent employment reached 180, a six-fold increase since the late 1960s. In addition the companies call on the services of 25,000 expert panelists across the nation.

Hill Top Companies' origins go back to 1947, when research bacteriologist Quisno, a 32-year-old Cincinnati native and UC microbiology graduate, left the William S. Merrell Company to found his own firm. Seeing the need for a new company to provide clinical testing services for area doctors and industrial microbiological services for food and beverage processors, he set up Hill Top Laboratories in a basement apartment at 921 William Howard Taft Road. A year later Hill Top Laboratories was incorporated.

By 1955 the staff had conducted tests for many of the nation's largest chemical and drug companies. Most of its business consisted of routine clinical analyses such as blood tests and pregnancy tests for doctors. Industrial microbiology was a sideline until May 1949, when Hill Top won a contract to do a toxicity and feeding study for The Procter & Gamble Company using animal test subjects.

P&G continued to employ Hill Top to do a series of increasingly complicated tests, enabling Hill Top to open a branch clinical lab on Auburn Ave. In October 1950 Hill Top moved into human testing for the first time, conducting a primary irritation screen test and later a sensitization patch test using samples of P&G's germicidal soaps. Continued study of the testing procedure led to adoption of Hill Top's innovative Repeated Insult Patch Test protocol and its patenting of the Hill Top Chamber®, a system for delivering test substances in patch tests that has been approved by the U.S. Food and Drug Administration to test foods and beverages.

In January 1953 Hill Top Laboratories incorporated the Hill Top Research Institute to take over industrial microbiology, animal toxicology and human clinical studies. Just over a year later the institute purchased a 20-acre site on the Little Miami northeast of Cincinnati in Miamiville, where it is located today.

Hill Top began an innovative series of tests for Procter & Gamble in the mid-1950s to develop and apply test methods for measuring the effectiveness of antiperspirants. The FDA recommended Hill Top's procedure for antiperspirant efficacy testing in 1978.

Cintest, Inc., now Hill Top Pharmatest, Inc., was established in 1964 to conduct proprietary clinical studies, including certain kinds of drug evaluations requiring especially close observation of test subjects. The medical lab made news in 1966 by installing the SMA-12 AutoAnalyzer, thus becoming Ohio's first semiautomated lab for blood chemistry.

Hill Top Research Institute reorganized in 1966, changing its name to Hill Top Research, Inc. and becoming the parent company for both Hill Top Laboratories, Inc. and Cintest, Inc. The following year Robert A. Quisno became chairman of the board of directors, and George Quisno succeeded him as president.

In 1968 Hill Top opened its first out-of-state laboratory in St. Petersburg, Florida to test sunscreen and tanning products during wintertime. The firm opened other branches in Scottsdale, Arizona (1976), New Brunswick, New Jersey (1979), Richmond, Virginia (1983) and Winnipeg, Canada (1988).

Hill Top founder Robert A. Quisno and Chief Executive Officer J. James Pearce at Hill Top's 40th anniversary celebration. Photograph. Courtesy of Hill Top Companies.

The American Biomedical Company acquired Hill Top Research, Inc. and its subsidiaries in December 1969. Quisno became a director of American Biomedical, and Hill Top Laboratories separated from Hill Top Research, Inc., with Jim Pearce as manager. But in 1978, when Revlon purchased American Biomedical, Quisno, Pearce and several other company officers repurchased most of Hill Top Research, Inc. and reestablished it as an independent company with Quisno as chairman of the board and Pearce, president and chief executive officer.

Hill Top Research has received worldwide attention for its development of testing techniques. Several international television documentaries have included segments on Hill Top's testing procedures. In August 1986 *National Geographic* carried an article called "The Intimate Sense of Smell" featuring Hill Top's odor-judging panel testing an underarm deodorant. The accompanying photograph appeared in a number of newspapers, and both local and national radio and television broadcasters interviewed the panelists.

Today Hill Top Research, Inc., with John E. Wild as vice president, director and general manager, is the largest of the Hill Top Companies, with 65% of the group's total sales. Concentrating on the household and personal care markets, it is the largest firm of its kind in the world, with 45% of the total world market of $40 million.

Hill Top Pharmatest, Inc., with Carl A. Bunde as director and general manager, continues to provide medical research and project management for pharmaceutical manufacturers. Although the smallest of the Hill Top Companies, it is the fastest growing, with 1% of a global market of $175 million.

Hill Top Biolabs, Inc., the newest of the companies, was created by combining Hill Top Research's oldest divisions, microbiology and toxicology. With Edwin V. Buehler as vice president, Biolabs provides varied testing services, including the milk and food analyses that were Hill Top's earliest products. Although Biolabs has only 25% of the group's total sales, it remains the largest firm in the industry, with 40% of a total world market of $5 million.

Hudepohl-Schoenling Brewing Company

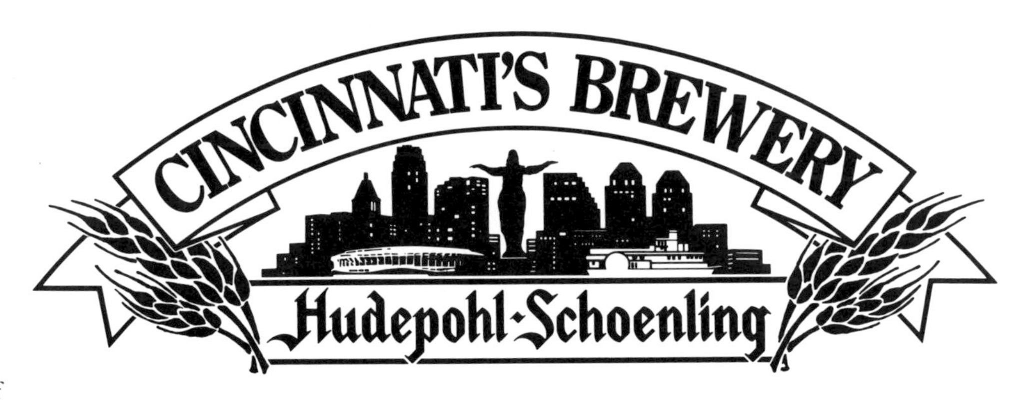

Along a section of Central Parkway just west of downtown floats the unmistakable, wonderful aroma of yeast and grain being transformed into fine beers and ale. For over 150 years the combined brewing heritage of The Hudepohl-Schoenling Brewing Company has provided Cincinnati with quality, fresh beer produced with pride by generations of family brewers.

Cincinnati was the nation's most famous and fabulous brewing center in the late 19th century. About 95% of the beer consumed locally was produced by one of the 36 local breweries, and Cincinnati consumed more beer per capita than any other city in the nation.

Today our proud heritage is preserved by The Hudepohl-Schoenling Brewing Company, the last of the Cincinnati breweries and fortunate combination of two arts—quality brewing and survivorship.

The Hudepohl-Schoenling Brewing Company was created in a 1986 merger of the 101-year-old Hudepohl Brewing Company and the 55-year-old Schoenling Brewing Company.

In 1885 Louis Hudepohl and George Kotte founded the Hudepohl and Kotte Brewing Company by purchasing the already thriving Koehler Brewery, popularly known as the Buckeye Brewery. The new owners continued producing a Buckeye beer along with its new labels: Dortmunder, Muenchener and, of course, Hudepohl.

Kotte died in 1893, but his wife remained a partner until she sold her interest to Hudepohl in 1900, leaving him the sole owner who incorporated the firm as The Hudepohl Brewing Company. Louis Hudepohl had a thriving operation — 100 employees and sales of 40,000 barrels of beer a year—when he died in 1902. His widow, Mary Elizabeth Hudepohl, took charge and called her son-in-law, William A. Pohl, to be general manager.

The 18th Amendment all but ended the era of family breweries. Hudepohl survived by producing "near beer" and soft drinks. After Prohibition was repealed in 1933, Hudepohl reopened and in 1934 purchased the Lachman Brewery at 505 Gest Street in Queensgate. By 1947 sales had reached a record 900,000 barrels.

In 1964 the original Buckeye plant near McMicken was closed, but Hudepohl continued to operate and expand the automated Gest Street brewery. Some untimely deaths then forced changes in the company management. However, a Hudepohl family member remained at the helm throughout its history: John O. Hesselbrock, 1923-1950; his son, John A. Hesselbrock, 1950-1973; William L. Pohl, son of William A. Pohl, 1973; Thomas A. Zins, Hesselbrock's nephew, 1973-1980; Louis G. Pohl, 1980-1985; and Robert L. Pohl, Louis Hudepohl's grandson, 1985-1986.

During the 1960s and 1970s, small local and regional brewers were closing or merging as the large national brewers expanded their distribution. During this period there were four local breweries—Wiedemann, Burger, Hudepohl and Schoenling. Wiedemann was absorbed by the G. Heilemann Brewing Company, and in 1973 Hudepohl purchased the Burger Brewing Company.

In 1983, as a salute to the fine history of the brewing industry in Cincinnati, Hudepohl brought back Christian Moerlein, a label that once belonged to the largest brewery in Cincinnati. Christian Moerlein was, in fact, one of the premier breweries in the country during its peak in 1895 and the first American beer to pass Reinheitsgebot, Germany's strict purity law.

While the Hudepohl brewery was thriving in the early 1900s, the Schoenling family was operating the Schoenling Ice and Fuel Company, an ice and coal company in the West End. By the time Prohibition was repealed, the Schoenling brothers and close family friend, Earl Lichtendahl, had grown tired of waiting in lines for their beer and decided to open their own brewery.

In 1933 Ed Schoenling Jr., who served as president until 1978, Arthur Schoenling, William Schoenling Sr., George Schoenling Jr., and Earl Lichtendahl opened the Schoenling Brewing Company at 1625 Central Parkway. High standards for quality and service and energetic distributors, some of whom are still selling today, characterized popular brands such as Schoenling Lager, known as Cincinnati's Finest; Top Hat; Sir Edward Stout; and Schoenling Cream Ale, which in 1958 became Little Kings Cream Ale.

Little Kings fueled the growth of the small, local Schoenling Brewery into a regional brewer selling in 44 states. Little Kings won a Gold Medal at the 1987 and 1988 Great American Beer Festival in Denver, Colorado. Competing in a blind taste test among brewing professionals, Little Kings was judged first in its class of American Cream Ales. It's become widely known for its superior flavor—and its distinctive seven-ounce green bottle.

In 1986 Hudepohl's local distribution strength and Schoenling's strong out-of-town sales were merged into one company that proudly became "Cincinnati's Brewery." The following year packaging and yeast handling equipment from the Gest Street plant was moved to the Central Parkway plant, where a $9 million expansion and modernization process was under way.

The plant is now totally controlled by a micro-processor automation system with brewing expertise being passed from generation to generation. Although today's brewing equipment has advanced from the coal boilers and kettles of old, traditional care and the brewmasters' personal art are still keys to success.

Hudepohl-Schoenling re-introduced 14-K in 1988 as a bicentennial birthday gift to the City of Cincinnati. As one of five major event sponsors of the year-long bicentennial celebrations, Cincinnati's Brewery was proud to feature 14-K at all the events.

Still a privately held company, Hudepohl-Schoenling is owned and operated by the nephew and great nephew of Earl Lichtendahl, one of the five original founders of Schoenling. Charles Lichtendahl, executive vice president and former brewmaster, started at the Schoenling Brewery in 1937. His son, Kenneth C. Lichtendahl, has been the president from 1978 to the present. Michael B. Schott, the third operational owner, is the vice president of sales and marketing.

With annual production of some 500,000 barrels, Hudepohl-Schoenling is currently the 10th largest brewery in the United States. Distribution of products covers 44 states, Canada and Taiwan. But the largest portion of Hudepohl-Schoenling sales is still right here in Cincinnati. Brewing beer for the Queen City is a tradition that will carry the company forward into the next century.

Although officially formed in 1986, the Hudepohl-Schoenling Brewing Company has roots going back to 1885. Illustration courtesy of Hudepohl-Schoenling.

Instant Replay Video Productions

Everything that Instant Replay Film and Video Productions, Inc. produces leaves a long-lasting impression.

From its award-winning commercials and special effects to its East Walnut Hills headquarters in the landmark Media Center, Instant Replay's commitment to the creation of innovative and memorable images is evident in every aspect of the young company's operation.

While Instant Replay has enjoyed notable success with its film capabilities, the company is better known for its achievements in the relatively young video industry.

From its inception Instant Replay has provided its talented staff with state-of-the-art equipment in an environment geared to nurture creativity and productivity.

The headquarters of Instant Replay in the Media Center, formerly the elegant Herman Schneider Foundation building, in East Walnut Hills. Photograph. Courtesy of Instant Replay Video Productions.

In 1976, with the advent of portable videotape equipment less than five years old, founder and president Terry Hamad transformed his personal interest in the medium's endless possibilities into a lean and aggressive company.

Instant Replay began its entry into a fast-paced and ever-changing business with initial projects including close-circuit television work for the Cincinnati Reds and work for Southern Ohio Television.

Countless projects later Ron Hamad joined his brother Terry in 1978, just as the company was expanding its equipment and services to accommodate its clients' post-production needs.

During the next few years, Instant Replay's client list grew to include Procter & Gamble, the General Electric Co. and many of the region's top advertising agencies. By dividing its services into four areas—commercials, corporate/industrial, post-production and graphics—the company found a unique way to provide a diverse range of highly specialized services.

Then in 1981, when the Hamads purchased the elegant Herman Schneider Foundation building in East Walnut Hills, their concept of full service was further strengthened by the expansive, luxurious space now known as the Media Center.

The 20,000-square-foot building was first renovated to accommodate an enormous amount of equipment, which now includes the region's first electronic paint box and three-dimensional graphics systems, as well as the area's best and brightest staff of producers, directors, designers, cinematographers, writers and animators.

Second, in the spirit of the bygone era of the all-encompassing Hollywood studio, the Hamads rented additional space in the building to media-affiliated companies.

In addition to the multitude of services offered by Instant Replay, clients enjoy the cost-efficient luxury of being able to fully complete projects under one roof. From audio production to still photography, an unprecedented range of the highest quality media services is available.

The results of Instant Replay's success are those with which Cincinnatians and the nation are quite familiar. The company's graphics division has worked with all Cincinnati's television stations to create powerful news identifications, as well as with the Cincinnati Reds and Bengals, the Cleveland Indians and the Atlanta Braves.

Vice President Ron Hamad's work, including the memorable and award-winning WARM 98 radio campaign, has helped him gain national recognition and representation. In 1988 alone Ron received citations for projects that he directed, including a Gold Award from the Houston International Film Festival, a Gold Camera Award from the U.S. Industrial Film & Video Festival, and a Silver HUGO, the highest honor given in the fund-raising category at the Chicago International Film Festival, for his direction of a film about the Museum Center at Cincinnati Union Terminal.

Jeff Heusser, director of post production, also brings a long list of credits to Instant Replay. Before joining the company in 1985, Heusser won two local Emmys for electronic graphics, created the city's first electronic graphics department at WLWT and directed the award-winning, nationally syndicated educational series "Zoo, Zoo, Zoo" while producer/director with WCET. Heusser now oversees the editorial staff and post production area, which features the region's finest, most specialized equipment.

Additionally Instant Replay was the recipient of a 1988 Crescendo Award. Sponsored by the Cincinnati Business Courier and Arthur Young & Co., this prestigious honor recognizes the fastest-growing, privately held corporations in the Cincinnati area.

With plans in the works to further expand the facilities to accommodate one of the largest stages in the Midwest, additional editing suites and client lounges, as well as a staff of nearly 50, this family company is sure to continue to create memorable images for Cincinnati and the nation.

The Jewish Hospital of Cincinnati, Inc.

The first Jewish Hospital at Betts and Cutter streets, 1854. Photograph courtesy of The Jewish Hospital.

The 138-year history of The Jewish Hospital of Cincinnati, Inc. closely parallels the growth and dramatic changes that medicine has undergone since the mid-1800s.

Medicine, like the hospital, was more personal and far less technical in 1850. Concerned about the plight of indigent Jews during the raging cholera epidemic of 1849, a group of Cincinnati Jewish people banded together to establish the very first Jewish hospital in the United States and guarantee care for their own.

The founders leased a modest house at the corner of what is now Central Avenue and Bauer Street downtown, bought the furniture and equipment necessary to run a hospital and employed Abraham Bettman, M.D. at $10 a month to see both men and women patients.

But the hospital did not break even and had to depend on fund-raisers to stay open. Through a bequest from the will of Judah Touro of New Orleans, however, the hospital board was able to purchase property downtown at Betts and Cutter streets in 1854. Articles of Incorporation of the Jewish Hospital Association were filed, and the hospital moved to its new two-story home that same year. Patients were treated and then transferred to other medical institutions.

For 12 years Jewish Hospital provided care at the Cutter Street location. Then at the urging of its physicians, a larger building was purchased near the waterworks in the East End and a 20-room house remodeled and expanded. The third Jewish Hospital was dedicated in March 1866.

How did Jewish Hospital get to its present Burnet Avenue location in Avondale? Just as the hospital had been founded because of a very personal concern for the welfare of the sick and poor, it filled a need to care for the elderly by purchasing and expanding the Home for Jewish Aged and Infirm on the corner of Burnet Avenue and Union Street. Dedicated in March 1890 this new, "suburban" hospital boasted Cincinnati's first modern operating room, featuring a steam sterilizing apparatus. Housewives and peddlers suffering from nervous prostration were the most common patients. However, the hospital could not accommodate people with contagious diseases because it had no isolation ward.

As the scope and quality of medical care grew, so did the building. Eventually Jewish Hospital encountered a problem that other area hospitals also were confronting: inadequate parking facilities for staff members' horses and carriages.

With the turn of the century Jewish Hospital established a School of Nursing—the first associated with a private hospital. Although its last class of registered nurses was graduated in 1988, an Institute for Advanced Nursing Clinical Education simultaneously was opened in its place to keep pace with the new educational needs of nurses.

What is known today as The Children's Psychiatric Center of The Jewish Hospital was founded in 1920 as the Psychopathic Institute for the Care of Abnormal Children, the first of its kind in the country. Designed to evaluate the problem child in a residential setting, the program has been a prototype for present-day child psychiatric study institutes.

By 1925 the hospital had 125 beds, including obstetrics and pediatrics. Of those, 35 were reserved for charity patients, maintaining a tradition that the founders had begun in 1850. Two years later Jewish Hospital installed the area's first electrocardiograph.

Expansion continued with the addition of a three-story maternity building, an eye clinic, a new power plant, a physiotherapy department and a heart clinic. In 1931 the city's first Drinker Respirator was installed at Jewish Hospital, marking a major advance in the treatment of respiratory problems. Through a gift of Mrs. David May in 1934, the May Institute for Medical Research was founded and has continued to support medical research.

Volunteer activity increased with the outbreak of World War II. About 30% of the nursing school graduates during the 1940s served in the armed forces. Jewish Hospital added a new emergency room, and improvements continued with new fervor after the war.

During the 1950s and early 1960s Jewish Hospital took many steps toward the technology of today's health care. The hospital expanded, opening the Emil Frank building; installed its first Isolette incubator; and introduced a new radiation therapy section with a Cobalt-60 Unit, which provides external radiation therapy for the treatment of cancer.

A new building on Burnet Avenue went up in 1970, providing a new entrance for primary patient care, and another building on Ridgeway opened in 1980. A telephone-teletype patient information system developed by Jewish Hospital and Cincinnati Bell marked another first toward more efficient patient care.

When the last of the old hospital buildings was closed in 1974, the 600-bed Jewish Hospital was well on its way to becoming a modern, full-service teaching hospital for all denominations. Progress in the next decade focused on expanding health care in other parts of town. The Midwest Medical Care Center started providing medical care downtown in the early 1980s. The Jewish Hospital Professional Building, a modern medical mall with physicians' offices and operating rooms, opened in suburban Evendale in 1988, and Jewish Hospital merged with Otto Epp Memorial Hospital northeast of Cincinnati.

Medical services took to the road with extensive diagnostic services such as echocardiography and mobile mammography made available to patients and physicians' offices. Jewish was the first Cincinnati hospital to take adult ECG's over the telephone. The hospital's cardiac rehabilitation unit, opened in 1980, provided the city's first complete three-phase service and, later, open-heart surgery and cardiac catheterizations.

Leon Goldman, M.D., known as the father of laser surgery, pioneered many breakthrough procedures at The Jewish Hospital in the 1980s. The region's first laser-assisted angioplasty, a procedure designed to clear arteries through the use of a laser probe, was performed at Jewish Hospital by Creighton Wright, M.D. Independent units within Jewish Hospital are helping to service current health care dilemmas, such as adolescent chemical dependency, aging and high cholesterol. A specific center for the treatment of chronic pain also was developed for inpatient and outpatient care.

High atop the Ridgeway building at Jewish Hospital is a brilliantly lit, blue Shofar, a "J" shaped logo symbolizing both a ram's horn once blown as a call to prayer and the hospital's original mission to help the needy.

Kahn's & Company

Cincinnati's day as the world pork processing city is long over, but Kahn's and Co. is bigger than ever.

Elias Kahn, a German immigrant, opened his meat market on Central Avenue in 1882. A year later he was slaughtering calves, lambs and poultry and making sausage in the rear of his store. For more than 40 years, Cincinnatians would know the high-quality retail markets which were to spring from this beginning. But Kahn's ultimate destiny was in meat packing.

Elias himself began slaughtering cattle at Findlay and John streets in 1885. By this time he had stores in downtown Cincinnati, Avondale and Walnut Hills.

He also had four sons—Louis, Nathan, Albert and Eugene—who joined him in the enterprise then known as E. Kahn's and Sons Co. All of them learned the business from the slaughter rooms to the business office.

Louis W. Kahn became president and was the company's general executive officer, but he had a reputation as a judge of livestock quality and skilled butcher. Newspaper accounts of September 2, 1898 report that he entered a competition which was part of the butchers' picnic at the Zoo. Fifteen thousand attended and saw three amateurs compete in a test of butchers' skills. Kahn, then 23, won a prize for dressing a 1,200-pound beef in 06:16.5. The professional record was exactly six minutes. Louis Kahn remained president of the company until his death in 1948.

Nathan Kahn, a director and vice president from 1907 until his death in 1936, also divided his time between administration and the field. He bought calves, lambs and poultry, supervised the poultry-dressing division and the slaughter of small stock at the packing plant.

Eugene Kahn worked in the meat packing plant until 1909, by which time the company had five retail food stores. He took over their management and purchased the groceries, fruits and vegetables. The retail stores were a major operation, but the meat-packing business came to overshadow them and the stores were gradually sold off. The largest, on the northwest corner of Reading Road and Forest Avenue, was Cincinnati's biggest and best-stocked grocery and meat market and remained part of Kahn's until it was sold in 1926. From then until his death in 1932, Eugene devoted his time to the meat packing operation.

The fourth son, Albert, became Kahn's treasurer and plant manager in 1907 and remained in that post until his death in 1948. He also had another job—soliciting and servicing clubs, hotels and other institutional customers. By 1927 he had built this operation into one which had customers over the entire area east of the Mississippi River.

The building at 3241 Spring Grove Avenue, which is now Kahn's main plant and home office, was opened in 1928. Kahn's had become a major employer—642 persons—and the building's dedication was a civic event. Mayor Murray Seasongood hailed it as an attempt to bring back the glories of Porkopolis. The plant was updated in 1949 and continuously thereafter. Of its 250,000 square feet, only 500 were left untouched by the remodeling crews.

The new plant did not restore Porkopolis, but it established Kahn's as a major factor in hams, bacon, wieners, lunchmeats and other sausages. In some east coast areas, Kahn's hams enjoy something of a cult following.

Kahn's enjoyed recognition in other areas. In 1981 it was recognized by the Association of Business and Professional Women for its progressive record in hiring and assigning work to women. The award was all the more telling for meat packing is traditionally a male-dominated industry.

When Louis Kahn died in 1948, the presidency of the company passed to Milton J. Schloss, a grandson of Elias, who—following the family tradition—had begun working in the slaughterhouse at age 14. His mother, Mathilda Kahn, also was trained as a butcher and had managed one of the retail stores.

Consolidated Foods Corp. of Chicago, now the Sara Lee Corp., purchased Kahn's in 1966. Nevertheless, Kahn's continued to expand its operations under Sara Lee and in 1974 increased its stockyard acreage in order to buy directly from hog breeders.

In 1988 Kahn's merged with Hillshire Farm to form a major meat division within the Sara Lee Corp. Consumer Foods Group. Robert Huber, president and chief executive officer of Kahn's, was named president and chief executive officer of the new division, which is headquartered at the Spring Grove Avenue offices.

Kahn's and Company operates three processing plants in addition to the one in Cincinnati: Springfield, Ohio; Claryville, Kentucky; and New London, Wisconsin.

Sausages packed by Kahn's and Company at its Spring Grove Avenue plant. Photograph courtesy of Kahn's & Company.

Kahn's opened this Spring Grove Avenue plant in 1928. Photograph of an architectural rendering. Courtesy of *The Cincinnati Post*.

A.M. Kinney Inc.

On February 4, 1929, a new engineering firm, Kinney & Ehlers, Inc., was started in Cincinnati. Aldon Monroe Kinney had attended Purdue University and learned the practical realities of his profession in various engineering offices and departments in town. Confident in their abilities and in the nation's continuing growth and productivity, Kinney and his partner retained a young attorney named Robert A. Taft to draw up the papers of incorporation.

Renting an office in the Dixie Terminal Building and employing a stenographer, the firm was ready for business as consulting engineers specializing in professional mechanical engineering services and power plant design and pioneering in the use of powdered coal. Neither man could have anticipated the stock market crash that would come nine months later.

The Kinney family had come from the Hebrides and Ulster to Massachusetts and New Brunswick, Canada. Successive generations of the family met the challenges of the New World experience along the eastern seaboard. Moving west they made Cincinnati their home in 1920.

Reared with a strong awareness of God's presence and purpose in his life, Kinney made his beliefs an integral part of the company's operations. In 1953 he established the company's Wednesday Devotional Luncheons, to which well-known Christian laymen were and continue to be invited as speakers.

A.M. Kinney led the corporation for 37 years, buying Ehlers' interest in 1931 and serving as president in 1955, then as chairman in 1966. He saw the firm grow from two employees to one of the largest professional firms in the country, from a one-room rented office to a large corporate headquarters building, and from a single firm offering services in a single discipline to a number of firms offering fully integrated and computerized services in many disciplines, with branches in New York, Chicago and other cities. He gave the company his expertise and infused it with his belief in hard work and a determination to excel. His influence on the business affairs of the company is still evident, as is the company's continuing commitment to the moral and spiritual principles by which he lived.

With the senior Kinney's retirement in 1966, his son, Aldon Kinney Jr., became chairman of the board. After studying liberal arts at the University of Cincinnati and serving in the Army, he returned to the university, studying both law and engineering. While in private law practice for many years, he worked as counsel to the firm and administrative assistant to the president.

Aldon Kinney III is also active in the company today, representing, as his name suggests, the third generation and continuing the close Kinney identification with engineering and architecture in the Cincinnati community.

The company moved from the Dixie Terminal Building to the Carew Tower in 1940, but by 1949 the company needed considerably more space. In that year it moved out of the downtown area into a building on Vernon Place, near the Vernon Manor Hotel in Avondale, where its headquarters is located today.

Kinney always looked to the time when the company could design a building for its own offices. In 1958 he presided at ground-breaking ceremonies for the first phase of the facility that the company now occupies at 2900 Vernon Place. Expansion of the corporate headquarters has continued to the present day, now providing over 140,000 square feet of space for A.M. Kinney and several of the companies with which it is affiliated.

Walter Kidde Constructors, Inc. and its subsidiaries joined the group in 1973, strengthening the overall capability in construction management. Vulcan Cincinnati, Inc. began its affiliation in 1975 and furnished technical design services, proprietary processes and process licensing in the chemical, methanol, petrochemical and solvent recovery industries.

Today the affiliated group of companies consists of firms providing an unusually wide range of total design capability, offering complete mechanical, electrical, structural, civil, sanitary, industrial and chemical engineering as well as planning, architectural, interiors design, construction management and energy conservation services nationally and internationally. For the sake of convenience, they are now called the A.M. Kinney Affiliation.

The bulk of drawings produced by the company is now prepared using high-powered, computer-aided drafting and design equipment, with alpha-numeric terminals and personal computers tied in as adjuncts to the main system. A long-distance, telephonic connection capability enables the company to communicate to client-owned or rented graphics terminals anywhere in the country day-to-day development of the drawings.

In 1953 A.M. Kinney, Inc. received the first of its many public recognitions for the quality of its work, the "Office of the Year Award" for the Mennen Company offices in New Jersey. The award was presented by Frank Lloyd Wright.

A.M. Kinney Affiliation firms have won more of the "America's Top Ten Plants of the Year" awards during the last 18 years of competition than any other firm in existence today. It has received 55 awards for design excellence, among which are 12 from the American Institute of Architects and three "Laboratory of the Year" awards. These awards have included such projects as the University of Cincinnati Renton K. Brodie Science and Engineering Center; the Cincinnati Children's Hospital Medical Center, Convalescent and Services Pavilion and Environmental Therapy Complex; the S.D. Johnson & Son, Inc. Biology Research Laboratory in Wisconsin; and the Nalco Chemical Company Technical Center in Illinois.

Today A.M. Kinney is a leading designer of laboratories for pharmaceutical, biological, chemical, industrial and food research as well as materials and science education laboratories.

Other major A.M. Kinney projects have included the American Museum of Atomic Energy in Oak Ridge; the National Environmental Research Center of the Environmental Protection Agency in Cincinnati; all site and support facilities of the Atomic Energy Commission uranium production complex in Portsmouth, Ohio, including joint design of the Gaseous Diffusion Plant; the Pike Island, Smithland and New Cumberland dams and locks on the Ohio River; Combined Fleet Command Headquarters of the Eastern and Western Fleets of the Royal Saudi Navy in Saudi Arabia; and the total renovation of the Cincinnati Gas & Electric Company corporate headquarters.

Leading designers of research laboratories, A.M. Kinney engineers are headquartered at 2900 Vernon Place in Avondale. Photograph courtesy of A.M. Kinney.

The Kroger Company

The Kroger Co., founded in 1883, has gone through at least two highly successful lives. The first was as the personal instrument of founder Bernard Henry Kroger; the second as a modern corporation.

Kroger's father, a German immigrant, owned a dry goods store with the family home on the second floor. B.H. was born in 1860. Kroger's father died just as the family's prosperity was wiped out by the panic of 1873, and the boy got a job in a drugstore. He had to quit because his mother would not allow Sunday work. He then got a job as a farmhand near Pleasant Plain. Overworked and poorly paid, 14 years old and ravaged by malaria, the boy decided that this was not his calling. In mid-winter he walked the 35 miles back home. He went to work the next day selling door-to-door for the Great Northern and Pacific Tea Co.

After similar selling jobs, he negotiated himself into the undisputed managership of a fading store called the Imperial Tea Co. He bought a cash register, hired a cashier and fired everybody else except a delivery boy. He worked as close to 24 hours a day as his body allowed. He tasted and tested everything, building a reputation of quality for the store and a reputation of being outrageously picky as a buyer for himself. When the store prospered, he tried to buy in as a partner. He was refused, so he and a friend—who could borrow $350—opened their own store at 66 Pearl Street. They painted the store front bright red and put the company name on it in gilt—The Great Western Tea Co. The year was 1883 and B.H. Kroger was 23 years old.

The Midwest is filled with elderly men and women who can remember Barney's red-fronted stores. The Pearl Street establishment was 17 feet wide, which was to remain typical of Kroger stores for almost 50 years.

Less than two months after its opening, the Pearl Street store was destroyed by a flood, but Kroger and his partner, B.A. Branagan, managed to make a profit that first year. Kroger soon bought out Branagan and was able to put his name on the store, "B.H. Kroger's Tea and Grocery Stores." He had four of them by 1885.

By 1893 he was rich, had 17 stores, had married above his station and was leading his seven children in front-yard parades. This life ended abruptly with Mrs. Kroger's unexpected death in 1899. His eldest son, age 12, died a few months later. Kroger would marry again, but for a time he apparently reverted to being the single-minded businessman.

He expanded to Hamilton, then to Dayton, then into the Midwest. He became a good story teller, took up golf and liked poker. Joseph Hall, a longtime president of Kroger, described him as having a military figure and qualities which "bespoke respectability, tried and trusted values, an uncompromising attitude toward life, and a freedom from inner doubt." Hall also credits him with an awesome command of profanity—followed by sheepish apology—and bursts of temper whose coming would be signalled by a softly whistled rendition of "Wait 'til the Sun Shines Nellie."

In 1928 he sold every share of Kroger stock he owned, although he remained on the board until 1931. Nor did he abandon his Cincinnati ties. He was a major supporter of charities and in 1933 was credited with stopping a run on the Provident Bank, which he had helped establish. During the depression he repurchased Kroger stock. He died in 1938 at the age of 78 and left an estate of $22,000,000.

The Kroger managements which followed him expanded the system of bakeries and packing plants and introduced a laboratory division which turned Barney's personal nitpicking into a science. Companies which wanted to sell to Kroger feared a Kroger inspector's visit more than one from a government agent.

The Kroger Co. did not invent supermarkets, but it began turning to them early; the narrow, red-fronted stores were disappearing well before World War II, although a few of them lingered on in small towns. The "official" Kroger color slowly changed from red to blue.

The average Kroger store today is under never-ending expansion and renovation and has evolved into a combination food and drug store, which offers a pharmacy as well as delicatessen departments, wine shops, fresh baked goods, even fresh-cut flowers.

Thus, Barney Kroger's first managerial attempt with two employees has grown somewhat. Kroger now employs 170,000 people, 11,000 of them in Cincinnati. It operates more than 1,300 grocery stores and 900 convenience stores; has plants producing such diverse items as coffee and pet food; and in 1987 grossed $17.1 billion.

It is no longer a one-man show, but is run by a pyramid of management. The man at its peak is Lyle Everingham, chairman and chief executive officer.

B. H. Kroger (1860-1938). Oil on canvas. Gift of the family of Gertrude Kroger Pettengill.

The first Kroger store opened in 1883 at 66 Pearl Street. Photograph. Gift of the Kroger Company.

LeBlond, Makino Machine Tool Company

The development of the R.K. LeBlond Machine Tool Company typifies the American success story. In 1887 23-year-old Richard Knight LeBlond started a manufacturing business in the type-making industry with a modest amount of personal savings. He rented a 20-square-foot room on Pearl Street and hired two employees. LeBlond brought together his family background as printers in England, his own apprenticeship in two type casting foundries and his experience with a machine tool company. To these talents he added an entrepreneurial spirit and a "head" for business and began to manufacture printing type molds, gauges and small tools.

One year later the business had grown so much that it had to move into new quarters more than seven times as large. In the new location at Second and Plum streets, LeBlond made the historic decision to enter the machine tool business as a lathe manufacturer. His brother, John A. LeBlond, joined the enterprise, and the business continued to prosper. A major lathe order from the Lodge & Davis Co. resulted in Nicholas Chard's leaving that firm and purchasing an interest in the fledgling LeBlond operation. Chard encouraged the company to raise its sights from simply manufacturing lathes to actually designing them as well. In 1892 the company introduced an innovative, 14-inch lathe of its own design, and the die was cast. Even though Chard left the company during the "Panic of 1893," R.K. LeBlond was firmly committed both to growth and to product development.

The "Gay '90s" saw a tremendous popular demand for bicycles throughout the United States. This in turn created a demand for machinery to be used in their production. R.K. LeBlond seized the opportunity, and in 1894 he hired the company's first full-time design engineer. That decision proved wise indeed, for in the next few years the company was producing not only several sizes of lathes, but also single- and multiple-spindle drills and milling machines. The growth resulting from these innovations necessitated new facilities. In 1897, a mere 10 years from its inception, the company built a new plant in what was then the suburb of Linwood, far from the congested center of the city. That same year the company was incorporated as the R.K. LeBlond Machine Tool Company, a name familiar to many Cincinnatians to this day.

Growth and creativity continued to be the watchwords as the company won a Bronze Medal for design at the 1900 *Exposition Universelle Internationale* in Paris and then in 1903 produced its first gear-driven lathe head-stock with a chain drive and an independent electric motor. These were radical innovations in a day when electricity was still in its youth.

Although the Linwood plant had been considered large when built, by 1916 the company had outgrown its facilities. This was due in part to the unprecedented production demands during World War I. A new factory was begun in 1917 on the site of a dairy farm at the corner of Madison Avenue and Edwards Road. The factory was a model manufacturing facility, even boasting a power plant with its own generator to produce electricity.

Among its many new products, the company developed a special lathe designed to make crankshafts for automobiles. The new factory made it possible for LeBlond to become the world's leading producer of these special machines, and over the next half century virtually every American car had a crankshaft made on a LeBlond lathe.

Beginning in 1927 the company began to diversify into other products and industries including the manufacture of small radial piston aircraft engines, small electric hand tools, buffers and grinders, trucks and fire engines, mixers used in the food and chemical industry, and many types of special purpose machinery. Yet none of these lines ever replaced the lathes for which the name LeBlond was famous.

During World War II the LeBlond plant was dedicated to the manufacture of gun boring lathes. Those lathes proved so vital to the war effort that several other factories throughout the country were converted to manufacture LeBlond lathes and lathe parts.

In the 1950s and 1960s, LeBlond made several technical breakthroughs. Among them was a special lathe used in making large jet engines. Another special lathe was used in the space program to form nose cones for missiles and to wrap fuel tanks for rockets. A joint project with the General Electric Company produced the first continuous-path, numerically controlled lathe, a major step in the development of automated manufacturing.

During the 1970s the company moved onto the international scene by building a new plant and foundry in Singapore to manufacture its Regal lathe line.

In 1981 the Makino Milling Machine Co., Ltd. of Tokyo, Japan purchased a major interest in the business, and the company became the LeBlond Makino Machine Tool Company. The marriage of the two has brought to Cincinnati the manufacture of a new line of highly sophisticated, computer-controlled machining centers. It has also brought to Cincinnati a special machining technique known as EDM (Electrical Discharge Machining) used in the production of such everyday products as toothbrush handles and plastic soft drink bottles.

As LeBlond Makino prepares itself for the 1990s, it is once again building a new plant. The modern, high-tech facility will be just north of Cincinnati in Mason, Ohio. This environmentally controlled plant will enable the company to manufacture high-precision, horizontal machining centers here in the United States. Under the leadership of Donald D. Bowers, president and chief executive officer, and Daniel W. LeBlond, chairman of the board, LeBlond Makino looks forward to a long and prosperous future in the greater Cincinnati community.

Richard Knight LeBlond founded his manufacturing business in the type-making industry in 1887 at age 23. Photograph courtsey of LeBlond-Makino.

This LeBlond 16-inch quick change, belt-driven lathe (1903) was an innovation in the early days of electricity. Illustration courtesy of LeBlond-Makino.

Mayfield Neurological Institute

Cincinnati is a city well recognized for its innovative medical pioneers. Among the most prominent is Frank Mayfield, M.D. He and the group practice he assembled over the last 50 years have been leaders in the treatment of diseases involving the brain, spinal cord, peripheral nerves, skull, spine and blood vessels of the neck and brain.

These innovations and advances, along with the group's uncompromising commitment to patient care and dedication to medical education, have earned the Mayfield Neurological Institute (MNI) world-wide recognition.

MNI's history spans more than half a century. Its roots trace to the solo practice established in 1938 by Dr. Mayfield. The group now has 20 highly specialized, acclaimed members who are leaders in a variety of subspecialties: neurology, neurological surgery and neuropsychology.

Dr. Mayfield first arrived in the Queen City in the spring of 1937. The 30-year-old Carolinian was appointed to head the section of neurological surgery at Good Samaritan Hospital and soon joined The Christ Hospital staff as well. He also developed a long personal and professional friendship with Dr. Joseph Evans, head of the neurosurgical program at the University of Cincinnati. The two men forged a close working relationship between MNI, University of Cincinnati hospitals and The Christ and Good Samaritan hospitals for cooperation in quality patient care, education and research in the neurosciences.

MNI quickly flourished. Within one year Dr. Mayfield was working 90-hour weeks and handling seven to eight surgical cases a day. He loved the drama and pace, and soon after returning from the armed services during World War II, he decided it was time to form a group practice.

Adding associates to MNI was something Dr. Mayfield would do several times throughout the coming years. Candidates were always carefully selected; many were graduates of the training program that Dr. Mayfield headed at The Christ and Good Samaritan hospitals.

This training program, affiliated with Dr. Evans' Division of Neurological Surgery, remained an important link between MNI and the hospitals. It is a link which continues today and exemplifies MNI's dedication to excellence in the neurosciences.

The 1950s and 1960s were certainly decades of growth for MNI. Achievements included the establishment of its principal location at 506 Oak Street, the addition of new partners and the invention and patent of the "Mayfield Clip Setter" and the development of the Mayfield Clip. Used to close an aneurysm during intracranial surgery, this clip won worldwide acclaim for Dr. Mayfield and the institute. The device saved the lives of countless patients and dramatically changed the course of history for such brain operations.

Development of the "Mayfield Clip," however, was only one of several medical advances attributed to members of MNI. The "Mayfield Headrest" and "Budde-Halo Retractor," two instruments that secure patient positions during surgery, are additional innovations that have been patented and used around the world.

MNI members are also pioneers in introducing new techniques to treat neurological diseases. One of MNI's surgeons was among the first in the nation to receive Food and Drug Administration approval to use a laser powered by a garnet crystal to treat brain tumors. Another MNI colleague was the first surgeon in Cincinnati to perform a stereotactic interstitial radiation treatment. In this therapy radioactive seeds are implanted by way of a catheter into malignant brain tumors.

The Mayfield Neurological Institute has had and continues to have a dramatic and beneficial impact on the medical well-being of the citizens of the Greater Cincinnati area. Seeing well over 14,000 patients a year from every Cincinnati area location and hospital, MNI is by far the largest and most renowned group of physicians in the Greater Cincinnati area specializing in the neurosciences.

Dedication to innovation—the desire to learn, teach and to share expertise—and, most important, uncompromising passion to improve patients' lives: these are the cornerstones upon which pioneer Frank H. Mayfield built a practice. That rich tradition continues in today's Mayfield Neurological Institute.

The main office of Mayfield Neurological Institute at 506 Oak Street. Illustration. Courtesy of Miller Communications.

Merrell Dow Pharmaceuticals

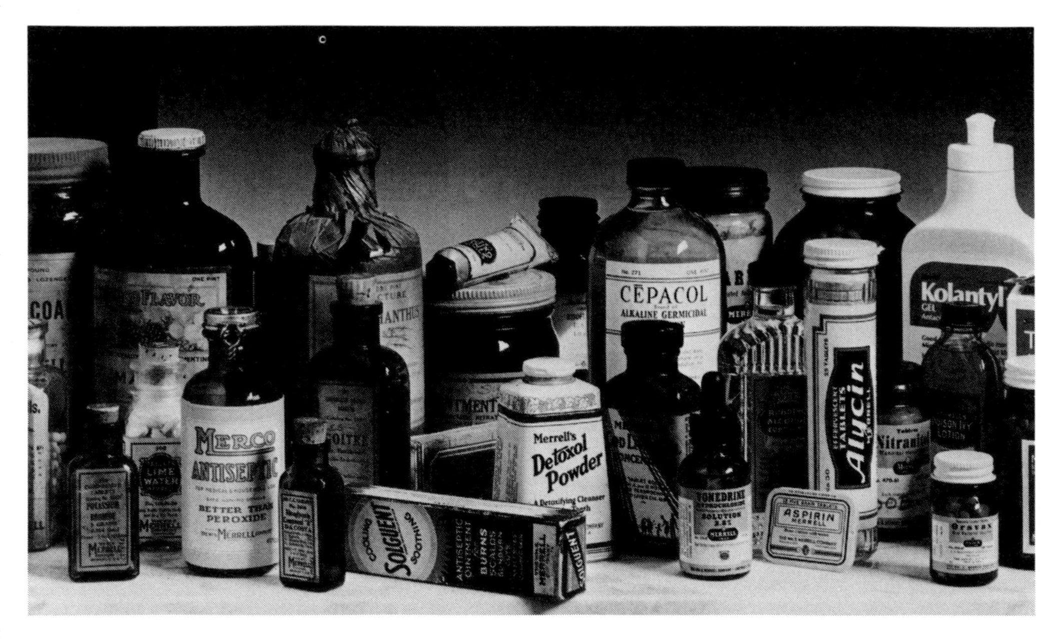

150 Years of Medicine For Mankind. Portion of photograph displaying products of Merrell Dow Pharmaceuticals, Inc. published in the corporation's 1978 *Annual Report.* Courtesy of Thurston Merrell, Jr.

William Stanley Merrell, born in 1798, made a slight correction in the course of his career, but for the rest of his life he seemed to know exactly what to do and how he wanted to do it.

He had intended to become a physician. He even attended some classes at the Medical College of Ohio that had been founded by Dr. Daniel Drake. Although he graduated from Hamilton College in Clinton, New York, he waited 27 years to pick up his diploma. With his usual attention to duty, he waited until a business trip took him back east.

In his early years he was a Presbyterian who started his days with Bible reading and who attended church three times on Sundays. In his middle years he joined the Swedenborgians. He was charitable, sometimes hiring unqualified people because they needed the work.

He gave the impression of frailty, because he weighed only 120 pounds, was five feet tall and seemed to be either ill or worn out by work for much of his life. The truth is he was made of leather and steel, fathered 11 children, worked 12 to 14 hours a day, lived to 82 years and founded the William S. Merrell Co., now known as Merrell Dow Pharmaceuticals.

Family business first brought him to Cincinnati and he soon found that physicians here needed a source for their medications. Merrell's move into pharmaceuticals took place on June 10, 1828, when he opened a retail drugstore at Sixth Street and Western Row (Central Avenue), then on the far edge of town. He took in all of $3.07 the first week and netted about $100 the first year. Business became so good that he took Mehitabel Thurston Poor as his wife and both family names persist in the business today in the person of Thurston Merrell Jr., the great grandson of William S. Merrell.

The pharmaceuticals of the time were for the most part made from substances found in nature. In 1832 Merrell made his first transactions as a wholesaler and manufacturer by shipping green elm to Philadelphia and setting up a still to make chloride of lime. Merrell's first big sales were of Podophyllin made from mandrake root, and Leptandrin, a resinous laxative. The firm became known for its "green" pharmaceuticals, which were made from a variety of plants preserved in alcohol as soon as they were picked. Merrell soon was attempting to supply druggists and physicians with every item they might need, and at one time the company carried approximately 2,000 products in its catalog.

As a result the company was forever running out of production space. New stores and mills were opened at several locations in downtown Cincinnati. Its final downtown location was wiped out in the 1930s by the construction of the Fifth Street viaduct and Columbia Parkway. The company moved to Reading, where Merrell now conducts its major activities at 2110 East Galbraith Road, in a proliferation of office, research and production buildings.

Shortly after William S. opened his first store, his brother, Ashbell, offered to come to Cincinnati to help. In general William and Ashbell made a good team. While William plowed new fields, Ashbell fretted over the economics of innovation. The company even went through a number of titles, beginning with the original store's "Western Market Drug Store." For a time it was the William S. Merrell Chemical Co., not because it produced chemicals in the modern sense, but because it supplied druggists who were used to the English terminology.

William led the company from 1828 until 1880. George Merrell, his son, was president from 1880 to 1914 and was succeeded by his son, Charles, from 1914 to 1937. Thurston Merrell, brother of Charles, was president from 1937 until 1949 and was the last president to bear the family name.

The Vick Chemical Company purchased the William S. Merrell Co. in 1938 and later changed its corporate name to Richardson-Merrell to honor William S. Merrell and Lunsford Richardson, who founded Vick. In succeeding years Merrell acquired the Loeser Laboratory Inc. of New York City, the National Drug Co. and Walker Laboratories. Nelson Gampfer became president in 1949, to be succeeded by Frank Getman (1957), Edmund R. Beckwith Jr. (1962), J.K. Lindsay (1966), John S. Scott (1970), Ivan Husovsky (1973) and David B. Sharrock (1980).

In 1981 the entire domestic and international operation of Merrell National Laboratories merged with the Dow Pharmaceuticals business under its current title with headquarters in Cincinnati.

Although the products, as well as the company, have gone through many changes, perhaps the biggest change involves people. William S. started with a single employee. Merrell Dow now employs 8,500 worldwide and 1,500 in Cincinnati.

To better service the increasing demands of customers and the health care industry in the United States, Merrell Dow Pharmaceuticals Inc. established two U.S. divisions, Merrell Dow U.S.A. and Lakeside Pharmaceuticals. Both divisions are committed to marketing therapeutically important drugs for both acute and chronic conditions.

Merrell Dow U.S.A. specializes in therapeutic prescription products. Lakeside Pharmaceuticals specializes in over-the-counter and prescription products dedicated to health improvement.

Joseph G. Temple was named president and retained that title until 1987 when David B. Sharrock was named president and chief operating officer. Temple became chairman of the board and chief executive officer.

The Merten Company

The Merten Company, located at 1515 Central Parkway in downtown Cincinnati, was organized in 1962 by Harold A. Merten Jr., who remains president of the firm. Previously known as the Alfred M. May Company, the firm originally consisted of a small letter press shop whose business was primarily general commercial printing. Organized before the turn-of-the-century as the May and Kreidler Company, it had long been respected in the industry but had not grown significantly.

But under the ownership of Harold A. Merten Jr., the firm experienced a dramatic new birth. As Merten recalled upon the occasion of the new company's 25th anniversary, "What we've worked to do over the years is build it [the company] into a shop where customers could obtain quality work. We look for the customer who is looking for a finished print job that is better than average. We work very hard to let our customers know that their business is appreciated, and that there is somebody here who is looking after their job, someone who cares and will make sure everything is right."

The company specializes in four and five color work. It prints house organs, newsletters and reports. Today only 10-15% of Merten's business remains in the general commercial printing category. Its motto reflects its concern with quality and customer satisfaction: "Our growth is propelled by the quality and service of our people."

The Merten Company has grown into a medium-size printing operation with customers in Cincinnati, Indianapolis and Louisville. In 1962, when Merten purchased the company, he rented 6,000 square feet of space at the firm's present location. In 1974 he purchased the building, gradually occupying more and more of the space until the last tenants left in June 1987 and the company occupied all 22,000 square feet in the building. Meanwhile the company opened a new 22,000-square-foot plant on adjoining land in 1985. Thus today The Merten Company occupies 44,000 square feet of plant space.

Over the same period of time, the company's financial success was equally impressive. Between 1978 and 1988 its business grew from $1.5 million to $5.5 million per year, a 25% annual growth rate.

Harold A. Merten III, executive vice president, and his father, Harold A. Merten Jr., president, come from a family with a long heritage in the printing industry. Photograph courtesy of The Merten Company.

Merten also began an ancillary business, Pagemakers, Inc., which does typesetting for about 25% of the Merten Company's clients as well as for outside firms.

The company's success is due in large measure to the hard work and attention to detail of its founder and president, but his prior experience in the printing industry undoubtedly played an important role as well. Merten comes from a family with a long and illustrious heritage in the industry.

Merten's grandfather, William H. Merten (1870-1951), began working for the Strobridge Lithographing Company of Norwood at the age of 14 and rose in the ranks until he reached the top. He served as president of the company from 1936 to 1951 and was elected chairman of the board of directors in January 1951.

William Merten was very active in the printing industry and was among the founders of the Lithographic Technical Foundation of New York, New York, in 1925 and served as president and board member of the National Lithographing Association for many years. His father, Harold A. Merten (1897-1973) had also served as president of the Strobridge Lithographing Company. His brother, John W. Merten, has published a scholarly account of the history of the Strobridge Lithographing Company.

Prior to purchasing The Merten Company, Harold Merten Jr. had worked for the Strobridge Lithographing Company from 1950 to 1961. He continued to work for the company even after it became a division of the H.S. Crocker Company during 1961-1962 but finally decided to branch out on his own.

The future of The Merten Company looks promising and, if tradition is served, the Merten family will continue to be represented in the industry for many years to come. Harold Merten Jr.'s son, Harold A. Merten III, is currently director for marketing and someday may succeed his father as president. If he does he will be the fourth generation of the family to head a major printing and lithographing company in the Cincinnati area.

Frank Messer & Sons Construction Company

One of the nation's largest general contractors, Frank Messer & Sons helped build much of the Cincinnati skyline. Photograph of its Bond Hill headquarters courtesy of Frank Messer & Sons.

Many of Cincinnati's largest and best-known 20th-century buildings have been built by firms begun by Frank Messer, an Austrian immigrant who settled in Cincinnati in 1909. Messer originally came to New York in 1901, working as a carpenter's helper at six dollars a week. At age 30 he left New York for Cincinnati and in a few years formed a partnership known as the Ohio Building and Construction Co.

During Messer's tenure as president, the Ohio Building and Construction Co. completed several large projects in the 1920s in downtown Cincinnati, including the Dixie Terminal Building, the Central Y.M.C.A. and the Keith Theatre building. After building the 11-story Belvedere Apartments in North Avondale, the business partnership was dissolved, and Frank Messer incorporated Frank Messer & Sons in 1932.

The new company grew steadily, overcoming not only the Great Depression, but also the death of Frank Messer in 1937. His son, Charles M. Messer, succeeded him. Shortly thereafter the company began construction of the Wright Aeronautical Company plant, now the General Electric Company, in Evendale. At that time the 1.4 million square foot project was described as "the largest ever let under one contract in the United States." During the World War II years, Messer completed many defense-related projects, including several buildings for Wright Patterson Air Force Base in Dayton.

After the war Messer's construction activities included industrial plant expansions, retail projects, hotels, motels and office buildings. The economic development of the post-war years also brought on an increased demand for energy. As a result Messer built power plants for the Cincinnati Gas & Electric Co., Kentucky Utilities, Dayton Power and Light Co., East Kentucky Power Cooperative, Indianapolis Power & Light Co. and American Power Co.

Among the large construction projects that Messer has completed in the Cincinnati area are: Shillito's Department Store; Procter & Gamble's first downtown Corporate Headquarters Building; the Terrace Hilton Hotel; the Quality Hotel Riverview in Covington; Cincinnati Gardens; academic and dormitory buildings at the University of Cincinnati, Miami University and Northern Kentucky University; hospital buildings and additions; Lytle Tower; the Hamilton County Justice Center; the corporate headquarters for Cincinnati Financial Corporation; Riverbend Music Pavilion and Colonnade; Sak's Fifth Avenue; The Beach waterpark; and the renovation of the Cincinnatian Hotel and the Alms and Doepke Building.

Although the Messer Company concentrates on a market area that includes Ohio, Kentucky, Indiana and West Virginia, it has worked in Texas, Kansas, Alabama, Tennessee, Pennsylvania and Massachusetts as well. To meet rapidly changing production schedule needs, Messer owns and maintains a substantial inventory of equipment and tools, ranging from sophisticated tower cranes to the basic material conveying and handling equipment and computerized accounting, estimating, cost control, and schedule control systems. Messer is currently ranked by *Engineering News Record Magazine* as the 159th largest general contractor in the United States.

The Messer Company has employed the principles of construction management through negotiated contracts with owners for more than 40 years. Now that the concept has come into general acceptance, Messer has broadened its personnel, systems and methods, offering many management services in addition to its expertise in construction methods.

Messer has proudly joined with William Cargile Contractors as part of the construction management team responsible for converting the historic Union Terminal building into the new Museum Center at Cincinnati Union Terminal.

Changes in the construction industry in recent years, including prefabrication, precutting, premachining, preassembly, and mechanization, have reduced the number of manhours required to construct new buildings along with the ratio of unskilled to skilled workers in the industry. Messer has a policy of recruiting young engineering and business college trainees and co-ops, many of whom become full-time employees that grow and develop within the company. This has produced a very stable firm, with an average tenure in the administrative and supervisory ranks of 16 years.

The organization is made up of 50 people in the main office on Paddock Road and more than 100 key personnel in field offices, including 30 project superintendents. Total employment, including foremen and tradesmen, sometimes reaches over 350.

Miami University

Established in 1809 as the second-oldest state university west of the Alleghenies, Miami University has grown to more than 19,000 students on four campuses. It is a residential liberal arts college dedicated to the quality education of undergraduate students.

The first 20 students who came to Miami in November 1824 traveled through dense forests to arrive at the stump-cluttered campus. In the high-ceilinged rooms of Old Main, rural scholars pursued an ambitious curriculum based on that of eastern universities. Miami's emulation of Yale in particular led to its nickname, "the Yale of the Early West."

The "triangular" curriculum, prevalent in universities until the late 1800s, included moral philosophy and history, ancient languages (Latin, Hebrew, and Greek), and mathematics and astronomy. Miami was unusual in that it also emphasized science.

Of the 29 young men enrolled in three college classes in those first few years, nine became clergy; five, lawyers; one, a physician; one, a college president; four, college and theological teachers; two, members of Congress; and one, a diplomat. By the 1840s Miami had earned a sound academic reputation in the South and old West.

One of Miami's more famous faculty members, William Holmes McGuffey, came to the university in 1826 as librarian and professor of Ancient Languages. During his 10 years here, he wrote the original four *Eclectic Readers*. The McGuffey home on Miami's campus is now a museum to his life and works, containing a collection of his *Readers* as well as his eight-sided revolving work table, where grammar school children gathered to try out his lessons.

Another famous Miamian was Benjamin Harrison, an "earnest, grave fellow" from the class of 1852 who became president of the United States in 1888.

During the Civil War, Miami students left to fight for both the Union and the Confederacy. Southern students did not return after the war; consequently Miami shared in the nation's post-war financial problems. "Impoverished in an impoverished land," the school closed in 1873, not to reopen until 1885, when it had marshalled financial backing and a substantial student enrollment.

"New Miami" would retain much of the tradition, charm and prestige of "Old Miami," but it also changed with the times. The curriculum began expanding beyond the classical courses offered from 1824 to 1873, and specialized academic departments were created.

By the turn of the century, women were receiving diplomas at Miami commencements. Female enrollment began to swell in 1902 with the establishment of the Ohio Normal College, the predecessor of Miami's School of Education and Allied Professions. Within 10 years the predominantly female student body in the teachers college represented about 40 percent of Miami's enrollment.

In 1927 the School of Business Administration was created and has grown to have the seventh largest undergraduate enrollment in the nation. The American Assembly of Collegiate Schools of Business has recognized Miami's advertising practice class, Laws Hall and Associates, as an innovation in teaching. The class combines the talents of Miami students from marketing, art and mass communications to create marketing campaigns for such companies as Marathon Oil, Avon and American Greetings. Laws Hall is one reason why the Association of American Colleges has named Miami as one of 40 colleges and universities successfully integrating career preparation and liberal arts programs.

The School of Fine Arts, with curricula in architecture, music, theater, painting, printmaking and design, was added in 1929. The School of Applied Science, organized in 1959, prepares students for careers in manufacturing engineering, health care and information systems. Its paper science and engineering program is one of only seven in the country.

In 1974, through affiliation, the Western College, a small, 120-year-old private institution adjoining the Oxford campus, became a new Miami division, the School in Interdisciplinary Studies (Western College Program). The school has been recognized by the National Institute of Education for its innovative approach to education.

Growing graduate programs were organized into the Graduate School in 1947, resulting in increased research and creative work for our faculty. An example of this is the Scripps Gerontology Center. Originally founded in 1922 to study population problems, the center officially changed its focus in 1972 to study the impact of aging on population and society.

The Ecology Research Center's teaching and research programs evaluate the effects of fire, radiation, pesticides and sludge on ecosystems. The Department of Architecture's Center for Building Science Research is one of a few research facilities in the country designed to study passive solar energy and architectural daylighting. And the Center for the Study of Writing involves faculty and students from various departments in researching composition to improve the quality of writing instruction in all disciplines.

Miami is the only state-assisted university in Ohio with an independently sited art museum. Designed by Walter A. Netsch of Skidmore Owings and Merrill, the building has received international recognition.

Miami also is known as the "Mother of Fraternities." It is the founding site of the famous "Miami Triad" of Beta Theta Pi, Phi Delta Theta and Sigma Chi, along with Phi Kappa Tau. The Delta Zeta sorority was also founded at Miami University.

In sports circles Miami has earned the name "Cradle of Coaches" for the number of coaches and athletic administrators trained here who have achieved national prominence.

The Miami University Alumni Association, founded in 1832, is the fourth oldest in the nation. Consistently alumni contributions have placed Miami among the top 10 public universities in the nation for percentage of alumni giving.

Miami has long been known in the midwest for the traditional beauty of its red brick campus, the excellence of its students and the quality of its academic programs. It increasingly has received national acclaim from publications such as *Money* magazine, *TIME, Newsweek* and the *Wall Street Journal*. Miami was one of eight public universities in Richard Moll's book *The Public Ivys* and is included in Edward Fiske's *The Best Buys in College Education.*

Old Main, Stoddard and Elliott halls, along with a one-room science building, comprised the Miami campus for more than 50 years. Built in 1818 Old Main was the heart of Miami University for more than a century. It was replaced in 1958 by Harrison Hall, but Stoddard and Elliott are still used as residence halls. Elliott, the oldest residence hall on any Ohio campus, was built in 1824, and Stoddard, in 1835. Both are included on the National Register of Historic Places. Illustration. Courtesy of Miami University.

The Midland Company

The Midland Co. is a Cincinnati institution that has shown an outstanding ability to find the mainstream of American life, especially its business life, and as a result has found success in a number of endeavors.

Though it shares the "mid" part of its name with a number of local firms, it is a unique company not to be confused with others with a sound-alike name. It has itself changed parts of its name through the 50 years of its existence.

The Midland Co. was founded as Midland Discount Co. in 1938 by J. Page Hayden and H.R. LaBar, who put up a total capital investment of $25,000. Hayden was a native of Baltimore and LaBar of the Adirondack region of New York. They came to Cincinnati and met while working for a local automobile finance company, Midland Acceptance Co. When this company was sold, they formed their own company.

Their infant project, Midland Discount, was an automobile finance company and, subsequently, a direct loan company. It became Cincinnati's largest in that field and opened branches in Toledo, Pittsburgh and Hamilton. After World War II it became one of the first companies to finance mobile homes. For a time mobile homes occupied most of its attention. In 1956 it sold its Cincinnati auto-finance business to The First National Bank and expanded the consumer loan and mobile home finance business with branches throughout midwestern and southern states.

J. Page Hayden and *H. R. LaBar,* founders of the Midland Discount Company. Photographs courtesy of The Midland Company.

To raise the capital for expansion, the firm was converted into a public stock company under the name of Midland-Guardian in 1961. The Hayden and LaBar families owned most of the shares and continue to do so despite several additional new issues of common stock.

The current management is the second generation, and it has mapped the expansion and diversification which has continued since the 1960s. Among the first major steps was the formation in 1965 of the American Modern Home Insurance Group. It specialized in casualty coverage in the mobile home industry and in credit life coverage for this and other industries. This division of Midland is its largest and today operates in every state.

Because of its experience in financing and insuring mobile homes, in 1965 Midland began manufacturing and selling them. By 1970 there were four manufacturing plants – in Georgia, Indiana and Virginia—operating under the name of Midland Industries, Inc. Retail sales were conducted at 70 locations in the South and Southeast under the name of Mustang Mobile Homes, Inc.

The biggest step toward diversification was made in 1968, when Midland bought a small barge line. As M/G Transport Services, Inc. this modest start has grown into one of the major operating divisions of the company and one of the nation's larger independent bulk carriers. Its principal business is transporting coal under contract with major utilities on the Ohio and Mississippi rivers. (Another company with "midland" in its name also operates river barge lines, but the two firms are not related.)

Between 1980 and 1982 M/G Transport Services added $38 million worth of new equipment to an already up-to-date fleet. The company acquired the operating assets of Harcon Barge Line in 1988. It operates 13 full-line towboats and 447 barges, representing a total investment of more than $100 million.

Midland's operations have continued to undergo sizable realignment. The recessions of 1973-1974 and of 1980-1982 seriously affected the mobile home industry and the extraordinary changes in the cost of borrowing money seriously cut into the ability of independent finance companies to compete. Midland decided to leave the manufactured housing business and sold its manufacturing plants and retail sales lots in 1982. Its consumer loan division had been sold two years earlier. The mobile home financing operation, with a loan portfolio that at one time had receivables at over $200 million, was sold in 1984.

Thus for the time being—and for the near future—Midland expects to expand in the insurance and river transport fields, where its management believes profitable growth will continue to be possible and to look at other industries for diversification.

In 1987 Midland dedicated its new headquarters building on Pete Rose Way in Cincinnati. Its growth has been profitable so far. The $25,000 stake of the founders has grown to annual revenues of more than $1 million, a net worth of more than $80 million and assets of $250 million.

Current officers of Midland are Joseph P. Hayden, Jr., chairman of the board; William F. Plettner, president; Michael J. Conaton, executive vice president; John R. LaBar, vice president and secretary; Robert W. Hayden, vice president; Grant Owings, vice president; Thomas J. Rohs, vice president; Edmund M. Graber, vice president; John I. Von Lehman, vice president and treasurer; J.P. Hayden III, vice president; and John W. Hayden, vice president.

Midland Enterprises Inc.

One of the largest companies in the barging industry is headquartered in Cincinnati. Although many Cincinnatians have seen its boats and barges in action, relatively few know the identity of the operator or its link to their city. With revenues over $203 million in 1987, Midland Enterprises Inc. ranks as one of the two largest barge carriers in the United States.

Located downtown in the 580 Building, Midland Enterprises also has sales offices or operating facilities in West Virginia, Kentucky, Pennsylvania, Illinois, Missouri, Louisiana and Florida. A subsidiary of Eastern Gas and Fuel Associates since 1961, Midland is composed of eight major operating companies.

The Ohio River Company, incorporated in 1925, is the foundation of Midland Enterprises. Its operations initially consisted of coal movements from the Kanawha River in West Virginia to the Cincinnati area. Today coal transportation to Cincinnati continues to represent a significant portion of all the company's business. From the beginning the Cincinnati Gas & Electric Co. has been one of its best customers. The Ohio River Company is responsible for transporting all of the coal burned at CG&E's generating units and also serves other major utilities on the Ohio River.

Along with Orgulf Transport Co., The Ohio River Company operates on the entire Ohio and Mississippi river systems as well as the Illinois, Gulf Intracoastal and Tennessee-Tombigbee waterways. Operating a fleet in excess of 2,000 open and covered hopper barges, the two companies are the dominant carriers of coal on the inland waterway system. Coal is not the only commodity handled, however. Iron, steel, scrap, stone, sand, gravel and coke are some of the other commodities that move in Midland barges. With the acquisition of Federal Barge Lines in 1985, Midland has also developed into a key transporter of grain and grain products.

Red Circle Transport Co. is Midland's ocean carrier of dry bulk commodities, operating in the Gulf of Mexico, the Caribbean and other coastal areas. Red Circle's specially designed tug-barge units are built with a notch in the stern to allow for efficient offshore transportation of dry bulk commodities.

Port Allen Marine Service Inc. (PAMS) is located on the lower Mississippi River near Baton Rouge, Louisiana. Towboat operators can look to PAMS for all their boat and barge repairs. PAMS is also a major builder of barges.

The Walker Companies were acquired by Midland in 1982. Located in Paducah, Kentucky, these firms provide a wide range of services to marine shippers. Walker Boat Yard's operations include a ship yard and a diesel shop for both boat and barge repair. In addition Walker's Midstream provides a delivery service to boats allowing them to take on fuel without stopping. R&W Marine provides towing on the Ohio, Tennessee, Green, Cumberland and Illinois rivers.

Midland also operates three terminals. Eastern Associated Terminals Company, located in Tampa, Florida, handles dry and wet phosphate rock for both domestic and export shippers.

Supporting the large volume of coal it moves on the inland waterway system, Midland operates two rail-to-barge transfer coal terminals in Huntington and Kenova, West Virginia. Coal is transported to the facilities by the two largest railroads serving the Appalachian coal fields. After coal is received at the terminals, it is loaded into barges for final delivery to utilities, steel companies and other consumers along the waterway system.

Midland is much more than boats, barges and buildings. As in all service-oriented businesses, the company's major asset is its people. To provide the prompt, reliable service required by our customers, Midland's boats operate 24 hours a day, 365 days a year. Such a demanding schedule requires the dedication and commitment of all our employees.

In total Midland employs over 1,400 people. About half are crew members aboard the company's 70-odd towboats. Working closely with our boat personnel as well as customers are the members of our transportation department who are responsible for coordinating and facilitating the efficient movement of our customers' shipments.

Through constant interaction and cooperation between our crew personnel and the company's Cincinnati-based administrative staff, our employees were responsible for delivering almost 49 million tons of bulk commodities in 1987, including 30 million tons of coal.

Omar was once the flagship of the Ohio River Company's fleet. It was built in 1936 and used primarily for hauling coal between Huntington, West Virginia, and Cincinnati. In 1939 it set a record for handling 28 barges of coal between those two ports.

The *Walter C. Beckjord* was built in 1955 and named for the president and board chairman of the Cincinnati Gas and Electric Company. It is 164 feet long, 44 feet wide and has 3,240 horsepower. Midland Enterprises operates 55 towboats on inland waterways in the United States.

Photographs courtesy of Midland Enterprises.

Multimedia Inc.

Multimedia Inc., the diversified media communications company that owns and operates Cincinnati's WLWT, has four operating divisions.

Multimedia Broadcasting Company is headquartered in Cincinnati. In addition to WLWT, Cincinnati's NBC affiliate, the division owns and operates KSDK-TV (NBC) in St. Louis, Missouri; WBIR-TV (NBC) in Knoxville, Tennessee; and WMAZ-TV in Macon, Georgia. These stations are powerful ratings and demographic leaders in their respective markets. Multimedia's seven radio stations, located in South Carolina, Georgia, Louisiana and Wisconsin, lead their markets in format innovations and provide both entertainment and information to the communities they serve. Multimedia Productions, the division's newest company, is located in Cincinnati at Production Plaza on Chickasaw Street. This unit has rapidly moved to the forefront of the video-communications marketplace, providing equipment and personnel for a prestigious client list.

Multimedia Newspaper Company, headquartered in Greenville, South Carolina, publishes 14 daily and 40 non-daily newspapers. Two dailies—*The Daily Sentinel* in Pomeroy and the *Gallipolis Daily Tribune*—are located in Ohio. Other properties are situated primarily in the Southeast. The 40 non-daily products include a variety of shopper, weekly, biweekly and triweekly newspapers. The division also publishes two monthly magazines devoted to the music industry. *The Music City News* has long been recognized as America's favorite country music publication. Recently introduced was *The Gospel Voice*, a trade magazine reporting on the gospel music business. Multimedia Newspaper Company's *The Alabama Journal*, an afternoon daily of less than 20,000 circulation, won the 1988 Pulitzer Prize for general news reporting with a series on the state's infant mortality rate.

Multimedia Cablevision Company is based in the historic Union Station facility in Wichita, Kansas. The division operates more than 100 cable television franchises in Kansas, Oklahoma, Illinois and North Carolina. Ancillary businesses include Multimedia Cable Security, the largest home security service in Wichita, and Multimedia Advertising Sales.

Multimedia Entertainment operates out of offices in New York City's Rockefeller Plaza. This division evolved from Multimedia Program Productions, headquartered in Cincinnati until 1984. Multimedia Entertainment has established a reputation as a leader in television program production and syndication. On air for over 20 years, *DONAHUE* continues as one of television's most enduring shows, an all-time great. *SALLY JESSY RAPHAEL* has grown dramatically in popularity and is now seen in 132 U.S. markets, Canada and parts of the United Kingdom. Telecast in many countries the *YOUNG PEOPLE'S SPECIALS* series has won almost every award for which it has been eligible. The production unit for this series also produces television programming for the networks and cable. *SWEETHEARTS* is a five-day-per-week comedy/game show hosted by Charles Nelson Reilly. Television specials are also produced by the division for the networks and syndication.

Multimedia Inc. is younger than most of its constituent divisions. It was formed in 1968 by the merger of three privately owned companies that had four newspapers, three TV and seven radio stations in the Carolinas, Georgia and Tennessee. The company now serves an audience in the tens of millions plus worldwide clientele for its syndicated products.

Multimedia acquired WLWT in 1976 from AVCO, which had bought the Crosley Broadcasting Corp. from Powel Crosley Jr. in 1945 when WLWT was still a pioneering experiment. It was a time when radio was dominant, and the movies had both color and the capacity to keep an actor's head and body on the same side of the screen at the same time. Only a true believer would bet on TV.

Crosley often insisted that he played things close to his vest, but he would take chances and had made a fortune doing so. He had made his first fortune selling accessories for Model T Fords and his second in appliances (the Crosley Shelvador refrigerator forced other manufacturers to advertise their product with the doors shut). Crosley had gotten into radio early both as a set manufacturer and a broadcaster; to sell the sets, he had to assure customers that there was something to hear.

Similarly WLWT was not only the first television station to go on the air in Ohio, it soon established a reputation for excellence and live programming. It put Ruth Lyons into the first talk show in television, and she made it the most popular. When she retired Bob Braun took over. The show was seen in five states.

WLWT's devotion to live programming was rarely matched other than by national networks. Its lively spirit was the impetus behind what would eventually become Multimedia Entertainment.

President and chief executive officer of Multimedia Inc., Walter Bartlett, joined Crosley (as the division of AVCO was called) as a time salesman in 1953 at its Columbus station. In 1964 he became vice president in charge of television for all Crosley stations and became general manager of WLWT when it was purchased by Multimedia in 1976.

In 1981 Wilson Wearn of Greenville, South Carolina moved up to chairman of Multimedia Inc.'s board of directors, and Bartlett became president and chief operating officer. James Lynagh succeeded Bartlett as president of Multimedia Broadcasting. Bartlett was elected to his present position in 1985.

Multimedia gained a great deal of national attention in 1985 when it pioneered the public "cash buy-out" by re-purchasing its existing common stock and issuing a combination of subordinated debentures and new common stock. Since that time the company has turned its energies toward increasing cash flow, paying off the debt incurred during the recapitalization and building the value of its assets, rather than acquiring new properties.

Multimedia holds an enviable portfolio of media properties and is guided by one of the finest management teams in the business. The future looks bright indeed for this corporation, which has been a mainstay of the Cincinnati business community for so many years.

Peter Grant gives the weather report on WLWT, the first television station to go on the air in Ohio. Photograph courtesy of Multimedia Broadcasting Company.

H. Nagel & Son Company

A Brighton Mills wheat flour sack displays the name of what is now the only mill in town: H. Nagel & Son Company.

H. Nagel and Son, also known as the Brighton Mills, has been in operation since 1857 when Johann Heinrich Nagel founded the company. It is currently located on Spring Grove Avenue in Camp Washington and sells flour to commercial bakeries and other customers.

Born in 1825 in Hanover, Germany, Nagel arrived in Cincinnati in 1844 and began working on steamboats that plied the Ohio and Mississippi rivers. In 1851 he settled in the city and became involved in the milling industry. Within two years he operated his own mill at the corner of Sycamore Road and Webster Street in Over-the-Rhine.

He continued the business until 1860 when he purchased 80 acres in Green Township and retired to the life of a farmer. Here Henrietta Meyer Nagel, whom Nagel married in 1853, gave birth to Edward, the only surviving child of six born.

In 1869 Johann Nagel reentered the milling business and opened a new feed and flour mill on Harrison Avenue in Fairmount near the family's new home on Tremont Avenue. In 1883, seeking to modernize the business, he moved the mill to Brighton at 2168 McClean Avenue (now Spring Grove Avenue) between Bank and Harrison streets. Steel roller mills replaced the old grinding stones for the making of flour, although mill stones still were used to grind corn for feed. Here the mill became widely known as the Brighton Mills.

Nagel remained active in the business until his death in 1902. When his son Edward took control of the firm, the mill was producing 50,000 barrels of flour a year, including the highest grade of wheat flour, called patent flour, and a rye flour. The mill also did a considerable business selling animal feed made from corn, as well as bran and other by-products from the milling process. A 1912 publication, *Cincinnati—The Queen City*, claimed, "The excellence of the product commends it to the patronage of the public."

Edward Nagel was very involved in the civic life of Cincinnati. He initiated the early effort to erect the old Harrison Avenue viaduct and later served on the dedication committee of the Western Hills Viaduct. He was a director of the Brighton German Bank and of the Central Trust Co., and he served as president of the Westwood Homestead Building and Loan Association. He and his wife, Matilda Gaefe of Cincinnati, had three children, Laura, Helen and Henry Edward.

Henry Edward Nagel joined the firm in 1917 following graduation from the University of Cincinnati and assumed control of the company after his father's death in 1941. His son, Henry Edward Jr., joined Brighton Mills after graduating from Ohio Weslyen College and serving in the Navy during World War II.

In 1958 the company hired Walter Gumpert, trained in the milling industry in Germany, to serve as head miller. Gumpert remains with the firm today, maintaining the mill machinery and blending the flour to the exact specifications required by the customer.

In the 1960s the mill was threatened by the construction of the Interstate 75 expressway, and the company moved to its present location at 2641 Spring Grove Avenue. Henry Jr.'s brother, William, a graduate of the Massachusetts Institute of Technology and engineering manager of Eaton Manufacturing Company's research center in Detroit, joined the firm, and the two created a partnership. Their father remained active in the business until his death in 1983.

The mill ceased grinding corn and producing custom feeds during the 1970s to concentrate solely on milling flour. It added a fleet of trucks and a grain elevator complex in Reading, Ohio, formerly the grain storage portion of the Cooperative Mills. This increased storage capacity enabled the company to keep more wheat on hand for manufacturing. Brighton Mills also purchased Loy's Flour Mill, an established mill in Pyrmont, Ohio, west of Dayton. The business was incorporated in 1980, and six years later Henry Nagel Jr. retired. His interest was purchased by Stewart Horn, a Cincinnati investor and owner of the Reading Feed Mill. Horn brought with him knowledge of finance and grain markets.

Brighton today mills a type of local wheat known as soft wheat. Planted in the fall and harvested in early July, the raw product is purchased from farmers and elevators in Ohio, Kentucky and Indiana. The wheat goes through four floors of milling machinery that roll, sift and blend it to meet customer specifications. The capacity of the two mills is 400,000 pounds of flour per day, much of which is sold to well-known national bakeries for their cookies, crackers and pie crusts. The flour is transported by bulk tank truck to the bakeries' factories in the Midwest. Long-term sales relationships exist with Keebler Company, Kroger Company, Nabisco and Blue Bird Pie Company.

A new product is breading mixes, which are made by blending spices with the flour. Brighton Mills also sells bran and other by-products of the milling process to feed mills for the manufacture of animal feed.

Some flour is also bagged for distribution. The company maintains a small retail outlet at the Spring Grove address where specialized flour such as cake and whole wheat flour and fresh wheat germ may be purchased. These products frequently have been recommended by local chefs and food critics.

H. Nagel and Son is the only mill in Cincinnati, the lone survivor of a important industry in the mid-1800s and a family-owned business for over 130 years. The family tradition is being carried forward by Edward S. Nagel, son of William and Carol, who currently is a student in the Milling Science Management Program at Kansas State University.

The Ohio National Life Insurance Company

Local business history is filled with incidents in which enterprise ignores adversity or the strength of an idea overcomes the weakness of the economy. Banks are founded during panics, factories launched without an order for their products. The Ohio National Life Insurance Company took its first steps under similar circumstances. It was founded in 1909, when the insurance industry was under a cloud because of a federal investigation. The faults were cured, but the process had left the public distrustful.

On September 9, 1909, a group of investment specialists took over a small insurance company named Ohio Mutual. They knew a great deal more about selling stock than about selling insurance, and for its first four years the company—renamed Ohio National Life—drifted until it found Albert Bettinger. Bettinger, an attorney, and other directors of the insurance company effected a management change that made him president. The company had six employees in a one-room office.

Bettinger continued his law practice and walked across town to the insurance company office every day. This was unsatisfactory if the company was to grow, so Bettinger hired Troy W. Appleby in 1914 to improve supervision of the insurance firm. Appleby was a former high school mathematics teacher who had become an insurance actuary.

Appleby's first job was to find agents, for the company was doing business only in Ohio and Kentucky. Appleby's agents were patient, ingenious salesmen. One successful agent always singled out the town's leading citizen to become his first customer. Another agent used an approving letter from his pastor which he showed to potential customers.

World War I, with its federal insurance for men in service and the catastrophic influenza epidemic, wiped out public reservations about insurance. Ohio National Life began to fly despite a postwar recession. In 1922 Bettinger died and the presidency passed to Appleby. He held the position until 1947, the longest tenure of any of the company's chief executives, and came to be recognized as an organizational genius responsible for the company's success.

The depression arrived late at Ohio National Life. The firm continued to advance cash to policyholders until 1932, when a moratorium that temporarily closed banks also held up policy loans. Although the company found it increasingly difficult to collect on its investments, Appleby's policy was to avoid foreclosure unless an owner abandoned his property.

During these difficult times Ohio National Life expanded. In 1930 it took over the business of Toledo Travelers; in 1931 it absorbed Omaha Life and American Old Line; and in 1933, having passed the $100 million mark for insurance in force, it doubled its size by taking over the Bankers Reserve Life Co. of Omaha. With this last development, the company had insurance in force of $200 million and was doing business in 20 states. It also had to find larger quarters. It moved from the Duttenhofer Building at Sixth and Sycamore streets into a renovated factory building on Reading Road just outside the downtown area.

In 1941 Ohio National Life's stockholders voted to change the company into a mutual company—a concern owned by those who held policies. There was almost no opposition, but litigation blocked the process until after World War II, when mutualization began. It was completed in 1959.

Shortly after the war, in 1946, the company purchased the site of its present headquarters on William Howard Taft Road. In 1959 the company moved into its Taft Road building, and its former headquarters were turned over to the Community Chest.

Appleby died in 1947, and John Evans became president. Appleby had recruited Evans in 1922 from the University of Michigan. Evans, in turn, had helped recruit M. Rey Dodson from the same university in 1932. Dodson was a Cincinnatian and had been a co-op student at the University of Cincinnati before entering the actuarial school at Michigan. Shortly after Evans became president, Dodson was made executive vice president, and in 1956 he became the company's president. During Evans' tenure Ohio National Life started its company-wide school for agents, a capstone for the sales organization which it had been building since 1909.

It took 50 years for Ohio National to reach $1 billion of insurance in force. Yet it reached $2 billion in the next 10 years during the Dodson presidency. It was also during this period that Ohio National established a broker-dealer subsidiary, O.N. Equity Sales Company, to market mutual funds, variable annuities and other equity-based products. These products now form a significant part of the company's product portfolio.

Dodson retired in 1972, and Paul E. Martin became chief executive officer, holding that position for most of the 1970s. During these years Ohio National Life Assurance Corporation, a wholly owned stock subsidiary, was established by the company to market low-cost term insurance. This subsidiary now also markets universal life and variable universal life insurance, both introduced during the 1980s and a major portion of the company's individual life sales.

Through the years Ohio National had expanded into additional product areas, including disability income insurance and group life and group medical coverage.

When Martin retired in 1979, Burnell F. Saum became president. Saum had begun his career with Ohio National as an agent and later distinguished himself in various sales and marketing management positions. Insurance in force continued to grow and by 1980 passed the $5 billion mark.

When Saum retired in 1985, Bradley L. Warnemunde became the company's chief executive officer. Like Saum he also rose through the sales and marketing ranks to the company's top position. Under Warnemunde's leadership, the company has continued to prosper and by 1988 had $12 billion life insurance in force.

In 1959 Ohio National Life moved from a converted Reading Road factory to the present corporate headquarters on William Howard Taft Road. Photograph courtesy of Ohio National Life Insurance Company.

Paxton & Seasongood

Cincinnati reform mayor Murray Seasongood, early partner in the firm of Paxton & Seasongood. Photograph. Courtesy of The Cincinnati Historical Society.

Paxton & Seasongood, a legal professional corporation, traces its Cincinnati origins to the 1870s. On June 15, 1875, the firm of Paxton & Warrington, consisting of Thomas B. Paxton Sr. and John W. Warrington, was formed with offices at 21 West Third Street between Main and Walnut streets. The firm moved from 21 West Third Street to the United Bank Building at the southeast corner of Third and Walnut streets in 1887. In 1890 John B. Boutet and Charles B. Warrington, a brother of John Warrington, were admitted as members of the firm. In 1894 it became known as Paxton, Warrington & Boutet, which continued through 1899, when the name was shortened to Paxton & Warrington.

In 1903 a young lawyer named Murray Seasongood from Harvard Law School joined the firm. In 1907 the firm moved to the second floor of the Citizens Bank Building at the southeast corner of Fourth and Main streets. The 1909 City Directory lists the firm name as Paxton, Warrington & Seasongood, with its partners as Thomas B. Paxton, Thomas B. Paxton Jr., George H. Warrington and Murray Seasongood. John Warrington had by then been appointed as a judge of the United States Circuit Court of Appeals for the Sixth Circuit. In 1927 The Citizens Bank & Trust Company, represented by Paxton, Warrington & Seasongood, merged with The Fourth and Central Trust Company under the name of The Central Trust Company. The bank's offices were located in the new Union Central Building at Fourth and Vine streets, and shortly after the merger Paxton, Warrington & Seasongood shortened its name to the present day Paxton & Seasongood and moved its offices to a portion of the 16th floor of the Union Central Building.

In 1927 the firm's partners consisted of Thomas B. Paxton Jr., Murray Seasongood, Robert P. Goldman, Lester A. Jaffe and Clyde M. Abbott. They along with several associates handled a variety of general civil matters with emphasis on trial work, corporate and banking law, real estate, and probate practice. The firm continued to grow and in 1965 took over the entire 17th floor of the Union Central Building.

From the time he began the practice of law, Murray Seasongood's career shaped the future of the firm as well as that of the City of Cincinnati. Perhaps the most well known member of the firm in its history, Seasongood distinguished himself as a brilliant legal scholar and practitioner with extraordinary advocacy skills. He established a tradition for excellence over the course of his long career which still guides the firm today. In civic affairs Seasongood organized and led the municipal reform movement that ousted the political machine of George "Boss" Cox and culminated in Seasongood's election to Council and as the first mayor under the new Charter. He was mayor from 1926 until 1930. Seasongood continued to practice law well into his nineties and came into the office regularly until close to his 100th birthday. He died in February 1983 at the age of 104.

In 1971 Paxton & Seasongood merged with the Cincinnati firm of Dolle, O'Donnell, Cash, Fee & Hahn, which had originated in 1910 with the partnership of Louis J. Dolle, Walter C. Taylor and James B. O'Donnell. The two predecessor firms had similar backgrounds and clientele, with Dolle, O'Donnell counting among its former members Albert D. Cash Sr., the mayor of Cincinnati at the time of his tragic death in 1952.

Today Paxton & Seasongood's 40 attorneys and staff occupy the 17th, 18th and 19th floors of the building at Fourth and Vine streets now known as Central Trust Tower. The firm engages in all areas of civil practice, with specialists in corporate law, litigation, mortgage lending, real estate, tax, estate planning and probate. In addition to these mainstream areas of law, the firm has developed a specialty and nationwide practice in catastrophe litigation defense. Among its clients in this area have been defendants in the litigation relating to the fires at the Beverly Hills Supper Club, the DuPont Hotel in Puerto Rico and the MGM Grand Hotel in Las Vegas. The firm's clients include major financial institutions, manufacturers, insurance companies, and service and retail businesses. Medium-size businesses comprise a substantial portion of the firm's clientele, along with public and closely held corporations, nonprofit corporations, partnerships, individuals, trusts and estates.

In keeping with the growing trend among law firms, Paxton & Seasongood announced in the fall of 1988 its intention to merge with the Cleveland-based firm of Thompson, Hine and Flory as of January 1, 1989. The new firm will have approximately 235 lawyers in offices in Cleveland, Cincinnati, Columbus, Washington, D.C., and Palm Beach, Florida. Although the firm contemplates introducing the name of Thompson, Hine and Flory to the community, it plans to memorialize the name and maintain the tradition of Paxton & Seasongood known for so long by Cincinnatians.

Pease Industries, Inc.

In 1893 Charles Harlow Pease began selling wholesale building materials out of a store within "horse and buggy" distance of Cincinnati's retail lumber yards. He probably never dreamed that the company he created would someday be a giant in the building industry or that the name Pease would become synonymous with the words "quality and dependability."

This growth through the years can be attributed to Pease innovation, the ability to recognize new trends in the building industry and a determined insistence on quality. In 1898 Pease published the first retail mail order catalog for building products, the well-known *Pricer*. Pease was also one of the first to handle "veneered panels," as plywood was called, and one of the leaders in the introduction of prefabricated wall sections and roof trusses.

In the 1960s Pease innovation again led the way. A young family member, David Pease Jr., solved one of the biggest problems of the modern home by inventing the world's first insulating steel door. Patented and trademarked Ever-Strait, this product was the first significant advancement in door technology in hundreds of years, resulting in the formation of a multibillion-dollar residential steel door industry in the United States.

The Ever Strait Door made obsolete leaky, drafty entry doors that had to be painted every year and swelled shut in wet weather. By marketing a pre-hung unit including door, frame and sill, Pease reduced much of the carpenter work required in the field and developed a complete door system. Homes could now have doors that were easy to install and operated flawlessly all year-round.

Builders and homeowners quickly realized the advantages of the new Ever-Strait Door System. With the wide acceptance of the Pease insulating steel door in the building industry, the Ever-Strait Division of Pease Company was established. In 1968 this division moved to a new plant on the corner of Route 4 and Mulhauser Road in Fairfield, Ohio. As home heating costs skyrocketed, the energy-efficient Ever-Strait Door became even more popular.

In 1981 continued growth resulted in the formation of Pease Industries, Inc., a free-standing, privately held corporation. Pease Company continues to manufacture and distribute building materials from its Hamilton, Ohio location.

Under the leadership of David H. Pease Jr., Pease Industries is devoted to the manufacture and sale of unique, high-performance building products throughout the United States and Canada. The Pease philosophy has always been to market a complete system, with all components engineered to work together for maximum performance.

In addition Pease has continued to develop innovative products and features. An impressive list of "firsts" resulting from Pease research includes: the first use of magnetic weatherstripping on an entry door, first adjustable sill/threshold, first plastic decorative door trim, first approval of a 45-minute fire rating and introduction of vented sidelights, first approval for 90-minute fire rating, and the first adjustable door frame.

Today with over 8 million door systems produced, Pease Industries, Inc. has manufacturing facilities in Fairfield, Ohio and Denver, Colorado, as well as many overseas joint ventures. An extensive research and development facility is also located in Fairfield. Major product lines include Ever-Strait and Homestead insulating steel entry and patio door systems and the Pease Retractable Awning.

Recently Pease has introduced yet another innovative product: Registry Entranceways. With many years experience in steel door systems, Pease has developed wood door systems so unique that they are patented. The Registry series includes hardwood doors with a warranted, factory-applied finish. Yet another "first" for Pease is the first use of magnetic weatherstrip on a wooden door.

Charles Harlow Pease would indeed be proud of the company he founded nearly a century ago and of his grandson David, who carries on his traditions.

David H. Pease Jr. is president and chief executive officer of the firm that his grandfather founded in 1893.

Pease Industries, Inc., shown here as it looked in the 1890s, markets door systems and other building materials worldwide.

Photograph and illustration courtesy of Pease Industries, Inc.

The Penn Central Corporation

Cincinnati's bicentennial year marks The Penn Central Corporation's first anniversary as a corporate resident. Indirectly, however, the relationship dates to a much earlier period.

In 1845 Philadelphians realized that their city was losing its status as a center for westward commerce to rivals New York and Baltimore. The Erie Canal had been completed for 20 years; the New York & Erie Railroad was building westward, and Baltimore was considering the conversion of its National Pike into a steam railroad.

In response the Pennsylvania Legislature approved a bill forming The Pennsylvania Railroad on April 13, 1846. The "Pennsy" built 249 miles of rail from Harrisburg to Pittsburgh by 1854, effectively tying Philadelphia with western states. Goods moving up the Ohio River, many from Cincinnati, were passed onto the eastward line at Pittsburgh.

No sooner was the Pennsylvania Railroad's line extended to Pittsburgh than the company's officers were advocating investment in Ohio and Indiana lines that could be tied into the system. Even while the track to Pittsburgh was supporting the river traffic that developed Cincinnati, the railroad was investing in the Ohio & Pennsylvania Railroad from Crestline to Fort Wayne, Indiana and finally the Fort Wayne & Chicago Railroad. These three lines were consolidated into a continuous, 468-mile line from Pittsburgh to Chicago. Within 15 years of the Pennsylvania Railroad's founding, the East and Midwest were linked by a solid "artificial artery" of iron rails that initially bypassed Cincinnati.

The original rail system shot westward, but the Pennsylvania Railroad grew swiftly to include trunk lines through Columbus to Indianapolis and St. Louis, and to New York and Washington, D.C. There were also auxiliary lines built to Cincinnati, Cleveland, Detroit and Louisville. Railroads proved both faster and cheaper than river travel, and rail hubs became the new boom towns of the west. Indirectly the Pennsylvania Railroad helped cap Cincinnati's growth and make Chicago the transportation center of the Midwest after 1860.

The New York Central Railroad officially was formed on July 6, 1853, under the direction of Erastus Corning, its first president. The new line consolidated 10 railroads with over 600 miles of track running from Schenectady, New York to Buffalo.

Although the New York Central and Pennsylvania railroads were fierce rivals and competitors for virtually all of their existence, their beginnings and characters were dramatically different. Where the Pennsylvania Railroad was initially owned and supported by the solid, stable citizens of Philadelphia, New York Central's early history is dominated by powerful and controversial characters, including Corning and his successor, Cornelius Vanderbilt.

Both the New York Central and Pennsylvania railroads prospered through the early 1900s. The Pennsylvania became known as "the standard railroad," a model of efficiency whose stock paid consecutive dividends for more than 120 years. Among Pennsy railroading "firsts" were steel rails, air brakes, block signals, train phones and multi-cylinder locomotives. The competition between the two was exemplified by the New York Central's Twentieth Century Limited and the Pennsylvania Railroad's Broadway Limited, twin high-speed, first-class trains that raced from New York to Chicago in 20 hours. The trains actually matched each other's time by mutual agreement, but in luxury and service they competed constantly.

Expansion of U.S. railroad mileage peaked in 1916. During the next six decades, the industry struggled with increasing overcapacity, federal regulation, rising labor costs and competition from the automotive industry. Even in 1916 more than 37,000 miles of track were in receivership. By 1940, when the worst of the Depression had passed, nearly a third of the nation's track was still being run by trustees or receivers.

Discussion of a merger between the two rival railroads began in 1957, and both boards of directors approved the idea in June 1962. Four years later the Interstate Commerce Commission approved their merger and incorporation as The Penn Central Transportation Company, effective February 1, 1968.

Only 872 days later, on June 21, 1970, The Penn Central Transportation Company filed a petition for reorganization in bankruptcy. It was not alone in succumbing to financial pressures; within two or three years, six other major northeastern railroads also declared bankruptcy. As a result Amtrak came into existence on May 1, 1971, when railroads were allowed to drop their unprofitable long distance passenger service.

In 1973 Congress enacted the Regional Rail Reorganization Act, making the federally sponsored and funded Consolidated Rail Corporation (Conrail) the freight service operating successor of Penn Central and the other bankrupt lines. Accordingly on April 1, 1976, Penn Central transferred 15,000 miles of track to Conrail and left the railroad business. A reorganization plan for its remaining assets was proposed in December 1976, and a new entity, The Penn Central Corporation, began its existence on October 24, 1978.

Cincinnati investor Carl H. Lindner soon appeared among the shareholders of the new corporation. He was named to the board of directors in 1982, became chairman of the board in 1983 and was made chief executive officer in March 1987, the year that Penn Central's headquarters moved from Greenwich, Connecticut to Cincinnati.

Today's Penn Central Corporation is a diversified holding company with assets of $2.5 billion as of December 31, 1987. Its General Cable and Guardian Products subsidiaries manufacture wire and cable products for the telecommunications and construction industries. Marathon LeTourneau builds enormous loaders and trucks principally used in the mining and timber industries. And Vitro Corporation provides systems and software engineering to the defense industry, relating primarily to ballistic and guided missiles, ship communications and air support systems.

Other businesses design and install computer-based tracking radar systems; manufacture aerial life trucks; make batteries for private, commercial and military aircraft; and build electromechanical connectors for the defense industry. The reshaping that has marked The Penn Central Corporation since 1978 is expected to continue as the company invests its assets in profitable and growing businesses.

Although only recently headquartered in Cincinnati, Penn Central's corporate roots include Cincinnati's first railroad, the Little Miami.

Procter & Gamble Company

Procter & Gamble Co., one of Cincinnati's oldest, largest and most honored companies, has grown in 150 years from a struggling soap and candle shop to a $20 billion, international corporation.

The company began in a makeshift backyard factory at Sixth and Main streets in 1837, when two immigrant tradesmen, English candlemaker William Procter and Irish soap-maker James Gamble, formed a partnership to sell soap, candles and lard oil.

The by-products of Cincinnati's booming pork-packing industry, principally lard, provided the raw materials for the soap and candle business. At the time Procter and Gamble launched their new concern, there already were 18 similar firms in the city. But over the next 50 years, the company made several important decisions and discoveries that clearly marked Procter & Gamble as the preeminent Cincinnati firm and a national leader as well.

The company rapidly outgrew the small factory and office at Sixth and Main. In the mid-1850s Procter & Gamble built a new plant on Central Avenue along the Miami and Erie Canal and a new office on Second Street. By 1859 it employed 80 workers and sales were nearing the $1 million mark.

In 1860 the company feared that its southern market for rosin, an important ingredient in making soap, might be affected if a war between the states erupted. Procter and Gamble's two young sons quickly traveled to New Orleans and bought a boatload of rosin for one dollar a barrel. Three months after the Civil War began, rosin soared from eight dollars to $15 a barrel, and rosin-rich P&G landed orders from the Union Army for 1,000 cases of soap a day, making P&G one of the best known soap companies in the nation.

In the mid-1870s the company launched a successful research project to develop a bar of white soap that would equal the finest dark castile soaps of the day. P&G "White Soap," as it was first called, sold well but did not take off nationally until 1878, when a worker happened to leave a soap mixing machine on too long during a lunch break. The extra air pumped into the mixture caused the soap to float.

Soon thereafter Harley T. Procter, son of the founder, renamed the soap "Ivory." The company launched its first national advertising campaign, championing the soap's buoyancy ("It Floats!") and its properties ("99-44/100 percent pure").

In 1884 a fire at the Central Avenue factory forced P&G to find a new home. It chose the relatively undeveloped Mill Creek Valley for its excellent rail facilities and proximity to the city's major meat packing plants. Two years later P&G's sprawling Ivorydale complex opened on 55 acres in what is now St. Bernard. It included more than 20 structures; today Ivorydale occupies five times more land, with 1,800 employees.

By the time Ivorydale opened, the operation of the business had passed from the founders to their sons and grandsons. James N. Gamble established P&G's first research laboratory. William A. Procter and Harley T. Procter ran the business side, but it was the leadership of William Cooper Procter, grandson of William Procter, that had the greatest impact on the company. Cooper Procter set the standard for P&G's emphasis on people: he inaugurated profit-sharing, guaranteed-work programs and led the move to a shorter work week by making Saturday a half-holiday. He was in top leadership positions for 44 years. His employees paid for a memorial to him on the Ivorydale grounds after his death in 1934.

P&G incorporated in 1890 and sold 45,000 shares of stock at $100 each. (One share of common stock purchased in 1890 would now be worth nearly $300,000.) The New York Stock Exchange began listing P&G stock in 1891. The company opened its first plant outside Cincinnati, in Kansas City in 1904 and its first international plant in 1915 in Canada.

Radio listeners in 1923 heard P&G's first electronic media advertisement. P&G introduced the daytime radio drama genre in 1932 to advertise its products. In the 1940s the company extended the genre to television, where thanks to P&G's ads it became known as the "soap opera." By 1987 P&G spent $1.44 billion a year on advertising.

Although P&G began as a soap and candle company, its success in the 20th century has been due in large part to its diversification into other household product lines. Cooper Procter moved the company into the food business in the early 1900s with the processing of salad oil. Crisco first appeared in 1911. After World War II, P&G introduced two new synthetic detergents, Tide and Joy. Crest toothpaste, Duncan Hines baking mixes and Charmin's paper products were added in the 1950s. P&G introduced Pampers disposable diapers and purchased Folger's coffee in the early 1960s. It also acquired beverage and drug companies in the 1980s. Research and development was a priority with the company, and P&G researchers introduced new products and improved old ones in four Cincinnati laboratories and technical centers.

P&G remained family operated until 1934, when Richard R. Deupree, who started work at P&G at age 12, became chief executive. During the Deupree era, following the death of William Cooper Procter, the company entered into large-scale advertising, including the television soap operas. Deupree was succeeded by Neil H. McElroy, who had introduced the concept of brand management, in which each brand competes as a separate business within the company.

Howard J. Morgens followed McElroy in 1957. Morgens' tenure as president and chief executive officer was marked by product diversification and the growth of P&G from a national corporation to a truly worldwide company. Edward G. Harness became president in 1971, having built the company's business in disposable paper products.

John Smale became president in 1974 and chief executive officer in 1986. Smale, who helped secured the American Dental Association's endorsement of Crest toothpaste in 1960, presided over several key acquisitions in the 1980s and the company's entry into new foreign markets, including China. The company opened its expanded international headquarters in downtown Cincinnati—the distinctive, 17-story twin towers fronted by a four-acre garden plaza—in 1985.

In 1988 the company's earnings exceeded $1 billion for the first time. P&G has 116 locations in 24 states and 24 foreign countries with 77,000 employees worldwide.

General View of the Ivorydale Plant (1890). Photograph of an architect's rendering. Gift of Procter & Gamble.

The Provident Bank

The Provident Bank would make a good model for anyone thinking of starting a new bank in Cincinnati because its history incorporates almost all the factors which the city's bankers have had to deal with at one time or another. It started as two institutions under the same management and doing business in the same offices, a routine practice because of banking laws. It was chartered on November 26, 1900, as both The Provident Savings Bank Company and The Provident Trust Company. In May 1928 the two institutions were consolidated as The Provident Savings Bank & Trust Co., and on January 30, 1959, that name was abbreviated to The Provident Bank. To Cincinnatians it has been "The Provident" all along.

The Provident opened for business on February 23, 1901, in offices at Vine Street and Baker Alley in the Old Chamber of Commerce Building. The building, on the southwest corner of Fourth and Vine streets, was destroyed by fire after the bank had moved out of it.

Business grew too large for the Provident's five original employees and the original quarters, and the bank built a new headquarters on the southeast corner of Seventh and Vine, an 11-story building most still call the Provident Bank Building. The bank moved into this new home on September 22, 1909 and began a long period of expansion.

First it acquired the Queen City Savings Bank on August 24, 1910; the next year, November 29, 1911, it purchased the Cincinnati Trust Co. and its six branches. (The Cincinnati Trust Co. had been housed in the Carlisle Building, which is now the site of the Dixie Terminal.)

Two more branches were added with the purchase of the Unity Banking and Savings Co. in February 1921. The entire decade was a busy one. Provident acquired the Madisonville Deposit Co. in 1925, the Liberty Banking and Savings Co. and the East End Bank in 1926 and on November 1, 1930 it added The Bank of Commerce and Trust Co. with two branches.

The 1940s brought two additions. Provident purchased the Sharonville Bank on April 25, 1947, and continued to operate it as a branch. On May 29, 1949, it purchased the deposits and mortgage loans of The Guardian Bank and Savings Co., which had started business as the Morris Plan Bank. The accounts were moved to the main Provident office and the Guardian was liquidated.

By 1967 Provident had prospered through some exciting times with the help of some exciting people. Among them was Barney Kroger. In his later years the founder of the Kroger Co. was giving as much time to banking as he was to groceries, and he remained a director of the bank during the years in which he had divested himself of Kroger stock. In 1933 he was given credit for stopping talk of a run on the bank with a typically Krogerian gesture. Using his personal resources to get the cash, Kroger raised between seven and 15 million dollars which he had stacked in the tellers' cages and along the walls of the bank's lobby. An associate, Joseph Hall, recalled in a memoir that Kroger and other Provident officials personally assured depositors their money was safe. Kroger, Hall recalled, held up two bundles of $100,000 and announced his money was staying in the Provident but that the bank would stay open after hours to give out cash to any depositors who were foolish enough to want it. That ended the crisis.

Cincinnatians in general thought of the staid and conservative Provident as "Barney Kroger's" bank long after his death and considered it as somehow peculiarly "Cincinnati" although all Cincinnati banks were thoroughly home-grown products.

These included a new home office on the southeast corner of Fourth and Vine, the bank's current headquarters. It offered new services—free checking for accounts with small balances and free checking to all senior citizens, electronic tellers, money market and checking account combinations and eventually a new ownership and an acquisition.

On October 31, 1980, American Financial Corp. divested itself of Provident by distributing its bank stock to AFC stockholders. At the same time Provident Bancorp Inc., a holding company, was formed. In 1982 Provident Bancorp purchased Midwest Bank and Trust Co. of Cleveland, making itself a regional bank.

Provident now has 38 branches and assets of $1.7 billion.

Provident Bank's home office on the southeast corner of Fourth and Vine streets completed in 1967. Photograph courtesy of *The Cincinnati Post.*

Quantum Chemical Corporation

Quantum Chemical Corporation (formerly National Distillers & Chemical Corporation) consists of the Emery and USI divisions, leading manufacturers of oleochemicals and petrochemicals headquartered northeast of Cincinnati in Sycamore Township, and the Suburban Propane Division, the nation's leading retail propane marketer.

Quantum's Cincinnati roots date to 1840, when Thomas Emery Sr. founded a business in downtown Cincinnati, near Fourth Street and Hammond Avenue. Using animal fat by-products of the city's meat-packing industry, the company manufactured tallow candles and lard oil for lamps. By 1850 these products had been replaced by an improved candle made from the solid portion of squeezed tallow and composed mainly of stearic acid. The liquid by-products, "Elaine oil" (oleic acid) and "sweetwater" (glycerine), were sold for use in soap manufacturing and wool yarn lubrication.

By 1860 the Emery Candle Company, as it was known then, had expanded manufacturing facilities four times to keep up with market demand. The company remained at Vine and Water streets near the Ohio River, the city's principal means of transportation, until the growth of railroads. In 1885 it relocated to the Cincinnati suburb of St. Bernard on the banks of the Mill Creek, adjacent to the main line of the railroads serving Cincinnati.

In 1886 the company hired its first full-time research chemist, Dr. Ernst Twitchell. A Cincinnati native, Twitchell carried out extensive investigations into the chemistry of fats and oils and the nature of emulsions. His discoveries revolutionized the industry and formed the basis of many of the products in use today. By the end of the century, Twitchell was recognized as an expert in his field. In 1917 he became the 11th recipient of the Perkin Medal, awarded annually by the American Chemical Society for the most original and valuable work in applied chemistry.

In 1931 the Emery Candle Company, with interests in chemicals, candles and dry-cleaning, reorganized as Emery Industries, Inc., giving new emphasis to process and applications research related to its chemical product line. The introduction of the Emersol Process in 1938 again revolutionized the fatty acid fractions from the more soluble liquid portion. Subsequent endeavors led the company into new products and markets—azelaic and pelargonic acids, dimer and trimer acids, plasticizers, synthetic lubricants, and ozone treatment of water – the foundation of the Emery Division's business today.

In October 1906 the U.S. Industrial Alcohol Company was organized to serve industrial users of ethyl alcohol. Within a decade demand had exceeded the industry's production capacity. In 1915 USI announced construction of the largest and most modern industrial alcohol plant in the world in Curtis Bay, Maryland. Equipment for this plant was fabricated and constructed by a Cincinnati-based subsidiary, Ansonia Copper & Iron Works. Upon its completion in 1916, USI's alcohol production had doubled to 22 million gallons, making it the nation's leading alcohol producer.

National Distillers Products Company was founded in 1924, the height of Prohibition, as an outgrowth of efforts to reorganize the bankrupt U.S. Food Products Corporation. Anticipating that repeal was inevitable, early management bought as much stock in pre-Prohibition liquor and distilling plants as it could.

When Prohibition ended in 1933, National Distillers owned 50% of the legal liquor production facilities in the country. In that same year it purchased the Carthage Distillery on Anthony Wayne Avenue in Cincinnati, which had opened in 1893 on land Major James Caldwell had purchased from John Cleves Symmes and operated a still as early as 1806.

Emery's fatty acids were in demand during World War II for soaps, candles and the synthetic rubber program, as well as for specialty derivatives used as rust preventatives and lubricant additives.

For its part in the war effort, USI stepped up production of its industrial alcohols used in manufacturing antiseptics, external pharmaceuticals and specialty products. By 1943, since its chemical activity exceeded its alcohol concerns, the company was reorganized and merged with its subsidiaries into U.S. Industrial Chemicals, Inc. Advances in derivatives research led to products used as antifreeze, insecticides, aerosol insect repellants, Sterno, and Vitol, a fuel injection fluid used in aircraft engines.

With all U.S. distillation of beverage spirits halted during wartime, National Distillers turned to production of industrial alcohol needed for war materials ranging from munitions to synthetic rubber. The firm was incorporated in 1948 as National Distillers and Chemical Corporation, marking its permanent expansion into chemical manufacturing. Emery meanwhile developed new specialty products such as synthetic lubricants and plasticizers.

NDCC purchased USI in 1951. The new corporation centralized its basic research efforts in Cincinnati and continued to grow by expanding its product line into the emerging polyethylene industry.

In 1983 the corporation announced plans to relocate USI's headquarters from New York to Cincinnati and centralize its chemical business offices in Sycamore Township. In 1986 NDCC purchased Enron Chemical Co., which moved to Cincinnati and merged with USI, now the nation's largest polyethylene producer.

NDCC purchased Cincinnati-based Emery Industries in 1978 to further expand its interests in chemical manufacturing. Emery has maintained its position of leadership over the past decade by extending its product line into new areas and expanding its existing manufacturing facilities. Its headquarters were relocated to Sycamore Township in 1985.

National Distillers and Chemical Corporation acquired Suburban Propane in 1983. Subsequent acquisitions and market expansions have made the Suburban Propane Division the largest retail propane marketer in the United States. From coast to coast Suburban serves more than 1 million customers, including many in Greater Cincinnati.

Having decided to concentrate on its chemicals and energy business, the corporation divested of its wine and spirits business in 1987. It adopted a new identity, Quantum Chemical Corporation, a year later to reflect this new emphasis.

Quantum is committed to playing a prominent role in the Queen City. Construction of a new, 245,000-square-foot, centralized research and development center adjacent to the Emery Division and USI Division headquarters is currently under way and scheduled for completion in 1991.

Sycamore Township serves as headquarters for Quantum's Emery and USI divisions, leading manufacturers of oleochemicals and petrochemicals. Photograph courtesy of Quantum Chemical Corporation.

Rendigs, Fry, Kiely & Dennis

The Cincinnati law firm that was to become Rendigs, Fry, Kiely & Dennis was principally founded by August A. Rendigs Jr. – or Gus, as he was called by many—who grew up in Cincinnati in the early 1900s. He graduated from Harvard Law School and began his legal career in 1919, following his return from active duty during World War I. Rendigs demonstrated an immediate expertise in trial law and set high standards that are both remembered and emulated today.

In the 1930s Rendigs became acquainted with William H. Fry, who had just graduated from Xavier Law School in the last year that Xavier offered an education in law. Fry joined Rendigs as an associate lawyer and became the first of many night school graduates to practice with the firm. With the outbreak of World War II, Fry left the practice of law in 1941 to join the Army Air Force. He served until autumn, 1945.

During the war years Rendigs practiced by himself and with various others from time to time. He corresponded with William Fry and suggested that the two of them form a partnership upon Fry's return to the city. Thus the firm of Rendigs and Fry came into being on January 1, 1946.

The firm's original offices were located on the seventh floor of the Union Central Building

(now the Central Trust Tower), one of the three floors that Rendigs, Fry, Kiely & Dennis occupies today.

Rendigs continued to display his expertise in civil trials. He virtually dominated the defense bar throughout the many years of his practice and developed a reputation far beyond the boundaries of Cincinnati. Rendigs was recognized for his patrician bearing and demeanor as well as his extensive preparation of facts and law. In that era lawyers could rely heavily on the personal art of advocacy as well as painstaking preparations. Rendigs excelled in combining these elements and, with Fry, established the high standards that exist in the firm today.

Fry assumed primary responsibility for the firm when Rendigs retired from his active practice in the early 1950s to devote more time to civic and family activities. Fry was uniquely qualified in many areas of the law. Although an active and capable trial lawyer, he also developed an expertise in corporate law and probate and domestic relations. Fry had the unique ability to undertake any challenge, regardless of its complexities. His high level of ability, high standards and willingness to take time to teach others in the firm has had a lasting effect.

As a consequence of the firm's extensive and successful experience in trial law, the work grew to unmanageable proportions, and it became necessary to employ associates. Between 1946 and 1949 Fry and Rendigs became acquainted with John A. Kiely of another firm. Kiely earned such respect from both Rendigs and Fry while on opposing sides of a number of trials that they decided to follow the sound proverbial advice: "If you can't beat him, join him." Thus Kiely became a partner in the firm of Rendigs, Fry & Kiely.

Against all probability Kiely—who was one of the kindest, gentlest and seemingly frailest of men—became *the* trial lawyer of his era in Cincinnati. He tried more cases in his career than anyone else in the history of the firm. As with Rendigs and Fry, Kiely added his distinct style and character to the partnership. To the erudition and drive of his partners, he brought a leavening and tempering influence, helping to create the attitude of the bench and bar not only toward the firm as it existed in the forties and fifties, but toward all those who have come afterward.

In 1950 another veteran of World War II and night law school graduate joined the firm as an associate lawyer. This youthful Irishman, Robert M. Dennis, added wit, humor, insight and character. Dennis also recognized the importance of firm growth, expansion into other areas of the law, and involvement in bar association, civic and charitable activities. Dennis himself was president of the Cincinnati Bar Association when he died in 1973.

Over the years Rendigs, Fry, Kiely & Dennis has become one of the larger law firms in Cincinnati. It now occupies three floors of the Central Trust Tower and has approximately 40 attorneys. Rendigs, Fry, Kiely & Dennis is now a general practice firm, maintaining its unique character as a trial firm. It handles all types of litigated matters and also offers legal expertise in corporate and commercial law, probate and estate planning, retirement plans, real estate and labor.

In addition to involvement in the law, members of the firm have participated in a wide variety of civic and charitable activities, including those sponsored by United Cerebral Palsy of Cincinnati, The Cincinnati Historical Society, Children's Dental Care and Family Service. Members also serve as adjunct professors at area law schools, public officeholders, and city and state bar association officials.

August A. (Gus) Rendigs Jr. (1895-1988) founded the firm in 1919 and retired from active practice in the early 1950s.

William H. Fry (1905-1975) became a partner of Rendigs in 1946 and assumed leadership of the firm after Rendigs retired.

John A. Kiely (1899-1986) was the third partner and one of the most successful trial attorneys in Cincinnati.

Robert M. Dennis (1917-1973) joined the firm in 1950; he was also president of the Cincinnati Bar Association.

Photographs. Courtesy of Rendigs, Fry, Kiely & Dennis.

Reynolds DeWitt & Company

Reynolds, DeWitt & Co. is a private, diversified investment firm formed in 1979 by Mercer Reynolds and William O. DeWitt Jr. Reynolds, chairman of the company, had been with a national investment firm prior to Reynolds DeWitt's formation. DeWitt, president of Reynolds DeWitt, also had been in the investment business prior to operating the Cincinnati Stingers, a major league hockey franchise that was sold in 1979. The time was opportune for both Reynolds and DeWitt to join in the development of a new investment banking-oriented enterprise.

From a two-man firm at its inception, Reynolds DeWitt has grown to over 50 employees. In addition to Reynolds and DeWitt, principals of the firm now include Joseph Beech III, vice president and general counsel, and John D. Peckskamp Jr., who heads Meridian Properties, Inc., the firm's real estate affiliate.

Initial focus in 1979 and the early 1980s was in the oil and gas exploration business, primarily in the Permian Basin of west Texas through an affiliated company, Spectrum 7 Energy Corporation. Originally responsible for approximately $50 million of exploration activities, Spectrum 7 merged with Bush Exploration in 1983, and George W. Bush Jr. became president and chief executive officer. In 1986 Spectrum 7 merged with Harken Oil and Gas, a large, publicly traded company.

Following the merger of Spectrum 7, Reynolds DeWitt became active in leveraged buyouts and corporate financings in a wide range of industries. A common element in each transaction was the presence of first-rate, experienced management.

In 1983 Reynolds DeWitt formed Seven Hills Communications to acquire Cincinnati's premier radio property, WLW-AM, along with a sister station, WSKS-FM. Led by three former Taft Broadcasting executives, Seven Hills grew to become Republic Broadcasting Corporation, acquiring additional stations in Nashville and Knoxville, Tennessee. Republic subsequently was sold for $34 million to Jacor Communications, which had effected a public offering through Reynolds DeWitt Securities, the registered broker-dealer affiliate of Reynolds, DeWitt & Co.

In 1984 Reynolds-DeWitt acquired the Cincinnati Coca-Cola Bottling Company, one of the country's largest soft drink bottlers and part of an even larger regional group that Reynolds DeWitt assembled in the following two years. With extensive industry consolidation taking place, however, the Coca-Cola group was sold for $165 million to another large, independent bottler in December 1986.

Through the early and mid-1980s, Reynolds DeWitt also was very active in the insurance industry. One of Cincinnati's oldest companies, Cincinnati Equitable Insurance Company, was acquired through a tender offer to its public shareholders and later sold to the Nathan Hale Insurance Company. Reynolds DeWitt then formed Midwest Employers Casualty Company with an experienced casualty insurance team. Midwest Employers has become one of the country's largest writers of excess workers compensation insurance for large, self-insured corporations and municipalities. Reynolds DeWitt also financed the Continental National Corporation, a regional, multi-line casualty insurance company headquartered and rapidly growing in Cincinnati.

In 1985 Reynolds DeWitt and several experienced industry operators were the founding shareholders of Mid-American Waste Systems, Inc., a non-hazardous waste disposal firm, one of the largest and fastest-growing in the industry with 1989 sales estimated at over $50 million. Based in Columbus, Ohio, the company has a sizeable division operating in the Cincinnati area.

Reynolds DeWitt entered the fast food industry with the 1988 acquisition of Restaurant Management, Inc. RMI is one of the country's largest Arby's franchises, with 34 restaurants in the Tri-State area. The company has over 1,000 employees and anticipates continued growth through the addition of several restaurants in the next few years.

The Reynolds DeWitt group also includes Charter Cable Systems, Inc., of Cincinnati. Led by a strong, experienced management team, Charter Cable has been very active in the acquisition and development of cable television systems in Ohio, Kentucky, Pennsylvania, West Virginia, Maryland and Tennessee. By the end of 1989, Charter is expected to be serving close to 50,000 subscribers in a consolidated cable group, placing it in the top echelon of regional cable companies.

A member of the National Association of Securities Dealers, Reynolds DeWitt Securities Company acts as a principal market maker for a variety of local and regional companies and provides investment research services for its institutional and retail clients. Reynolds DeWitt has concluded a number of public offerings, notably Jacor Communications, Skyline Chili, and Health Images, an Atlanta-based medical diagnosis company.

In the last several years, Reynolds DeWitt has also entered the real estate development field through its affiliate, Meridian Properties, Inc. Ventures have included the development of an apartment complex in Naples, Florida; the construction of St. James at the Park, a 15-story, luxury condominium project near Eden Park; and the historic renovation of a three-building office complex at Third and Main streets that is home for the Reynolds DeWitt operation.

Reynolds DeWitt has agreed to acquire The Future Now Corporation, one of Cincinnati's premier distribution and service companies in the fast-growing commercial computer market. It also anticipates entering the publishing business and is currently negotiating for the acquisition of several newspaper properties.

Acquisitions and financings of companies with superior management that either complement existing investments or serve as entries to additional fields will continue to be the main thrust for the future for Reynolds, DeWitt & Co.

The renovated three-building complex at Third and Main streets houses the investment firm of Reynolds, DeWitt & Co. Photograph courtesy of The Cincinnati Historical Society.

ROTEX INC.

ROTEX INC. manufactures industrial screening machines used by the process industries for sizing granular materials. Its products are manufactured in Cincinnati and also in England, Belgium, South Africa and Australia. This is in sharp contrast to the company's origin in 1844.

The company was founded by a Scotsman named Isaac Straub, who invented a unique grist mill which he called the "Queen of the South." He named his company The Straub Mill Company, and located his plant at Front and John streets in the heart of Cincinnati's thriving riverfront area. Although new technology eventually would surpass Isaac Straub's mills, the "Queen of the South" remained the backbone of the business until the turn of the century. Straub imported French buhrstones from the Seine River basin for use in his mills and, in later years, Frenchmen skilled in the art of redressing the stones were employed by the company. Used for grinding various grains, as well as drugs, spices, plaster and starch, the last "Queen of the South" mill was shipped during World War I.

In 1864 Robert Simpson from Davenport, Iowa, became the first general agent in Cincinnati for the Mutual Benefit Life Insurance Company of Newark, New Jersey. Almost immediately Simpson began investing in other local enterprises. He was president of the Cincinnati Northwestern Railroad and a principal stockholder in the Farmers' College, later known as Ohio Military Institute. Simpson also purchased Isaac Straub's grist mill company and hired a man named George Gault to operate it. The company's reputation for excellent mills grew as evidenced by medals won for unique mill designs during Cincinnati's expositions of the 1870s.

In 1885 Robert Simpson's son, Orville, age 25, became president of the company. Orville's brothers, Robert, Frank and William, were to contribute to the formation and management of several companies, including Duplex Paperbag, Armco Steel, Multicolor Type and Printing Machinery Corporation.

As steel roller mills became the new technology for grinding grain during the late 1800s, buhrstone grist mills were rapidly becoming obsolete. This prompted the purchase of two competitors to obtain a line of roller mills and the business of recorrugating the worn rolls. The Bradford line of cereal mill equipment and the Richmond City Mill Work were acquired.

In 1894 the company's Front and John streets plant was sold, necessitating a move to an old distillery warehouse located at 1956 West Sixth Street. This facility was used until 1910 when a new plant, designed by Walter Rapp, was completed in Cumminsville—the company's present Knowlton Street location. Concurrent with the move to the new plant, the company name was changed to The Orville Simpson Company.

Orville's son, Lowe, joined the company in 1906 when he was 19 years old. That same year he demonstrated his native mechanical genius by designing and building roll-mill corrugators, which were to continue in service for some 45 years.

In 1912 a Chillicothe, Ohio, flour miller's request of a favor changed the company's future. The miller wanted a "sifter" to go with his newly acquired grist mill. Lowe Simpson responded with his own design—a sifting device new in the art at the time. The new design was highly successful, and other millers soon wanted sifters "like the one in Chillicothe." The new sifter, or screener, was called "ROTEX." As word spread ROTEX Screeners found success in new applications and markets in such diverse fields as chemicals, fertilizer, food products, grain and forest products. The flour-mill supply business was to fade away as Lowe Simpson's favor to an Ohio flour miller took the company in a new direction.

Management of the company passed to the fourth generation of the Simpson family in 1957, when Lowe Simpson's son, Jeremy, became president at age 25. Through the 1960s ROTEX screeners were further developed to meet changing market requirements. New products have been introduced as extensions of the company's knowledge of sizing and separation. The original Knowlton Street plant is now dwarfed by the expansions necessary to accommodate manufacturing of the company's current products. And the firm flew a new banner in 1974 when it was given its current name—ROTEX INC.

Additions to the single ROTEX screener line of the 1960s include LIQUATEX Separators for liquid and solid separation and wastewater cleanup; HI-CAP Chip Screeners for large-volume sizing of wood chips for the pulp and paper industry; MEGATEX, a high-capacity grain cleaner that will handle 1,500 tons of grain per hour; and, the most recent product introduction, the GRADEX Particle Size Analyzer, a microcomputer-controlled device used for particle analysis and process control.

Alex C. Young, appointed president of ROTEX INC. in 1988, became the first president outside the Simpson family since 1864. Today, ROTEX INC.'s products are used to size a variety of materials. A walk through a home would reveal an almost endless list of items processed on ROTEX screeners—detergents, flooring tile, food and paper products, pet food, plastic, salt, sugar and more. And the sky's not the limit—ROTEX screeners have been used to screen solid rocket fuel as well as a granulated orange drink used by U.S. astronauts in space.

An early "Queen of the South" grist mill.

ROTEX Screeners in use in a modern paper mill.

Photographs courtesy of ROTEX INC.

Schiff, Kreidler-Shell Inc.

The Schiff, Kreidler-Shell, Inc. insurance company was created in 1984, when Robert Schiff purchased Kreidler-Shell from the Cincinnati Equitable Insurance Company. However, the firm's history began over 100 years earlier and involved some of the most prominent names in the Cincinnati insurance business.

Schiff, Kreidler-Shell's oldest ancestor is the A. R. Witham Co., established in 1876 and originally located on West Third Street. By the turn of the century, Witham Co. had moved its offices to the Masonic Temple building and specialized in fire insurance. H. Raymond Smith, a leading alumnus of Woodward High School, was a long-time president of the company in the first half of the 20th century. Witham Co. primarily sold personal insurance and remained in business until 1970, when it was purchased by Cincinnati Equitable Insurance Company. The A. R. Witham Co. was later merged into the firm that became Schiff, Kreidler-Shell.

In the early 1970s Cincinnati Equitable also purchased the William H. Kreidler Insurance Agency. Kreidler, a member of the board of elections and a former vice chairman of the Hamilton County Republican Party Executive Committee, began his agency in 1955. The Kreidler Agency was primarily a bonding agency, writing surety bonds for contractors.

With the purchase of the Kreidler Agency and the A. R. Witham Co., Cincinnati Equitable, one of the city's oldest financial institutions, hoped to broaden its insurance offerings. Cincinnati Equitable was organized in 1826 for the sole purpose of insuring commercial buildings and private dwellings against loss or damage by fire. In so doing it became the first insurance company west of Philadelphia to write fire insurance policies. Its first policy was written in 1826 for a private, three-story brick house on Walnut Street with an outhouse, wash shed, frame stable and carriage house. Cincinnati Equitable also insured businesses, including chair making, tobacco manufacturing and tavern keeping, but considered these hazardous trades and charged them a higher fee.

By the early 1970s Cincinnati Equitable specialized in "perpetual policies," which are one-time deposits or fees. The acquisition of the Kreidler Agency and the Witham Co. gave Cincinnati Equitable new openings in bonding and surety and personal insurance lines. Needing new management to oversee the expansion, Cincinnati Equitable purchased the insurance company of A.W. Shell & Co. in 1975.

A.W. Shell & Co. was one of the four leading insurance companies in Cincinnati in the post-World War II period. The company's predecessor, the Henry C. Shell Agency, opened at Third and Main streets in 1877. When Albert W. Shell took over the agency from his father, he renamed it. By 1928 its offices were in the First National Bank building, and it sold fire, tornado, marine, boiler, accident, casualty, automobile and public liability insurance. Among its clients were many large commercial firms, including the Cincinnati Union Stockyards, Andrew Jergens Company, Gibson Art Company and the Baldwin Company. West Shell, A. W.'s son, succeeded his father as president, and in 1969 he was succeeded by Louis Hellming.

Cincinnati Equitable merged the firms of Kreidler, Witham, and Shell; renamed them Kreidler-Shell; retained Hellming as president of the new company; and operated Kreidler-Shell as a subsidiary. In 1984 Cincinnati Equitable sold Kreidler-Shell to Robert Schiff.

Schiff started in the insurance business in Columbus, Ohio in 1945. He subsequently moved to Cincinnati and helped found the Cincinnati Insurance Company in 1951. Cincinnati Insurance Company grew into Cincinnati Financial Corporation with assets of $2 billion. Schiff is currently president and chief executive officer of Schiff, Kreidler-Shell. The firm has 70 employees, among them Senior Vice President Richard Shell, the fourth generation of Shells to serve in the insurance business. Schiff, Kreidler-Shell is active in all insurance lines, specializing in commercial insurance. It provides insurance for all phases of the transportation industry, including aviation, ocean cargo and inland marine operations.

Lobby of the downtown offices of Schiff, Kreidler-Shell, Inc. Photograph. Courtesy of The Cincinnati Historical Society.

The E.W. Scripps Company

A publisher, broadcaster and supplier of newspaper services, The E.W. Scripps Co. can trace its Cincinnati connections back a century. Its oldest component is *The Cincinnati Post*, which published its first edition on January 3, 1881. The company also is represented in this area by *The Kentucky Post*, WCPO-TV and its own national headquarters.

Scripps is a corporate structure of daily and weekly newspapers and suppliers of editorial, circulation and advertising services. It also is the parent company of Scripps Howard Broadcasting and operator of WCPO-TV and other radio, television and cable systems across the nation.

Edward Willis Scripps, the founder, was born in Rushville, Illinois in 1854. His father and grandfather had been publishers and bookbinders in England, and his older siblings had preceded him in the newspaper business. E.W. himself entered journalism on *The Detroit News* as the employee of his brother, James. With his brother's help he launched *The Cleveland Press* in 1878 and set the penny-paper style that was to be widely copied. Among the copiers was a pair of brothers who founded *The Cincinnati Post* but who ran out of capital almost immediately. The Scripps brothers rescued the paper, and E.W. eventually purchased full control.

During these early years E.W. was plagued by illness, but from 1883 on he gave his full attention to *The Post*. The paper championed reform in Cincinnati city government for 40 years, and E.W. lived to see the adoption of charter government in the November 1924 election. His successes in Ohio allowed him to launch about 30 other newspapers in various cities, and his search for editorial freedom led him into two experiments with ad-free publications, neither of which was able to survive without his financial help. Many of his newspapers were launched in partnership with local residents and in the face of entrenched publications. As a result some were short lived.

When he began to expand to other newspapers, the Associated Press was the only nationwide news service, available to a new publisher only on the favorable vote of his competitors in the community. To offset the odds against getting a favorable vote, Scripps purchased three small regional wire services in 1907 and merged them into United Press, which became an international service competing with AP.

United Press International was sold in 1982, but long before, The E.W. Scripps Co. had established three other news and feature services. One is the Newspaper Enterprise Association, founded in 1902, which since 1924 has supplied its services to many papers in addition to Scripps Howard publications. Another is Scripps Howard News Service, established in 1924 to supply national and international news commentary. The third was United Feature service, originally an offshoot of United Press but which became a separate corporation in 1923. The latter two recently merged into a new corporation, United Media. All supply newspapers in addition to Scripps Howard papers.

The "Howard" in Scripps Howard was Roy W. Howard, a native of Gano, Ohio who became an assistant managing editor of *The Cincinnati Post* in 1905 after working on papers in Indianapolis and St. Louis. Howard became president of United Press in 1912 at age 29. In 1920 he resigned to help manage the Scripps newspapers, a career that lasted more than 30 years. Howard's son, Jack, became president of The E.W. Scripps Co. in 1953, the same time that Charles E. Scripps of Cincinnati became chairman of the board.

Following E.W. Scripps' death in 1926, all holdings in The E.W. Scripps Co. were assembled into a trust that owns most of its stock, for at that time, heirs to his estate were very young. Charles E. Scripps, a grandson of E.W., now is chairman of the trust. Although the trust maintains control, shares of the company were sold to the public for the first time in June 1988.

Roy W. Howard managed the Scripps newspapers for more than 30 years, beginning in 1920. Photograph. Courtesy of the Edward W. Scripps Trust.

The E.W. Scripps Co. does business under the trade name of Scripps Howard and maintains controlling interest in the stock of Scripps Howard Broadcasting Co., which owns nine TV stations and five radio stations. In addition, Scripps Howard owns and operates 20 daily newspapers in 12 states and Puerto Rico and 70 cable systems in 10 states.

The company supplies a variety of services to the publishing industry. The largest of these is United Media, which provides comic strips, commentaries, games, pictures and graphics to daily and weekly newspapers. Its most widely known features include "Peanuts," "Garfield" and "Miss Manners." United Media also publishes *The World Almanac* and provides TV schedules and other features for local television program guides.

Lawrence A. Leser is president of The E.W. Scripps Co.; William R. Burleigh, senior vice president for newspapers and publishing; Daniel J. Castellini, senior vice president for finance and administration; and Gilles R. Champagne, senior vice president for corporate development. Richard J. Janssen is president of Scripps Howard Broadcasting Co., and Michael W. Callaghan is vice president of cable. Paul Knue is editor of *The Cincinnati Post*; Judith Clabes, editor of *The Kentucky Post*; and Frank Gardner, general manager for WCPO-TV.

Edward Willis Scripps not only founded the company carrying his name, but also started United Press, one of the leading international wire services today.

Seasongood & Mayer

Seasongood & Mayer's offices at the southwest corner of Third and Walnut streets (c. 1898). Pictured, left to right, are Charles Doepke and Gordon Reis Sr. (seated). Grace Wilcox is one of the women in the foreground and Adolph Seasongood, Charles Mayer and Julius Reis are behind the screen. Photograph courtesy of Seasongood & Mayer.

Jacob Seasongood and Jacob Netter established the Seasongood and Netter Company, a private bank, in 1870. From 1872 until 1889 the bank, later known as Seasongood and Sons and Seasongood and Mayer, was located at 74 West Third Street. Engraving. From D. J. Kenny's *Illustrated Cincinnati*...(Cincinnati, 1875), p. 124.

Ohio's oldest investment banking firm, Seasongood & Mayer enjoys a distinction rare among firms that trace themselves back to Civil War days. Its ownership still rests with the descendants of one of its founders.

Its offices in the Mercantile Library Building are at its eighth address since it was founded, but all of them have been within a block of Fourth and Vine, and for almost 50 years, its name spread along the second floor windows on that corner was a downtown landmark. Its current quarters, decorated with pictures of the founders and mementoes of early-day Cincinnati, instantly banish any feeling that one might be dealing with a Johnny-come-lately. It also provides one more example of a custom often followed in Cincinnati: its founders were brothers-in-law.

A merchant-turned-banker named Jacob Netter set the stage for Seasongood & Mayer. Netter, a French Alsatian, was a successful merchant when he married Amelia Kuhn, a member of the family which was to establish Kuhn, Loeb in New York. Both died in the mid-1870s, but not until Netter and Jacob Seasongood opened one of the 50-odd private banks which Cincinnati has had at one time or another.

The Netters had four children, two of them daughters who married Charles Mayer and Adolph Seasongood. Meantime Julius Reis, a native of Baden, was doing well as a merchant with his brother and had married yet another Seasongood, Julia, the daughter of Jacob.

In 1887 after a series of preliminary excursions into banking and finance, Seasongood, Mayer and Reis opened business as Seasongood & Mayer, dealing in bonds. As a by-product they unwittingly gave birth to a network of cousinships which permeates Cincinnati history.

The decision that turned these merchants, bankers and importers to selling bonds was sound. The day of private banking was fading (the original Netter enterprise eventually became part of what is now Star Bank). Municipal bonds represented a booming present and a solid future. There was a great demand for money to finance the rapid growth of cities, and there was little compensation for the business.

In the early days Julius Reis visited the public produce markets in Cincinnati and sold bonds to farmers as the sun rose. Today tedious research precedes issuance of bonds. But in the flush times of America's growth, government credit was never questioned. Reis' marketplace clients did not trouble with financial reports. Many chose to buy a pink bond because they already owned a green one.

No record of the very first issue handled by Seasongood & Mayer remains, but the first bond it handled for a project in Hamilton County is shown as $15,000 for Mitchell Avenue. The nature of the project, done in 1899, is not specified, but the company assumes it was a street repair. A few years later Seasongood & Mayer shepherded the bond issue for the present county courthouse and jail.

Shortly before World War I, Mayer died and Seasongood retired, although he stayed on for a time as a special partner. The business was continued by Julius Reis and his sons, Gordon and James. Since then Seasongood & Mayer virtually always has been operated by a series of partnerships involving members of the Reis family. In 1920, after the death of founder Julius Reis, the partners were sons, Gordon and James, plus Robert Stark. Two of Julius' daughters married doctors named Stark. With the death of Stark and the retirement of James Reis, Gordon operated the company as a proprietorship, the single exception to the series of partnerships.

A third generation, Gordon Jr. and Thomas, joined the partnership in 1944. In 1948 Gordon Sr. died, and Robert Reis became a partner, joining Thomas and Gordon Jr. Edgar J. Mack Jr., who had been associated with the Red Top Brewing Co. from 1934 until 1954—eventually becoming president of that firm—joined Seasongood & Mayer as a special partner in 1959 and remains one now.

In 1967 Gordon Reis III became a partner, but in 1978 Robert's death once more reduced the number of general partners to three. The partnership set up when Thomas retired in 1979, consisted of Gordon Jr., Gordon III, Richard Reis (the son of Thomas) and R. Lee Mairose, the first person outside the founding families to become a partner. Since then three more individuals have joined the general partnership: Joseph P. Magdich, Todd I. Braff and Paul T. Stubbins. There also are special partners, some of whom bear the Reis name, as well as the fifth generation of the Reis family.

Seasongood & Mayer handles all types of bonds. Its most recent annual report lists 180 municipal, corporate, federal or general bond issues which it helped launch either as a manager, co-manager or participant.

Many Cincinnati firms can claim a history of a century or more, but very few can boast so enduring a family name in their management.

Senco Products, Inc.

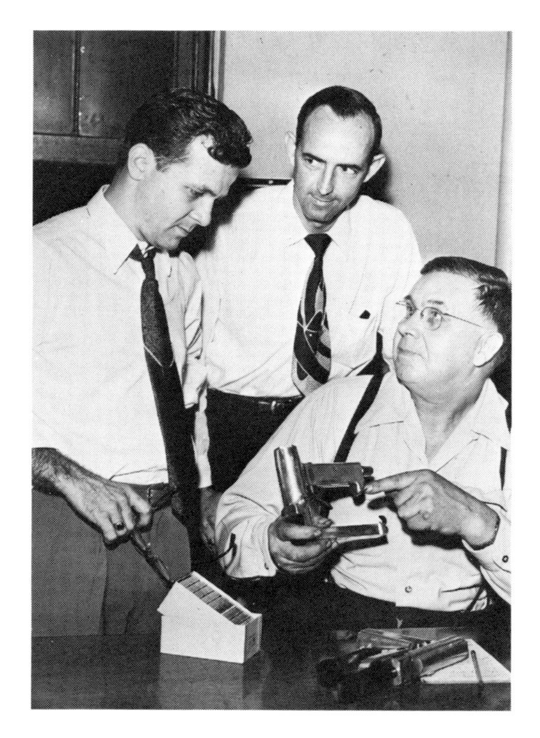

William Tillinghast, left, George W. Kennedy and A. G. Juilfs are pictured in 1951, the year of Senco's incorporation, with their pneumatic tacker. Although the machine was then only 3½ years old, it "fire[d] tacks or staples like a revolver" and was already in wide use, especially in the automobile industry for installing upholstery and other accessories inside of cars.

Senco Products, Inc. is not Cincinnati's oldest company but its origins contain exactly the same elements of old-fashioned success found in the histories of firms a century older than it is. There was a happy meeting of partners whose combined talents made the whole greater than its parts; energy and ingenuity were investments more important than money; and the founders approached their undertaking with the zeal of evangelists.

Senco's official age is 38 years, and its roots are not much older. The story begins in Newtown.

A.G. Juilfs (pronounced jewel-fs) was the operator of a small job shop in what had been a three-room Newtown schoolhouse. During World War II the little shop made a variety of things on government contract and the business was known as the Springtramp Eliminator Co. after an automotive part which Juilfs had designed. The name Senco is derived from this small beginning.

Juilfs was a mechanical genius who had accumulated approximately 100 patents on his designs. A schoolteacher friend, George Kennedy, translated Juilfs' notes and sketches into mechanical drawings for the shop. Among the things Juilfs had invented was a foot operated stapler.

William Tillinghast meantime was making his own start in business as a fastener salesman and distributor in Detroit, but he had heard about the Juilfs design genius. In 1946 he came to Juilfs with an order from Federated Department Stores for a stapler which would seal cardboard packages. Juilfs designed one with Kennedy's assistance, and the three founders of Senco had found each other.

Because of his Detroit location, Tillinghast knew a great deal about the automotive industry. At his urging Juilfs designed a pneumatic tacker for attaching upholstery to automobile interiors, and in 1948 they sold 125 of these machines to General Motors.

While they were still in the old schoolhouse at Plum and Debolt streets in Newtown, the partners began turning out the staples as well as the staplers. This decision turned the company's expansion into an industrial mushroom. The company was incorporated into Senco Products Inc. in 1951 by the three men, with Juilfs as the majority shareholder.

In 1952 the company moved to Fairfax into a plant which was to be expanded five times. In 1967 it began operations in a new building at 8485 Broadwell Road. The plant was expected to take care of all foreseeable expansion, but expansion of it had to be started within three years. By 1973 a new building was erected across the street and that building has since been remodeled to increase space by one-third.

Senco products no longer are limited to government or automotive products. They range from a nearly invisible staple in Polaroid camera film packs to three-and-a-half inch giant staples and nails; from a two-and-a-half pound stapler to a 12 pound nailer. They also design and produce disposable instruments that apply stainless steel staples which surgeons use to close incisions.

All the tools are manufactured in the local plants, but fasteners are made over much of the world by branch plants, subsidiary companies or licensees. The Senco name is on installations in Australia, Brazil, Canada, France, West Germany, Holland, Israel, Italy, Japan, New Zealand, South Africa and Spain. Over 1,500 are employed in the Greater Cincinnati area, many of them persons who can boast that they were there at the beginning.

Senco's growth into a global company started in the early 1950s when the company began selling products in Europe. Senco was first in the Tri-State area to be awarded the Presidential "E" (1962) and "E-Star" (1970) for international trade.

A.G. Juilfs, the senior of the founding partners, died in 1970. Upon his retirement his son George Juilfs became Senco's president and chief executive officer. Tillinghast became chairman of the board. Kennedy lives in Atlanta, where he owns Senco Southeast Inc., a distributorship which covers Georgia, Alabama and part of Tennessee selling Senco products.

In October 1983 a new parent company known as SENCORP was formed, with Senco Products, Inc. being a wholly-owned subsidiary. George C. Juilfs is the SENCORP president and chief executive officer and William C. Tillinghast, chairman of the board. William Hess serves as president of Senco Products, Inc.

The company continues to be locally owned and managed. Although it is the leader in its field, it intends to keep growing and expanding into new markets and products.

South-Western Publishing Company

Headquartered in Cincinnati since 1910, South-Western Publishing Co. is the largest publisher of business education textbooks and related instructional materials in the secondary and proprietary school markets and a major publisher in business administration texts for colleges and universities. Its *Century 21 Keyboarding, Formatting, and Document Processing* and *Century 21 Accounting* books are the dominant high school texts in their disciplines, and *College Accounting* has been a leader in its field for more than 50 years.

South-Western was founded in 1903 by James W. Baker, a 28-year-old bookkeeping teacher at Knoxville Business College in Tennessee. Unhappy with the text he was using in his classes, Baker wrote to the publisher in Baltimore suggesting changes that could improve it. The publisher's reply didn't satisfy Baker, so he wrote his own book.

Colleagues at the college were so impressed by his work, that they urged him to make his materials widely available. And so a company called Southern Publishing Co. was born.

The book that started it all was *20th Century Bookkeeping and Office Practice*, the predecessor of today's *Century 21 Accounting*. In the 85 years since Baker first published his text, more than 100 million high school students have learned the fundamentals of accounting from its many editions.

Baker spent his first several years as a publisher writing and editing all his own materials; overseeing typesetting, printing and distribution; and handling all sales. The company's first office, consisting of a desk and some shelves, was over a stairwell in Knoxville Business College.

In 1904, when the company incorporated, Baker discovered that a Southern Publishing Co. already existed. He changed the firm's name to South-Western because he expected to serve the southern and western areas of the United States. Little did he know that South-Western eventually would serve more than 250,000 customers nationwide.

Sales reached $50,000 in 1910, when the firm moved to Cincinnati to save on freight charges for paper, secure a better source of supply for printing and operate from a more central distribution point for the large area being served.

South-Western's first Cincinnati office occupied 8,000 square feet at 222 Main Street. In 1916 it doubled its space by moving to 309 West Third Street. In subsequent years it relocated to Third and Vine streets (1924); 201 West Fourth Street (1936); and 634 West Broadway (1947).

The current 316,346-square-foot headquarters building and warehouse opened in 1955 at 5101 Madison Road, about nine miles from downtown. The company built a high-density warehouse in 1986 to provide 80% additional storage, increasing total capacity to 15 million books. Two new floors on the main building, comprising another 36,148 square feet, are scheduled for completion in 1990.

South-Western also has regional offices and warehouses in Cincinnati; Dallas; Livermore, California; Mt. Kisco, New York; and West Chicago, Illinois.

In 1919 the company began publishing *The Balance Sheet, A Magazine for Commercial Teachers*. This magazine is now distributed five times during the school year, free of charge, to more than 150,000 educators.

As South-Western's reputation grew, other authors wanted Baker to publish their materials. Some of the early books published included Peters' *Speller* and *Commercial Law*; Hausam's *Pedagogical Writing Course*; Grisso's *Typewriting*; and Holmes' *Personality and Salesmanship*.

In 1927 South-Western published a breakthrough text in typewriting: *20th Century Touch Typewriting* by D.D. Lessenberry. In later editions it became the most widely used secondary typewriting text. Now titled *Century 21 Keyboarding, Formatting, and Document Processing*, the text continues as the leader in its field.

Accounting Principles, an introductory text for colleges and universities, was released in 1930. Now in its 15th edition, it is the most popular accounting textbook and the largest-selling collegiate text of all time. It was the first collegiate accounting book to have a correlating workbook, achievement tests and practice sets, and it introduced the use of the computer to augment instruction in accounting.

In 1934 South-Western became the first publisher to prepare and market a special line of books for private business schools.

James Baker died in 1938, leaving behind his legacy of service to customers. Because he felt that a publishing business did not deserve to survive if it did not put something back into education, he often was responsible for sponsoring speakers, assisting with conventions and giving advice— a tradition that South-Western continued. During World War II, for instance, South-Western provided more texts for the United States Armed Forces Institute than any other publisher.

Founder James W. Baker named the South-Western Publishing Company for the regions of the country that he intended it to serve. Photograph courtsey of South-Western.

In 1964 the first "Gold Books" were awarded to 10 authors whose titles had sold a million copies. Today a total of 69 Gold Book awards have been presented to South-Western authors.

South-Western was acquired in 1967 by Scott, Foresman and Co., one of the nation's largest publishing houses, represented internationally. South-Western entered the 1980s under the leadership of C. LeMoyne Smith, the current president and chief executive officer.

The company welcomed the computer age in business education with the 1982 introduction of its first microcomputer "courseware" package, printed text and program software, South-Western's fastest growing product line.

To better serve its educational markets, South-Western created three new divisions— the College, School and Electronic Publishing divisions— each with its own specialized editorial and marketing staff. Back in the 1950s two editors and five assistants comprised South-Western's entire editorial operation. Today the editorial staff of the three divisions numbers 220 talented individuals.

The current South-Western product line includes more than 2,500 textbooks, supplementary items and software packages for a variety of academic disciplines.

As the leader in business education publishing, South-Western attracted the attention of International Thomson Organisation, Ltd. of Toronto, Canada. In December 1986 this multibillion-dollar corporation with worldwide publishing interests acquired South-Western. A year later South-Western sales exceeded $100 million for the first time.

As South-Western looks forward to the next century, its more than 700 employees continue to carry on the traditions of its founder, providing high-quality materials and service to improve the process of education. James Baker would be proud.

Star Bank

With $2.9 billion in assets and 125 years of service, Star Bank, N.A., Cincinnati, formerly The First National Bank of Cincinnati, is the Queen City's biggest holding company. Founded on July 13, 1863, the bank was born as the nation was reeling from the horrors of Gettysburg. Cincinnati had its own problems: business was stagnant, river traffic at a standstill. The city was under martial law as Confederate General John Morgan and 5,000 of his raiders reportedly headed toward the city. Ohio Governor Dennison had issued a call for volunteers to defend Cincinnati. After many uncertain hours word came that Morgan's raiders had bypassed the city.

On that same day the charter for Star Bank was signed, and its first newspaper advertisement appeared announcing the availability of government bonds. The bank was chartered as number 24, but because of mergers and acquisitions, Star Bank now ranks among the four oldest in the national system.

As a tribute to Samuel P. Chase, Lincoln's Secretary of the Treasury and an architect of the National Bank Act, Star Bank's founding fathers had raised $1 million in capital, making Star the most highly capitalized national bank of the time. Its capital strength has remained a distinction throughout its history, even in troubled times like the Great Depression.

The governor of Ohio proclaimed a state banking holiday on February 27, 1933, and the following day the Cincinnati Clearing House authorized banks to restrict withdrawals to 5% of the amount on deposit. Star Bank was the only major bank in town that continued to pay out in full.

In the days that followed, several small business depositors walked out with brown paper bags containing withdrawals of $10,000 or so in cash. Companies had to make payroll, and Star Bank was the only bank in the city permitting withdrawals of such magnitude. Other banks in the trade area also came to obtain the cash needed in their own communities. And several national companies in other cities also approached Star Bank. Despite the extremely high demand, Star stayed its course. The high liquidity policy that the bank had pursued for several years had paid off.

Large commercial depositors, the bulk of the bank's business, demonstrated their confidence in Star Bank by not withdrawing more than was absolutely necessary. Soon, it is said, the nervous withdrawals of other customers ceased, and those brown paper bags, as yet unopened, were returned for deposit. A week later President Roosevelt ordered a national bank holiday, but the point was made: Star Bank was not only a strong institution, but also one ready to serve when other banks could not.

At the time of the bank's formation, Cincinnati was the third largest manufacturing city in the country. Its growth, however, had been financed by a series of what now seem like makeshift banking systems in a West chronically short of hard money. All of Cincinnati's private banks, once mainstays of finance, would be absorbed into new banks. First National's early acquisitions were the products of that implosion.

Its next expansion was the purchase of the Central National Bank in 1870. In 1904 it acquired the Ohio Valley National Bank and a year later, the National Lafayette Bank. In 1909 First National took over the Merchants National Bank. All of these institutions were themselves the results of earlier purchases or mergers. Ohio Valley National's components included the private bank of Smead, Collard & Hughes, the oldest of First National's roots, established in 1850.

The city's financial centers have been moving northward for a century, and First National has been part of the parade. Its first building was on the northwest corner of Third and Walnut streets, and its first office, on Second Street between Walnut and Vine. In 1903 a new building was constructed at the southeast corner of Fourth and Walnut. At 17 stories it had its day as the city's tallest skyscraper.

Star Bank Center overlooks the Tyler Davidson Fountain, named for the same man who received the bank's first loan in 1863. Photograph courtesy of Star Bank.

Long recognized as a premier business bank in the region, Star Bank primarily served businesses and other banks during its first century. However, the dispersal of business, industry and people to the suburbs after World War II dictated First National's move into retail and branch banking.

In 1951 Star purchased the Second National Bank, with its eight branches. Expansions then came swiftly. In 1951 First National of Norwood and Norwood Savings Bank were added to First National; in 1953, First National of Lockland; in 1954, Atlas National; and in 1960, Farmer's State Bank of Miamitown and First National of Elmwood Place. In 1956 it acquired Midland Discount, and in 1964, Walldon Inc., a mortgage banker.

Through subsequent acquisitions (including five offices of the failed Home State Savings Bank following Ohio's so-called S&L "crisis" in 1985) and geographic expansion, Star Bank, N.A., Cincinnati now operates a network of 41 branch offices in Greater Cincinnati.

In 1974 Star Bank became the lead bank in the newly established bank holding company, First National Cincinnati Corporation. The $5.4 billion corporation now operates 16 subsidiary banks in Ohio, Indiana and Kentucky with 154 offices. All subsidiary banks of the corporation began operating under the shared name "Star Bank" on July 1, 1988.

Oliver W. Waddell is chairman of the board and chief executive officer of Star Bank, N.A., Cincinnati and of First National Cincinnati Corporation. Samuel M. Cassidy is president of Star Bank, N.A., Cincinnati, and Mark T. Johnson is president of First National Cincinnati Corporation.

In 1981 the bank moved north again, this time into the new Star Bank Center at Fifth and Walnut streets across from Fountain Square. The bank lobby itself looks across Fifth Street to the square and its Tyler Davidson Fountain.

In August 125 years ago, the bank made its first loan: $5,000 to a Cincinnati businessman named Tyler Davidson.

Strauss & Troy

As Cincinnati celebrates its bicentennial, Strauss & Troy is celebrating its 35th anniversary.

On August 1, 1953, the partnership Strauss, Troy & Ruehlmann was formed by Lucien Strauss, Orville Troy and his son, Ken, and Eugene Ruehlmann. Senior partners Samuel Allen and Mark Berliant joined the firm in 1957 and 1959, respectively.

Over the years the firm has developed certain areas of expertise while retaining its full service, general practice orientation. Strauss & Troy represents a variety of clients with national and local interests, including numerous Ohio and Kentucky corporations, financial institutions, general and limited partnerships, charitable organizations, trusts, families, and individuals.

Strauss & Troy's growth has paralleled that of the City of Cincinnati. The firm originally was located in tiny offices in the Fountain Square Building at the northwest corner of Fifth and Walnut streets, but these were demolished in the early 1960s, when Fountain Square was renovated and the Fifth Third Center built.

The firm moved to the First National Bank Building (now the Clopay Building), where it grew to occupy two floors. These offices included a large library and a kitchen, where Ken Troy cooked gourmet breakfasts for his partners every Thursday morning.

After a 1976 merger with Goldman, Cole & Putnick brought Douglas Cole, Charles Atkins and two associates to the firm, Strauss, Troy & Ruehlmann became one of the first tenants in the Central Trust Center at the corner of Fifth and Main streets, where the Greyhound Bus Terminal had been until the mid-1970s. Senior partner Douglas Cole's grandfather had owned a horse stable on the site many years earlier.

In its current location the firm has changed its name to Strauss & Troy, merged with the eight-attorney firm of Arthur Heckerman and Gordon Hood, and grown to 49 lawyers. The firm opened a branch office in Covington, Kentucky in 1987. Its offices on both sides of the Ohio River are graced with widely acclaimed photographs of Cincinnati and Northern Kentucky by Gregory Thorp.

Although Orville Troy died in 1967, Strauss practiced until his late seventies but died in 1982, and Ken Troy retired to Florida in 1986, the firm's lawyers have continued to combine personal service with the sophisticated resources and legal skills necessary to handle complex transactions.

Strauss & Troy expects to continue its steady growth into the future while at the same time maintaining its tradition of high quality, imaginative, personal service for individuals, businesses and institutions in Greater Cincinnati and Northern Kentucky.

The law firm of Strauss & Troy periodically commissions photographer Gregory Thorp to take pictures of Cincinnati for display at its offices. Thorp photographs courtesy of Strauss & Troy.

Structural Dynamics Research Corporation

Structural Dynamics Research Corporation (SDRC) is a pioneer in the development of mechanical computer-aided engineering (MCAE), technology used in the design, analysis and testing of sophisticated mechanical products.

Headquartered in Milford, Ohio, SDRC is a leading supplier of MCAE software and engineering services used by automotive, aerospace and industrial manufactures worldwide to automate design engineering. The company's products and services significantly reduce product development time and cost, resulting in superior product quality by enabling customers to optimize product designs prior to production.

SDRC was founded in 1967 by a group of mechanical engineers from the University of Cincinnati who were dedicated to providing advanced mechanical engineering consulting services. In doing so the company developed MCAE software products. In 1971, after determining that there was a broad market demand for software products to automate design engineering, the company began to market the software it had created. Since then SDRC has led the MCAE industry in the development and support of software products and services.

In 1986 Ronald J. Friedsam was named chairman, president and chief executive officer. Prior to joining SDRC Friedsam was an executive with Burroughs Corporation (now Unisys). In 1987 SDRC completed its initial public stock offering.

SDRC employs more than 700 people and has offices in nine countries throughout North America, Europe and the Far East. More than half of SDRC's personnel is located at the Ohio corporate headquarters. SDRC's leadership in the MCAE software market attracts top engineers from around the world to the Cincinnati area.

The demand for MCAE software is being driven by worldwide competition among all industries to develop better products faster and at lower cost. To meet this challenge, manufacturers are turning to new methods of product development based upon MCAE technology.

The MCAE process begins with a concept design of a new product. Using software from SDRC, engineers create a computerized, three-dimensional solid model of the product, which can be visualized and evaluated before building expensive physical prototypes. This complete geometric description of the product can be used to perform computer simulation of the new product's performance early in the design process when alternative designs are being considered. Using the solid model as the basis for their evaluations, representatives from engineering, marketing and manufacturing can work together to achieve an optimum product design that meets all criteria for aesthetics, performance and manufacturability.

SDRC's software system, I-DEAS (Integrated Design Engineering Analysis System), addresses the complete product development process by automating design, analysis, testing, drafting and manufacturing capabilities. As of October 1988 there were approximately 7,500 I-DEAS licenses installed at more than 2,400 customer sites worldwide. The current I-DEAS product represents more than 900 "man-years" of research and development and 4.5 million lines of computer code. SDRC's research and development staff will continue to add new software capabilities while ensuring support for the leading computer systems and graphics devices.

In addition to offering industry leading software, SDRC also provides customers with advanced consulting engineering services. Across all major industries worldwide, SDRC engineers are working as integral members of customers' design teams, helping to improve the design of their products as well as their engineering and manufacturing processes. The company provides several types of engineering consulting services, including design audits, product design, engineering process development and trouble-shooting.

Companies worldwide are experiencing the benefits of MCAE technology, helping them to remain competitive in the international marketplace and meet sophisticated engineering challenges. For example SDRC has been working with NASA to create a customized space station preliminary design system. When astronauts find a comfortable, well constructed, near-earth home, they will have SDRC, in part, to thank for it.

More "down to earth" products are being developed with SDRC's products and services as well. Automobile manufacturers are using SDRC products to design safer, higher performance cars. Computer manufacturers are developing better, more reliable terminal housings for their sophisticated electronic circuitry. Makers of industrial robots are designing machines to perform more complex tasks by simulating their performance with SDRC products.

In 1988 the company received one of the largest single software orders in its history—more than 250 software licenses from the Fermi National Accelerator Laboratory, which operates the world's largest particle accelerator laboratory. The Chicago lab will use software to design superconducting magnets for high-energy physics research.

The horizons of MCAE technology seem unlimited. And as the use of computer-aided design and engineering becomes more prevalent and sophisticated, SDRC will continue to meet the need by providing leading edge MCAE software coupled with extensive engineering across many industries.

Representatives from engineering, marketing and manufacturing use SDRC's I-DEAS software to generate a three-dimensional solid model of a product design that can be analyzed to simulate product performance. In this case a point-of-sale terminal was redesigned to be marketed in the fast food industry. Photograph courtesy of SDRC.

United Brands Company

The newest Fortune 500 company to make Cincinnati its home is United Brands Company, one of the world's leading producers, processors and distributors of quality food products. United Brands' products are marketed worldwide under the Chiquita, John Morrell and other brand names.

Chiquita Brands, famous for its bananas, also markets pineapples, melons, grapefruits and other fresh fruit; frozen desserts and beverages sold under the Chiquita name; as well as margarine, shortening, salad dressings and dehydrated soups sold under various regional brand names. John Morrell products include fresh, frozen and processed beef, pork and lamb, including sausage, frankfurters, bacon, canned hams and luncheon meats sold under the John Morrell, Rath Black Hawk and various regional brand names.

Chiquita Brands began operation in 1899, when two groups of fruit companies in Boston and New York, spurred by the growing popularity of the much-sought-after banana, joined to form the United Fruit Company. Bananas received considerable national publicity at the Philadelphia Centennial Exposition in 1876 when they were wrapped in tin foil and sold for 10 cents apiece.

The United Fruit Company soon became the world's dominant banana company, in great part due to the ingenuity and tenacity of one of its founder, Minor Keith, who constructed railroads throughout the tropics despite many dangers and rampant disease. The company established operations in Latin America, transforming tropical jungles and swampland into huge banana plantations. United Fruit built new towns, schools and hospitals for its workers.

The first refrigerated ship from United Fruit made its maiden voyage in 1903, marking the beginning of the company's famous Great White Fleet. By 1933 the Great White Fleet had grown to 95 ships, and its fame was legendary. Though primarily involved in the shipment of bananas, the fleet also delivered mail for the U.S. government, and several of the huge vessels doubled as luxury passenger ships. During World War II the Great White Fleet delivered troops, ammunition, food and supplies for the United States. A ship from the fleet even was at Normandy on D-Day.

After the war the company began an expansion program, which included a new radio advertising jingle called "The Chiquita Banana Song." The jingle and the Chiquita Banana cartoon figure quickly became two of America's most popular corporate symbols.

In 1967 the company merged with John Morrell & Co. and two years later was purchased by AMK Corporation. The parent company's name was changed to United Brands Company in 1970 to better reflect its diversity.

John Morrell & Co. began in 1827 in Bradford, England when George Morrell opened a fruit and vegetable trading business. His son, John, brought the company to the United States 50 years later and specialized in pork-packing. He opened plants in Ottumwa, Iowa; Chicago; and Sioux Falls, South Dakota.

By the 1950s Morrell had become one of the four largest meat packers in the United States. Since then Morrell has acquired several smaller firms, enabling the company to expand its scope and brand presence in local markets. As part of this growth, the Chicago-based Morrell acquired the H.H. Meyer Company of Cincinnati and its Partridge brands in 1964.

Cincinnati financier Carl H. Lindner first became associated with United Brands in the early 1970s, first as a major shareholder and then in 1976 as a member of its board of directors. In 1984 Lindner's American Financial Corporation acquired the stock of other board members, and Lindner was elected chairman of the board and chief executive officer. Recognizing the potential of the highly recognizable Chiquita name, Lindner changed the name of the United Fruit Company to Chiquita Brands, Ltd. and introduced new products including frozen dessert bars and fruit juices under the Chiquita name.

In 1987 United Brands consolidated operations in New York, Boston, and Montvale, New Jersey and established its headquarters in downtown Cincinnati. The company occupies the former Columbia Plaza building at Fifth and Sycamore streets. Renamed the Chiquita Center the building features different colored lights on the top floor that are changed depending on the weather forecast (green for clear skies, blue for precipitation and orange for storms).

To further its position as a market leader, United Brands built a technical center in 1988 to provide state-of-the-art research and development, engineering and analytical services to both John Morrell and Chiquita.

The royal blue Chiquita Brands symbol means more than just bananas the world over. Illustration courtesy of United Brands.

United Brands is capitalizing on trends toward more healthful diets by adding fruit-based items and premium processed meats to its line of food products. Photograph courtesy of United Brands.

United Dairy Farmers

In 1938 Carl H. Lindner Sr. had the idea to start a small dairy in Norwood, Ohio. At a time when almost all milk was home-delivered and paid for on a weekly or monthly basis, Carl Sr. had a new concept: he would process milk and other dairy products and sell them, cash-and-carry, at his own dairy store. Since he would not extend credit to his customers nor incur delivery costs, he could afford to sell these products at a significant discount versus home delivery.

Carl Sr. and his wife, Clara, had four children: Carl Jr., Robert, Richard and Dorothy. During the Depression the entire family worked together to run several small milk and ice cream companies. Although the children had attended night school to complete their formal education, they received their real education working closely with their father in a succession of dairy enterprises.

This experience led Carl Jr., the eldest son, to run milk delivery routes for Lindner Quality Milk in Mariemont and Beechwood Farms Dairy in Silverton. Robert ran the small milk pasteurizing plant in Mariemont while Richard hauled milk from neighboring country farms to area dairies. Enterprising children, their days started at 4 a.m.

The Lindner family dedicated itself to making Carl Sr.'s idea a reality. Over the next two years, Richard and his father sought and purchased used dairy production equipment which they rebuilt and installed at 3955 Main Avenue (now Montgomery Road) in Norwood. Carl Jr. ran a milk route and Robert delivered eggs and poultry throughout Norwood. Together the family fashioned cabinets and signs for the new store, which they would call United Dairy Farmers in recognition of their valued milk suppliers.

Finally on May 8, 1940, the little dairy plant and the 20- by 50-foot store adjacent to it opened. United Dairy Farmers' cash-and-carry retail operation was a first, as was the availability of milk in gallon and half-gallon bottles (home-delivered milk was bottled exclusively in quarts). Moreover the company-owned store had most unusual hours: 8 a.m. to 10 p.m., seven days a week.

What housewives found most appealing about the new United Dairy Farmers store was the price of its milk. At 28 cents per gallon, they could save up to 24 cents of the cost of home-delivered milk. Other high-quality dairy products, butter, cottage cheese, eggs and buttermilk, were also available at low prices. First-day receipts totalled a respectable $8.

Home-delivery dairymen, however, were displeased by the Lindner family's newest venture and reacted to the price competition immediately. After closing up that first night, Carl Sr. was held and beaten by two dairymen in the store's driveway. He broke away, and later settled out of court for $1,000.

Using formulas Carl Sr. had developed and refined over some 30 years, United Dairy Farmers' ice cream soon became a local favorite. Slowly but surely United Dairy Farmers' popularity spread. A second store was opened in Norwood, a third in Silverton and a fourth in St. Bernard. Even with the expansion the business remained a family concern. Dorothy managed the bookkeeping from an "office" in the corner of the boiler room. Carl Jr. developed an interest in financial matters and directed market expansion efforts and real estate acquisitions. Robert oversaw the ice cream and milk production. Richard managed the physical facilities and maintenance; he designed and oversaw plant expansions and renovations that quickly increased production capacity. By 1950 there were nine United Dairy Farmers stores, and Dorothy's "office" moved to the house next door.

In 1958 a major plant expansion was completed, equipping the plant with two continuous ice cream freezers, half-gallon and pint ice cream fillers, a half-gallon milk bottle filler, a bottle washer and 12 stainless steel milk holding tanks adjacent to a new receiving dock. The chain now was composed of 22 stores.

Also at this time the family's interest in banking led to the formation of American Financial Corporation (AFC) followed by the acquisition of the Thriftway grocery chain. Dorothy, whose husband was a restaurant-owner, applied her management skills at that business, leaving management of these companies to her three brothers.

By 1960 United Dairy Farmers owned and operated some 30 stores in and around Cincinnati, many of which now carried expanded product lines of bread, cookies, lunch meat and cheeses to complement the selection of fresh dairy products.

By 1960 many United Dairy Farmers stores carried bread, cookies, lunch meat and cheeses in addition to fresh dairy products. Photograph courtesy of United Dairy Farmers.

In 1965 Richard left United Dairy Farmers to pursue his interest in grocery retailing at Thriftway. Carl Jr. and Robert continued to expand AFC holdings while operating United Dairy Farmers. A major United Dairy Farmers store remodeling program added merchandising space for some 1,200 convenience grocery products to the existing dairy and food sections.

United Dairy Farmers continued to grow during the 1970s while major family emphasis now focused on the development of AFC.

In the early 1980s the second generation of the Robert Lindner family—sons Bob Jr., Jeff, Brad and, most recently, David—became actively involved in the management of United Dairy Farmers.

Jeff and Brad, convinced that ice cream sales could be expanded significantly by adding a premium line, developed Homemade Brand premium ice cream in 1982. Homemade Brand offered exotic flavors, chock-full of costly condiments.

People magazine rated Homemade Brand Cookies 'N' Cream ice cream "Number One Exotic Flavor" in a 1984 competition. Over 890 flavors were submitted by 245 competitors nationwide. Other city, state and national awards followed, including a *Cincinnati Magazine* Best for Homemade Brand's Cherry Cordial ice cream.

By 1986 sales of United Dairy Farmers Homemade Brand ice cream were expanded to major grocery chains and independent stores in five states, and the company's wholesale enterprise was firmly established. Meanwhile the retail chain flourished under new management. Bob Jr., formerly executive vice-president of Provident Bank, became president. Under his leadership the chain grew to over 200 stores. New superstores with self-serve gasoline islands and fast-food sections were featured, in addition to expanded ice cream fountains and sit-down parlors. With over 225 stores and a wholesale ice cream business that ranks among the top 15 U.S. brands, United Dairy Farmers is listed within the top 100 privately-owned companies in the Tristate.

Lindner family members credit this outstanding achievement to Carl Lindner Sr., whose boundless energy he often expressed this way: "You can do anything you want to, children; the sky's the limit."

The United States Playing Card Company

Household words among even the most casual card players, U.S. Playing Card brands include:

BICYCLE

Since 1885, the most famous and largest-selling brand of playing cards in the world.

BEE

In play since 1895, the highest quality card produced anywhere and a favorite in over 200 casinos worldwide.

CONGRESS

The choice of sophisticated bridge players since 1881.

TALLY-HO

An East Coast favorite introduced in 1890.

The U.S. Playing Card Company sells these and many other playing cards and games throughout the United States and Canada and in more than 75 countries overseas.

The firm's founding dates back to 1867, when the vigorous Cincinnati partnership of Russell, Morgan & Company, a leading printer of labels, show cards, circus posters and state fair placards, purchased *The Cincinnati Enquirer's* printing shop. The company started manufacturing playing cards in 1880, laying the foundation for what would become The United States Playing Card Company. This initial venture proved so successful that by 1889, more than 630 people were involved in producing 30,000 decks per day.

The parent company, by then known as The United States Printing Company, further expanded its playing card business by acquiring Consolidated Card Company, New York, and The National Card Company of Indianapolis in 1890. The United States Playing Card Company was officially formed in 1894.

Booming business led to the need for more space, so U.S. Printing purchased 22 acres in suburban Norwood in 1899 and began construction on a new manufacturing plant that is still in use today. In order to bring employees so far out from the city, the company subsidized the extension of trolley lines that looped in front of the new facility.

A bell tower complete with a fine set of bells imported from Holland was added to the plant in 1926. Another building was outfitted in the early days of radio to broadcast "Bridge by Radio" and other musical acts. This became the original WSAI, which was sold to Powel Crosley Jr. in the 1930s and subsequently became WLW-T. Ultimately the plant was expanded to its present total of 600,000 square feet, spread over four stories.

During World War II U.S. Playing Card provided decks of cards showing poisonous plants, insects and reptiles to troops overseas for survival purposes. In addition BICYCLE cards with German maps laminated within the card itself were supplied to the Office of Strategic Services, which sent them to prisoners of German POW camps to aid in their escape.

At the request of NASA, USPC designed flameproof BICYCLE decks for the Apollo 14 mission and other orbital and underseas operations. Also, during the Vietnam War, millions of BICYCLE Aces of Spades were donated to U.S. troops to wear on their hats, for the North Vietnamese were superstitious of the so-called "death card." The firm also supplied specially-printed decks for aircraft and naval ship recognition.

Since then U.S. Playing Card has acquired other card companies, the most recent being Arrco Playing Card Company in 1987. In 1986 it also acquired Fournier, the largest playing card manufacturer in Europe. Located in Vitoria, Spain, Fournier also is a well-known quality publisher of fine books and postage stamps used in many smaller countries. Most domestic manufacturing remains concentrated in Cincinnati, although the company also operates the International Playing Card Company, Ltd. in Windsor, Ontario, Canada.

The Norwood plant maintains a museum featuring the finest collection of playing cards and memorabilia in the world. The collection is open to the public by appointment and free of charge. Among the 80,000 decks that the museum contains are cards from the 15th, 16th and 17th centuries; many original editions of cards that the company has purchased over the past 100 years; and books related to playing cards.

The United States Playing Card Company has remained a Cincinnati enterprise through a series of ownership changes during the past several years. In 1969 it merged with Diamond International Corporation, and in 1982 it was sold to the New York investment firm of Jesup & Lamont. Controlling interest remains with a new corporate entity created in 1987, The Jesup Group, Inc., a publicly traded company listed on the NASDAQ-OTC.

Ronald C. Rule is the company's current president and CEO. Since 1986 he has successfully managed a return to profitability for this premier supplier of playing cards and revitalized a major segment of its overseas markets. Cincinnati has every reason to be proud to be the home of the world leader in the playing card business.

The main entrance of the U.S. Playing Card Company plant on Beech Avenue in Norwood, Ohio. Illustration. Courtesy of U.S. Playing Card Company.

The United States Shoe Corporation

The United States Shoe Corporation, founded in 1931, is a consumer goods company engaged in two broad types of business: footwear and specialty apparel retailing. U.S. Shoe rose from its beginnings in the Depression to become one of the largest suppliers of quality-branded footwear in the United States. It is listed as one of the nation's top 50 retailers by *Forbes* magazine.

Red Cross Shoes, which has no connection whatever with the American National Red Cross, is the oldest and largest division at U.S. Shoe and was originally established in 1891 by Irwin Krohn. He joined with Samuel Fechheimer to form the Krohn-Fechheimer Shoe Co. in 1896. Red Cross developed a strong brand identity by advertising in the prestigious *Ladies' Home Journal*. In later years Red Cross Shoes generated only moderate sales—until it became a division of U.S. Shoe in 1931.

U.S. Shoe was founded with the merger of two Cincinnati shoe manufacturing companies. The United States Shoe Company, owner of Red Cross Shoes, had struggled to stay in business throughout the 1920s. Joseph S. Stern Sr. and A.B. Cohen of the Stern-Auer Company recognized the potential of owning a well-known brand name like Red Cross Shoes, especially in difficult economic times. In 1931 the United States Shoe Company and the Stern-Auer Company merged and became the United States Shoe Corporation. Stern was named chairman and Cohen president of the newly formed corporation.

The merger that created U.S. Shoe Corporation was a turning point for Red Cross Shoes. Management agreed that in a depression-era economy, dropping the price of shoes was imperative. In a daring merchandising move, U.S. Shoe reduced the retail price of Red Cross Shoes, previously $10 to $12, to $6 per pair. The industry was skeptical, but within two years production soared to 3,000 pairs per day . No U.S. Shoe employee lost a day's work because of the Depression and by 1939 Red Cross Shoes was the world's largest selling brand of quality footwear.

For the next 30 years, Stern and Cohen guided U.S. Shoe to growth and prosperity unparalleled in the footwear industry. In 1934 U.S. Shoe moved to a factory, warehouse and office facility on Herald Avenue in Norwood, Ohio. As the organization grew additional factories and warehouses were purchased and built throughout the Ohio Valley area, Midwest and East. Foreign shoe factories were also utilized to supplement domestic production.

Although Red Cross Shoes temporarily changed its name to Gold Cross Shoes during World War II, the brand never waned in popularity. Today the division includes four lines of quality footwear: Red Cross Shoes, Socialites, Cobbies and Cobbie Cuddlers.

In 1946 shareholders voted to go public, and common stock was registered with the Securities and Exchange Commission. U.S. Shoe was listed for the first time on the New York Stock Exchange.

For the last 30 years, planned expansion and acquisitions have led to prosperity at U.S. Shoe. The corporation began by acquiring additional brands of women's shoes—Selby shoes in 1957 and Joyce shoes in 1960. In 1962 Marx & Newman, Inc. was purchased. A leading importer of high fashion women's footwear, the New York-based division handles Amalfi, Bandolino, Evan-Picone and Liz Claiborne shoes. Pappagallo, Inc. was acquired in 1968, and Capezio was purchased in 1974. In addition to women's footwear, U.S. Shoe acquired Texas Brand Boots of Lebanon, Tennessee, which makes footwear for the entire family.

The company expanded into retailing in 1963 with purchase of the Wm. Hahn & Co. shoe stores. Today U.S. Shoe owns three retail footwear operations: Cincinnati Shoe, Corporate Concept and Banister Shoe stores.

In 1968 Phil G. Barach was elected president of U.S. Shoe, and in 1969 the company branched out into another area of the fashion industry, specialty apparel retailing. U.S. Shoe bought Casual Corner, a small chain of clothing stores designed for fashion-conscious young women. U.S. Shoe has continued to expand and add more apparel retailing divisions, including August Max, Caren Charles, Petite Sophisticate, Ups 'N Downs, T.H. Mandy and Cabaret.

U.S. Shoe celebrated its 50th anniversary in 1981 by moving to a new corporate headquarters in Eastwood Village, Cincinnati. A raw materials warehouse, finished goods distribution center and corporate office building operate from three new buildings on the 50-acre site.

In 1984 U.S. Shoe entered the eyewear field with the purchase of LensCrafters, then a three store chain. The stores feature an on-site optical laboratory enabling LensCrafters to promise finished eyewear in about an hour.

U.S. Shoe has continued to expand, with over 1,700 apparel stores, 250 superoptical stores and 400 footwear stores now in operation. The corporation that began in 1931 with 160 people now employs nearly 40,000, and it has paid cash dividends for 56 consecutive years.

On August 15, 1988, U.S. Shoe announced that it is in the process of evaluating various strategies for maximizing shareholder value, including the possible sale of the entire company or parts of the company, or a restructuring. The company noted, however, that while it will explore a number of alternatives, there is no assurance that any transaction will result from the process.

Advertisement for Red Cross Shoes from *The Saturday Evening Post* (May 26, 1917). Red Cross Shoes became a famous brand name because of advertisements such as this which were run in national magazines. Irwin Krohn and Samuel Fechheimer, who founded the Krohn-Fechheimer Shoe Company in 1896, pioneered in the development of a "brand philosophy." Their branded shoe gave the retailer a saleable item which he could count on year after year. It gave these shoe manufacturers an edge in the fiercely competitive national market. By the time the National American Red Cross was incorporated in 1905, the Red Cross Shoe was an established brand sold by leading merchants all over the country. Clipping courtesy of U.S. Shoe Corporation.

University of Cincinnati

The University of Cincinnati traces its origins to 1819, the year of the founding of the Cincinnati College and the Medical College of Ohio. In 1870 the City of Cincinnati established the University of Cincinnati, which later absorbed the earlier institutions. UC created the first cooperative education program in the United States in 1906 through its College of Engineering.

For many years UC was the second-oldest and second-largest municipal university in the country. In 1967 it became a "municipally-sponsored, state-affiliated" institution, entering a transitional period that culminated on July 1, 1977, when UC became one of Ohio's state universities.

Cincinnatians have always had a desire for education. The first attempt by the citizenry to create a college occurred in 1805, when the city was less than 20 years old and its population was under 1,000. In 1809 another attempt was made— this time through a lottery. Yet both efforts were unsuccessful, as was a Lancasterian Seminary, founded in 1815.

In 1819, due to the tireless energy of the indomitable Daniel Drake— physician, scholar, teacher and lecturer— the Ohio Legislature chartered Cincinnati College and the Medical College of Ohio, the two oldest units of UC.

The two stone lions that stand in front of UC's McMicken Hall have become the most recognizable symbols of the university. "Mick" and "Mack" originally guarded the Hoffner estate in Cumminsville and are copies of statues in the Loggia del Lanzi in Florence, Italy.

News of the incorporation was acclaimed by the citizens of Cincinnati. They took great pride in the college building. A faculty of three members was secured, and within three years after the college opened, the first commencement was held and three students graduated. But lack of funds and internal friction handicapped both the Cincinnati College and the Medical College of Ohio, and they languished.

In 1835 Cincinnati College was revived with medical and law departments and an observatory that boasted the largest telescope in the world at that time. The institution's president was William Holmes McGuffey, author of the famous readers. But financial trouble, internal friction and the coming of war again prevented the institution from achieving success.

An unexpected boost to higher education in Cincinnati came in 1858 when Charles McMicken, a wealthy merchant and landowner, bequeathed the bulk of his estate to the city to establish a university. McMicken's munificent gift provided the foundation of the University of Cincinnati, which the Ohio Legislature chartered as a municipal university in 1870.

During the course of the next century, a number of local educational institutions merged with the University of Cincinnati, including the colleges of Medicine, Law and Pharmacy—each of them the oldest colleges of its kind west of the Alleghenies. Also merging with UC before 1970 were the esteemed College-Conservatory of Music; the College of Applied Science, founded in 1828 as the Ohio Mechanics Institute; and the Cincinnati Observatory.

During its first century UC developed colleges of Engineering, Business, Education, Nursing and Art. But by the mid-1960s it was apparent that its days as a municipal institution were numbered. The city's resources could not accommodate the rapidly growing student body and aging physical plant. The State of Ohio offered relief through state affiliation, but a decade later even this partial adaption had run its course. UC joined the ranks of Ohio's state universities on July 1, 1977.

UC has been the source of many contributions to society, including the oral polio vaccine, the first program of cooperative education, the first electronic organ, the first safe anti-knock gasoline and the first antihistamine.

McMicken Hall, shown here as it looked 1894-1947, is named for Charles McMicken, who bequeathed the bulk of his estate to the city to establish a university. Photographs courtesy of University of Cincinnati.

In recent years UC has gained international attention for studies on the vibration analysis of structures, lipid research and laser brain surgery.

The U.S. Department of Education has commended UC for recruiting and graduating an exceptional number of minority graduate students compared to other predominantly white institutions.

The university has received a major technology incentive grant through the Thomas Alva Edison Program of the Ohio Development Office. This grant supports the activities of the UC-affiliated Institute for Advanced Manufacturing Sciences, an organization established to conduct research and technology transfer of manufacturing innovation to Ohio industries.

Eight of UC's undergraduate programs have been recognized through the Ohio Board of Regents' Program Excellence Awards— more than any other state university. Nine of UC's graduate programs have been honored through the state's Eminent Scholars program.

Sponsored research awards have increased dramatically in recent years, solidifying UC's standing as one of the few urban universities in the country that can also be called a comprehensive research institution. Of the 5,000 American colleges and universities, UC is among only 75 receiving the prestigious Research I standing from the Carnegie Commission.

The University of Cincinnati has become an intellectual magnet for southern Ohio, contributing to the prosperity of the city, state, nation and world through its faculty's distinguished teaching and research and the accomplishments of more than 130,000 living alumni.

A key word in any description of UC is "diversity," a term that accurately describes UC's 36,000 students, who represent all 50 states and 83 foreign countries, and the 500 degree programs offered by UC's 18 colleges and divisions.

An outstanding feature of many of UC's colleges is the cooperative education, or "professional practice" program, first offered in the United States at UC in 1906. It allows students the opportunity to alternate academic quarters of classroom instruction and salaried, on-the-job experience. Today UC's 4,000 co-op students work in 36 states and 11 foreign countries for 1,100 employers.

University of Cincinnati Medical Center

In 1800 a 15-year-old boy named Daniel Drake arrived in Cincinnati to begin a four-year "apprenticeship" in medicine. The town then was a settlement of about 150 people, and Drake, like everyone on the Northwest Frontier, was expected to be a jack-of-all-trades. Besides learning medicine the conditions of his indenture to Dr. William Goforth required him to keep the physician's books, compound medicine, make pills, and feed, water, curry and saddle his master's horse. He had "but little time to study," Drake wrote to his father, up river in Mays Lick, Kentucky.

Luckily for today's medical education, research and care, the young Drake found the time.

After a year Dr. Goforth awarded him a diploma in medicine, the first issued west of the Alleghenies. Drake then rode for 18 days on horseback to Philadelphia for another six months' medical study at the University of Pennsylvania. Two years later, after practicing medicine in Kentucky, he returned to Cincinnati and began the phase of his career that was to permanently influence the life of the community.

Within a few years of his return, Drake had helped found Cincinnati's first circulating library, opened a drug store and published observations on local plant life and environmental health. He established a medical society and a literary group, and he urged City Council to adopt public health legislation. Then he left once more for Philadelphia to complete his medical degree.

Drake again returned to Cincinnati in 1818 with a new and significant vision—to establish a medical school that would be affiliated with a public hospital. On January 19, 1819 he obtained a charter from the Ohio General Assembly to establish his school, the Medical College of Ohio. It was only the second such school west of the Alleghenies. The first, at Transylvania University in Lexington, later went out of existence.

The Medical College's first class of 24 students met for the first time on November 1, 1820 in a room over a store owned by Drake's father. By the time that first meeting took place, the entrepreneurial Drake was already planning his next move.

Two months later he persuaded the Ohio Legislature to pass a second charter, this time establishing a hospital where medical students could practice the medicine they were studying. In Drake's words, "It is in hospitals that lectures on practical or clinical medicine must be delivered."

The Commercial Hospital and Lunatic Asylum became the first public hospital in the nation whose charter gave clinical teaching rights to a specific medical college. Thus it was in Cincinnati that the concept of the teaching hospital was born, and the nation's great academic medical centers grew out of it.

The Commercial Hospital was built on a four-acre lot at the corner of 12th Street and Central Avenue, where the Music Hall parking garage now stands. It served as a refuge for the city's elderly, orphaned and poor. The orphans moved out in 1833, when the Cincinnati Orphan Asylum was built. The poor and elderly transferred to the Cincinnati Infirmary in 1852, and the next year a separate institution for the insane was built.

Despite changes in name and location and tremendous strides in the scope and quality of care provided, the same relationship continues between the college and the hospital as was forged by Daniel Drake in the early 1800s. The Medical College of Ohio is today the University of Cincinnati College of Medicine, and the Commercial Hospital has become the University Hospital. Together with the colleges of Pharmacy and Nursing and Health, they are major components of what is now the University of Cincinnati Medical Center.

On January 1, 1962 the City of Cincinnati handed over administration of the hospital to the University of Cincinnati's board of directors, and in 1967 the hospital's tax support base was extended to all Hamilton County residents. The current main University Hospital building opened on Goodman Street in 1969.

The medical center has come a long way since the days of Daniel Drake, but his pioneering spirit persists and has made the center the site of many national and international "firsts." The most widely known achievement, perhaps, is Albert Sabin's development of the oral polio vaccine that saved the lives of countless thousands of children throughout the world. But this great Cincinnati institution also started the country's first training program for emergency medicine physicians, and it boasts the region's only verified Level-1 trauma center and Level-3 perinatal research and treatment center for high-risk mothers and their infants, both of which are the top categories in their fields.

The UC Medical Center started the first university-based environmental research center in the United States, and it has pioneered studies on the environmental hazards of radioactivity and lead poisoning.

University Hospital is one of the major treatment centers for adult burns in the country. The hospital has the most modern operating rooms and anesthesia services, and its surgeons have pioneered laser surgery for previously inoperable brain tumors and run the region's only heart transplantation program.

The College of Medicine, direct descendent of Daniel Drake's brainchild, trains 80% of the physicians in the Greater Cincinnati area, and its College of Pharmacy and 100-year-old College of Nursing prepare most of the area's pharmacists and nurses.

Cincinnati's bicentennial year saw the opening of the Barrett Center for Cancer Research and Treatment, which will consolidate the medical center's many cancer services in one single and easily accessible facility. It will soon open a new trauma center with state-of-the-art emergency, surgery and intensive care facilities. And to keep pace with consumer demand for comprehensive health care that is also convenient and close to home, the medical center will open a new Medical Arts Building adjacent to University Hospital, as well as satellite facilities in suburbs throughout Cincinnati.

Today's medical center continues its commitment to social and scientific innovation, the intellectual legacy of a pioneer doctor described by historian James Flexner as "a frontiersman of the mind." The pioneering spirit continues on medical frontiers that Daniel Drake at his most insightful could never have imagined.

Today's University Hospital, dynamic successor to the General Hospital, is expanding rapidly. In the left foreground is the new Charles M. Barrett Center for Cancer Research and Treatment, which houses all of the University of Cincinnati Medical Center's cancer services and is the most comprehensive and advanced cancer center in the region. Photograph. Courtesy of the University of Cincinnati.

Western and Southern Life Insurance Company

The story of Western and Southern Life Insurance Company is not one of fits and starts. The company has been growing ever since William J. and Charles F. Williams incorporated it on February 23, 1888.

With $100,000 in capital the Williams brothers started one of the first insurance companies that wrote policies with premiums collected on a weekly basis at home. William, the elder brother, wrote the application for the first policy, issued on May 7, 1888. Eleven policies were issued the first week, and nine of these remained in force until maturity. Western-Southern expanded into Louisville the same month.

During the next two years the company opened offices in several major Ohio and Kentucky cities. Today it operates in 42 states through 250 sales and service offices.

Assets have skyrocketed from $104,307 the first year to more than $4.7 billion for the company and its affiliates today, and insurance in force from $889,073 to $36.3 billion, making Western-Southern the largest mutual life insurance company in Ohio and 46th in the country.

Over the years the company's Cincinnati headquarters have reflected this growth. Western-Southern began operations in a three-room suite in the Bodmann Building at 621 Main Street. By 1894 the six-year-old concern had outgrown those quarters and moved to a three-story stone building at 634 West Sixth Street. Seven years later the company bought the site of its current location at Fourth and Broadway. It was the former Edmund Dexter home, a fine private residence that hosted many luminaries. Western-Southern built a new headquarters building on this spot in 1916 and added to it in 1923, 1935, 1949, 1958 and 1961.

William J. Williams followed Dr. Frank Caldwell as the second president of the company and oversaw its expansion until he died in 1930. His brother, Charles, succeeded him.

Charles F. Williams once attributed the strong growth of the company to hard work and close attention to details. "My brother and I watched every investment and nearly every policy," he said. "For 21 years we got no cash dividends and very little salary."

Charles also said that he would not want the insurance in force to get so large that it precluded personal supervision. "I would like to pass the billion dollar mark," he said, "but we would not want to get much larger than that." A decade later, however, with Williams still presiding and Western-Southern going into its first year as a mutual company, insurance in force reached $2 billion.

Following Charles' death in 1950, his son, Charles M., a vice president since 1934, succeeded him. William C. Safford became the president of Western-Southern in 1957, when Charles M. moved up to chairman of the board.

In the three years after Safford took over as president of Western-Southern, the company grew as much as it had in the first 55 years. Assets increased by $280 million to more than $1 billion, fueled in part by the acquisition in 1957 and 1958 of four strategically located companies that increased Western-Southern's operating territory from 15 states to 42 plus the District of Columbia.

During Safford's remarkable tenure Western-Southern also bought Southern Ohio Bank and Eagle Savings Association (both later sold) and became heavily involved in downtown construction. The insurer financed construction of two downtown parking garages and the 580 Building at Sixth and Walnut streets. It also built luxury apartments at 550 East Fourth Street.

Safford advanced to board chairman in 1973 when Executive Vice President Dr. Charles M. Barrett, a practicing physician and a 30-year veteran of the company, became president and chief executive officer. Charles M. Williams moved over to chairman of the executive committee.

In 1988, during the company's 100th year, another William J. Williams, the second son of Charles F. Williams, ascended to president and chief executive officer upon Barrett's retirement as chief executive officer.

Barrett continues to serve as chairman of the board. During his 15 years of leadership, Western-Southern and affiliated companies' assets increased from $2.1 billion to $4.7 billion, and insurance in force grew from $10.6 billion to $36.3 billion, ranking the company as one of the giants in the industry. Policyholders' surplus of $541.5 million places the company as one of the most financially strong of all mutual life insurance companies in the country. Barrett's humanitarian achievements in the fields of medicine, education and business earned him the "Great Living Cincinnatian" Award in 1987.

Williams, the son of one of the founders, has been associated with the company since 1937. He has served on the board of directors of many business, educational, charitable, sports and civic organizations and is an outstanding executive to lead the company into its second century.

Between 1901 and 1914 the offices of The Western and Southern Life Insurance Company were in the grand Edmund Dexter house at the corner of Fourth Street and Broadway. When expanding business required new headquarters, the company built on the same site. Western-Southern preserved a relic of the old mansion by engaging Charles F. Williams' father, a former cabinetmaker, to convert the massive doors of the Dexter house into a director's table for the new building.

This dignified structure with elegant ionic columns anchors the Fourth Street and Broadway corner of the Western-Southern block. It was described as the "main office" in 1916 when it was designed by Harry Hake and Charles Kuck. Courtesy of The Western and Southern Life Insurance Company.

Whiting Manufacturing Company Inc.

The Whiting Manufacturing Company Inc., maker and marketer of quality bedspreads, comforters, pillows and other domestic textile products, was founded in 1949 by Carson Ross Whiting.

Born in 1910 Carson Ross graduated from Norwood High School in 1928 and the University of Cincinnati, where he received a degree in Commercial Engineering, in 1933. In 1937 he married Kathryn Townsley. The couple had a daughter, Clair Ann Sharpless, and twin sons, Richard Townsley Whiting and David Ross Whiting.

Following his graduation from the University of Cincinnati, Whiting began working for the Cincinnati Bell Telephone Co. in 1933 and a year later joined Gano and Cherrington, a local accounting firm that later merged with Arthur Andersen & Co. He left this position to become the assistant controller of McAlpin's department store in 1935, becoming store superintendent a year later and home furnishings buyer in 1937. From 1941 to 1949 he was national home furnishings buyer for the Montgomery Ward Company in New York City.

Through these positions he learned enough about manufacturing and marketing textile home products to convince himself that he could do as good a job as any in the industry. Montgomery Ward apparently agreed with him, for in 1949 the firm gave him a contract to produce several thousand satin and taffeta bed comforters despite his lack of experience, employees and a factory. He made delivery on time.

Whiting quickly demonstrated his independent spirit by choosing to locate his plant on a three-acre site at 9701 Kenwood Road in then-rural Blue Ash when most American textile manufacturers were moving their plants to low-wage areas in the rural South. Today the firm is the major remaining textile manufacturer outside the South.

From its first year of operation, when the Whiting Manufacturing Company's sales were under $2 million, sales grew to over $15 million by 1970. A 1980 *Cincinnati Enquirer* article ranked the company with private firms enjoying $15 million to $24 million in annual sales. It is now one of the larger 100 family owned firms in Cincinnati.

To keep pace with the rise in sales, the company had to expand nearly two dozen times. Between 1949 and 1970 alone, Whiting enlarged his original plant space 11 times, to 80,000 square feet. His first manufacturing plant and office building soon gave way to more elaborate facilities. Having outgrown the Kenwood Road site, he moved to a new, 12-acre site at 9999 Carver Road in the Blue Ash Industrial Park, where he erected a 120,000-square-foot building and 5,000-square-foot office. Between 1970 and 1977 additions to the building expanded space to 210,000 square feet. Today the firm occupies 300,000 square feet on 23 acres.

The number of Whiting employees grew equally dramatically, from six in 1949 to 225 in 1970 and about 450, including 50 office personnel, in 1988. Most of its employees are women, which generally is the case in the textile industry. In 1958 the company adopted a profit-sharing plan for its employees, whom Whiting credited as the primary reason for his company's success.

Whiting has also greatly expanded its range of products. In the 1950s it stopped making satin and taffeta comforters, changing over to cotton and polyester. Today all its comforters are polyester-filled, and it uses 100-150 different printed covers styles. In 1954 the company began making polyester-filled pillows; a year later, bed spreads and drapes, and in 1958 it added a line of down and feather-filled pillows and patchwork quilts. Whiting had established a nationwide distribution system by 1960.

The company patented, manufactured and marketed a "comforter pouch," an indoor sleeping bag which can be used as a body garment, or be unsnapped and used as a bed cover. This item was invented by Richard Whiting and became a very big seller for a time during the energy crisis of the late 1970s. The company continues to seek new products and is now marketing flannel and cotton/polyester bed sheets.

By 1980 Whiting's sales staff had grown to include 22 independent sales representatives and a New York showroom on Fifth Avenue. Here the company conducts "major market weeks" four times a year for major buyers. Rather than employ high-priced, big-name, outside designers, the company established its own designer/stylist staff in New York and began to market its products as "Whiting Fifth Avenue." The company regularly sells to Sears, Roebuck & Co., Montgomery Ward, J.C. Penney and other fine department stores nationwide. And since 1979 Whiting has marketed its overrun products through three outlet stores in the Cincinnati area.

The Whiting Company specializes in customer service, offering very fast delivery to large buyers, which allows them to maintain smaller inventories. It targets the middle of market rather than making the highest or lowest priced products in the industry. The firm has built its reputation on high quality; fashion consciousness, introducing new styles every six months; superior marketing and advertising techniques; and advanced management.

Whiting could produce 35,000 to 40,000 comforters a week in 1980 by running two shifts in certain seasons. Many high-speed production techniques were developed by the company itself. However, the firm continued to seek ways to improve efficiency. In 1985 it began using advanced, high-speed, automated sewing machines imported from Sweden. From 1983 to 1988 the company produced an average of 1 million to 1.2 million comforters annually. A new state-of-the-art computer system currently being installed and scheduled to become operational in 1989 will add to productivity and customer service.

Technically the company operates a single plant in Blue Ash, but it also has a very close relationship with Barkley Home Products of Cherokee, North Carolina, which makes similar bedroom products. Wholly owned by his son, Richard Townsley Whiting, this firm shares production facilities with Whiting Manufacturing from time to time.

Beginning in the mid-1960s, both of Carson R. Whiting's twin sons joined him in the firm. David Ross Whiting served as executive vice president from 1964 until his untimely death at age 35 in 1978. Richard, who began working at the Whiting Manufacturing Company in 1966, rose to become president of the firm and, since his father's retirement in 1987, has succeeded him as president and chief executive officer. Richard's wife Donna currently serves as treasurer of the company. And a third generation of Whitings is waiting in the wings.

The Whiting Manufacturing Company, with 450 employees, is situated on a 23-acre site on Carver Road in the Blue Ash Industrial Park. Photograph courtesy of Whiting Manufacturing Company.

The Williamson Company

Andrew Wilson Williamson helped finance the Bennett & Peck Heating and Ventilating Company, later renamed The Williamson Company, featured in this 1891 ad. Illustration courtesy of the City of Cincinnati; published by Times Star Publishing.

Cincinnati was fertile soil for The Williamson Company, which will celebrate its 100th anniversary in 1990.

The fascinating story began with the birth of the founder, Andrew Wilson Williamson ("A.W."), on a small farm outside of little Russellville, Ohio. One of six children, he shared the business insights of his father, a village entrepreneur. The boy was caught up in the action and developed a remarkable sensibility to opportunities. Eventually he held stock in 26 corporations, and at the time of his death in 1931, his personal fortune was well over $1 million.

Something of a whiz at school assignments as a youngster, he spent 24 years as an educator before becoming an executive at Bennett & Peck in 1890. The firm, a partnership of C.H. Bennett and George Peck, was located at 245-249 West Fifth Street. It had commenced operations the previous year to manufacture and sell furnaces for homes and industry. It's clear that Williamson jumped in with both feet. In 1890 "Bennett & Peck Heating and Ventilating Company" was incorporated with a total capitalization of $100,000, and a quarter of that amount was provided by A.W.

The following year his younger brother, William Carey Williamson ("W.C."), joined the enterprise. The tide was with them, and the company became respected for its integrity and superior designs. In just two years the firm's name was changed for a second time to The Peck, Williamson Heating and Ventilating Company, since Bennett had withdrawn. A surge of growth brought about physical expansion in 1895. A site at 335-339 West Fifth Street, only a block west of the prior location, was chosen for the erection of a six-story structure, reputedly the first reinforced concrete building west of the Alleghenies.

A third name change occurred in 1903 when George Peck became too ill to manage. The Peck, Williamson Foundry Company had A.W. as president and W.C. as secretary.

In 1908 the firm bought a farm on Madison Road in Oakley, about eight miles from its downtown offices. The next year the Wellston Foundry, purchased in 1902, was moved to the new site. Five years later, in 1914, the firm was officially named The Williamson Heater Company. This appellation appeared on the new Oakley main office building, next to the factory at 3500 Madison Road, when it was completed in 1952.

Two years later, in recognition of the air-cooling and filtering features in some of Williamson's furnace systems as well as the expansion of its product line, a fifth identity tag was devised. The Williamson Company designation has lasted to the present day, and the simplification goes well with its modern logo, a low, double dipped "W."

Williamson's has long been regarded as a good, stable place to work. A self-made man, A.W. and his management philosophy could be summed up in his statement: "Believe in somebody; then back him to the limit." He clearly took pleasure in promoting from within.

The company also hired minority group members. In the early 20th century, the Oakley foundry was known as the largest employer of blacks in the Cincinnati region. In 1943 *The Cincinnati Union*, a black newspaper, credited the company with being "first in the city to hire blacks for industrial work." Moreover, this was said to be "over the opposition of fellow businessmen who scoffed at this attitude and tried to discourage them from continuing these practices."

Another well-publicized personnel effort took place between 1938 and 1965. Based on Charles P. McCormick's multiple management approach, a plan that came to be known in Cincinnati business circles as "The Williamson Way" was initiated. Essentially, junior boards, composed of lower-level managers, took part in upper-level decision making.

Top managers who followed the term of the founder are: William C. Williamson (1931-1943); William L. McGrath (1943-1961); Lawrence B. Murphy (1961-1965); Robert L. Hermann (1965-1975); William D. Wilder (1974-1986); Mary J. Boone (1986-1988); and, under new ownership, John D. Carroll (1988-   ).

The founding Williamson was a research enthusiast. While still teaching school in the 1870s, he developed plans for a new furnace grate. The firm's later product innovations include: the underfeed furnace (1893); the two-piece radiator, flat grate and water pan (1908); the pipeless furnace (1920); gas or coal combination furnace (1924); the cast iron furnace with one-piece radiators (1930).

Other product changes included restyled furnace castings; shifts to steel from cast iron; introduction of blowers and thermostats; and oil or gas combination furnaces. Total heating and cooling units, which first appeared in the immediate post-World War II period, have been developed into ever more efficient systems. Present company research concentrates on exceeding government energy specifications and on some revolutionary breakthroughs.

The product line was also expanded. The Madison plant, built for steel furnace fabrication after World War II, continues today with the manufacture of containers for the military and special products for communications and other industries. Still another plant, in Hillsboro, Ohio, makes pipe and fittings for the parent Oakley plant as well as custom work for outside firms. Despite rising costs The Williamson Company has held to its traditional virtues of quality, durability, value and individualized services.

All things change, and new-style winds cooled the board's resistance to a stack of takeover offers. Laws, interest rates and increased operating costs in the 1980s had popularized this hard decision both nationally and locally among some of Cincinnati's most respected firms. In March 1988 Williamson reached an agreement with the Jay Carroll Co., an energetic team of management specialists headed by John D. Carroll, Robert L. McGrath (son of an earlier president), Robert H. Carroll and James J. Carroll (John's brothers).

The Carroll approach is calculated to ensure the firm's survival and enhance its capital creating ability through new management techniques. A revealing glimpse of its performance came immediately in the form of more stylish advertising. An overall pattern of operations updating is gradually being put into place.

Anniversaries are occasions for celebrating accomplishments and voicing dreams. They enable us to take stock and move forward into an intentional future. As part of its centennial celebration, the firm will publish a detailed corporate history, *The Williamson Company: A Century of Caring*, by Dr. George Gore.

Witt Industries, Inc.

There's a lot of Witt around Cincinnati. It's a matter of knowing where to look, for the company's history is evident both high and low—from decorative metal cornices on 19th-century buildings to new swing-top waste receptacles on city sidewalks. In many respects Witt Industries exemplifies the old-fashioned ingredients that made so many Cincinnati manufactures successful: it built upon the craft tradition and adapted its operation to changing social and economic conditions.

George C. Witt, born in Cincinnati in 1851, founded The Witt Cornice Co. in 1887. Located in the old Eureka Hall on Walnut Street, the firm originally did roofing and custom-made decorative cornices for homes and commercial buildings. Construction work in those days was limited to the summertime, and very soon George Witt was investigating other products to give year-round employment to his skilled workers.

Witt recognized the need for a sturdy covered container that could provide for the safe and sanitary disposal of ashes and garbage. At that time uncovered wooden barrels and boxes were standard set-out containers for waste collection, and the crowded 19th century city was plagued by fires resulting from hot ashes placed in wooden containers and health hazards from uncovered garbage. He designed a corrugated metal hot-dip galvanized can with a tight-fitting cover. Metal made it fire-proof; corrugation provided strength; galvanization provided rust protection. Patented in 1899, Witt's first mass-produced line was a great success.

The Witt cinder guard was another turn-of-the-century product which, like the ash can, was designed to control the danger of hot ashes. The cinder guard was attached to railroad cars. It shielded the mail clerk's face and eyes from flying cinders while he retrieved mail bags from the moving train. Witt sold thousands of cinder guards to railroads across the country before the conversion to diesel engines made the product obsolete.

As sales grew the company abandoned custom work in favor of manufacturing. George Witt's son, J. Wilbur (commonly known as J.W.), joined the firm in 1907. When his father died in 1910, he became general manager of the company. George's widow, Mary, became president. J.W. Witt expanded product lines and increased production capability with a move in 1912 from its second location on Broadway to its third home on Winchell Avenue near Redland Field. That year the company also changed from a partnership to a corporation.

J.W. launched a successful sales and advertising program which soon put Witt cans in leading hardware and home-furnishing stores across the nation. He became president in 1921 and continued to look for new ways to make use of the company's unique capabilities. He expanded the galvanizing operation to take jobs from other manufacturers of steel products. Galvanizing protects steel from rust and corrosion by sealing it with a zinc coating. Then and now, Witt's galvanizing jobs are all about the city and the nation. It treats items as large as structural steel members for piers, bridges and high-rise buildings, and items as small as nuts and bolts. In 1926 the Winchell Avenue site was expanded onto Patterson Street in a new plant equipped with two larger galvanizing kettles.

The great depression had an adverse effect upon Witt but the company managed to give at least part-time employment to all of its people. In those years Witt went into direct-mail retailing with a revolutionary canning device, "Mrs. Bunting's Cold Pack Canner." While the canner had distinct practical and safety advantages over the volatile hot-pack canners, it never generated sufficient demand to keep it in production.

J.W. Witt's son, Jim, joined the firm in 1947 and succeeded his father as president in 1957. The custom galvanizing aspect of the business expanded in the late 1950s and 1960s with the acquisition of galvanizing operations in Indianapolis and Muncie, Indiana. Witt had become the largest independent job-galvanizing company in the Midwest by 1958 when the Cincinnati operation moved from the old West End to a new plant on Steel Place in Oakley. The company also changed its name from The Witt Cornice Co. to The Witt Co.

A complete line of wastebaskets was introduced in 1964. And in recognition of the diversification and expansion of product lines, the name of the parent company was changed to Witt Industries, Inc. The Witt Company became a subsidiary for job-galvanizing work; Witt Products, Inc. became a subsidiary for manufacturing and marketing galvanized and painted products for the office and janitorial markets.

Witt's national reputation has been built upon the quality of its galvanizing work and the dependability of its products. The motto, "If the lid fits, it's a Witt," was developed to point up the superiority of the galvanized trash can with the tight-fitting lid and a lifetime guarantee. It was put to a light-hearted but memorable test at the Cincinnati Zoo. Witt cans were filled with fish and honey, then placed in the bear pits. The Kodiaks growled, chewed and pawed, but got nowhere. The polar bears, at long last, succeeded in prying open the cans but only with a team effort that is unlikely to be replicated in the wilds. Maybe that's why Witt containers are in so many national parks today.

Through the years the Witt Company has remained a family operation. Jim Witt died in 1971 and J.W. Witt asked his son-in-law, a member of the board of directors since 1954, to become chief executive officer. Bob Wydman's background prepared him well for the task. The grandson of H. Edward Brunhoff, founder of a Cincinnati metal specialties company, Wydman was also one of the founders of The Ohmart Corporation. Under his direction Witt's galvanizing markets were expanded and the waste container and receptacle product lines were updated and enlarged. Bob Wydman died in 1984, and Mary Witt Wydman, Bob's wife and J.W.'s daughter, became chairman and chief executive officer.

In 1987 The Witt Company proudly celebrated its 100th anniversary. Under Mary's direction the beginning of Witt's second century has been explosive. In 1988 Witt acquired the painted receptacle line of the F.H. Lawson Company, more than doubling Witt's product sales; Witt also built a new state-of-the-art galvanizing plant in Muncie, Indiana; and the fourth generation of the family entered the business. Bob and Mary's daughter, Marcy R. Wydman, joined Witt as vice president of finance/business development. Marcy joins Mary in building the company's future, driven by Witt's newest corporate motto: "If you rest, you will rust."

Polar bears at the Cincinnati Zoo attempt to pry loose the tight-fitting lid from a Witt galvanized can filled with honey and fish. The Witt design was patented in 1899 and has made a national reputation for the Cincinnati company. Witt containers are used in many national parks throughout the United States. Photograph courtesy of *The Cincinnati Post.*

Thomas E. Wood, Inc.

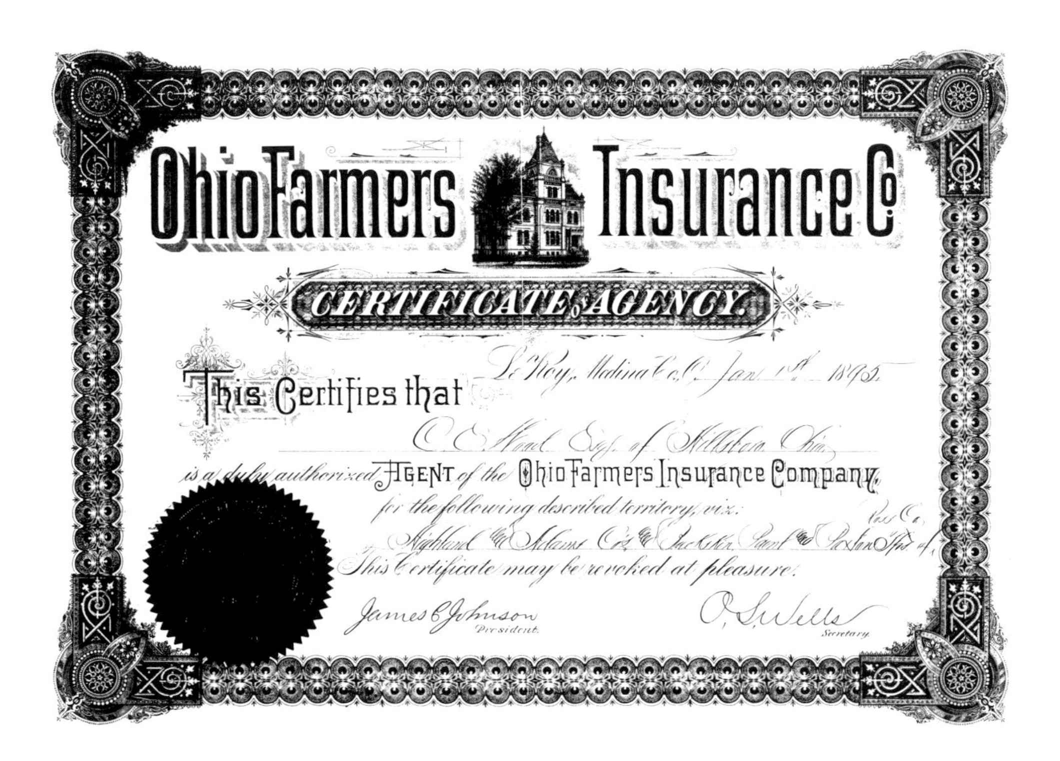

Ohio Farmers Insurance Co

CERTIFICATE OF AGENCY

Le Roy, Medina Co. O. Jan 1st 1895

This Certifies that C. E. Wood Esq. of Hillsboro Ohio

is a duly authorized AGENT of the Ohio Farmers Insurance Company, for the following described territory, viz:

This Certificate may be revoked at pleasure.

James Johnson, President

Secretary

This original certificate from the Ohio Farmers Insurance Company, dated 1895, designated Thomas E. Wood an authorized agent in three Ohio counties.

The Thomas E. Wood, Inc. insurance agency has been active in Cincinnati since 1902 and is currently one of the 50 largest privately owned agencies in the United States. In 1988 Thomas E. Wood was asked to be the insurance advisor and consultant for all Cincinnati Bicentennial activities.

The agency began in Hillsboro, Ohio, 50 miles east of Cincinnati, in 1895 when C.E. Wood, father of Thomas E. Wood, opened a one-man office. C.E. Wood specialized in farm insurance and represented only one company, the Ohio Farmers Insurance Co.

At the turn of the century, C.E. Wood's business consisted primarily of insuring barns and horses against fire and storm-related damages. In 1902 Wood moved his family and his business to Mt. Healthy.

Thomas Wood's start in the insurance business came on the seat of a buckboard wagon, listening to his father as they traveled over country roads to meet with farmers in southwestern Ohio. After World War I the elder Wood became ill and was about to sell the company when Thomas, just out of the Marine Corps, asked for a chance to run the business.

Thomas expanded the business by concentrating on the rapidly growing automobile insurance market. The company payroll jumped from two to nine, and in 1927 the firm moved to downtown Cincinnati to the Atlas Bank Building on Walnut Street.

That year also marked the company's largest single contract to date. The insurance carrier for a local automobile finance company was about to cancel all its coverage. Wood immediately contacted the finance company's president and delivered a forceful presentation. The next morning he won the contract. First-year premiums from that single account netted as much or more than all the other company's business put together and is considered the firm's critical transition point.

In 1932 the agency became one of the original tenants in the Carew Tower and remains one its largest. During the 1930s and 1940s, the company expanded by purchasing the Cincinnati Underwriters Agency, which was heavily involved in placing insurance for large industrial and mercantile accounts, and by forming the Wood Underwriters Agency in Covington to handle insurance on distilleries throughout Kentucky.

The Cincinnati Underwriters Agency occupied the old Cuvier Press Club Building on Garfield Place before moving to Carew Tower in 1940. Wood Underwriters Agency has remained in Northern Kentucky, presently in Edgewood.

Since the 1940s Thomas E. Wood, Inc. has purchased many other agencies, including the W.E. Lord Company in 1975; Perkins and Geohegan Agency in 1984; and Brunsman, Curry, and Shepherd in 1985.

In the 1950s Thomas Wood gained prominence locally for his activities outside the insurance business; he was president of the Cincinnati Gardens, chairman of the board of the Cincinnati Royals and a director of the First National Bank. He died in 1961 and was succeeded as president by Leslie C. Graham, who served until 1968. Thomas J. Klinedinst Sr. headed the agency from 1968-1988, when he became chairman of the board and chief executive officer and his son, Thomas Jr., assumed the office of president and chief operating officer.

The officers of the company remain active in community activities and in the national insurance industry as well. The agency has had five presidents of the National Association of Insurance Agents, four presidents of the Ohio Association of Insurance Agents and three presidents of the Cincinnati Insurance Board.

Under the present leadership, Thomas E. Wood, Inc. employs 125 people and has emerged from being principally a property and casualty insurance agency to a multi-line agency with a growing presence in the life and employee benefit areas.

Xtek, Inc.

Many of Cincinnati's industries were started by men who had found a better way to do something. In the case of Xtek, the man was Russell C. Bloomfield, who experimented in a Chicago bicycle shop until he found a better way to harden steel.

Bloomfield's original goal was to make a tougher bearing for bicycles in a town whose cobbled streets were hell on wheels. He built a furnace in the basement of the bicycle shop and perfected his method of hardening steel.

In 1905 his father-in-law, Charles E. Sawtelle, helped him start up in an old blacksmith shop in North Bend, Ohio. Their first job, a set of gears, was for the U.S. Pipe and Foundry Co. at Addyston. After the plant foreman encouraged them to go into the business of making special hardened gears, Sawtelle and Bloomfield incorporated the Tool Steel Motor Gear and Pinion Co. on August 16, 1907.

For most of its life the company that became Xtek was known to Cincinnatians as Tool Steel Gear and Pinion. It was renamed Xtek—short for "exact technology" – in 1976. Its basic product was gears, including pinions, the drive gears in a train of gears. The "tool steel" in its name came from an early laboratory report, which said that the wearing surface of the gear being tested was of tool steel, or cutting steel quality.

The new company's first major customer was the Cincinnati Traction Co. More investors were found, and a new plant was set up in rented space in Carthage. The furnaces for treating steel were new, but the rest of the machinery was second hand. Bloomfield and four men ran the plant; Sawtelle took over sales and office work. Edward E. Dwight, a Cincinnati businessman, and his nephews, Edward L. Brooks and Leroy Brooks Jr., supplied $50,000 working capital to the enterprise.

On March 17, 1909—the day from which Xtek counts its birthday—the company was reorganized as The Tool Steel Gear and Pinion Co. Edward Dwight became president; Leroy Brooks Jr., secretary-treasurer; and Charles Sawtelle vice president and general manager. Dwight did not take an active part, and Leroy Brooks Jr. became the guiding force of the company and its president in 1929. In 1952, after 43 years with the firm, he became chairman of the board.

Edward L. Brooks, a member of the board, became secretary-treasurer in 1923 and later vice president of Sawbrook Steel Castings Co., which had been formed to supply the foundry products needed in Tool Steel's processes. In 1929 he became secretary-treasurer, and in 1940 he was elected vice president of Tool Steel.

Russell Bloomfield eventually left the company to live in California, but Sawtelle remained as senior vice president until his death in 1935. His son, E.S. Sawtelle, eventually became vice president and general manager.

The reorganized company struck it rich in 1910 when the Chicago Street Railway Co. ordered a railroad carload of gears. Tool Steel Gear and Pinion did all of the tool steel processing. (Everything the company made bore one or both of its trademarks: The Tool Steel name or a groove cut either into the side of the wheel or the face of the gear. There never was any debate about the source of a "TSP" product.)

In 1911 the company bought the site of its current Plant #1 on Township Avenue, Elmwood Place. The new plant was ready for production when World War I started. The Elmwood Place plant was enlarged several times, and in 1952 Plant #2 was opened in Sharonville. That plant, too, has undergone several expansions and is now also the site of corporate headquarters.

Product expansion began with an order for electric locomotive gears from a coal mine. Then came inquiries from steel mills and a man named J.P. Biggert. As the company's first independent sales agent, he generated an entirely new range of gear products for the Tool Steel Process in the steel industry.

Xtek's product lines have been expanded over the years and, in addition to gears, now include rolls for cold steel processing, track and brake wheels, and geared spindle couplings. The steel industry is still its major market (Armco was one of its first customers), but it also produces items for mining, paper and cement production. Xtek has two plants outside Cincinnati: the Xtek-Goldman Division of Tempe, Arizona; and Xtek-Canada, Ltd. of Rexdale, Ontario.

The company has had only six chief executives in its long history. Its first president, Edward E. Dwight, was succeeded in 1919 by a lawyer, Lewis N. Gatch. Leroy Brooks Jr. became president in 1929, followed in 1952 by his cousin, LeRoy R. Brooks. In 1961 Sanford M. Brooks, son of Leroy Brooks Jr., was named to the office. James D. Kiggen was elected president in 1979 and in 1985 added the position of chairman, in which capacity he leads Xtek today.

Xtek began a new era in 1986 when it became employee-owned. Given the additional motivation and teamwork achieved through employee equity participation, the company is well positioned to meet the opportunities and challenges of the future.

The Tool Steel Gear and Pinion Company plant in Carthage, Ohio. Photograph (1911). Courtesy of Xtek.

Xtek's Sharonville headquarters and plant opened in 1952. Photograph. Courtesy of Xtek Inc.

Cincinnati: The Queen City Acknowledgements

Cincinnati: The Queen City Bicentennial Edition is a revised and updated version of the book published in 1982 by The Cincinnati Historical Society. Virtually every member of the Society staff had some input on compiling the book. Daniel Hurley, then head of the education department, was the principal author. Director Gale E. Peterson served as managing editor; Laura L. Chace, then and now the Frederick A. Hauck Librarian, wrote captions for the illustrations and compiled the index; and Sue S. Brunsman, Director of Community Development, wrote sidebars.

The textual editor was Edward J. Bedinghaus; proofreader, our now retired reference librarian, Frances Forman; and photographer, Michael Isaacs, who was staff photographer at that time. Leo Hirtl, who had just retired as managing editor of the *Cincinnati Post*, wrote most of the histories for 57 corporate sponsors of the first edition. Mark Eberhard of Eberhard + Eberhard designed the book, and The Hennegan Company printed it.

At the time of its appearance in December 1982, no general history of Cincinnati had been published since the early 20th century, and the Society's beautiful coffee-table book was very well received. The first printing of 15,000 sold quickly, and the second printing of 10,000 is in short supply. Faced with the prospect of a third printing, the Society's staff and board concluded that the occasion of the city's 200th birthday, plus some significant changes in the past six years, particularly in the corporate world, argued for a revised edition.

Once again the staff of the Society worked cooperatively to produce this version of *Cincinnati: The Queen City*. Some of the original team members of the first edition have been involved: Mark Eberhard and The Hennegan Company have given us a handsome product. Gale Peterson headed an invaluable committee of board members who secured the support of more than 80 corporate and community sponsors; Sue Brunsman Painter served as managing editor and with her co-worker in the Community Development Department, Bronwen Howells, edited this expanded sponsor section. Staff historian Greg Rhodes and Manuscripts Supervisor Jonathan Dembo researched and wrote several of the new sponsor histories; Dottie Lewis edited the Bicentennial Essay; and Robin Lippelman and Karen Regina read proofs.

Joseph S. Stern, Jr., who has served as the chairman of the Greater Cincinnati Bicentennial Commission from its inception in 1983, facilitated the inclusion of photographs from the community's bicentennial celebration in this edition. In 1988 he was named a trustee emeritus of the Society, having served as a trustee since his election to the board in December 1972.

The dedication of the Bicentennial Edition of *Cincinnati: The Queen City* to retiring board president John Diehl is a fitting tribute. He joined the board in December 1962, when the membership of the Society was 1,283, became its president in 1974 and stepped down in October 1988. John not only led the Society through years of growth and maturity, he reflected the essence of what the institution should strive to be.

The Society itself was founded in 1831, and its purpose continues to be that of collecting, preserving and communicating information about the history of the Cincinnati region. Within several areas of personal interest ranging from early Cincinnati clocks made by Luman Watson to information about Ohio's covered bridges, John Diehl does all of those things himself. Thus, he has been an ideal leader for the Historical Society as it expanded its membership base to nearly 4,000 and broadened its collecting interests to include three-dimensional artifacts in preparation for launching a museum of Cincinnati history in Union Terminal in 1991.

Virtually all of the illustrations incorporated into the text of this book are drawn from the Society's extensive collections of printed and visual material donated, over a span of 150 years, to help the Historical Society fulfill the mission that John Diehl has cared so much about and served so effectively.

Notes on Sources

The historical overview of *Cincinnati: The Queen City*, the Bicentennial Edition, remains for the most part unchanged. The sources cited below are as valid now as they were for the original, 1982 version. However, there has been an important addition insofar as general works about Greater Cincinnati: *The Bicentennial Guide to Greater Cincinnati: A Portrait of Two Hundred Years* (Cincinnati: 1988).

This encyclopedic study of Greater Cincinnati employs a tour format to trace the development and interrelationship of more than 100 neighborhoods. The book was published by the Society, with staff historians Geoffrey Giglierano and Deborah Overmyer the principal authors. It surely will become an indispensable reference work for Cincinnati history.

Cincinnati: Urban History Sourcebooks, written by School Education Director Karen Regina with Staff Historian Greg Rhodes and published by the Society, are directed toward elementary and middle school children, but the abundant use of original documents and insightful text make these award-winning books useful and stimulating for adults as well.

The name of *The Cincinnati Historical Society Bulletin*, which is referred to frequently below, was changed to *Queen City Heritage* in 1983. It continues to publish articles of scholarly and popular interest, though its new design reflects the warm welcome accorded this book.

Primary sources in the Society library, as well as the works cited above, were used in writing and editing this edition of *Cincinnati: The Queen City*. In 1982 the book attempted to fill a void in the literature available to the general public about the history of the city. Several books of historic photographs were on the market, but none included a substantial narrative text. Numerous scholarly studies also were available as monographs or as articles in journals, but these were not easily accessible for most people. *Cincinnati: The Queen City* drew upon the scholarship of the monographs plus a great body of unpublished research contained in master's theses and doctoral dissertations available at the Cincinnati Historical Society and University of Cincinnati libraries. While many of the illustrations that complement the text had appeared in other works, all of the items shown were drawn from the Society's own collections.

Although researchers from across the United States have contributed to our understanding of Cincinnati's development, Zane L. Miller, professor of history at the University of Cincinnati, deserves special recognition. Not only has he published some of the most insightful and useful research available about Cincinnati, Professor Miller has also directed the work of dozens of graduate students. While much of their research remains unpublished, some of it has appeared in *The Cincinnati Historical Society Bulletin* and other journals, and other parts of it can be found in manuscript form at the University of Cincinnati Library and at the Society.

Several general works published early in the 20th century remain indispensable to the study of Cincinnati's history. Most important of these are: Charles T. Greve, *Centennial History of Cincinnati,* 2 vols. (Chicago, 1904); Charles F. Goss, *Cincinnati: The Queen City,* 4 vols. (Chicago, 1912); Federal Writers' Program of the Work Projects Administration, *Cincinnati: A Guide to the Queen City and Its Neighbors* (Cincinnati, 1943) and Wendell P. Dabney, *Cincinnati's Colored Citizens* (Cincinnati, 1926). A recently published book prepared primarily for use in schools is also valuable: Iola Hessler Silberstein, *Cincinnati Then and Now* (Cincinnati, 1982). The *Cincinnati Historical Society Bulletin,* which began its quarterly publication in 1943 as the *Historical and Philosophical Society of Ohio Bulletin,* is also a useful source of information on Cincinnati's history, containing both scholarly and popular articles on a wide range of subjects pertaining to the city's history. Between 1906 and 1923 the Society issued the *Historical and Philosophical Society of Ohio Quarterly* which reprinted portions of manuscript collections from the library's holdings.

In selecting books and articles for further reading in connection with each chapter, the works were selected both for their importance and their availability. Most are published works, but serious and scholarly investigation of any topic touched upon in *Cincinnati: The Queen City* will require use of primary documents found at the Cincinnati Historical Society, the Rare Books and Special Collections Department of the University of Cincinnati Library and in other area archives as well as the extensive collection of the Public Library of Cincinnati and Hamilton County.

Chapter 1.

Taming the Ohio Wilderness

1788-1830

For a general introduction to early Cincinnati and its relationship to other midwestern cities, see Richard Wade, *The Urban Frontier* (Chicago, 1959); Henry D. Shapiro and Zane L. Miller, eds. *Physician to the West: Selected Writings of Daniel Drake* (Lexington, 1970); Charles N. Glaab, "The Idea of the City and Early Ohio Growth," in *Toward an Urban Ohio,* John Wunder, ed. (Columbus, 1977); and Richard T. Farrell, "Cincinnati 1800-1830: Economic Development Through Trade and Industry," *Ohio History* 77 (Autumn 1968): 111-29. For an interpretation of Indian policy at the time of settlement see Reginald Horsman, "American Indian Policy in the Old Northwest, 1783-1812," *William and Mary Quarterly 18,* series 3 (January 1961): 35-53.

Early development in transportation is explained in Sherry O. Hessler, "Patterns of Transport and Urban Growth in the Miami Valley, Ohio, 1820-1880" (Master's thesis, Johns Hopkins University, 1961) and Harry N. Scheiber, *Ohio Canal Era* (Athens, Ohio, 1969).

The political development of Cincinnati in the early period is discussed in Daniel Aaron, "Cincinnati, 1818-1838" (Ph.D. diss., Harvard University, 1942) and Irwin F. Flack, "Who Governed Cincinnati?" (Ph.D. diss., University of Pittsburgh, 1977).

Chapter 2.

Of Visions and Dreams

1830-1880

For information about the city's major industries and its economic development see Carl Abbott, *Boosters and Businessmen* (Westport, 1981); Stephen C. Gordon, "The City as 'Porkopolis'" (Master's thesis, Miami University, 1981); Margaret Walsh, "The spacial evolution of the Midwestern pork industry, 1835-75," *Journal of Historical Geography* 4 (January 1978): 1-22; and George A. Wing, "The History of the Cincinnati Machine-Tool Industry" (Ph.D. diss., Indiana University, 1964).

For the impact of the railroads on the city see Sherry O. Hessler, " 'The Great Disturbing

Cause' and the Decline of the Queen City," *Historical and Philosophical Society of Ohio Bulletin* 20 (July 1962): 170-85 and John F. Stover, *Iron Road to the West: American Railroads in the 1850s* (New York, 1978).

The nature of mid-19th century Cincinnati society is explained in Walter S. Glazer, "Cincinnati in 1840: A Community Profile" (Ph.D. diss., University of Michigan, 1968); William A. Baughin, "Nativism in Cincinnati Before 1860" (Master's thesis, University of Cincinnati, 1963); Ann D. Michael, "Origins of the Jewish Community in Cincinnati, 1817-1860" (Master's thesis, University of Cincinnati, 1970); Virgil A. Rogers, "The Irish in Cincinnati, 1860-1870" (Master's thesis, University of Cincinnati, 1972); Leonard Harding, "The Negro in Cincinnati, 1860-1870" (Master's thesis, University of Cincinnati, 1967); David L. Calkins, "Black Education in Nineteenth Century Cincinnati," *Cincinnati Historical Society Bulletin* 38 (Summer 1980): 115-28 and Geoffrey Giglierano, "'A Creature of Law:' Cincinnati's Paid Fire Department," *Cincinnati Historical Society Bulletin* 40 (Summer 1982): 79-99.

Information about the cultural flowering of the 1870s may be found in Zane L. Miller, "Music Hall: Its Neighborhood, The City and The Metropolis," in *Cincinnati's Music Hall* (Virginia Beach, 1978); Cincinnati Art Museum, *Art Palace of the West* (Cincinnati, 1981) and Judith Spraul-Schmidt, "The Late Nineteenth Century City and Its Cultural Institutions: The Cincinnati Zoological Garden, 1873-1898" (Master's thesis, University of Cincinnati, 1978).

Chapter 3.
Scramble Up the Hills
1870-1914

The late 19th century reorganization of the city and the formation of new communities or transformation of existing ones are discussed in Richard Rhoda, "Urban Transport and the Expansion of Cincinnati, 1858-1920," *Cincinnati Historical Society Bulletin* 35 (Summer 1977): 130-43; Steven J. Ross, "Workers on the Edge: Work, Leisure and Politics in Industrializing Cincinnati, 1830-1890" (Ph.D. diss., Princeton University, 1980); Henry D. Shapiro and Zane L. Miller, *Clifton: Neighborhood and Community in an Urban Setting* (Cincinnati, 1976); Doris Dwyer, "A Century of City-Building; Three Generations of the Kilgour Family in Cincinnati, 1798-1914" (Ph.D. diss., Miami University, 1979); Margaret Childress, "Norwood, Ohio 1787-1915" (Master's thesis, University of Cincinnati, 1970) and James E. Cebula, "Kennedy Heights: A Fragmented Hilltop Suburb," *Cincinnati Historical Society Bulletin* 34 (Summer 1976): 79-101.

For the political impact of these changes, see Zane L. Miller, *Boss Cox's Cincinnati, Urban Politics in the Progressive Era* (New York, 1968) and Christopher B. Hett, "Political Boss of Cincinnati: The Era of George B. Cox" (Master's thesis, Xavier University, 1968).

Chapter 4.
New Ways to Cope
1914-1945

The first half of the 20th century saw the dissolution of the German community, political reform efforts, the Depression and increased government involvement in the provision of social services. For a discussion of the German-American community see Guido A. Dobbert, "The Disintegration of an Immigrant Community: The Cincinnati Germans, 1870-1920" (Ph.D. diss., University of Chicago, 1965). Political reform efforts are discussed in Louis L. Tucker, *Cincinnati's Citizen Crusaders* (Cincinnati, 1967); William A. Baughin, "Murray Seasongood" (Ph.D. diss., University of Cincinnati, 1972); Forest Frank, "The Disestablishment of the Charter Committee," *Cincinnati Historical Society Bulletin* 33 (Spring 1975): 27-47 and Louis L. Tucker, "Mike Mullen, Saint or Sinner?" *Cincinnati Historical Society Bulletin* 27 (Summer 1969): 107-22.

Early 20th century social reforms are outlined in Robert B. Fairbanks, "Better Housing Movements and the City" (Ph.D. diss., University of Cincinnati, 1981); Patricia Mooney-Melvin, "Mohawk-Brighton: A Pioneer in Neighborhood Health Care," *Cincinnati Historical Society Bulletin* 36 (Spring 1978): 57-72 and Geoffrey Giglierano, "The City and the System: Developing a Municipal Service, 1800-1915," *Cincinnati Historical Society Bulletin* 35 (Winter 1977): 223-47.

Information about Cincinnati during the Depression may be found in Alden N. Monroe, "Effects to Causes: The Evolution of a Social Agency," *Cincinnati Historical Society Bulletin* 37 (Fall 1979): 191-216; Tyrone Tillery, "Cincinnati Blacks and the Great Depression, 1929-1938" (Master's thesis, University of Cincinnati, 1972) and Carl W. Condit, *The Railroad and the City* (Columbus, 1977).

Chapter 5.
My Neighborhood and Our City
1945-1982

During the years after World War II the city continued its commitment to urban planning, included neighborhood participation in governmental policy decisions and was involved in the civil rights movement. Most of the information on the city planning and renewal efforts is drawn from primary sources including City Planning Commission, *The Cincinnati Metropolitan Master Plan* (Cincinnati, 1948); City Planning Commission, *The Plan for Downtown Cincinnati* (Cincinnati, 1964); City Planning Commission, *Cincinnati 2000 Plan* (Cincinnati, 1982); the Citizens' Development Committee Papers, 1922-1972, Cincinnati Historical Society Library; Charles Phelps Taft II Papers, 1922-1977, Cincinnati Historical Society Library and the Society's newspaper clipping files on the Cincinnati Planning Commission and Cincinnati buildings.

Sources dealing with the rise of the neighborhood movement are Susan Redman-Rengstorf, "A Neighborhood in Transition: Sedamsville 1880-1950," *Cincinnati Historical Society Bulletin* 39 (Fall 1981): 175-94; Phyllis Myers and Gordon Binder, *An Issue Report: Neighborhood Conservation: Lessons From Three Cities* (Washington, 1977); William K. Woods, *Cincinnati's Community Councils: An Assessment* (New York, 1979); Martha S. Reynolds, "The City, Suburbs, and the Establishment of the Clifton Town Meeting, 1961-1964," *Cincinnati Historical Society Bulletin* 38 (Spring 1980): 7-32 and Gary P. Kocolowski, "The History of North Avondale" (Master's thesis, University of Cincinnati, 1971).

Material on the effects of racism is included in the Urban League of Greater Cincinnati Papers, 1921-1975, Cincinnati Historical Society Library; S. Arthur Spiegel, "Affirmative Action in Cincinnati," *Cincinnati Historical Society Bulletin* 37 (Summer 1979): 79-88 and the Society's newspaper clipping files on riots and Avondale.

In 1895 McMicken Hall was dedicated on the University of Cincinnati's new campus in Burnet Woods Park. By 1903 the Hanna and Cunningham wings had been added and, to the north, the Wan Wormer Library constructed. Photograph. Eugene F. Bliss fund purchase.

Index

In December, 1963 The Historical and Philosophical Society of Ohio changed its name to The Cincinnati Historical Society. A few months later, the library was moved to the Cincinnati Art Museum's Adams-Emery wing. Photograph.

The Historical and Philosophical Society of Ohio moved its library, which included 17,000 volumes and 64,000 pamphlets, into the Van Wormer Library in November 1901. By 1930 the University had completed a new library building and the Society moved into quarters with an adequate reading room and stack space (1935). Photograph.